Why We're All Romans

Why We're All Romans

The Roman Contribution
to the Western World

Carl J. Richard

ROWMAN & LITTLEFIELD PUBLISHERS, INC.
Lanham · Boulder · New York · Toronto · Plymouth, UK

Published by Rowman & Littlefield Publishers, Inc.
A wholly owned subsidary of The Rowman & Littlefield Publishing Group, Inc.
4501 Forbes Boulevard, Suite 200, Lanham, Maryland 20706
http://www.rowmanlittlefield.com

Estover Road, Plymouth PL6 7PY, United Kingdom

Distributed by National Book Network

British Library Cataloguing in Publication Information Available

Library of Congress Cataloging-in-Publication Data

Richard, Carl J.
  Why we're all Romans : the Roman contribution to the Western world / Carl J. Richard.
    p.   cm.
  Includes bibliographical references and index.
  ISBN 978-0-7425-6778-8 (cloth : alk. paper) — ISBN 978-0-7425-6780-1
(electronic)
  1. Rome—Civilization—Influence. 2. Civilization, Modern—Roman influences. 3.
Rome—History. I. Title.
  DG77.R53 2010
  937—dc22

                                                                    2009043889

Printed in the United States of America

In memory of the great Meyer Reinhold

Contents

Illustrations

Preface

$\mathcal{W}$hen the British poet Percy Shelley wrote, "We are all Greeks," he was certainly correct. The Greeks deduced the core of modern scientific and mathematical knowledge and developed the very method that has allowed modern scientists to surpass them. They established the Western forms of drama, poetry, art, and architecture. By articulating all of the principal metaphysical and ethical problems and proposing a dazzling variety of solutions, their philosophers set the terms for subsequent philosophical discourse. They invented research-based historical writing. Most important, they formulated the theories of popular sovereignty, natural law, and mixed government that undergird modern democratic government.

Yet it has often been noted, with equal justification, that we are all Hebrews too. The Judaic concept of a single, omniscient, omnipotent God who was not only ethical Himself but who also demanded ethical behavior from His human creatures, a concept unique to the Hebrews in the ancient world, has become so much a part of the Western mind that even the unorthodox or irreligious can only challenge it, not escape it. Combined with the related Hebraic doctrine of the spiritual equality of all people, it forms the core of Western consciousness. Thus, we Westerners are all Hebrews in the crucial areas of ethics and spirituality, Greeks in nearly everything else.

What is noted far less frequently is that it is the Romans who made us Greeks and Hebrews. From the Middle Ages on, most Westerners learned of Greek art from Roman copies, not original works; of Greek mythology from Ovid, not Hesiod; of Stoicism from Seneca and Marcus Aurelius, not Zeno or Cleanthes; of Epicureanism from Lucretius, not Epicurus; of Greek comedy from Plautus and Terence, not Aristophanes and Menander; of the Greek novel from Apuleius, not its forgotten originators; of the Greek conception of history from Sallust, Livy, and Tacitus, not Herodotus or Thucydides; and of the Greek theories of popular sovereignty, natural law, and mixed government from Cicero, not Plato or Aristotle. It was the Roman republic, not Athenian democracy, that most Westerners long regarded as the greatest model of government.

Not until the Renaissance were many of the original Greek texts recovered and studied in the West, and even thereafter, Latin continued to dominate the Western educational system at both the grammar school and college levels until the nineteenth century. The most influential of the Greeks—Homer, Plato, Aristotle, Thucydides, Polybius, and Plutarch, for instance—owed their survival and influence largely to their translation into Latin (and later into the vernacular languages), translations that long continued to be read in preference to the original texts. After a brief heyday during the philhellenic movement of the first half of the nineteenth century, the Greek language resumed a subordinate role to Latin in Western curricula. Despite the general decline of classical education in the twentieth century, hundreds of thousands of Americans continued to study Latin in high school each year until the 1960s.

Likewise, when the Western world adopted the ethical monotheism of the Hebrews, it did so at the instigation of a Roman citizen named Paul, who took advantage of the peace, unity, stability, and roads of the Roman Empire to proselytize the previously pagan Gentiles who quickly became a majority of the religion's adherents. Though the Roman government of the first century crucified Christ and persecuted Christians, its descendant of the fourth and fifth centuries encouraged the spread of Christianity throughout the Western world. The three greatest of the so-called Early Church Fathers, Jerome, Ambrose, and Augustine, were all Roman citizens. For over a millennium, most Westerners who read the Scriptures read them not in their original Hebrew and Greek texts but in the Latin Vulgate Bible of Jerome. "Jesus" became known by his Latin name, not by his Hebrew or Greek names ("Yeshua" or "Iesous," respectively). Latin continued to be the language of the Catholic Mass until the 1960s and continues to be the official language of the Roman Catholic Church, whose billion members constitute the largest Christian denomination in the world.

If the Romans were not as innovative as the Greeks or Hebrews, it is partly because their civilization reached its zenith at a later time. All Westerners who came after the Greeks and Hebrews were, and continue to be, inheritors and adapters. But great ingenuity is required to adapt what is inherited to one's own historical context successfully, and the Romans certainly succeeded in that endeavor. What is most remarkable about the Romans is that, unlike so many other imperial peoples before and since, they did not dismiss the past and present civilizations of the peoples they conquered as inherently inferior. This willingness to adapt elements of other civilizations to their own needs was the product of self-confidence rather than humility. Immensely proud of their enormous empire, and convinced of its divine destiny, they felt little need to denigrate other civilizations or to forgo the advantages of borrowing their best aspects, a practice that also appealed to their renowned pragmatism. Virgil was not ashamed to learn from Homer, nor Cicero from Plato, nor Augustine from the psalmist. Even as proud a Roman as Horace acknowledged, "Greece, the captive, held her savage victor captive."

What the Romans assimilated they also modified and often improved. Though Virgil learned epic poetry from Homer, his gods were more dignified and ethical than Homer's. The greatest didactic poem ever written, Virgil's *Georgics*, far surpassed its Greek models. Ovid developed an imaginative and playful way of presenting classical mythology that was worlds apart from, and far more influential than, the somberness of Hesiod. The Roman agricultural writers Cato, Varro, and Columella took the bare shell of a genre begun by the Greek Xenophon and converted it into an effective means of transmitting sound, useful information concerning the most vital of subjects, the production of food. Roman architects used the Greek column as an ornament to decorate the far larger spaces they were able to enclose with their own invention, the concrete dome. Lucretius presented Epicureanism in a poem whose elegance and passion proved essential to the philosophy's enduring influence on Western intellectuals. Seneca and Marcus Aurelius ensured the survival of Stoicism by bringing it down to earth through the employment of direct, colloquial language and through a greater emphasis on ethics. Plautus revived the Greek New Comedy, which had grown stale and formulaic, by lampooning its conventions and introducing an ironic self-awareness in its characters. Terence developed a more sophisticated and urbane form of comedy filled with psychological insight and moral musings. The Romans invented the equally influential genre of satire and carried the epigram to its height. Tacitus surpassed the jovial Herodotus in presenting the horrors of totalitarian monarchy in a way that continues to haunt readers even today.

The Roman modification of Christianity was even more profound. Beginning in the fourth century, the period of the greatest expansion of the religion—when the Roman emperor Constantine became the first Christian emperor and proceeded to shower the Church with his favor, and when Theodosius made Christianity the state religion, prohibiting all others—Roman influence transformed the Church. Its hierarchical structure increasingly reflected that of the empire. The bishop of Rome became the widely acknowledged leader of the Western Church. As bishops began to hold public office and emperors began to intervene in religious matters, Church and

State became as inextricably entwined as they had been in the days of Roman paganism. The ritualistic elements of the liturgy increased, reflecting the traditional Roman obsession with ritual. The veneration of Mary and the saints arose first among the newly converted, who missed certain aspects of paganism, such as the worship of goddesses and of specialized deities from whose ranks they could claim a personal patron by virtue of practicing a particular craft. The veneration of relics and the practice of pilgrimages to holy sites appealed to the deeply ingrained Roman tendency to invest material objects and places with magical powers. It was almost inevitable that as Christianity conquered the Roman Empire, the Romans should conquer Christianity. The rapid incorporation of so many new converts could not help but alter the religion, placing the Roman stamp on it.

The Romans also made original contributions to administration, law, architecture, and engineering. The degree of peace, law, and order they established within the inner provinces of their empire, conditions vital to the transmission of Greco-Roman culture and Christianity, was unprecedented. The most capable administrators and lawgivers in history, they effectively administered an empire of unprecedented size with minimal technology and bureaucracy and bequeathed to the West a system of law whose principles of equity and justice, as represented in the ideals of fairness and impartiality in the application of the law and in the concept of the prosecutorial burden, endured long after the fall of their empire. Roman law remains the basis for the civil law codes in Italy, France, Spain, Quebec, and Louisiana, and its revolutionary principles have exerted a considerable influence even on English common law. Employing the arch and concrete, the Romans constructed buildings of unprecedented size and complexity, preparing the way for Gothic and neoclassical architecture. They were the greatest engineers of the ancient world; some of the roads, bridges, and aqueducts they constructed are still in use even today.

The pragmatic Romans brought Greek and Hebrew ideas down to earth, modified them, and transmitted them throughout western Europe. Without Roman conquest, these ideas probably would not have gained a hearing in most of the West. Furthermore, without the Roman sense of social responsibility to temper the individualism of Hellenistic Greece, classical culture might not have endured, and without the Roman masses to proselytize, Christianity might not have survived. Neither the political record of Hellenistic Greece nor the religious record of Christian proselytizing among the Jews was very hopeful.

In the chapters that follow, I will summarize the history of Rome; explore the Romans' original contributions to Western administration, law, engineering, and architecture; examine their clever and influential adaptations of Greek poems, speeches, letters, agricultural manuals, philosophical treatises, histories, comedies, epigrams, and novels, and the new genre of satire that they created; discuss the continuing contributions of Greeks and Jews in the Roman era; and conclude with an examination of the rise and Romanization of Christianity, two distinct but interrelated developments that were crucial to the formation of Western civilization. Hopefully, these chapters will demonstrate the various, sometimes surprising ways in which we modern Westerners are indeed still Romans.

I would like to thank Rowman & Littlefield Publishers for allowing me to reproduce material from my previous book, *Twelve Greeks and Romans Who Changed the World* (2003), throughout this volume. I would also like to express my gratitude to my colleagues Thomas Martin, Eran Shalev, and Bruce Thornton for their sage advice. Additionally, I would like to thank my editor, Susan McEachern, for her unfailing enthusiasm and wisdom. As always, I would like to thank my precious wife, Debbie, my other half, for her unceasing prayers and support.

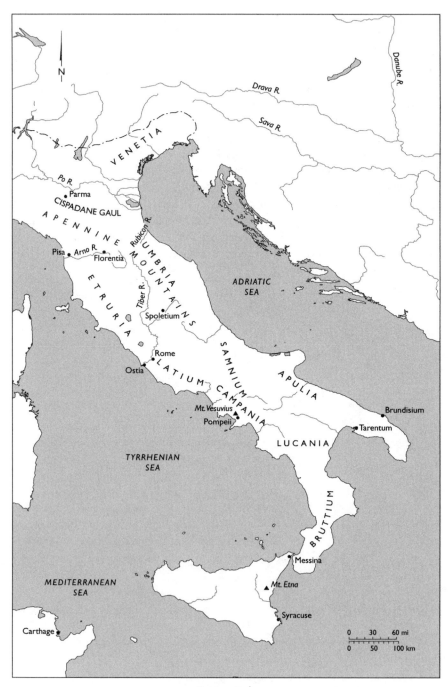

Roman Italy

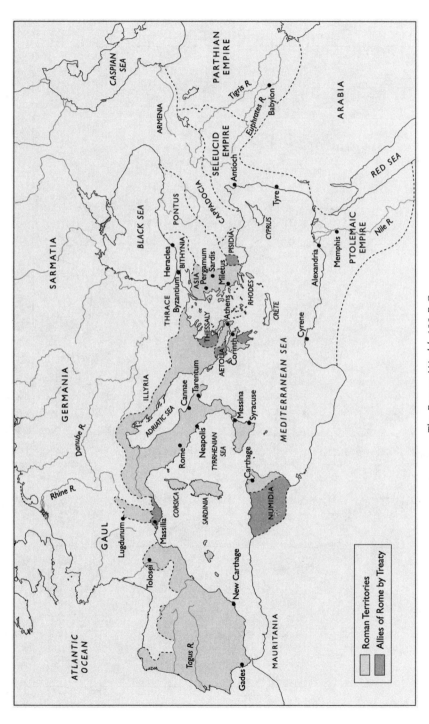

The Roman World, 133 B.C.

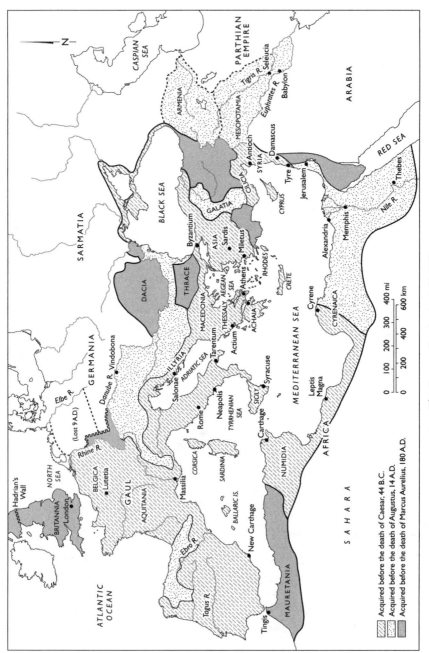

The Roman Empire to A.D. 180

Acquired before the death of Caesar, 44 B.C.

Acquired before the death of Augustus, 14 A.D.

Acquired before the death of Marcus Aurelius, 180 A.D.

Roman History in Brief

*I*n 1,200 years the tiny village of Rome established a republic, conquered all of the Mediterranean basin and western Europe, lost its republic, and finally, surrendered its empire. In the process the Romans laid the foundation of Western civilization.

THE REASONS FOR ROMAN SUCCESS

How is it that a small people possessing relatively poor soil and harbors came to rule over the largest empire in the world, spanning several million square miles and containing seventy-five million people? The Romans' geographical advantages and cultural traits account for much of their success.

Location

Around 1000 B.C. various Latin tribes migrated from the Balkans into central Italy and intermarried with the locals. Though familiar with iron, the Latins were mostly shepherds and herdsmen. During the ninth century B.C. some of these tribesmen settled on the Palatine and Esquiline hills, two of Rome's famed seven hills, overlooking a convenient crossing of the Tiber, the second largest river in Italy. Twenty miles from the sea, Rome was close enough for transportation and communication but distant enough to have warning of raiders. Located near valuable salt beds, Rome's hills were easily defensible and free from flooding. Most significant, Rome was located at the crossroads between the Etruscans to the north and the Greeks to the south. The Romans learned much from both of these peoples.

By 700 B.C. the Etruscans had settled in Etruria, the land northwest of Rome. Their precise origins are uncertain, but their language was not Indo-European, and in all probability they came from Asia Minor.

The Etruscans expanded southward to the Bay of Naples, intermarrying with the locals and organizing much of northern and central Italy and some of southern Italy into three different confederations of Etruscan-dominated city-states. By about 625 B.C., an Etruscan adventurer from Tarquinia, the wealthiest and most powerful of the Etruscan cities (forty miles north of Rome), had become king of Rome.

The Etruscans contributed much to Roman civilization. Etruscan kings transformed Rome from a collection of huts into a real city possessing streets, public buildings, markets, and temples. The Etruscans taught the Romans the art of construction, including the use of the arch. Their temples, shrines, private homes, aqueducts, and roads greatly influenced Roman architecture and engineering. When one of the kings drained the Forum, Rome's marshy central valley, which had previously been used as a burial site, it was the first step toward the Forum's eventual fame as the greatest marketplace in the world.

Between 775 and 400 B.C., the Greeks colonized parts of southern Italy and Sicily, converting this region into what the Romans called *Magna Graecia* (Greater Greece). From these Greeks, via the Etruscans, the Romans learned the Greek alphabet, which they adapted into the Latin alphabet now used throughout the Western world. The Romans assimilated virtually the entire Greek religion (also via the Etruscans), merely changing the names of the gods. The Romans would later assimilate Greek art, literature, science, and philosophy as a result of their conquest of the eastern Mediterranean.

Cultural Traits

The Romans possessed important cultural traits that also contributed to their success. They were pragmatic, tough, and frugal. They subordinated themselves to the family and to Rome. The patriarch of an extended family (the *pater familias*) theoretically possessed absolute authority over the entire clan, including the power of life and death, but, in reality, exercises of this power were extremely rare and sometimes punished as murder if a court deemed the cause insufficient.

The Romans utilized a large collection of stirring myths to instill courage, selflessness, honesty, and patriotism in their children. The greatest of these myths was that of the founding of Rome. According to Virgil's *Aeneid*, Aeneas, son of the Trojan aristocrat Anchises and the love goddess Venus, had led a few refugees out of Troy before it fell to the Greeks. The refugees encountered many hardships before reaching Italy, where they settled down with local Latin tribesmen. Thirteen generations later, two of Aeneas' descendants, Romulus and Remus, established Rome. Romulus and Remus were the sons of the war god Mars and of Rhea Silvia, a priestess sworn to chastity. Rhea Silvia's uncle, the king of Alba Longa, angry with her for breaking her vows, rejected her claim that the father was Mars, imprisoned her, and had her infant sons exposed on the banks of the Tiber. But a wolf found and suckled Romulus and Remus until a herdsman discovered and raised the brothers. According to the myth, in 753 B.C. the brothers returned to the site where they had been exposed as infants and Romulus traced the outlines of Rome with his plow. Romulus killed Remus in a fit of rage over an insult and became the first king of Rome. This myth gave the Romans a noble origin and lineage; they were descended from Trojan heroes and from the god of war himself.

From such myths the Romans learned courage, discipline, persistence, patience, self-restraint, hard work, endurance, honesty, piety, dignity, and manliness. The last of these qualities was *virtus*, whence comes "virtue." Indeed, most of the English terms listed above are Latin in origin.

Most important, perhaps, the Romans possessed a sense of invincibility. The Roman historian Livy wrote, "It is as natural for Romans to win battles as for water to go downhill." This feeling of invincibility stemmed from the Roman belief that the gods would support them completely as long as they performed the proper rituals.

For this reason perhaps no other people has ever been so obsessed with ritual. The Romans never went to war without performing the same rite. If a mistake was made during any ritual, however time-consuming, the Romans began again from the beginning. It did not even matter that, in some cases, the meaning of the ritual had been forgotten. If the college of priests found fault with the rites performed by a consul or praetor with regard to a public act, and the Senate concurred, the act was declared invalid.

Many rituals originated in elaborate family rites, handed down from father to son, for the purpose of appealing to Ceres (the goddess of agriculture), Vesta (the goddess of the hearth), and the Lares (the household gods). Even the family meal was a religious ceremony during which the Romans offered prayers, incense, and libations to the gods.

Military victories reinforced the Roman sense of invincibility, which, in turn, produced more victories. On the few occasions when the Romans lost battles they believed that the gods were merely trying to teach them a lesson in order to keep them from becoming too proud. Nearly all Roman authors cited piety as a crucial factor in the city's success.

THE ROMAN CONQUEST OF ITALY

Between the sixth and third centuries B.C. the Romans conquered all of Italy and established a republic. These two momentous developments were interrelated. The growing recognition of the rights of commoners created the internal harmony necessary for the defeat of external enemies, and the constant warfare highlighted the need to keep commoners happy by recognizing their rights.

The last of the seven kings who ruled Rome during its first two and a half centuries was Tarquin the Proud, an Etruscan who seized power and ruled without senate consultation. In 509 B.C. Tarquin was expelled from Rome. The Romans so hated Tarquin that the very title of "king" (*rex*) became odious to them. Even centuries later the Roman emperors, who had more power than Tarquin ever dreamed of possessing, adopted the designation *imperator* (victorious general) to avoid the title of king.

In 496 B.C. the Roman infantry suppressed a rebellion of other cities of the Latin League, defeating a force composed mostly of cavalry at Lake Regillus. In 396 B.C. the Romans captured and destroyed the rival city of Veii. After surviving a Gallic invasion of Rome in 387 B.C., the Romans waged a series of successful wars against the rebellious Latins, subduing the last tribe in 338 B.C. The Romans conquered Tarquinia by 311 B.C. and defeated the fierce Samnites of southwestern Italy decisively by 290 B.C., though the Samnites were aided by the Etruscans and the Gauls.

It was during the Samnite Wars that the Romans moved from the phalanx, learned from the Greeks via the Etruscans, to the more maneuverable formations that later enabled them to conquer the entire Mediterranean basin and all of western Europe. Roman armies were now organized around small units called centuries, led by centurions. A century consisted of sixty to one hundred men. Two centuries constituted a maniple. Three maniples formed a cohort. Ten cohorts (3,600 to 6,000 men) and three hundred cavalry constituted a legion. When a Roman legion marched into battle, its sixty centuries did so in three lines, each able to coalesce into a mass or disperse into smaller contingents. Roman soldiers generally cast seven-foot javelins, then ran to meet the enemy with a razor-sharp, double-edged short sword (the *gladius*). They often used their rectangular shields offensively, as battering rams. The second line cast their javelins over their comrades' heads to impale the enemy behind.

The Roman conquest of the Samnites left only the Greeks of southern Italy to conquer. In 282 B.C. the Greek city of Tarentum, fearful of the growing Roman power, sank part of a Roman flotilla and called on the brilliant Greek general Pyrrhus of Epirus for aid. Though Pyrrhus defeated the

Romans several times, he could not afford his casualties as well as the Romans could (hence the term "Pyrrhic victory"). Thus, by 275 B.C., the Roman army had subdued all of the Greek city-states of Italy. Only the conquest of the Po valley, shortly after 200 B.C., remained to complete Roman control of the Italian peninsula.

THE GROWTH OF REPUBLICAN GOVERNMENT

Until 509 B.C., the Romans were ruled by monarchs selected by the Senate and approved by the people. The Senate was a council of approximately three hundred former officeholders called patricians (fathers) who advised the king. Nearly all of the senators were landed aristocrats.

After the Romans expelled Tarquin, the senators established an oligarchy. The chief magistrates were three to six military tribunes. By the fourth century B.C., the military tribunes had been replaced by two consuls (colleagues). The consuls were elected annually from the patrician class by the people, subject to ratification by the Senate. In times of emergency, they could appoint a dictator whose term lasted no more than six months. But, in reality, since the consuls were fatally weakened by their fractured power (they could veto each other's decisions) and short terms, the real power in the Roman republic was held by the life-tenured Senate, which decided public policy and controlled the treasury, foreign policy, and religious affairs. The Senate could veto any action taken by the consuls. If the consuls disagreed with each other, the Senate could make executive decisions. The Senate also served as the supreme judicial body. Common Romans, the plebeians, possessed little power.

Within a few centuries, however, Rome moved from an oligarchy to a more republican system. In 494 B.C., stung by the threatened secession of the plebeians, the patricians allowed them to elect two tribunes. Eventually, these tribunes were granted the authority to veto senate measures they considered unfair and to block any magistrate from exercising his office, including the punishment of a citizen. The number of tribunes was gradually increased to ten.

Around 450 B.C. the plebeians demanded a written code of law so that officials could no longer interpret Rome's customary law to suit their own interests. Like most of its contemporaries, the Law of the Twelve Tables was harsh. But its very existence constituted an important reform, and its terse sentences represent the first indication of the Romans' uncanny talent for legal definition. It was exhibited in the Forum for all to see and was memorized by schoolchildren for centuries.

In 445 B.C. plebeians were granted the right to marry patricians. In 421 B.C. the office of quaestor, the consuls' finance manager, was made elective and opened to plebeians. In 366 B.C. plebeians were allowed to run for consul; in 342 B.C. one of the consulships was reserved for them. In 326 B.C. enslavement for debt was abolished. Livy later referred to this measure as "a new birth of freedom," a phrase immortalized by Abraham Lincoln in the Gettysburg Address.

In the mid to late fourth century B.C., new offices were created and opened to the plebeians. Most of the new offices possessed powers previously held by the consuls. One office was that of aedile (supervisor of the marketplace, public buildings, archives, traffic, water and grain supplies, and weights and measures, and sponsor of games), while another was that of praetor (supervisor of courts). A third new office was that of censor (administrator of the census every five years, assessor of taxes, supervisor of public morals, awarder of state contracts, and confirmer of the lineage of senators). At about the same time some wealthy plebeians were admitted into the Senate and the priesthood.

In 300 B.C. every citizen was granted the right to appeal to the people against a death penalty. At about the same time the college of pontiffs and augurs was opened to plebeians. The pontiffs presided over rituals and maintained the lore, while augurs recorded omens and predicted the future. Nevertheless, since none of these positions was salaried, only wealthy plebeians could afford to serve.

Most significant, in 287 B.C., temporary dictator Quintus Hortensius transferred supreme legislative authority from the Senate to the three popular assemblies of Rome, each of which was organized differently and authorized to vote for different offices and measures. The Romans called the new system of government a *res publica* (commonwealth).

Though the patricians still possessed much greater economic and judicial power than the plebeians had, the republic certainly granted plebeians greater rights than they had ever known. Hence the plebeians felt that they had a stake in Roman military success. It was no accident that the growth of the republic coincided with the Roman conquest of Italy.

THE FIRST AND SECOND PUNIC WARS

The First Punic War (264–241 B.C.)

The word "Punic" is derived from *Punicus*, the Latin term for Phoenician, since Carthage had been founded as a colony by settlers from the Phoenician city of Tyre (in what is now Lebanon). The Phoenicians had colonized the western Mediterranean (western Sicily, Sardinia, Corsica, Spain, and northwestern Africa) by about 800 B.C. By 500 B.C. Carthage, located on the coast of what is now Tunisia, had become wealthy and powerful enough to dominate the other Phoenician colonies. The chief source of Carthaginian wealth and power was trade (especially in metals) protected by a large navy. Thirty merchant princes played the leading role in governing Carthage. The Carthaginian Senate, controlled by the aristocracy, possessed most of the power. The popularly elected magistrates (called suffetes) possessed only one-year terms, and the popular assembly was consulted only when the senators and suffetes could not agree. The Carthaginians possessed little art or literature but did produce explorers who traveled to Britain and a considerable distance down the Atlantic coast of Africa.

The First Punic War began as a struggle over the strategic city of Messana (Messina) on the northeastern tip of Sicily. The Romans feared that if the Carthaginians controlled the Straits of Messina, the narrow strip of water that separates Sicily from the Italian mainland, they would be able to cross over into Italy without warning and to block Rome's most important sea lane.

During the course of the war the Romans, who were completely inexperienced in naval warfare, lost several large fleets. But each time the Romans built more ships and worked harder at rowing in unison, while the overconfident Carthaginians allowed their training to diminish. As a result, the Romans were able to sink fifty Carthaginian ships and capture seventy vessels containing ten thousand men at the Aegates, off the coast of Sicily.

Carthage was forced to surrender Sicily and 3,200 talents over a ten-year period. A few years later, taking advantage of a rebellion against Carthage launched by mercenaries and Libyan slaves, Rome seized Sardinia and Corsica and demanded another 1,200 talents. The Carthaginians were furious but were in no position to resist the Romans.

The Second Punic War (218–201 B.C.)

Between 237 and 229 B.C., Carthage's greatest general, Hamilcar Barca, expanded Carthaginian territory in Spain. By 219 B.C. Hamilcar's brilliant son Hannibal had further extended Carthaginian rule northward to the Iberus (Ebro) River. When news reached Rome that Hannibal had besieged Saguntum, an important Roman ally in Spain, the Romans were furious. When Carthage refused to repudiate Hannibal's act and turn him over to the Romans, Rome declared war.

Hannibal then surprised the Romans by crossing the Pyrenees Mountains, the Loire River, and the Alps, among other obstacles, to assault Rome from the north. Hannibal then stunned the Romans by defeating them in a series of battles, in each case drawing Roman generals into an ambush.

The Senate appointed Quintus Fabius Maximus dictator to deal with the crisis. Fabius adopted the controversial strategy of avoiding conflict with Hannibal, merely following him at a distance and pouncing on any detachment Hannibal sent out to forage. Hannibal's losses were imperceptible to most observers, but not to Fabius and Hannibal, both of whom understood the wisdom of Fabius' strategy. Since Hannibal, unlike the Romans, could not get reinforcements, he could not afford the gradual attrition of his army.

Unfortunately, Fabius' term as dictator expired, and the rash and incompetent Gaius Terentius Varro engaged Hannibal at Cannae (216 B.C.). Rather than taking advantage of his numerical superiority to outflank the Carthaginians, Varro massed the bulk of his army in the center along a one-mile front, thereby fatally reducing his soldiers' ability both to get at the enemy and to escape Hannibal's trap. Varro compounded this error by filling his wings with his least experienced troops. Hannibal had placed his best soldiers on the wings and personally supervised the rest in the center, so that the center held long enough for Hannibal's wings to crush the Roman wings and surround the Roman center. Hannibal slaughtered fifty thousand Romans, including eighty senators, and captured another ten thousand soldiers, while losing fewer than six thousand troops of his own. But Hannibal, who was not equipped for siege warfare, failed to march on Rome.

Of equal importance to Roman survival was the loyalty of the Italian allies. Except for the Gallic villages of northern Italy (which was not then considered a part of Italy), only a few Italian cities joined the Carthaginians. The most remarkable and most crucial fact about the Second Punic War was that the vast majority of Italians suffered death and destruction alongside the Romans for sixteen years rather than defect to the enemy.

The Romans then turned the tide of the war through victories in Spain. In 209 B.C. Publius Cornelius Scipio captured New Carthage (Cartagena), the chief Carthaginian supply center in Spain. Over the next three years Scipio defeated the Carthaginians at Baecula and Ilipa, driving them from Spain entirely.

Though he lacked the support of jealous senators, Scipio then launched an invasion of North Africa that forced Hannibal to return to Carthage, having failed in his fifteen-year effort to subdue Rome. A master at inspiring troops, Scipio used as his core soldiers the remnants of the legions that had been humiliated at Cannae. Understanding that that calamity had been the fault of the imbecilic Varro and not the result of any cowardice on the part of the troops, Scipio was fully prepared to take advantage of these soldiers' intense desire for revenge and redemption. Thus, Scipio won a series of battles against the Carthaginians that threatened Carthage itself.

In 202 B.C. Hannibal faced off against Scipio's legions at Zama, eighty miles southwest of Carthage. Neither general had ever been defeated. Recalling that the Carthaginians' elephants at Ilipa had become so confused at one in point in the battle that they had charged into the Carthaginian center, Scipio ordered a tremendous blare of trumpets along the front lines as Hannibal's elephants charged into battle. Frightened by the trumpets, the elephants turned and collided with Hannibal's cavalry, throwing it into chaos. Scipio's cavalry then charged Hannibal's disoriented horsemen, driving the Carthaginian cavalry from the field and pursuing them to ensure that they would not return. Though the rest of the battle proceeded as Hannibal planned, with his soldiers getting the best of the fighting, Scipio's cavalry returned and surrounded Hannibal's soldiers. Twenty thousand Carthaginians were killed, and almost as many captured, to the Romans' fifteen hundred.

Under the terms of the treaty of 201 B.C., the Carthaginian fleet was destroyed and the Carthaginians were forced to pay a huge indemnity of 10,000 talents. Carthage also had to cede its territory in Spain and southern France to the Romans. Henceforth, Carthage could not wage war outside of Africa and could not wage war within Africa without Roman consent.

ROMAN EXPANSION IN THE EASTERN MEDITERRANEAN

The destruction of Carthaginian military power during and after the Second Punic War opened the Mediterranean world to Roman expansion. When King Philip V of Macedon allied himself with the Carthaginians during that war, the Romans defeated him and, in the process, conquered Illyria (the northwestern Balkans). After the war, the Romans responded enthusiastically to the call of Pergamum (in Asia Minor) and Rhodes for aid against Philip. In 197 B.C. a Roman legion under Titus Flaminius defeated Philip at Cynoscephalae in Thessaly, killing twenty thousand Macedonians and capturing another eleven thousand.

As in most of the Romans' other battles against the Macedonians and Greeks, the chief cause of Roman victory was their ability to take advantage of the phalanx's woeful lack of maneuverability. Relying on the careful overlapping of heavy, twenty-one-foot spears, the phalanx was highly effective in opening charges but required level ground without obstructions and a perfect coordination between soldiers that the Romans, with their more maneuverable maniples, quickly learned to disrupt. The Romans surged into the inevitable gaps in the phalanx that formed during battle and assaulted the enemy from the side and rear. When the enemy had to turn their bulky, unwieldy spears to face such threats, they inevitably lost the close coordination on which the phalanx depended.

In 190 B.C. the Romans halted a Seleucid invasion of Greece under King Antiochus III. Though outnumbered seventy-four thousand to thirty thousand, Scipio and his brother Lucius defeated Antiochus at Magnesia in Asia Minor. In 168 B.C. the Romans defeated a coalition of Greeks, led by Philip V's successor Perseus, at Pydna in Macedon. In 148 B.C., when anti-Roman sentiment flared in Greece as a result of the Senate's policy of supporting oligarchies there, the Romans burned Corinth. The Senate then converted all of Greece into a collection of provinces governed by a Roman proconsul. The Romans looted Greece for slaves, books, and art. The employment of well-educated Greek slaves as tutors to Roman children was one of the means by which Roman aristocrats were Hellenized.

Meanwhile, from 149 to 146 B.C., the Romans engaged in the Third Punic War. Made paranoid by Carthage's economic recovery from the ravages of the first two Punic Wars, senators like Cato the Elder demanded the destruction of Rome's nemesis. In 149 B.C. Rome presented a series of outrageous demands to Carthage, including one that all Carthaginians leave the city and settle at least ten miles inland, a move that would destroy the Carthaginian economy. When the Carthaginians refused, the Romans besieged the city. Though often on the verge of starvation, the Carthaginians fought heroically for three years. When the Romans took the city in 146 B.C., they killed every male Carthaginian and sold every woman and child into slavery. Rome then annexed the remaining Carthaginian territory.

In 133 B.C., when Attalus III, the king of Pergamum, died without an heir, he left his kingdom to Rome. Fearing a popular revolt when he died, he knew that the Romans would maintain order and would continue to follow his policy of favoring the aristocrats over the masses. The Romans had now conquered almost the whole Mediterranean basin.

THE EFFECTS OF THE NEW ROMAN EXPANSION

In contrast to the Romans' gradual conquest of Italy, which helped produce a republican form of government, the Romans' rapid subjugation of the Mediterranean helped destroy the same republic. By further increasing the already vast inequalities of wealth between the rich and poor, the new Roman expansion generated class warfare, which, in turn, produced the chaos and violence that paved the way for the emperors.

The Decline of Popular Assemblies

The sudden and extensive expansion of Roman territory transformed Rome from a village into an imperial center, housing a host of foreign and domestic supplicants. It is estimated that the city possessed four hundred thousand adult male citizens by the mid-second century B.C., yet the Campus Martius, where voting occurred, held seventy thousand people at most. Under such conditions, the average Roman citizen found it difficult to participate in government, even to the small extent that he had before. Those who lived far from Rome found it difficult to vote. The popular assemblies became far too large to make the swift decisions required of an empire. Hence both the Senate and the aristocratic proconsuls whom they appointed to govern the provinces wielded great power. The commoners were now losing the little political power they had once possessed.

Economic Inequalities

Ever increasing numbers of commoners lost their land and became the clients of aristocrats. Moving to Rome, they were forced to support their patrons' political interests in order to earn a living. Long-term military service overseas forced many commoners to neglect their farms. Nor could the commoners compete with the massive amounts of produce grown on the aristocrats' plantations (*latifundia*), which depressed prices. The Senate sold aristocrats these plantations in the conquered territories at a relatively low price. The Senate sold the land in large blocks so that only the wealthy could afford it. Enslaved people from the conquered provinces provided the labor force for the latifundia; wealthy landholders shifted from hiring free laborers to employing slaves, partly because the latter were not subject to military conscription. Those whom the overseas wars had enriched exploited those whom they had impoverished.

Moral Decline

Rome suffered a general moral decline that observers attributed to the "Punic Curse," since the incredible wealth that helped produce the decline was the indirect result of the Roman conquest of Carthage. Newfound luxury undermined the traditional Roman values of frugality, discipline, honesty, and respect for law, the values on which the republic rested. Aristocrats sought profit with ruthless abandon. Vote buying and ballot box stuffing proliferated. The crushing poverty and slum environment of the commoners rendered them equally cruel and lazy. The new class of merchants, moneylenders, tax collectors, and government contractors spawned by the rapid growth of the empire proved corrupt as well. These low-born wealthy were called *equites*, members of the equestrian order, because they could afford to serve in the cavalry with their own horses.

The Romans also treated their slaves harshly. As a result, there were several major slave revolts. From 135 to 132 B.C., a slave rebellion in Sicily was led by shepherd-slaves who were both ill fed and armed to protect their flocks from predators, animal and human. A second slave revolt occurred in Sicily from 104 to 100 B.C. But the largest and most famous slave revolt occurred on the Italian mainland in 73–71 B.C., when the Thracian gladiator Spartacus, who had served as an auxiliary in the Roman army, led seventy thousand slaves in revolt. The slave army defeated five separate Roman forces and plundered much of Italy before the rebels were finally overwhelmed at Lucania, their leader killed in battle. The Romans crucified six thousand of the rebels and lined the Appian Way, Rome's main highway, with their rotting corpses.

Tiberius and Gaius Gracchus, the grandsons of Scipio, tried to halt the decline of the republic by restoring its traditional backbone, the yeoman farmer. The Gracchi pushed through the Tribal Assembly various measures to limit estates in the public lands, so that the excess land could be distributed among the landless poor. The Senate used its control of the treasury to block the implementation of these laws and even resorted to violence, eventually having both brothers and their followers killed.

THE DEATH OF THE REPUBLIC

Rome endured a full century of bloody civil wars that eventuated in the rise of the emperors. Exploited by ambitious aristocrats, these civil wars were largely the result of Rome's division into two factions, the Optimates, who favored the aristocrats, and the Populares, who favored the poor. Although the aristocrats who led both of these factions generally placed personal ambition above all other considerations and, thus, were quite capable of shifting their allegiance from one faction to another, the underlying economic divisions that produced the factions persisted.

Marius versus Sulla

An eques from the country town of Arpinum, Gaius Marius rose to power by defeating Jugurtha, the king of Numidia in northwestern Africa, and Germanic tribes that threatened Rome. In the process of waging war against Jugurtha's brother for complete control of Numidia, Jugurtha's soldiers had massacred Roman merchants who sided with his brother. Partly because Jugurtha had bribed some of the senators, the Senate had been reluctant to act against him at first. Furious at the Senate, the Tribal Assembly had taken the unprecedented act of ordering Marius to proceed to North Africa and crush Jugurtha, which he eventually did in 106 B.C. In 102 and 101 B.C., Marius followed this triumph with a successful defense of Italy against two large Germanic tribes.

Marius' army was composed of landless citizens (he disregarded the small property qualification for service in the army) whom he personally equipped. Marius transformed the army from a militia equipped by, and loyal to, Rome, into a professional army equipped by, and loyal to, its commander. Marius used the threat of armed force to overcome senate opposition to the distribution of land in North Africa to his veterans—a tactic unheard of during the early days of the republic. But at least Marius did not yet take the opportunity to seize Rome. He contented himself with being elected consul six years in a row between 105 and 100 B.C., though Roman law prohibited consuls from holding office two consecutive terms.

When King Mithridates of Pontus (northeastern Asia Minor) revolted in 88 B.C., both the Senate and Tribal Assembly claimed authority to suppress the rebellion, and each selected its own general. While the Tribal Assembly chose Marius, the Senate selected Lucius Cornelius Sulla, who had once served as Marius' quaestor but was now his rival. As Sulla went east to suppress the revolt, Marius joined with the consul Cinna and others, including slaves whom they freed, to seize Rome. They executed a consul and others without trial. They finally had to kill some of the slaves they had freed as well because the latter would not stop murdering and looting.

After suppressing the revolt of Mithridates, Sulla returned to Rome to rout Marius' army, which had been weakened by the death of its leader. Sulla was the first to march troops inside the city limits of Rome and the first to kill a tribune, both illegal acts. Thousands of Romans died in this civil war, including many senators.

In 82 B.C. the Senate appointed Sulla dictator for an unlimited term, another unconstitutional act, and assigned him the task of revising the Roman political system. Sulla strengthened the Senate and rendered the popular assemblies and the tribunes virtually powerless. Sulla also "proscribed" (listed for execution) his own enemies, the enemies of his friends, and some whose only crime was the possession of wealth that could then be legally confiscated. Whoever brought the heads of the proscribed received a large reward. Although estimates of the number of Sulla's victims range widely, from nine thousand to fifty thousand, there were enough that even the Senate begged him to stop.

But Sulla was not personally ambitious. He wanted only to "cleanse" Rome by restoring the Senate to a dominant position. In 81 B.C. he voluntarily surrendered power and retired to his estate, where he died three years later. When abdicating, Sulla allegedly declared that it would be the last time a Roman surrendered the supreme power. If Rome had escaped a permanent dictatorship, it was due solely to the fact that Marius and Sulla possessed a few scruples about openly assuming such power. Rome would not be so fortunate in the future.

Pompey versus Caesar

In 67 B.C. the Tribal Assembly authorized Pompey (Gnaeus Pompeius) to clear the Mediterranean of pirates. Pompey succeeded in three months but spent another four years conquering the remaining part of the Seleucid Empire, which included Syria, Armenia, Phoenicia, Pontus, and Cilicia (southeastern Asia Minor). He also conquered Judea (Israel), an independent country that had successfully revolted against the Seleucid king Antiochus IV a century earlier.

When Pompey returned to Rome in 62 B.C., the Senate refused to grant his soldiers the land he requested for them. Pompey had made the mistake of disbanding his army too quickly, leaving him with no leverage over the Senate. In frustration Pompey then formed with Crassus and Julius Caesar what historians call the First Triumvirate (60 B.C.). Seven years later Crassus was killed while fighting Parthia, a new empire east of the Euphrates River. When combined with the death of Julia, Caesar's daughter and Pompey's beloved wife, the same year, Crassus' death removed a powerful motive for cooperation between the remaining triumvirs.

In the meantime Caesar had set about conquering much of Gaul (what is now France, Belgium, southern Holland, Germany west of the Rhine, and most of Switzerland). In the process Caesar proved himself Pompey's equal as a general. On one occasion, at Alesia in 52 B.C., Caesar succeeded in capturing an impregnable town held by a large Gallic army while simultaneously warding off an even larger army that had surrounded him. In conquering Gaul, Caesar acquired a fortune in plunder, which he used to bribe Roman officials and to curry favor with the Roman masses.

Jealous of his success and fearful of his motives, the Senate, with Pompey's acquiescence, demanded that Caesar disband his army and return to Rome. Fearing for his life should he disband his army, his sole protection against his enemies, Caesar crossed the Rubicon and invaded Italy instead.

Pompey and most of the Senate fled eastward. Caesar defeated Pompey at Pharsalus in Thessaly in 48 B.C. Pompey then fled to Egypt, where he was murdered by Egyptian officials seeking to curry favor with Caesar. But Caesar wept at the sight of his severed head and ordered the murderers put to death. He then dallied with Cleopatra VII, the Macedonian queen of Egypt, who gave birth to a son, Caesarion (Ptolemy Caesar). Caesar's mopping-up operations against scattered republicans and followers of Pompey continued for three more years, raising the total number of casualties in the second civil war to about a hundred thousand.

Caesar's Rule

From 48 to 44 B.C., Caesar proved an effective dictator of Rome. He was magnanimous—in retrospect, more than was wise—even appointing some of his former opponents to high office. He subdued the street gangs that had paralyzed the city and reduced Rome's debt through efficient administration. He decreased unemployment and established colonies for his veterans and for eighty thousand poor Romans. He introduced the "Julian calendar" of 365 and one-quarter days, replacing a calendar of 355 days that had left Rome three months off the solar year. He removed many incompetent and corrupt proconsuls from office and ejected them from the Senate. In a momentous move Caesar extended Roman citizenship to numerous non-Italians (mostly Gallic chieftains) for the first time, even admitting some Gauls into the Senate, along with businessmen, the sons of freedmen, and former centurions. He annexed Numidia and rebuilt Carthage as a Roman city.

Caesar's Assassination

But Caesar's arrogance offended some aristocrats, who had good reason to suspect that he intended to make himself a king. Although the Senate agreed to extend his dictatorship from the initial ten years to life in February 44 B.C., some senators began plotting his assassination. One month later a group of conspirators led by Marcus Junius Brutus and his brother-in-law Gaius Cassius Longinus stabbed Caesar to death with daggers.

The assassins made two mistakes. First, on the insistence of Brutus, they decided not to kill Caesar's chief lieutenant, Mark Antony (Marcus Antonius). Second, the assassins allowed Caesar a public funeral, at which Antony delivered a passionate speech and waved Caesar's bloody and tattered clothing about. The people had already been moved to tears on learning that Caesar had willed to each Roman citizen a tidy sum and the use of one of his gardens. Driven to a frenzy by grief when a wax effigy of Caesar featuring his twenty-three wounds was raised, the mourners carried Caesar's blood-stained body through the Forum, where they burned it on a pyre. The crowd then ignited the Senate House and attempted to burn the houses of Brutus and Cassius. The assassins were forced to flee Rome.

The Second Triumvirate

Caesar's chief supporters, Antony, Marcus Aemilius Lepidus, and Octavian, eventually formed the Second Triumvirate. Lepidus was the proconsul of Spain. Octavian, newly arrived from educational and military training in Apollonia (in Macedon), was Caesar's grandnephew and (as the will revealed) adopted son. Caesar had no legitimate son of his own, and his daughter had died childless. Octavian's mother and stepfather thought he should renounce his dangerous status as Caesar's heir, but he refused.

The triumvirs slaughtered all opponents, including as many as three hundred senators and two thousand equites, confiscated their property, and redistributed it among their supporters. In fact, it has been estimated that one-fourth of all Italian land changed hands as a result of the Second Triumvirate's proscriptions and evictions. Each triumvir even allowed relatives of his own to be proscribed by the others.

After crushing the republican army of Brutus and Cassius at Philippi in 42 B.C., the triumvirs divided the empire between them. Octavian received the western empire, except for northwestern Africa, which went to Lepidus, and Mark Antony received the eastern empire. At the same time Antony married Octavian's sister, Octavia, to cement the alliance between them. Octavian evicted Lepidus from the triumvirate in 36 B.C., after Lepidus attempted to seize Sicily from him.

Antony versus Octavian

Antony then sealed his fate by falling in love with Cleopatra. When Antony dispatched formal letters of divorce to Octavia, a kind and virtuous woman much beloved by the Roman people, Octavian used the act as a pretext for waging war against Antony. He seized Antony's will from the Vestal Virgins and publicly revealed its contents. In the will Antony made his sons by Cleopatra his heirs, even declaring that they would inherit Parthia, which had not been conquered. Many Romans were outraged at the prospect of being ruled by men who were only half Roman. The people also discovered that Antony's will ceded control of three Roman territories to Cleopatra. Finally, the will declared that if Antony died in Rome, his body must be returned to Cleopatra in Alexandria. Octavian cleverly used Roman xenophobia to attract broad support, claiming that Antony would transfer the capital of the empire to Alexandria. For propagandistic purposes, Octavian declared war on

Cleopatra, not Antony, claiming that Antony was acting under some sort of spell cast by this evil eastern woman.

In 31 B.C. Octavian's navy, under the leadership of Marcus Vipsanius Agrippa—a brilliant admiral of low birth who had built a fleet from scratch and trained its crews—destroyed or captured three-quarters of Antony's fleet at Actium in Greece. Antony and Cleopatra fled to Egypt, both committing suicide in 30 B.C.

Octavian then annexed Egypt, the breadbasket of the Mediterranean world, and placed it under his personal control, the first such arrangement in Roman history. Octavian returned to Rome with so much gold that the interest rate immediately plunged from twelve to four percent. After a full century of chaos and violence, in which the Roman republic had proved incapable of maintaining any semblance of peace or order, Rome was now thoroughly prepared for the rule of an emperor.

WOMEN OF THE REPUBLIC

Roman women possessed a higher status than most Greek women and, indeed, more than any women before the modern age. Although subordinate to men, they were not secluded or denied an education based on their gender, and they exerted considerable influence within the family. Aristocratic girls attended elementary schools with their brothers, though early marriage deprived them of higher education. Yet, as in Greece, fathers arranged marriages (and, sometimes, divorces), and a daughter could refuse a marriage only if she could demonstrate that the potential groom was morally unfit.

By the late republican era, the vast majority of women wed under a new form of marriage that did not place them under the authority of their husbands but allowed them to remain under the authority of their pater familias, who was generally their father or grandfather and who, because of high mortality rates, seldom exercised such control for very long. Women without a live pater familias required a legal guardian but could manage most of their own financial affairs with little hindrance from the guardian and could apply to have the guardian replaced. Unlike minors, women could marry without their guardians' consent. Vestal Virgins and mothers with three or more children were exempt from the necessity of a guardian. Women could also divorce easily, forcing their husbands to return the dowry to the wife's family (minus one-fifth for each child produced by the marriage, one-sixth for adultery), a factor that gave even relatively poor women some economic leverage in the marriage. (The same held true if either the wife or husband died. The dowry belonged to the wife's family and was managed by the husband only for the term of the marriage; the husband was liable for the dowry's entire value, which averaged about one year's income for the bride's family.) On the other hand, until the late empire, the children of divorced parents remained with the father (unless he was ruled "depraved") because, unlike their mothers under the new form of marriage, they were considered part of his household. Roman husbands had no legal right to discipline their wives physically or to require them to have sex.

Some women were revered for their virtue. One of the most famous women of republican Rome was Cornelia, the mother of the Gracchi. Widowed early, she rejected a marriage proposal from the king of Egypt and raised her sons alone. When a frivolous lady asked to see her jewels, Cornelia presented her sons. After her youngest son, Gaius, was murdered, Cornelia retired to Misenum to study Greek and Latin literature. The Roman people later erected a bronze statue of her. Nearly a century later Brutus' wife Porcia secured a similar glory when she killed herself in imitation of her husband after the Battle of Philippi.

Although Roman women could not vote and were discouraged from any involvement in politics, in 195 B.C. a group of women gathered to demand repeal of the Oppian Law, passed during the Second Punic War, which had imposed restrictions on female extravagance in clothing, jewelry, and carriages. The stern Cato the Elder opposed repeal of the law, telling the senators regarding their wives: "The very moment they begin to be your equals, they will be your superiors. . . . Is it your wish, citizens, to start such a competition between your wives, so that the rich will desire to possess what no other woman can possess; while the poor will stretch themselves beyond their proper means to avoid being looked down on for their poverty? Let them once begin to be ashamed of what should cause no shame, and they will not be ashamed of what is truly shameful. . . . Once the law has ceased to place a limit on your wife's spending, you yourself will never do it." A tribune who favored repeal of the law retorted, "You should want to be called fathers and husbands rather than masters." The law was repealed. Nevertheless, Cato exaggerated when he made the famous statement, "We rule the world and our wives rule us."

In 42 B.C. a group of women burst into the Forum to protest a tax levied against them to pay the expenses of the latest civil war produced by the assassination of Caesar. Their leader, Hortensia, declared: "Why should we pay taxes when we do not share in the offices, honors, military commands, nor, in short, the government, for which you fight between yourselves with such shameful results? Let war with the Celts or Parthians come, we will not be inferior to our mothers when it is a question of common safety. But for civil wars, may we never contribute nor aid you against each other." The speech made Hortensia famous, won the applause of several male commentators, and caused the Second Triumvirate to reduce the number of women affected by the tax by more than 70 percent.

Female slaves and poor women lived hard lives and had no time for even the limited political involvement in which aristocratic women engaged. In fact, because of the greater demand for male slaves, infant slave daughters were often exposed.

THE EARLY ROMAN EMPIRE, 27 B.C.–A.D. 180

Augustus (27 B.C.–A.D. 14)

When Octavian returned to Rome in triumph after defeating Antony and Cleopatra, he declared before the Senate that the republic was restored. Of course, this was a charade. Everyone knew that Octavian wielded the supreme power and that it rested on his status as imperator, commander of the army, whose soldiers took an oath of allegiance to him. Fearful of Octavian's power and, even more, of the continual civil wars that had nearly destroyed Rome, the Senate heaped awards, honors, and titles on him. The most famous of these titles was Augustus, or "consecrated one," a title previously reserved for the gods. Augustus called himself the *princeps civitatis* (first citizen), a title which had been granted to elder statesmen during the republican period. For this reason historians often refer to Augustus' reign as the Principate.

Augustus gradually accrued to himself the powers of tribune, consul, and *pontifex maximus* (chief priest). He controlled the outer provinces through the army and through the legati he appointed to govern them, and controlled the inner (senatorial) provinces through his power to reject the proconsuls appointed by the Senate, his authority to intervene there, and his ability to appoint new senators. His tribunician power allowed him to veto the acts of magistrates. He could draw from the treasury any time he wanted, as well as from the vast personal wealth he had acquired during the civil war. Because of these enormous powers, continued by Augustus' successors, senate resolutions became little more than expressions of the imperial will. While the Senate became a rubber stamp, the popular assemblies gradually withdrew from view altogether.

But perhaps the greatest source of Augustus' power was his own humility. Unlike his granduncle and adoptive father, Julius Caesar, Augustus generally eschewed even the appearance of arrogance. Even while consolidating power beyond the dreams of most kings, Augustus was careful to avoid the trappings of monarchy. He understood that although Romans of all classes thirsted for the stability offered by one-man rule, centuries of republican tradition had instilled in them a fierce hatred of the very word "king." Augustus' humility and magnanimity, when joined with his fiction of a restored republic, set the exhausted Romans at ease.

The reign of Augustus was one of unprecedented peace and prosperity. During his reign the doors of the temple of the god Janus, closed only in times of complete peace, were closed three times. The doors had been shut only twice in the centuries before Augustus. When combined with the construction of durable roads throughout the empire, peace made extensive trade and travel possible.

During the few periods of war in Augustus' forty-year reign, his generals extended the northeastern frontier from the Alps to the Danube River and completed the conquest of Spain, an operation that had taken two centuries to complete, owing to the mountainous terrain and hardy tribesmen of the Iberian Peninsula. The gold, silver, copper, tin, and iron mines of Spain, all monopolies of the imperial government, enriched Rome, much as Latin America would later enrich Spain.

Augustus established a professional army of twenty-eight legions, stationed it on the frontier, and largely succeeded in keeping it out of politics. The army proved a tremendous Romanizing influence. Towns, such as Lyons, Bonn, Cologne, and Mainz, sprouted around its camps, as Roman soldiers intermarried with native women, settled down on sizable pensions (equal to thirteen years' pay), and became local dignitaries. After twenty-five years of service, foreigners who served in the auxiliary forces were issued a pair of bronze tablets called a *diploma* (double tablets) that granted them full citizenship. The soldiers of auxiliary units that distinguished themselves in battle sometimes received immediate citizenship, gifts, and special emblems (eagles or wreaths) on their shields in reward for their valor. Augustus also maintained fleets throughout the Mediterranean to transport troops and to suppress piracy.

Augustus reduced the number of senators from one thousand to six hundred, making the Senate more efficient. He assigned equites, as well as members of the senatorial class, to financial posts, to the governorship of small provinces, to the command of armies, and to the Praetorian Guard, the palace guard of nine thousand men.

Augustus rebuilt eighty-two temples destroyed during the civil wars, revived old priesthoods, and restored religious festivals. Holding to traditional Roman frugality, he lived in a modest house, ate sparingly, and dressed in simple clothes made by his female relatives. Concerned about the decline of traditional Roman values and fearing depopulation, he passed laws rewarding the production of legitimate children and penalizing adultery, bachelorhood, and childlessness. He even exiled his own daughter and granddaughter, both named Julia, for adultery.

Aside from the exile of his daughter, Augustus' greatest source of sorrow was the loss of three Roman legions under Publius Quinctilius Varus in the Teutoburg Forest in A.D. 9. The Romans were attempting to conquer Germany when a group of Germanic tribes, led by Herman (Arminius), chief of the Cherusci, who had served as a Roman auxiliary and had been granted Roman citizenship, ambushed and slaughtered Varus' army in an unfamiliar bog. The Roman failure to conquer the Germanic tribes allowed these tribes to conquer Rome four centuries later.

But perhaps Augustus' very success as a ruler constitutes his greatest failure. At best, his reign was a mixed blessing for Rome: by making the Roman people content to live under an emperor, Augustus paved the way for the likes of Tiberius, Caligula, and Nero.

Tiberius (A.D. 14–37)

Augustus' stepson Tiberius began as a mild and capable ruler but became so paranoid that he spent the last eleven years of his reign secluded on the island of Capraea (Capri). While Tiberius was hiding from potential assassins, his administration languished under the cruel and arrogant direction of Lucius Aelius Sejanus, prefect of the Praetorian Guard. When Tiberius received evidence of Sejanus' treachery, he executed Sejanus and his family. Thereafter, Tiberius was even more paranoid, executing people on the basis of the dubious claims of paid informers.

Caligula (37–41)

Tiberius' grandnephew Caligula was even worse. The demented emperor forced the Romans to worship him as a god. (Augustus had been deified by the Senate after his death and, while alive, he had tolerated his own worship in eastern provinces where there was a long tradition of worshipping rulers, but neither he nor Tiberius had insisted on worship by their fellow Romans.) Disdaining the long hours of administrative work his office required, work he considered beneath a god, Caligula devoted his time to lavish entertainment. Having exhausted the vast treasury left by the frugal Tiberius on palaces and other grand (often ludicrous) projects, Caligula forced many aristocrats to declare him their heir and then killed them. He pressured others into bidding ridiculous sums they could not afford at palace furniture auctions. Everyone and everything was taxed. Caligula established a state brothel at which even boys and married women were required to work. In 41, officers of Caligula's own Praetorian Guard killed him.

Claudius (41–54)

Caligula's uncle Claudius was a fairly effective emperor. Under his rule the Romans conquered southern Britain. He expanded and improved Rome's chief port at Ostia. Claudius' principal administrators were two of his freedmen.

Nero (54–68)

Claudius' fourth wife, Agrippina the Younger (who was also his niece), poisoned his mushrooms so that Nero, her son by a previous marriage, could become emperor. Nero had his mother executed, killed his aunt for her money, had his first wife executed on false charges, kicked his second wife to death while she was pregnant, and killed his third wife's husband in order to marry her. He forced people to attend concerts at which he sang and played the lyre. Some suspected him of ordering the burning of Rome in 64 so that he could rebuild the city to his glory. Whether or not this was true, Nero used the new sect of Christianity as his scapegoat, executing some Christians in a grisly fashion. The extravagance of Nero, including his vast and gaudy palace the Domus Aurea (Golden House), led to higher taxes, the devaluation of coinage, and the quasi-judicial fleecing of rich victims. Nero told one magistrate: "You know my needs! Let us see to it that nobody is left with anything." As a result, several Roman armies revolted, causing the Senate to condemn Nero to death by flogging and the emperor himself to commit suicide.

Civil War (68–69)

In 68–69 there were four emperors. Galba, the commander of the Roman army in Spain, lasted less than seven months on the throne after he reneged on a promise of large bonuses to the army and dismissed some of the Praetorian Guard. He was assassinated and replaced by Otho, prefect of the Guard, who lasted only three months, at which time the Roman army in Germany, under Vitellius, marched on the capital. Vitellius' army defeated Otho's force, and Otho committed suicide. The fourth emperor, the ultimate victor in this civil war, was Vespasian (Titus Flavius Sabinus Vespasianus), the founder of the Flavian dynasty, who had barely avoided execution after falling asleep at one of Nero's infamous concerts.

Vespasian (69–79)

At the time that Nero committed suicide, sixty-year-old Vespasian, who had commanded Claudius' left wing in the invasion of Britain, stood at the head of Roman legions attempting to suppress a rebellion in Judea, a province that had been most troublesome to Rome since the time of its formal annexation in A.D. 6. In 66 the Jews had driven Roman forces out of Jerusalem and had routed a legion that had come from Syria to reestablish Roman control of the province. While Vespasian was in the process of suppressing the Jewish revolt, the legions in Egypt, Judea, Syria, and the Balkans proclaimed him emperor. After Vespasian's army defeated that of Vitellius, the Senate recognized Vespasian as emperor. Few voices called for the return of the republic any more.

Vespasian was the first emperor of low birth and the first to be succeeded by his biological son. He was a simple and honest man who took vacations at the purposely unchanged Sabine farmhouse of his forefathers. When a sycophant tried to trace Vespasian's ancestry to one of Hercules' companions, Vespasian burst out laughing.

Vespasian appointed his son Titus coemperor in order to ensure a smooth succession and assigned him the task of ending the Jewish revolt. In 70 Titus captured Jerusalem following a horrific siege. Hunger within the city became so great that bandits began torturing people to find out where their food was hidden. The leaders of the revolt executed not only those suspected of treachery but those suspected of trying to flee as well. Many of the Jews trapped within the city were there for the Feast of Unleavened Bread; they were not revolutionaries but innocent civilians. When the Romans finally stormed Jerusalem, they destroyed most of it, including the Second Great Temple. The Romans burned the temple on the same month and day in the Jewish calendar that the First Temple had been destroyed by the Chaldeans in 586 B.C.

After the rebellion the site of the Great Temple was closed to Jews, and the Jewish priesthood and council of rulers (the Sanhedrin) were abolished. While some of the spoils from the war, including the Menorah and the silver trumpets of the Great Temple, were deposited in Vespasian's fabulous new Temple of Peace, other golden and silver items were sold to fund construction projects throughout the empire, including the Colosseum.

Some Jewish rebels had occupied the stronghold of Masada, situated on a rock 1,300 feet high, thirty miles southeast of Jerusalem. After a difficult siege, the Romans finally succeeded in storming the bastion in 73, but were shocked to discover that 960 rebels within the fortress had committed suicide, preferring to die rather than live under Roman rule. Each man killed his own wife and children. Ten men chosen by lot killed the rest of the men, and one man chosen by lot killed the remaining ten and himself. Only two women and five children who had hidden themselves during the killings escaped death.

Vespasian extended Roman citizenship to Spanish nobles and replenished the ranks of the senatorial and equestrian orders, which had been decimated by imperial murders and civil war, with Italians and provincials. He strengthened the frontier forts and improved the roads leading to them. He saved Rome from bankruptcy by reducing expenses. He improved the civil service. He exempted teachers and physicians from taxation. He expanded Roman territory in northern England and Wales.

Titus (79–81)

Titus was handsome, graceful, dignified, talented, and much beloved. He discontinued all prosecutions for treason based on mere expressions of disrespect for the emperor and imposed severe punishments on professional informers, who had been responsible for many deaths under Nero. Titus even spared two senators who had plotted against him. He was generous to Romans afflicted by fire and plague. After bearing much of the burden of administration during his father's reign, he ruled alone for only two years before dying of the plague. Titus dedicated the Flavian Amphitheater, later known as the Colosseum, begun under his father, at the site where Nero's Golden House had stood.

Domitian (81–96)

Domitian (Titus Flavius Domitianus), Vespasian's younger son, began as a hardworking administrator whose armies extended Roman control into Scotland. But, like Tiberius, whose notebooks and memoirs he often read, Domitian eventually succumbed to paranoia. He built a huge palace, the Domus Augustana, to better protect himself (whence comes the word "palace," since it was situated on Palatine Hill). He executed numerous senators for idle remarks, which he always interpreted in the darkest light, and confiscated their property. He even killed his own cousin because a herald mistakenly announced him as the emperor. He had the genitals of suspected traitors scorched to get them to reveal their accomplices. After he impregnated his niece, he forced her to submit to an abortion that killed her. He adopted the title *dominus et deus* (lord and god). He erected so many triumphal arches to commemorate his slightest achievements that someone scrawled, "That's enough!" on one of them. He was finally stabbed to death as the result of a conspiracy hatched by his wife and court officials. For the first time, the Senate purged an emperor's name from all monuments and other public records and selected his successor.

Nerva (96–98)

The emperors of the late first and second centuries, the Antonine dynasty minus Commodus, have been termed "the Five Good Emperors." They brought the Roman Empire to its zenith of power and prosperity. They generally considered themselves the servants of Rome rather than its masters. Looking back on their dynasty, the historian Edward Gibbon once claimed, "If a man were called to fix the period in the history of the world during which the condition of the human race was most happy and prosperous, he would, without hesitation, name that which elapsed from the death of Domitian to the accession of Commodus."

Proclaimed emperor by the Senate in 96, Nerva (Marcus Cocceius Nerva) was a sixty-six-year-old lawyer. He suppressed the informers who had flourished in the latter years of Domitian's reign. Nerva also established the *alimenta*, a fund that provided aid to the poor children of forty Italian cities. Nerva funded the program with the interest from public land sales and loans to farmers. He also purchased land for the landless poor of Italy. Nerva adopted the able, attractive, affable, half-Spanish general Trajan (the first emperor born outside of Italy) as his heir.

Trajan (98–117)

The Roman Empire reached its greatest extent (3.5 million square miles and seventy-five million people) under Trajan (Marcus Ulpius Trajanus). He added fertile, gold-rich Dacia (Romania), Armenia, and Mesopotamia (Iraq) to the empire. He appointed aristocrats from the eastern portion of the empire to the Senate. One year Trajan set aside the entire imperial budget for the loans that financed the alimenta, thereby allowing him to expand the number of its beneficiaries dramatically. He was so proud of this achievement that he highlighted it on his coins and on his Arch of Beneventum. Trajan's own generosity encouraged private philanthropists to fund the construction of roads, temples, theaters, public baths, and aqueducts. Legend has it that he once tore his own cloak into strips when there was a shortage of bandages for his wounded soldiers. It was later alleged that Pope Gregory the Great had prayed for and won the pagan emperor's salvation, and Dante depicted him in paradise.

Hadrian (117–138)

Long before his death, Trajan had adopted his deceased cousin's ten-year-old son, Hadrian (Publius Aelius Hadrianus), as his heir. Hadrian had later married Trajan's grandniece, thus solidifying his position as Trajan's successor. Realizing that the empire was growing beyond the ability of Rome to defend, Hadrian returned most of Mesopotamia to Parthia and made Armenia a client kingdom.

Hadrian also built Hadrian's Wall, a twenty-foot-high, eight-foot-wide wall, consisting of over one million cubic yards of stone, that extended seventy-three miles between the Tyne River and Solway Firth in northern England. The wall was fronted by a ditch that was ten feet deep and twenty-five feet wide. Every five miles along the wall stood a full-sized fort, with towers in between. Manned by fifteen thousand auxiliaries, the wall successfully held off the Celts of Scotland, as well as serving as the starting point for occasional operations in enemy territory. Hadrian built a second wall in Germany in the angle between the Rhine and Danube rivers that extended 345 miles in order to fend off the Germanic tribes.

Hadrian traveled extensively, personally investigating conditions in every part of the empire. He spent more than half of his reign outside of Italy.

Intellectually inclined, Hadrian surrounded himself with poets and philosophers, wrote skillful verse in both Latin and Greek, and built lavishly in his favorite city, Athens. His villa in Tibur (Tivoli) outside Rome was an entire town, graced with splendid buildings that recalled the best he had seen on his travels and containing some of the finest sculptures of the ancient world. So great was his love of Greek culture that some resentful Romans called him "the Greek," especially after his Hellenic beard started a trend that violated the Roman tradition of clean-shaven chins.

The greatest of Hadrian's public works projects in Rome was the Pantheon, a domed temple to "all of the gods" based on a shrine built by Marcus Agrippa. Hadrian also constructed a massive tomb for himself, renamed the Castel Sant'Angelo during the Middle Ages when it served as a papal fortress. He expanded the alimenta even further. During his reign, Roman traders reached China by sea.

The dark spot in Hadrian's reign was yet another Jewish revolt (132–135), after Hadrian decided to establish a colony for Roman veterans at Jerusalem, to prohibit circumcision, and to erect an altar to Jupiter on the site where the Great Temple had stood. Led by Simon Bar-Kokhba (Son of the Star), whom a popular rabbi had proclaimed the Messiah, the rebels succeeded in defeating two Roman armies and capturing Jerusalem and fifty other towns in Judea. But in 135 the Roman general Julius Severus crushed the rebels at Bethar near Jerusalem. Bar-Kokhba was killed in the battle. The Romans destroyed hundreds of villages and slaughtered 580,000 Jews during the rebellion and sold thousands of women and children into slavery. They renamed Jerusalem, Aelia Capitolina, and Judea, Syria Palaestina, and banished Jews from the city on pain of death.

The banishment accelerated the *diaspora* (dispersion) of the Jews that had begun after the destruction of Jerusalem in 70. The Jews wandered for centuries, suffering great persecution at the hands of Christians and others. In the nineteenth century Zionists began a movement to re-create the state of Israel in the Holy Lands, a movement that finally achieved success in 1948.

Antoninus Pius (138–161)

Fifty-one years old on taking the throne, Antoninus Pius (Titus Aurelius Fulvius Antoninus) continued the policies of his predecessors. Born and raised at Nimes (in southern France), he admitted North Africans into the Senate. He was humble, tolerant, hardworking, and, yes, pious. He temporarily expanded Roman territory into Scotland, building a thirty-seven-mile wall there (the Antonine Wall), between the River Clyde and the Firth of Forth, that was almost as grand as Hadrian's.

Marcus Aurelius (161–180)

Of all the Roman emperors Antoninus' nephew, son-in-law, adopted son, and successor, Marcus Aurelius (Marcus Aelius Aurelius Antoninus), came the closest to Plato's ideal of the philosopher-king (though he considered Plato's utopian *Republic* impractical). Marcus was so magnanimous that when presented with evidence of a conspiracy against his life, he ordered the incriminating letters burned so that he could not learn the names of the conspirators and, therefore, have a reason to dislike them. He even sold some of his personal possessions to assist victims of famine and plague.

Though he preferred books to battles, Marcus faced a three-pronged invasion soon after taking the throne. In 162 the Parthians crossed the Euphrates River. Taking advantage of the resultant transfer of Roman troops to the East, various Germanic tribes then crossed the Rhine and Danube rivers. One tribe even crossed the Alps into Italy, while another lay waste to the Balkans. Marcus Aurelius was able to repel each of Rome's enemies, though at great cost. He lost so many men to wars and to an epidemic of the plague that he was forced to invite ten thousand Germanic tribesmen to settle within the empire, south of the Danube, hoping to use them as a buffer against the other Germanic tribes. His measure foreshadowed the decline of Rome, which no longer possessed enough native troops to defend its borders. It marked the beginning of a gradual process of German infiltration of the empire.

Like any good Stoic, Marcus Aurelius died at his post at Vindobona (Vienna) in 180. At Rome his equestrian statue still stands, returning the salute of legions that have been dead for almost two thousand years.

LIFE IN THE EARLY ROMAN EMPIRE

The City

The center of a vast empire, the city of Rome boasted a population of one million by the second century A.D. Within its confines, the most magnificent luxury coexisted with the most degrading squalor. The city bustled with Italians, Egyptians, Syrians, Jews, Gauls, and Spaniards—both commoners and kings. Frequent squabbles and brawls erupted between carriage drivers, the Roman equivalent of modern taxicab drivers. The barber shops overflowed with gossip, since affluent men who lacked a slave skilled in the use of a razor visited every day.

The Aristocrats

Wealthy Romans could escape the hustle and bustle of the imperial city by retiring to their rural villas on weekends and during the summer. Buried and preserved by thirteen feet of ash that covered the city after the eruption of Mount Vesuvius on August 24, A.D. 79, Pompeii, located a few miles from Naples, reveals much about the lives of Roman aristocrats during the imperial period. A prosperous commercial center of between ten thousand and twenty thousand people, Pompeii possessed spacious streets, an elegant forum, a stone amphitheater, impressive temples, delicate statues, public baths, concert halls, and brothels. (A famous sign, in the form of an erect phallus, pointed tourists to the brothels.) Election posters covered the city walls. One poster declared, "Vote for Bruttius: he'll keep the tax rates down." (Read my lips, Romans.) The forum, a large market for selling fish, utensils, wine, olive oil, and bread in flat loaves (like modern pizza bases), was closed to vehicular traffic. The houses of the aristocrats featured bright, Hellenistic-style frescoes designed to bring good fortune (including fertility) to the household. Elaborately sculpted gardens, sheltered from the noise of the streets in the back of the house, were graced with elegant fountains and Greek statues and sometimes flanked by bedrooms, libraries, and private baths. Upstairs dining rooms looked down on the street or courtyard through large windows. In the last years of the city, many old patrician houses were subdivided and converted into lodging houses or commercial enterprises.

Commoners

Commoners, both in Rome and in rural areas, lived more difficult lives. In order to escape their troubles, the unemployed of the city sought pleasure as fervently as the wealthy. Plebeians formed social clubs called *collegia*. The collegia involved themselves in feasting, celebrating, and giving decent burials to members (who no doubt died of too much feasting and celebrating). One member named Vitalis (meaning "alive") chose as his punning epitaph: "While still Vitalis, I built myself a tomb, and every time I pass I read with these two eyes my own epitaph." Even these clubs, dedicated to celebration, reflected the Roman love of order. Their leaders took an oath and rendered accounts at the end of their terms, new members were advised to read the club's rules, which were couched in the formal language of Roman law, and minutes were taken at meetings.

Of course, the government provided its own "bread and circuses" to placate the masses. It furnished grain free of charge, wine and olive oil at subsidized prices. There were over eight hundred public baths in Rome alone. The larger baths contained gardens, gymnasia, libraries, works of art, and even *baths*. An old inscription reads, "The bath, wine, and love ruin one's health but make life worth living."

Slaves

Slaves constituted approximately one-sixth of the population of Italy, one-tenth of the imperial population as a whole. Slaves were generally prisoners of war or captives purchased from "barbarian" tribes. Slave traders were obligated to reveal to potential buyers if a female slave could not bear children, if a slave had ever committed a capital offense or tried to commit suicide, and the ethnic origin of the slave. A slave could reclaim his freedom if he could prove to a Roman magistrate that pirates had kidnapped him. Rural slaves were generally employed as farm workers, herdsmen, or shepherds.

Urban slaves were used as litter bearers, secretaries, messengers, musicians, doorkeepers, cooks, butlers, nurses, and even teachers, physicians, and financial managers. Their work was less strenuous than that of rural slaves, their discipline less strict, and they had more opportunities for recreational activity. Urban slaves were kept as much for prestige as for economic benefit. State-owned slaves worked in the public baths, cleaned sewers, and maintained roads.

Slavery was less harsh in the imperial period than in the republican era. It was less humiliating to be a slave in an imperial culture in which everyone was, in a sense, a slave to the emperor. The emperors' slaves maintained the aqueducts, and freedmen formed the core of the seven thousand *vigiles*, Rome's fire brigade. Some emperors issued edicts that improved the lot of slaves or sought to protect them from extreme cruelty in other ways. Augustus once freed a young slave at a dinner party when the boy's furious master ordered him thrown to some giant lampreys he kept in a pond because the boy had broken a crystal cup. When the boy fell at Augustus' feet and begged to be allowed to die in a more humane fashion, Augustus freed the boy, ordered all of his master's crystal cups shattered before his eyes, and ordered his pond filled in with dirt. Claudius made it legal for imperial slaves to marry female citizens, in which case their children had certain civil rights.

Already more common among the Romans than among the Greeks, the manumission of slaves became even more frequent during the imperial period and was often accompanied with annuities or other property for the freedmen's maintenance. Freedmen did not become full Roman citizens (they could not serve in a legion or join the senatorial or equestrian orders) and continued to have certain social and economic obligations to their former masters. But if they married citizens, their children became full citizens. The increase in manumission, when combined with the decrease in the supply of new slaves as the rate of Roman territorial expansion slowed, led the owners of rural estates to begin to rely more on tenant farmers for agricultural production.

Yet vestiges of cruelty remained. As late as the reign of Nero, after an urban prefect was murdered by one of his slaves, all four hundred of the household's slaves were executed in compliance with an ancient custom intended to encourage slaves to inform on conspirators. A senator explained: "Nowadays our huge households are international. They include every alien religion—or none at all. The only way to keep down this scum is by intimidation. . . . Exemplary punishment always contains an element of injustice. But individual wrongs are outweighed by the advantage of the community." In some cases slaves were tortured for evidence.

Yet a few freedmen rose to a high status. Claudius promoted his freedmen to the highest positions in government. Some freedmen owned property—land, ships, businesses, and slaves. Aristocrats sometimes established their freedmen in a trade and invested in that business, since it was considered disgraceful for aristocrats to engage in trade but not to invest in it. Thankful for the education and training his master had given him, training that had allowed him to buy his freedom and, ultimately, to own and operate a successful business, a wealthy freedman in Petronius' *Satiricon* declares: "Thank heaven for slavery. It made me what you see now."

Yet mistreated slaves had little recourse. As in the Old South of the United States, they could and did sabotage equipment, delay the performance of tasks, and steal goods. But to flee successfully was difficult since the law penalized those who aided runaways, since masters had the right to search others' estates for runaways, and since some masters hired slave catchers. Slave catchers sometimes bought runaways from their former masters at a discount, so that they could sell whatever runaways they captured to different masters at full price, thereby making a nifty profit. Runaways could take refuge at a shrine. Such a runaway did not become free but could remain there until sold to a (presumably) more humane master. Rebellion usually brought swift and merciless punishment.

Women

Though poor women continued to lead difficult lives, aristocratic women enjoyed greater property rights during the early imperial period. Augustus prohibited husbands from selling land in Italy that was acquired by dowry. In the second century, some wealthy women, like Plancia Magna of Perge in Asia Minor, became famous as public benefactors, whose generosity was honored with statues and other memorials. Aristocratic women often managed their husbands', fathers', or brothers' estates in their absence. Electoral graffiti in Pompeii reveals that though women could not hold political office they often endorsed candidates.

An increase in adultery was among the factors that led some women to seek out and practice often unreliable forms of birth control and abortion. The poet Ovid chastised: "Women, why will you thrust and pierce with the instrument, and give dire poisons, to your children yet unborn? . . . This neither the tigress has done in the jungles of Armenia, nor has the lioness had the heart to destroy her unborn young; yet tender woman does it—but not unpunished; often she who slays her own dies herself. All who behold cry out, 'She deserved it!'"

There was also an increase in divorce among the upper classes. Seneca complained that many women counted the years not in the traditional Roman way, by the terms of the consuls, but by the tenures of their many husbands.

Spouses often possessed genuine affection for one another. An early first-century eulogy of a husband for his infertile wife refers to the fact that she loved him so much that she offered to divorce him so that he could marry a fertile woman and have children. He refused. An epitaph for another couple records, "For fifty years together they shared agreement unbroken." Though wives did not technically belong to their husbands' households in the most common form of marriage, husbands often willed their widows the use of property until death, at which point it reverted to the husbands' sons and daughters.

By the second century, girls in various cities could be taught by publicly funded teachers. But the subjects taught were limited to reading, writing, and grammar. Even aristocratic women were barred by custom from pursuing more than a smattering of learning, a situation that must have been frustrating to intelligent women. Writing to console his mother, Helvia, over his own exile, Seneca recalled that she had once engaged in study with her son "with a pleasure beyond" her gender. He added:

> I could wish that my father, excellent man that he was, had not been so set on following the practice of his elders and had allowed you to acquire a thorough grounding in philosophic doctrine instead of only a smattering. . . . His reason for not indulging you in deeper study was that some women do not use literature for philosophic ends but trim themselves with it for luxury's sake. But thanks to your acquisitive intellect, you imbibed a great deal for the time you spent; the foundations for the various disciplines have been laid. Return to them now; they will keep you safe, they will console you, they will cheer you.

Similarly, the famous rhetorician Quintilian wrote, "As for parents, I should like them to be as well educated as possible, and I am not speaking just of fathers."

A few women became philosophers, artists, and physicians. A second- or third-century inscription to Domnina of Neoclaudopolis in Asia Minor declares, "Men will say that you have not died but that the gods stole you away because you have saved your native fatherland from disease." The husband of Panthia of Pergamum left her a similar epitaph: "You guided straight the rudder of life in our home and raised high our common fame in healing—though you were a woman, you were not behind me in skill. . . . I myself will lie here when I die; since with you alone I shared a bed when I was alive, so may I cover myself in ground that we share."

During the imperial period, some women of the royal family (e.g., Livia, Agrippina the Younger) engaged in as much political intrigue as the men, though generally to secure the accession of their sons. The Senate still occasionally debated gender matters. During the reign of Tiberius, a senator named Aulus Caecena Severus proposed a prohibition on governors bringing their wives with them to their provinces. He declared: "My wife and I are good friends, and have produced six children. But I have practiced what I preach, by keeping her at home in Italy during all my forty years of service in various provinces! . . . Relax control, and they become ferocious, ambitious schemers, circulating among the soldiers, ordering company-commanders about. . . . The wives attract every rascal in the province. . . . [There develop] two centers of government—and the women give the more willful and despotic orders. They . . . are rulers everywhere—at home, in the courts, and now in the army." But many senators opposed the measure. One senator said of the governors: "When they return from their labors [in war] they are surely entitled to relax with their wives. Some women, we hear, are schemers or money-grubbers. But officials themselves show every sort of imperfection; yet governorships are filled. . . . The weakness of one or two husbands is no reason to deprive all of them of their wives' partnership in good times and bad. Moreover, that would mean abandoning and exposing the weaker sex to its own temptations and to masculine sensuality. Marriages scarcely survive with the keeper on the spot—what would happen with some years of virtual divorce to efface them? When reforming abuses elsewhere, remember the immorality of the capital." Tiberius' son Drusus also spoke against the measure, noting that Augustus had always traveled with his wife Livia. The matter was dropped.

Games

The emperors subsidized athletic contests, such as foot races, boxing matches, wrestling contests, and chariot races, as well as gladiatorial combat. By 180 the cry for "bread and circuses" from the roughly 15 percent of the Roman public that was unemployed grew so loud that 135 days per year were set aside as holidays, most of them devoted to public games. Such games often constituted the closest contact between the emperor and the people; emperors who chose not to attend the games were generally unpopular.

The most popular competition, by far, was the chariot race. Most races were held in the six largest racecourses in Rome. The largest was the Circus Maximus, reconstructed several times, which seated 150,000 spectators under Augustus, 250,000 under Trajan. Ovid recommended it as one of the best places for singles to meet. As many as twelve teams of two to four horses generally made seven counterclockwise rounds of the circus, a total of roughly five and one-quarter miles. Each race lasted about fifteen minutes. Since this indicates a speed of about twenty-one miles per hour, it is not surprising that chariot crashes were often fatal. There were as many as twenty-four races in a day, presided over by the emperor or one of his representatives.

Chariot drivers, who usually began as slaves, could become wealthy celebrities, and the owners of victorious horses were honored highly. Horses could become popular too; the mosaic floor of an African bathhouse possesses the inscription to one equine, "Whether you win or lose, we love you still, Polydoxus!"

A constant betting mania surrounded the races, and fans of the competing Blue and Green teams often came to blows. Rare was the Roman who was immune to the lure of the races, such as the aristocrat Pliny the Younger, who complained, "If they were attracted by the speed of the horses or the drivers' skill one could account for it, but in fact it is the racing-colors they really support and care about, and if the colors were to be exchanged in mid-course during a race, they would transfer their favor and enthusiasm and rapidly desert the famous drivers and horses whose names they shout as they recognize them from afar. Such is the popularity and importance of a worthless shirt."

Gladiatorial contests arose first among the Etruscans, who made their prisoners of war fight to the death as a way of honoring and appeasing their own dead. Even in later times, dead gladiators were hammered on the forehead and hauled out of the arena by a slave dressed as the Etruscan death-demon Charun (Virgil's Charon). The first known Roman gladiatorial games had formed part of the funeral proceedings for Decimus Junius Brutus in 264 B.C. During the First Punic War, 242 Carthaginian elephants were captured at Palermo and taken to Rome to fight with men in the Circus Maximus. By the late republican period, the sponsoring of such games had become a common way for the dedicators of temples, victorious generals, and politicians to celebrate their achievements and to curry favor with the masses. Thereafter, the emperors adopted the practice of sponsoring ever more lavish games. Before the construction of the Colosseum, the gladiatorial contests often took place in the Forum, where gladiators waited in tunnels before emerging to fight in a temporary wooden arena. Caesar became the first Roman to sponsor a gladiatorial contest in memory of a woman (his daughter Julia). Sponsors used colorful posters and heralds to advertise the games. Programs were printed; Ovid suggested borrowing a program as a good way to meet a woman.

The gladiatorial contests generally took one of three forms: gladiator versus gladiator; gladiator versus hungry, ferocious animal; and hungry, ferocious animal versus hungry, ferocious animal. The gladiators were usually trained slaves, sometimes criminals sentenced to death. Gladiators who faced animals were generally armed, unless they were terrible criminals, charged with murder, treason, arson, or being a Christian. Domitian once compelled a group of women to fight a group of dwarves and, on another occasion, had a spectator who was witty at his expense tossed to the dogs in the arena. During Trajan's various celebrations of the Dacian Wars (106–114), eleven thousand animals were slain, and ten thousand pairs of gladiators fought. By the time wild beast hunts were abolished in the sixth century, North Africa had witnessed the extinction of its elephants and hippopotami, Mesopotamia its lions, and the Caspian region its tigers.

Gladiators sometimes fought individually, sometimes in groups, each side using different weapons and armor. If a gladiator was disarmed or prostrate and raised a finger on his left hand as a plea for mercy, the emperor or the host of the games decided his fate with a thumbs-up or thumbs-down motion, with input from the screaming crowd. If a gladiator had fought well, he might be spared to entertain again. Boys raked over the blood-stained sand between contests. A basic record of outcomes was kept. Some gladiators found ways to kill themselves, though under constant guard, rather than fight in the arena. If a fighter's performance was poor, or his death was desired by the host, he could be made to fight twice in a single day. Victorious gladiators were presented with palm branches and prize money, counted out in front of the public, who counted along.

As gladiators became more expensive in the second century, more untrained criminals were used. A few free men chose to work for wages as gladiators; they were more popular with audiences because they tended to fight more enthusiastically. There were a few female gladiators before A.D. 200, when they were prohibited.

Although there were gladiatorial arenas and schools in every part of the empire, the leading schools in the capital were owned by the emperors and possessed their own arenas for training purposes. Training, often led by former gladiators, generally involved thrusting at a straw man or post with a wooden sword.

Caesar, Augustus, Claudius, Titus, and Domitian all staged sea battles involving thousands of gladiators at various lakes and in the Tiber. Caligula and Hadrian both dabbled in gladiatorial combat themselves. Supposedly, when a gladiator who was helping Caligula practice with a wooden sword fell down on purpose, onlookers were horrified to see Caligula draw a real dagger, stab the man to death, and run around waving the palm of victory. Marcus Aurelius drafted gladiators into the army to face the growing German threat, prompting fears that he was trying to force the Roman people to turn to philosophy for recreation by depriving them of their regular entertainers.

Most gladiators died in the arena; only a few ever secured their freedom and retired. Epitaphs for gladiators included: "Killed not by man but fate"; "Won but died of wounds"; "Avenged by my comrade"; and, from one killed by a rival he had spared earlier, "Take warning from my fate. Give no quarter, whoever the fallen foe may be."

Not all Romans approved of gladiatorial combat. Cicero asked: "What pleasure can a cultivated man get out of seeing a weak human being torn to pieces by a powerful animal or a splendid animal transfixed by a hunting spear?" He reluctantly financed such games when compelled by custom, but argued that it was better to spend money on walls, docks, harbors, aqueducts, and other useful things. But even Cicero saw some value in having gladiators demonstrate courage for an audience and in having criminals receive well-deserved punishment before the public.

For all of its horrible abuses, the system of imperial government established by Augustus created unprecedented security, stability, and prosperity throughout the Western world for over two centuries. In the process it saved the political, social, and cultural heritage of Greece and Rome, which had been threatened by the instability, chaos, and violence of the late Roman republic. Yet the abuses made possible by the imperial system were significant too, foreshadowing the eventual decline and fall of the empire.

THE DECLINE AND FALL OF THE WESTERN ROMAN EMPIRE

Political Decline

While it is often difficult to separate cause from effect in a society as gravely ill as that of the late Roman Empire, the cancer that ultimately killed the empire appears to have been political. Constant warfare between rival generals seeking the throne undermined the Roman economy and sapped the sense of patriotism that had been the Romans' greatest source of strength.

Commodus (180–192), the son of Marcus Aurelius, brutalized and murdered his subjects and confiscated their property. Portraying himself as Hercules (albeit one with dyed and powdered hair), the patron of gladiators, Commodus fought 1,000 bouts in the arena, 365 before he became emperor, the rest after. Though killing and mutilating some opponents in private fights, he and his adversaries fought only with wooden swords in these public bouts. But he slaughtered large numbers of animals, including one hundred bears shot from his platform in a single day. Like Caligula, he demanded that his subjects worship him as a god and, also like Caligula, he was murdered by his own Praetorian Prefect (in combination with Commodus' mistress and a professional wrestler).

After Commodus' assassination, the virtuous Pertinax (193), a friend of Marcus Aurelius, ruled for only eighty-six days before being murdered by the Praetorian Guard. The guards then offered the empire to the highest bidder.

Though Julianus won the auction, a horrifying civil war ensued. The North African general Septimius Severus (193–211) won it by offering his army twice the amount of money that Julianus paid the guards. Once in power, Severus reorganized the Praetorian Guard and transferred control of finances, the provinces, and the law to his Praetorian Prefect. While Severus dramatically increased the size of the army, he failed to increase its effectiveness; Scottish tribesmen easily repelled Severus' ill-fated invasion of their homeland. Severus summarized for posterity the reigning philosophy of third-century emperors, "Take care of the Army, and everything else will take care of itself." The Severi dynasty, consisting of Caracalla (211–217), Macrinus (217–218), Heliogabulus (218–222), and Alexander Severus (222–235), consisted of corrupt and ineffective emperors who met bad ends.

In the forty-nine years between the death of Alexander Severus and the reign of Diocletian, there were twenty-six emperors, only one of whom died a natural death. Nearly all of these emperors suffered violent deaths at the hands of the very soldiers who had placed them on the throne. There was no suitable system of succession, and "barracks emperors" (army commanders) terrorized the people. Even in the late third and fourth centuries, when the imperial succession was more stable, warfare between rival generals and their armies frequently distracted Rome from defense against invading tribes.

The Economic Decline

The inability of the emperors to control the army contributed greatly to the economic crisis of the late empire. Emperors sometimes had to tax the people at an extremely high rate in order to pay the ever-increasing bribes required to pacify the army and its generals, though no amount ever proved sufficient to ward off the ceaseless coups. Taxes became so difficult to collect that the provincial nobility, who had once sought positions on municipal councils, now went to great lengths to avoid them, since the Roman government compelled council members to make up any shortfalls in tax revenues from their own property. The avoidance of government service proved impossible, however, as Roman administrators forced those with any wealth (even children who had inherited property, in a few cases) to serve. Added to the formal taxes was an informal levy: corrupt officials frequently demanded protection money from citizens.

When even high taxes proved insufficient to raise the required revenue, the emperors (beginning with Severus) devalued the coinage, a form of taxation by inflation. The resultant hyperinflation caused the hoarding of silver, which led to the further devaluing of the coinage, which further accelerated the inflation. A single modius of wheat (8.6 liters), which had cost two sesterces in A.D. 150, cost four hundred in 300. By the fifth century, silver comprised only 2 percent of Rome's so-called silver coins, which had been 75 percent silver under Marcus Aurelius. For most of the late imperial period Roman currency was so worthless that the Roman government refused to accept it for taxes, requiring goods instead. These goods were distributed to soldiers as bonuses, since inflation had decimated their wages.

Hyperinflation discouraged all forms of economic activity and caused a decline in the population of western cities, as members of both the middle and lower classes were forced to move to great estates, where they became the serfs (*coloni*) of aristocrats, and their children inherited this status. In fact, a host of both high and low positions in the government, even including that of common soldier, began to be passed down hereditarily, and guilds were given legal control of various crafts. Feudalism did not begin in the Middle Ages, as is commonly thought, but in the late imperial period (though the empire's collapse greatly reinforced it, as each region was forced even further into military and economic self-sufficiency).

Other factors contributed to the Roman economic decline, of course. The end of territorial expansion prevented the acquisition of new resources and markets, thereby limiting economic growth. Furthermore, Rome made very few technological improvements in manufacturing, transportation, or agriculture. Once, when an engineer offered to haul some columns up to the Capitol using a mechanical device, the emperor Vespasian paid him but destroyed his device, saying, "I must always ensure that the working classes earn enough money to buy themselves food." (The notion that a labor-saving device could increase rather than decrease overall employment through greater productivity was slow in developing, even in modern times.) In addition, roads were allowed to fall into disrepair, badly injuring trade. The Romans followed a wasteful two-field system of crop and fallow that depressed agricultural production. A cold spell in the global climate exacerbated this problem and attracted unwanted attention from the Germanic tribes of the even colder north.

The Psychological Decline

The chaos, destruction, and inflation produced by political instability undermined traditional Roman confidence and patriotism. Many Romans deserted both the army and politics. By and large, they turned to religion for consolation. The cults of the Roman Bacchus, the Persian (originally Indian) Mithras, the Phrygian Cybele, and the Egyptian Isis all achieved popularity within the empire.

Like the other religions, Christianity profited from the psychic crisis. But Christianity also helped destroy the empire by turning many intelligent and desperately needed Romans from a life of political leadership to an ascetic lifestyle focused on the next life. Christianity may also have exacerbated the economic crisis; much of the late empire's private and public wealth gravitated to the Church, which was exempt from the taxes needed to fund the common defense and whose clergy were exempt from military service. Indeed, some pagan aristocrats even joined the Church and became bishops to escape the fighting.

The Military Decline

These political, economic, and psychological crises produced a military crisis that proved fatal to the empire. The absence of that confidence and patriotism that had always formed the foundation of Roman military success forced the emperors to rely increasingly on foreign enlistees and mercenaries, a common sign of a declining power. Indeed, by the fourth century, most barbarian generals in the Roman army retained their Germanic names, rather than adopting Roman names like their predecessors. Roman soldiers of the late imperial period often had to be conscripted and were so undisciplined that they sometimes refused to wear armor and helmets or carry weapons, and when forced to do so, deserted. In some instances Romans even severed a thumb to avoid military service. Soldiers began to resist the manual labor (the raising of walls, the digging of ditches, the draining of swamps, and road construction) that had been central to a Roman soldier's life for centuries, viewing such work as beneath them.

As a result of the psychological crisis, the Romans suffered a series of military disasters. In 231 the Persians, having overthrown the Parthians, defeated the Romans and terrorized the eastern part of the empire. In 251 the

Germanic Goths crossed the Danube River into Dacia, defeated a Roman army, terrorized the Balkans, threatened Italy, and brought trade in the eastern Mediterranean to an abrupt halt through piracy. In 267–268, the Heruli, a Germanic tribe from southern Russia, plundered the coasts of the Black and Aegean seas, burning Ephesus and Athens.

Although two emperors, one a persecutor of Christians named Diocletian, the other a convert to Christianity named Constantine, managed to slow the decline of the ailing empire, they were unable to save it. In fact, Diocletian's division of the empire into two parts worsened the economic situation by replacing the one imperial court with four new lavish courts. (The emperor of each half possessed a deputy emperor, who possessed his own court.) Constantine's transference of the imperial capital to the Greek city of Byzantium, which later became known as Constantinople, added further expense, as great treasure was lavished on the city. By looting pagan temples of their gold, Constantine managed to restore a sound gold currency, but this significant advancement was more than counteracted by the excessive taxation needed to fund his massive spending.

In 372 the Huns, a large, nomadic tribe of superb horsemen who had originated in central Asia, crossed the Volga River in what is now Russia and defeated the Ostrogoths of the Ukraine, setting their fields and villages aflame. Surviving Ostrogoths were forced to join the rampaging Huns as allies. The terrified Visigoths then received Roman permission to cross the Danube and settle in Thrace. Rather than combining with the Visigoths to oppose the Huns, the Romans oppressed them.

The generally tolerant Romans never made a serious effort to assimilate the Germans as they had so many other peoples, considering them hopeless barbarians. This was a mistake, because the Germanic tribes were beginning to perceive their own relative power and the Romans' relative weakness.

The Visigoths finally erupted in rebellion and, with the help of the Ostrogoths and of some Romans, devastated much of the Balkans. In 378 the emperor Valens was killed and lost two-thirds of his army at Adrianople while attempting to suppress the Visigothic rebellion. Valens' successor, Theodosius I (378–395), was forced to accept an unprecedented migration of Visigoths into the empire and to recognize them as part of the Roman army.

In 410 the Visigoths, under Alaric, besieged Rome, causing so severe a famine in the city that there were rumors of cannibalism. When Alaric's demand for all of the city's gold, silver, and silk cloth was rejected, he entered a city gate that had been opened for him by slaves and domestics at midnight. The Visigoths murdered or enslaved many Romans, but left after only six days to plunder southern Italy.

The Western world was shocked. Foreign conquerors had not entered Rome since the Gauls had occupied part of the city eight centuries earlier. Even the great Hannibal had never entered it. Alaric died the same year, but his successor carved out a sizable kingdom for the Visigoths in southern Gaul and Spain, a kingdom the Romans were forced to recognize in 419.

In the 420s the Germanic Angles and Saxons were allowed to settle in Britain, only to rebel and conquer the province two decades later. Also in the 420s the Alemanni and Franks crossed the Rhine and settled in Gaul.

In the 430s the Vandals, a Germanic tribe that had assumed control of parts of Spain, conquered most of North Africa. They destroyed cities and tortured people to locate their hidden wealth.

In 447 Attila and the Huns, who had since forged an empire from the Baltic Sea to the Danube, plundered Illyricum; only the Huns' lack of siege equipment and experience prevented them from capturing Constantinople. The Eastern Emperor Theodosius II was forced to cede land south of the Danube to the Huns and to pay them tribute.

In 452 the Huns sacked Milan and advanced on Rome. Pope Leo I managed to convince Attila, who had great reverence for priests of all religions, to turn away from the city. He was planning another invasion of Italy when he died of a burst artery the following year.

In 455 the Vandals sailed across from North Africa and sacked Rome, hauling away nearly all of its remaining wealth, public and private. Among the items the Vandals looted were the Menorah and other items the Romans had taken from the Great Temple of Jerusalem almost four centuries earlier. (These items were later taken from the Vandals by a Byzantine army.) Every spring thereafter the Vandals, accompanied by Roman converts to piracy, sailed forth from Carthage with a massive fleet to plunder a different part of the ever-dwindling empire.

The usual date for the fall of the western part of the Roman Empire is 476. In that year Odoacer, the Herulian commander of the Roman army (by then most of the army was German), demanded that one-third of Italy be allotted to his men in reward for their service. When Orestes, who was acting as regent for his young son, Romulus Augustulus, refused, Odoacer dropped the pretense of Roman rule and seized control of the city. Orestes was put to death, Romulus sent into exile at a villa near Naples. Thus did Rome begin with one Romulus and end with another.

Only the Western Empire fell. The more prosperous, populous, and geographically secure Eastern Empire continued, though greatly diminished by the Arab conquests of the seventh century, until the Turks conquered it in 1453. Constantinople (Istanbul), the capital of this Byzantine Empire, remained one of the largest, most splendid, and most learned cities in the world.

CONCLUSION

This summary of 1,200 years of Roman history has hopefully provided an adequate background for the chapters that follow, chapters devoted to delineating Rome's numerous contributions to the Western world. This tale of a tiny village in central Italy that rose to an unprecedented height of power and wealth was the story that inspired Roman jurists, engineers, architects, poets, philosophers, and historians to create incredible works of genius.

· 2 ·

Administration and Law

*T*he Romans were not merely the modifiers and transmitters of Greek culture and of Christianity. They also made original contributions to the Western world. They not only provided the conditions of peace and prosperity necessary for the transmission of Greco-Roman culture and Christianity but also proved themselves the most capable administrators and lawgivers in human history. They effectively administered an empire of unprecedented size with minimal bureaucracy and technology and bequeathed to the West a system of law whose principles of equity and justice endured long after the fall of the empire.

THE PAX ROMANA

The term *pax Romana* was first used by Pliny the Elder, who exulted in "the immense majesty of the Roman peace." During the days of the early Roman Empire, the seventy-five million subjects of Rome enjoyed a greater degree of peace than the Mediterranean world had ever known. The inner provinces of the empire experienced an end to the constant warfare that constituted life before. Although the Romans still waged periodic wars along their far-flung borders, most of the provinces remained tranquil.

While it is true that the Romans secured this peace through conquest—according to Tacitus, a Celtic chieftain once complained, "They make a desert and call it peace"—peace, however acquired, was a rare and priceless commodity in the ancient world. A second-century Greek named Aelius Aristides was exaggerating but also making a valid and important point when he declared:

Only those, if there are any, who are outside your Empire are to be pitied for the blessings which they are denied. Better than all others, you have demonstrated the universal saying that the earth is the mother of all and the fatherland of all. Greek and barbarian, with his property or without it, can go with ease wherever he likes, just as though going from one homeland to another. The Cilician Gates hold no terror, nor the narrow and desert approaches from Arabia to Egypt, nor inaccessible mountains nor uncrossed expanses of rivers, nor tribes inhospitable to the stranger, for safety it is enough to be a Roman or one of your subjects. In very deed you have made real Homer's dictum that the earth is the property of all; you have measured the whole world, spanned rivers with bridges of divers kinds, cut through mountains to make level roads for traffic, filled desolate places with farmsteads, and made life easier by supplying its necessities amid law and order. Everywhere are gymnasia, fountains, gateways, temples, factories, schools, and it could be said in technical phrase that the world which from the beginning has been laboring in illness has now been put in the way of health. . . . Cities are radiant in their splendor and their grace, and the whole earth is trim as a garden.

PROSPERITY

The Roman consolidation of the Mediterranean basin and western Europe resulted in the abolition of tariffs between states, a dramatic reduction in piracy and highway robbery, the construction of cities and roads to connect them, and the establishment of a sound, standardized coinage. Using Greek weights and designs, the Romans began minting their own coins as early as the Pyrrhic War (282–275 B.C.). As dictator, Caesar was the first living Roman to allow his own image to be used on coins. One such coin featured a globe on the opposite side to depict his aspirations for world power. Augustus established an efficient monetary system, made possible by elaborate mining facilities and augmented by local small change. Gold and silver coins were minted at Lugdunum (Lyons), while the senatorial mint at Rome produced copper and bronze coins. The images on coins were frequently changed, allowing emperors to highlight their own accomplishments, or to introduce their chosen successor to the provinces. Some coins discovered at military posts are stamped with the commander's name as well.

Together, these developments generated an explosion in trade in the first and second centuries, which, in turn, produced prosperity. Roman coins found in every part of the empire show that barter virtually disappeared. Merchants even dispatched 120 ships per year to India via the Red Sea to trade their pots and other goods for Indian spices, jewels, and ivory and for Chinese silk. Amber was imported from the Baltic coast, incense from Arabia, and ivory from Africa. Roman coins have been discovered as far away as South Korea. Banks were established to hold money on deposit, make payments on behalf of depositors according to written instructions, and transfer funds between depositors.

It is important to note, however, that the economy of the empire still rested squarely on agriculture, and the cities (particularly in the west) consumed more than they produced. Without a revolution in agricultural production like that which occurred in late-eighteenth-century Europe, there could be no industrial revolution like that which occurred in the nineteenth century. The western cities lived on borrowed time, supported by a prosperous empire.

EFFICIENT ADMINISTRATION

The Romans were administrative geniuses who organized a vast empire with little bureaucracy and limited technology. Roman administration of conquered territories passed through three distinct phases. In the early days of the republic, when the Romans conquered Italy, administration was extremely minimal. The Romans won the loyalty of the conquered Italians through relatively lenient treatment. Although most subject states had to adhere to Rome's foreign policy, to supply auxiliaries for the Roman army, and to surrender 20 percent of their land, the Romans demanded no tribute and allowed each city to retain its local self-government. Some cities were even allowed full Roman citizenship and given loot and land. Such leniency was extremely uncommon in the ancient world. Even the "enlightened" Greeks often slaughtered or enslaved conquered peoples. Roman leniency in Italy proved wise. During the Second Punic War, when Hannibal and the Carthaginians invaded Italy, their failure to entice Italians into widespread rebellion saved Rome and proved fatal to Carthage.

In the mid to late republican period Roman administration of newly conquered territories outside of Italy was harsher. Beginning with the islands of Sicily, Sardinia, and Corsica, Rome's overseas provinces were taxed and disarmed. Sicily and Sardinia were placed under the rule of Roman praetors. Local leaders, operating under Roman direction, were allowed to continue governing most other territories until 146 B.C., at which point they were replaced by Roman military governors, who were called proconsuls because they acted "for the consuls." Some client kingdoms remained in eastern territories, though nearly all were converted into provinces by the second century A.D. Alliances between allies and subjects of Rome were forbidden, so that each dependent community had legal relations only with Rome.

In the late republican era Roman proconsuls and tax collectors plundered their provinces shamelessly, both for Rome and for themselves. Provinces paid an annual tribute in addition to other taxes. Far from the prying eyes of the Senate, and largely ignorant of local cultures, the underpaid and overworked proconsuls extorted as much wealth as possible from the helpless inhabitants of their provinces. One proconsul explained that he needed to extract three fortunes from his province: one to pay the debts incurred in bribing senators to obtain the position, another to bribe the jury at his inevitable trial for corruption, and a third fortune to last the rest of his life. Even Cato the Elder, famed for his virtue, plundered Spain mercilessly after the Second Punic War. Tax-collecting syndicates used their political influence in Rome to pressure even honest governors into giving them free rein. Such companies issued bids to the Roman treasury; the highest bidder received the tax-collection contract for a province, but then had to pay the entire amount in advance before collecting taxes from the province. These tax collectors could then collect excess taxes as profit. Since governors served only one year, they knew little about their provinces and had little emotional investment in them. They often followed the advice of the most powerful provincials in order to avoid trouble. Provincials who attempted to prosecute governors after their term (they could not be prosecuted during their term) were rarely successful.

But the imperial period witnessed a considerable improvement in Roman administration of the provinces, despite the fact (because of the fact?) that the government remained incredibly small. In the first century A.D. the Roman administrative departments that oversaw the vast empire consisted of only 150 to 350 officials. Even in a crucial province like Egypt, it has been estimated that the proportion of imperial officials to the overall population was less than one in ten thousand. Unlike the republican magistrates of the past, officials now received salaries and often served much longer than a year, lending more professionalism and continuity to the civil service.

With a few exceptions, the early Roman emperors governed capably. Augustus, the most capable of them all, marveled at the fact that Alexander the Great had devoted so much care to conquering his empire and so little to administering it properly. Both Augustus and the Antonines of the following century made a point of removing corrupt or inefficient proconsuls and of appointing honest and efficient legati to govern the outer provinces. Roman governors emphasized, as much as possible, provincial autonomy and local self-government. Cities retained their own magistrates, senates, popular assemblies, and legal codes. Local dignitaries acted as liaisons for their cities in Rome. In the east, Roman administrative correspondence, conducted via a reliable postal service, was conducted in Greek, the literary language of the Eastern Empire, and important records often featured parallel texts in both Greek and Latin.

Beginning with the Italians in the first century B.C., the Romans adopted a policy of extending citizenship gradually throughout the empire, a policy that culminated in Caracalla's edict granting it to virtually the entire free population of the Roman Empire (A.D. 212). By that time, about half of the senators came from the provinces.

This policy of assimilation affected even the imperial throne. The second century witnessed the accession of Spanish emperors (Trajan and Hadrian), the third century of North Africans (the Severi), and the fourth and fifth centuries of emperors from the Balkans (Diocletian and Constantine).

This pluralism was one of the wisest of Rome's policies. It enabled the Romans to hold together a vast empire of innumerable ethnic groups with a minimum of rebellion and to avoid an inefficient, centralized bureaucracy, thereby allowing them to maintain taxes at a tolerable level until the late imperial period. The Roman army benefited as well from the added expertise introduced by Syrian archers, North African light cavalry, and Gallic heavy cavalry, and the navy consisted largely of provincial sailors and rowers.

Augustus established the precedent of the census. Conducted by each community independently but collated and transmitted to the Roman archives by imperial officials, the census allowed emperors to monitor changes in the population, wealth, and resources of each province. Thus, emperors were generally able to preserve the goodwill of the provincials by shifting the tax burden from those provinces least able to pay. Augustus issued annual financial statements and, at the time of his death, left an exhaustive account of the armed forces and revenues of the empire.

Most revenue raised in the provinces remained there, to cover the expenses of local administrations. There was virtually no increase in taxes in the two centuries between Augustus and Septimius Severus. Rather than raising taxes, most of the early emperors who were faced with budgetary crises either altered their policies, as in the case of Hadrian's territorial retrenchment, or economized, as with the frugal Tiberius and with Marcus Aurelius, who auctioned off palace furniture. Private tax collectors played a smaller and smaller role in taxation. Those who felt unfairly taxed could sue the treasury, although after Hadrian there were lawyers to defend it. Even those emperors who became infamous for their tyrannical behavior largely restricted themselves to victimizing the leading aristocrats of Rome, which is why aristocratic Roman historians so despised them; the typical provincial hardly noticed any change from one emperor to the next.

Beginning with Claudius, there was a move toward specialization and professionalism within the bureaucracy. Claudius established a research department to help the emperor draft documents and speeches. Just as the Julio-Claudians and Flavians made wide use of capable and loyal freedmen, the Antonines employed capable and loyal equites, who became the pillars of imperial administration, serving as governors, postmasters general, supervisors of the corn supply, and Praetorian prefects. The Antonines dispatched representatives (*curatores*) to the cities to monitor and advise local officials and to exert fiscal discipline. A Greek orator spoke for many when he declared, "The whole world speaks in unison more distinctly than a chorus; and so well does it harmonize under this director-in-chief [Augustus] that it joins in praying this empire may last for all time."

LAW

Roman law emphasized two important principles. The first was equity, the idea of fairness and impartiality in the application of the law. This did not mean complete equality before the law, since Roman law distinguished not only between free and slave but also between various classes of free people. But it did mean that the law should be applied fairly and impartially within the context of these legal categories. The second principle was that of the prosecutorial burden to prove the guilt of the defendant. The emperor Trajan was speaking out of a long Roman legal tradition when he asserted that it was better that a guilty person should go unpunished than that an innocent person should be punished.

The *ius civile*, or civil law, which had begun with the Law of the Twelve Tables around 450 B.C., pertained only to Roman citizens, since the provinces were allowed to retain their own laws and legal systems. Like most early legal codes, the Twelve Tables possessed features that were harsh by later standards. It granted the pater familias, or male head of the household, absolute authority, including the rarely used right to kill children or sell them into slavery. It decreed that "a notably deformed child shall be killed immediately." It placed even adult women under the strict guardianship of fathers or husbands due to their alleged "levity of mind," though allowing the loophole that, "If any woman is unwilling to be subjected in this manner to her husband's marital control, she shall absent herself for three successive nights in every year and by this means shall interrupt his prescriptive right of each year." It allowed fathers and husbands, under certain conditions, the right to kill daughters and wives caught in the act of adultery. It also prohibited burials or cremations in the city (hence the large numbers of tombs immediately outside Rome), hostile demonstrations, and nocturnal assemblies. In a nod to earlier systems of private vengeance, victims of crime were allowed to impose the legal penalty against the perpetrator, which was generally intended to fit the crime (e.g., a murderer would be killed, an arsonist would be burned alive, and a thief who stole crops would be hanged in the field as a sacrifice to Ceres). It mandated death for judges convicted of taking bribes. As befitted the law of a primitive, agricultural society, it possessed few stipulations concerning commercial law.

By the third century B.C., territorial and commercial expansion necessitated the *ius gentium*, or law of nations, which was applicable to dealings between Romans and foreigners, or between foreigners present in Rome. After 242 B.C., the urban praetor retained jurisdiction over Roman citizens, while the foreign praetor assumed it in cases involving foreigners. A century and a half later, the dictator Sulla greatly increased the number of praetors to deal with the enormous increase in lawsuits.

The law of nations derived from Roman legal principles like equity and from the mercantile law long employed in Mediterranean commerce. It was necessarily broad and tolerant, since it applied to diverse cultures. By the early third century A.D. the large-scale extension of Roman citizenship had eroded the distinction between the civil law and the law of nations.

The Roman legal system was flexible enough to incorporate such changes, since the praetors were given some degree of freedom in interpreting the law, yet it was also stable enough to ensure a degree of predictability and fairness. Praetors began their terms of office by displaying lists of the causes of action they would recognize and the remedies they would adopt on a whitewashed tablet (*album*). These "edicts" were theoretically alterable but, in practice, became fairly standardized and changed little over time. Every new praetor had the opportunity of deleting what was antiquated and of including new remedies, which, if they proved themselves over time, would then be copied by other praetors and become standard elements of the praetorian edict. This combination of flexibility and stability, so essential to law in all times and places, was one of the keys to the success of Roman law in meeting the needs of the day. Unfortunately, the praetorian edict was fixed into a final form under Hadrian in A.D. 130, and, thereafter, could only be altered with the consent of the emperor.

Praetors, like judges and juries, often consulted *jurisprudentes*, those "skilled in law." Beginning with Augustus, the opinions of the emperors' legal experts were sometimes published and given the imperial stamp of approval, thereby reducing the potential for praetorian corruption by giving litigants an authoritative standard to which they could appeal. Thus, Augustus created a source of guidance for the administration of justice that operated in much the same way as do the highest courts today. Some jurists taught law courses, and law schools developed, thereby increasing knowledge of the law.

In criminal cases the praetor's principal task was to supervise the selection of a jury. Political offenses, such as dereliction of duty by a proconsul, were generally tried by a jury of senators (and, later, equites) chosen by the praetor himself. After 149 B.C., in most other criminal cases, the accuser and accused jointly selected jurors from special lists, each pertaining to a different type of crime. Juries might contain as many as seventy-five members. Jurors listened in silence and were forbidden to speak to one another. The presiding praetor restricted himself to ensuring an orderly conduct of the trial. The accused could have up to six legal advocates, who were given 50 percent more speaking time than the accuser. The jurors' voting tablets were placed in an urn and counted. Since a juror could abstain, the tally for each side was sometimes equal, a result that led to acquittal. A large number of abstentions, the equivalent of a hung jury, led to a new trial.

Unlike the Athenians, the Romans permitted defense by legal advocates. In fact, the foreign praetor might even assign an advocate to a foreigner, though these public defenders were not always the best attorneys. When assigned a stupid lawyer, a Sicilian said, "Praetor, please assign that gentleman as counsel to my opponent, and then I will not ask you to assign any counsel to me."

Trials before the construction of basilicas (the Roman term for public buildings), like gladiatorial contests before the erection of the Colosseum, were held in the open air of the Forum and often attracted crowds of spectators. They were so popular that aristocratic boys sometimes staged mock trials. Pliny the Younger complained, however, that unskilled attorneys paid some audience members, who were not even listening, to cheer their horrid speeches at various points when given a signal. The sober Pliny called the cheers "howling," for "no other word can express this applause, which would be indecent even in the theater."

Attorneys could not accept fees but generally received gifts, loans, and other favors, including inclusion in wills, from defendants. As in Athens, there were no professional prosecutors; whatever citizen proffered the charge prosecuted the case.

Attorneys were often allowed numerous hours to speak over many days. Pliny epitomized Roman seriousness about trials: "One of the first duties of a magistrate under oath is patience. . . . You will protest that a good deal is said which is irrelevant. That may be, but it is better than leaving out essentials, and it is impossible to judge what is irrelevant without first hearing it." Any citizen in good standing could bring a charge, but if he was found guilty of making an accusation in bad faith, he was branded on the forehead with the letter *K* (for *kalumniator*, or "slanderer").

In criminal cases, an attorney could generally gain more glory and wealth by defense than by prosecution. Cicero wrote: "The side of the defense is more honorable. . . . It requires a heartless man, it seems, or rather one who is well-nigh inhuman, to be arraigning one person after another on capital charges. It is not only fraught with danger to the prosecutor himself but is damaging to his reputation, to allow himself to be called a prosecutor."

By the first century B.C., aristocratic convicts were generally allowed to escape into exile rather than face execution. Nevertheless, their property was confiscated and they lost the rights of citizenship, including inheritance. Vestal Virgins and emperors' wives (who possessed the rights of Vestals) could pardon individuals.

By contrast, criminal defendants in republican Rome who were of low or slave origin were generally tried not by the praetors and their elite juries, but by the *tresviri capitales*, magistrates of lower rank who also had the task of policing the city, superintending the state jail, and carrying out executions. Augustus replaced these *tresviri capitales* with urban prefects, who had the authority to try multiple offenses at once and whose judicial knowledge exceeded that of most praetors. Thus, not only were the urban prefects' trials swifter, but their quality of justice was generally superior. Although low-born convicts might now be sentenced to gladiatorial schools, mines, or public works projects, there were fewer death sentences than under the republic. Sacred temples (*asyla*) offered sanctuary to those who fled there to escape punishment.

In civil cases the praetor's principal task was to settle between the parties the exact nature of their dispute and of their claims and counterclaims. The praetor then issued a formula that appointed a specific judge to try the action and contained a precise statement of the question the judge had to decide. A typical formula might read: "Let Titius be judge. If it appears that the defendant ought to give ten thousand sesterces to the plaintiff, let the judge condemn the defendant to the plaintiff in that sum; if it does not so appear, let him acquit." Through such formulae, praetors managed to extend civil law beyond the rigid confines of the Twelve Tables and other statutes to new areas, such as the protection of foreigners from theft and the enforcement of "good faith" pledges in business deals, both necessary preconditions to commercial prosperity.

A praetor could dismiss a case he considered flimsy, but, in such an instance, the plaintiff could always resubmit the case to a different praetor the following year or appeal to the tribunes or to the emperor. The emperor Claudius, who frequently attended praetorian sessions to ensure their fairness, created a legal office to help him adjudicate such cases. (Emperors could also hear appeals from citizens in criminal cases, and provincial governors could hear the criminal cases of foreigners if local leaders requested it, as in the case of Pontius Pilate and Jesus.)

Praetors selected the same sort of men (at first only senators, later equites as well) to serve as judges in civil cases as they chose to serve as juries in criminal cases, based on the suggestions of the plaintiff and defendant. In civil cases there was generally a single judge and no jury. (In rare cases there might be three or five judges.) Like the juries in criminal cases, judges in civil cases served free of charge, as a public service, and had to be officially excused by the praetor if they wished to be released from service. Conscientious judges asked to be excused from cases in which there was a danger, or even sometimes the appearance, of partiality. Only in the later empire did judges become paid magistrates organized in a bureaucratic hierarchy.

Inheritance disputes among the wealthy might go before a jury of one hundred. All descendants could expect to inherit a share of their father's estate unless specifically disinherited, which was rare.

Laws were kept in a record office in the Forum and at various archives, including in provincial capitals. Cities had archives of their own laws.

While the degree of influence of Stoicism on Roman law is open to debate, it seems clear that many Roman jurists accepted the Stoic concept of natural law, a universal code of ethics ascertainable by all humans through intuition and reason, and attempted to conform their verdicts to its ideals of reason and equity. The Roman belief in natural law was reinforced by the discovery of similarities in the legal codes of different cultures. Nevertheless, natural law concepts did not always prevail in civil law. For instance, the second-century jurist Florentinus noted, "Insofar as civil law is concerned, slaves are deemed nonpersons; but not so in natural law, since insofar as natural law is concerned, all men are equal."

In the early third century the great jurist Ulpian (Domitius Ulpianus) of Tyre wrote approximately two hundred books that helped explain Roman law to the many people who had recently become citizens under Caracalla's edict. Ulpian wrote: "Justice is a steady and enduring desire to give every man his due. The basic principles of the law are these: to live honorably, not to injure any other person, and to render to each his own. Jurisprudence is the knowledge of things divine and human, the science of what is right and wrong." He wrote large commentaries on numerous civil-law topics, including the praetor's edict, as well as on the duties of provincial governors. His comprehensiveness and willingness to entertain the divergent views of earlier jurists earned him a prominent place in the study of the civil law. He argued for the crucial theory of popular sovereignty, claiming that even the edicts of the emperors were law not merely because they represented the will of the emperor, but also because the people had supposedly consented to that particular mode of legislation. Ulpian declared, "The will of the prince has the force of the law because the people conferred on him all its power." Thus, the principle of popular sovereignty, however poorly implemented in Western practice for centuries, survived to reemerge as a cornerstone of modern democracy.

By contrast with classical civil law, the simplified law of the late imperial period (the "vulgar" or "popular" law) tended toward verbosity and harshness. It was this law that dominated the early Middle Ages, just as medieval Latin was largely derived from the "vulgar Latin" of the late empire. Still, it is a remarkable testimony to the efficacy of both the Roman law and the Roman language, even in their declining states, that the Germanic tribes that overthrew the western portion of the Roman Empire should have borrowed so heavily from both. Ironically, once defeated, the Romans finally achieved what they had failed to achieve at the height of their power: the imposition of their law and language on the German people.

An additional irony is that it was the Eastern Empire, which remained largely Greek in culture, having never assimilated Roman culture as fully as the less developed West, that came to the rescue of classical Roman law. The sixth-century Byzantine emperor Justinian established a commission of legal scholars to codify the civil law. Led by Tribonianus, the commission was heavily influenced by teachers from the law schools at Berytos (Beirut) and Constantinople, which, by then, were (along with the jurists of the higher courts) about the only easterners still using Latin. It is difficult to exaggerate the influence of Justinian's *Corpus Iuris Civilis* (Body of Civil Law, 529–533), composed of the *Institutes* (an elementary treatise on law based on the second-century *Institutes* of Gaius), the *Digest* (which contained the basic Roman statutes and commentaries on them by past eminent lawyers), and the *Code* (which contained imperial statutes since the time of Hadrian).

Classical Roman law revived powerfully in western Europe in the late eleventh century when the *Corpus* was rediscovered in the West. For centuries thereafter, French, Spanish, and German students studied Roman law at Italian universities. Roman law became the basis of a common western European legal culture.

Roman law remains the basis for the legal codes of most western European and Latin American countries, as well as Quebec and Louisiana, and for some of the canon law of the Roman Catholic Church. Even in English-speaking countries, where common law prevails, Roman law has exerted substantial influence. One of the few opinions Thomas Jefferson and Alexander Hamilton shared was their reverence for Roman civil law, whose influence in the United States increased after the Revolutionary War. Many of the founders of the United States considered Roman law more rational and more truly based on natural law than the common law. The Supreme Court justice Joseph Story led a nineteenth-century movement to use Roman legal concepts to reform the more chaotic common law and to provide guidance in those areas in which the common law was silent. Roman civil law greatly influenced water and commercial law in the United States and provided the foundation for international law.

CONCLUSION

For all of the imperfections in the Roman effort to realize the ideal of fairness and impartiality in the application of the law, the very introduction of this ideal into Western civilization made it more just and humane than it would have been otherwise and led eventually to the broader ideal of equality before the law. Such ideals are crucial. Though they are, by their very nature, unattainable, the very effort to attain them improves those societies that undertake the effort. Furthermore, the concept of prosecutorial burden has proved essential in maintaining the rights of defendants. When combined with peace, prosperity, and efficient administration, Roman law proved a crucial basis for the success of the Roman Empire and an important foundation of Western civilization.

• 3 •

Engineering and Architecture

$\mathcal{T}$ he Romans were the greatest builders in the ancient world. They constructed the most durable roads, bridges, aqueducts, and buildings that had ever been built. Indeed, many of their structures are still used today. Employing the arch and concrete, they constructed marvels of unprecedented size and complexity.

ENGINEERING

Roads

By 244 B.C. the first and most famous Roman highway, the Appian Way, extended 230 miles southeastward from Rome to Brundisium (Brindisi). Begun in 312 B.C. by Appius Claudius, the Appian Way was constructed to aid the Roman army. Consisting of smoothly fitted blocks of lava resting on a heavy stone foundation, some of it still survives. (See photo 3.1.)

It was long believed that all Roman roads were made the same—three to four feet thick, consisting of three layers of successively finer stones set in mortar, topped with a layer of fitted stone blocks. But it is now clear that there was no "standard Roman road." Gravel, stone, cement, earth, pebbles, and broken tile were all used in the construction of various highways. Roman engineers varied both their materials and their methods, even along the same road, according to the degree of support in the subsoil and the available resources. Some roads consisted of a timber framework, pinned to the ground with vertical stakes, on which rested tree trunks topped by limestone cemented with clay, in turn covered with gravel and pebbles. The widths

Photo 3.1.   Via Appia (Appian Way). *Scala/Art Resource, NY*

of even neighboring roads could vary from eleven and a half to twenty-five feet. Some, like the streets of Pompeii, had well-marked ruts made by wagons, which used poles for braking. Some intercity roads were flanked by leveled verges; it is perhaps along these shoulders, rather than on the roads themselves, that the largely unshod draught animals pulled their springless wagons. The roads themselves, with their paving stones, were clearly built for pedestrians, horses, and pack animals, not wagons, though some mountain roads featured artificial ruts intended to provide vehicles with traction on steep inclines.

Most Roman highways began as tools of military conquest, though quickly utilized by merchants. They were built so as to allow legionaries firm footing in all sorts of weather. First in Italy and later in England and North Africa, the Romans established a ladder pattern of roads, in which two main highways formed the shafts of the ladder and cross-links formed the rungs, to connect their armies and exploit their successes. London first became an important city not only because it was the first convenient crossing place of the Thames, but also because it was the chief modal point of the Roman road system in England.

By A.D. 200 the Romans had constructed over fifty-three thousand miles of major highways and two hundred thousand miles of secondary roads (the latter comprised mostly of gravel). Twenty-nine highways radiated from Rome itself. The Aurelian Way proceeded northwest from Rome to Pisa, from which the Way of Aemilius Scaurus continued to Genoa, from which the Julian-Augustan Way continued into southern France, from which the Domitian Way passed into Spain, ending at Gades (Cadiz) on the Atlantic coast. This series of connected highways was known collectively as "The Great West Road." One branch of the Domitian Way reached Bordeaux, offering a faster path to the ocean, while another coursed northward to Lugdunum (Lyons). Eastward from Rome the Flaminian Way proceeded to Remini on the Adriatic coast. The Egnatian Way, the first Roman highway outside of Italy, proceeded through Macedon, thereby connecting the Adriatic with the Aegean. As a result, one of the favorite routes from Rome to the East, for soldier and civilian alike, was down the Appian Way to Brindisi, then by ship across the Adriatic, then via the Egnatian Way to Thessalonica, then by ship to Ephesus, which served as the hub of another network of highways. In the Forum stood the *milliarium aureum* (the Golden Milestone), the starting point of the Roman road system. Thus began the famous expression, "All roads lead to Rome."

Provincial governors often oversaw the construction of major highways, not to mention bridges, tunnels, forts, walls, canals, and even markets and baths. For such projects, the governors generally appointed a director who was a combined surveyor, engineer, and architect. Among his tools were a portable sundial for fixing directions and a cross-staff to lay down straight lines. The labor force consisted largely of soldiers aided by locals.

Wherever possible, Roman engineers plotted direct routes, building embankments through marshland, bridging or filling in depressions, and tunneling through hills, which was no easy task before the invention of dynamite. Their mountain roads in the Alps and the Apennines were superbly planned and engineered. They could construct steep highways in the mountains since they were built for pedestrians, pack animals, and horses, not motorized vehicles.

Couriers could now travel up to fifty miles per day overland. Roman road construction design and techniques, and the speed of land travel they made possible, were not surpassed until the nineteenth century. The road system was the foundation on which Roman prosperity and defense rested.

Aqueducts

Most Roman aqueducts consisted largely of an underground conduit made of stone or terra-cotta pipe. Only a small portion of their length was comprised of an aboveground conduit that carried water across valleys on stone, brick, or concrete arches. Gravity was made to perform the arduous work of carrying the water; the elevation of the aqueducts dropped very gradually from the water source to the city. Engineers had to tunnel through intervening mountains when the fall from the source to the delivery point was too slight to accommodate the longer circuit around the mountain; in such cases, vertical shafts were sunk into the tunnel every 116 feet to allow ease of access for maintenance in case of subsidence, leakage, or flooding of the tunnel. The water generally flowed in an open channel, in order to reduce obstructions, but sometimes in enclosed pipes, in a decline of two or three feet per mile. The waters of the various aqueducts were channeled into covered basins outside the city, where they deposited their sediment, and were then piped into water towers, from which they were made to flow into smaller reservoirs around the city. Pipes distributed the water to consumers.

The first Roman aqueduct was constructed by Appius Claudius, the same censor who authorized the Appian Way. The second aqueduct, the Old Anio (272 B.C.), was financed by the booty captured from Pyrrhus. In republican times the water system was operated by private contractors and overseen by censors, who fined illicit use by large-scale private users. As censor, Cato the Elder once made enemies by severing the pipes by which such people diverted the public water supply illegally.

Under Augustus, the system was overseen by an imperial water commissioner, who determined how much water should go to public structures (including baths), to the public fountains from which ordinary Romans drew their water freely, and to private users (both commercial establishments and wealthy homeowners), who had to pay. Water grants issued to private users specified the reservoir from which the water must be taken and its destination point. Standardized pipes, stamped by the imperial government, were designed to ensure that only the amount of water specified in the grant was taken. (Although Roman engineers knew that pressure affected flow, they did not know by how much, so they had no choice but to estimate usage from the size of the pipe aperture, an incomplete gauge.) So crucial was the water supply that aqueducts had an automatic right-of-way; private landowners could not stop them from traversing their land and were fined if they obstructed access to them by planting trees or erecting buildings within a few feet of them or if they tapped into them.

The first imperial water commissioner, Marcus Agrippa, not only repaired Rome's five aqueducts, but also provided the city with a large number of fountains. His slaves, trained to maintain the system, passed to Augustus when Agrippa died and became the basis for the imperial aqueduct service. Numbering seven hundred by the second century, these slaves served as overseers, reservoir keepers, inspectors, pavers, and plasterers. The emperor Claudius added another two aqueducts that provided two-thirds of Rome's water supply in his day.

Many eminent men held the position of water commissioner. Besides Agrippa, Augustus' son-in-law and chief advisor, another prime example is Sextus Julius Frontinus (35–103), the commissioner under Nerva and Trajan, who had served as urban praetor, consul, and provincial governor of Britain, during which time his military campaigns had been crucial in subduing Wales. Educated in mathematics, Frontinus wrote seminal works on surveying and military tactics, but is known principally for *The Aqueducts of Rome*, an invaluable study of the Roman water supply. The conscientious Frontinus collected and published information concerning the course of each aqueduct, its water quality, its various maintenance needs, and the elevation at which it reached the city. Frontinus gauged the water in all of the aqueducts at various points in order to ascertain the quantity and location of water that was being lost to leaks and thieves, in the process correcting records that had become grossly inaccurate. The reduction of waste and fraud doubled Rome's water supply. Districts previously supplied by a single aqueduct now received the water of several, in case repairs to one caused an interruption of its flow. Frontinus ordered repairs in the spring or autumn, rather than the summer, when demand for water was at its peak, and decreed that aqueducts should be repaired one at a time to minimize disruption in water supply. Basins were connected to aqueducts by more than one pipe in case an accident put one out of commission. The waters of different aqueducts were allotted for different purposes, from drinking to gardening, based on water quality. Proud of the aqueducts, which he viewed as emblems of Roman practical benevolence, Frontinus wrote, "With such an array of indispensable structures carrying so many waters, compare, if you will, the idle Pyramids or the useless, though famous, works of the Greeks."

At the height of the system, aqueducts carried approximately two hundred million gallons of water per day from springs in the Apennines, as well as from various lakes and rivers, to the city of Rome. Rome's water supply was superior not only to that of any other city in antiquity but even to that of many modern cities. In fact, the ancient aqueducts still supply some fountains in Rome.

Roman aqueducts were by no means confined to the capital. In fact, surviving examples may be found in Spain, Algeria, and Greece. A prime example is the famous Pont du Gard (20–16 B.C.), a three-tiered aqueduct in southern France, sponsored by Agrippa. Standing 160 feet above the Gard River, it channeled thirty thousand cubic meters of fresh water per day to Nimes from springs thirty-one miles away. Its largest arches, constructed of stone blocks weighing as much as twelve thousand pounds and held together without clamps or mortar, spanned eighty-two feet. The Pont du Gard's gradient is less than one one-hundredth of an inch per foot. (See photo 3.2.) Aqueducts were also used at state-owned mines for prospecting and for washing away the overburden.

Other Engineering Feats

The Romans also constructed multispan bridges, dams, lighthouses, harbors, canals, drains, and sewers. Bridges often consisted of masonry supported on stone piers driven into the riverbed. For added stability, many bridges were equipped with storm-water apertures in the masonry between the arches. In Roman bridge abutments the narrow face was placed perpendicular to the current, the long face parallel, and the blunt end was placed upstream, the tapering end downstream, which was the optimum streamlined shape for minimal turbulence. In order to reduce the number of spans obstructing the current, arches gradually became wider toward the middle of the bridge. Most bridges also possessed numerous projecting bosses to support the scaffolding required for maintenance and repair.

Built by Diocletian in 284, a dam at the Lake of Homs in Syria created a reservoir fifteen square miles in area, the largest man-made lake to that date. Still in use today, the core of the dam wall consists of rubble made from basalt quarried locally. Also still in use, the Cornalvo dam near Merida in Spain (second century) was protected from seepage by a powerful sealant consisting of hydrated lime and crushed brick and pottery. Dams like these provided domestic and irrigation water, controlled floods, and prevented soil erosion.

The emperor Trajan ended Rome's dependence on Puteoli, a distant port on the Bay of Naples, by converting nearby Ostia into a reliable harbor. Claudius had made a little progress toward this goal through dredging and

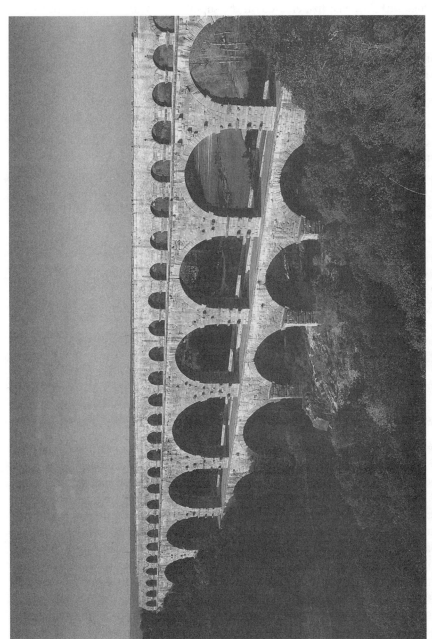

Photo 3.2.   Pont du Gard, Nimes, France. *Copyright © DeA Picture Library/Art Resource, NY*

by having two enormous travertine blocks weighing six or seven tons, tied to-gether with iron clamps, erected on the supertanker Caligula had built to im-port an obelisk (the one that now stands before St. Peter's Basilica) and then sunk at Ostia to form a barrier. (The left mole also served as the foundation for a lighthouse.) But this failed to solve the problem, and a harbor that was truly safe from storms awaited Trajan's excavation of an enormous, hexagonal basin inland of Claudius' harbor. With facilities for over one hundred ships, Ostia became a world-class port filled with miles of warehouses and mercan-tile establishments fronted by colorful mosaics that illustrated the business of each. Over fifty thousand people lived there. The Romans also constructed intricate canal systems for military transport throughout northern Europe.

By the late republican era, a number of public latrines connected to the Roman sewage system were flushed by water from the public baths and full-ers' shops. Shortly thereafter, Agrippa toured the sewers in a boat in order to catalog the necessary repairs, thereby demonstrating that even Augustus' son-in-law and closest advisor did not consider it beneath his dignity to oversee personally the most basic needs of the city.

Roman engineers drained much of the Po valley in northern Italy, con-verting it from a swamp into a productive center of agriculture and livestock production. They also developed the water mill, which utilized water power to grind grain.

ARCHITECTURE

The Arch

By the first century A.D., Roman buildings were able to enclose vast areas by combining the arch with a new building material, concrete. Beginning in the third century B.C., the arch liberated the Romans from the constraints imposed by the Greeks' lintel-and-post architecture. The arch, which placed wedge-shaped stones into compression, thereby channeling pressure outward, was superior to the horizontal lintel, which placed stones into tension, for spanning great distances. The barrel or tunnel vault, a series of arches, be-came the means for enclosing large spaces in a continuous curve. By the first century, Roman architects had discovered that two vaults could be made to intersect at right angles without any danger to the stability of either. These groined vaults could be used to roof a large rectangular space, the roof being supported only by piers at each of the four points of intersection. The use of such vaults for circular spaces was close behind.

Concrete

Although the Sumerians and Etruscans had used the arch, they had been limited by their principal building materials: stone, marble, and mud bricks. By contrast, the Romans were able to construct huge domes without internal supports through the use of concrete, an inexpensive, strong, adaptable, water-resistant, and fireproof material. Roman concrete consisted of an amalgam of lime, pozzolona (a reddish volcanic sand—in essence, a very finely ground silica—from the Bay of Naples), and rubble, which consisted of broken brick and tile and was used for its bonding strength. (Nero's architect incorporated broken material from the great fire of 64 into the concrete of his Golden House.) When used as mortar, concrete allowed the Romans to make their joints as strong as the materials joined. Roman bricks were slim and lightly baked to increase their porosity, so as to absorb the mortar and create a stronger bond. The earliest concrete vaults and domes were presumably supported on full wooden centering until the concrete dried and the centering was removed. The carpentry skill involved in producing such scaffolding must have been as impressive as the skilled use of the cement itself.

Concrete walls faced with brick or marble became popular in the first century B.C., as the population of Rome grew rapidly, and became even more popular after the fire of 64. Concrete foundations replaced square masonry with rubble infill. The result was the construction of massive, freestanding theaters and amphitheaters (since they no longer had to be set in a hillside for structural support), baths, apartment buildings, and warehouses.

Vitruvius and the Roman Architect

Some of what we know about Roman architecture comes from *On Architecture* (ca. 26–14 B.C.) by Marcus Vitruvius Pollio, who participated in Augustus' reconstruction of Rome. Vitruvius claimed that a Roman architect also had to be a town planner and a civil engineer and had to possess knowledge of warfare (since architects were often employed by the military), languages, painting, and sculpture. In addition, an architect must be a student of mathematics, history, science, philosophy, music, medicine, law, and astronomy. Musical knowledge was necessary to recognize the tone that artillery ropes had when stretched properly, medical expertise to ascertain the healthiness of potential building sites and local water supplies, legal knowledge to comprehend the laws pertaining to common walls and water rights, astronomical expertise for the construction of clocks, and scientific knowledge to understand the principles of nature, such as the existence of air pockets in water courses. Vitruvius explained, "All studies are related to one another." He placed special emphasis on philosophy, since it taught the architect to be humble, urbane, fair-minded, loyal, and "what is most important, without avarice."

Vitruvius was the first to concede that many architects failed to meet these high standards. After noting that an Ephesian law penalized architects who exceeded their budget by more than 25 percent by deducting the remainder of the cost from their own property, Vitruvius added: "Would that the gods had impelled the Roman people to make such a law not only for public, but also for private, buildings! In that case, unqualified persons would not swagger abroad with impunity, but persons trained in entirely accurate methods would profess architecture with confidence. Nor would owners be led on to unlimited and lavish expenditure, so that they are even dispossessed of their property, and the architects themselves, controlled by the fear of a penalty, would be more careful in calculating and declaring the amount of the cost."

Vitruvius also reported on the machines needed for raising, storing, and transmitting water, as well as on civil defense, siege engines, and catapults. He was aware that the ingestion of lead was dangerous to health and, hence, warned Romans about the use of lead pipes, though with little success. He also understood that sound traveled in waves and possessed a sophisticated understanding of cloud formation.

Vitruvius declared that Roman buildings should "correspond to the grandeur of our history" and serve as "a memorial to future ages." His discourse on the Greek columnar orders and rules of architecture was considered authoritative into the nineteenth century, and his discussion of arches furnished medieval builders with the chief principles of Gothic architecture. His speculations about the relationship between circular and square forms in architecture and the human figure inspired Leonardo da Vinci's famous drawing of the reach and spatial envelope of a man.

Basilicas

The Christian cathedrals of a later age were often modeled on Roman basilicas, concrete public buildings used for business transactions (especially monetary exchanges) and legal proceedings. Large rectangular structures, basilicas generally featured high domed ceilings, a central aisle or nave flanked by side aisles set off by colonnades, a raised platform enclosed by an apse, clerestory windows, and a monumental stairway leading up to the façade. The long nave came to be crossed just before the apse by a shorter transept, creating the cross-shaped plan that remains a standard church form. The name "basilica" derived from the Greek word for king (*basileus*), in reference to the kingly porticoes of Greek columns that generally fronted these buildings. But Roman basilicas, unlike Greek stoas, were roofed and, hence, closed off from external noise and foul weather.

The earliest basilicas were the Porticus Aemilia (193 B.C.) and the Basilica Porcia (built by Cato the Elder in 184 B.C.). Under Augustus, the Basilica Julia, home to four panels whose members adjudicated inheritance cases, was divided into five parts by three rows of piers, so that, through the use of partitions, the courts could meet simultaneously. Modeled on basilicas though not one itself, Domitian's palace, the Domus Augustana (A.D. 81–92), with its apse and double row of columns, was indirectly influential in the layout of future Christian churches.

Theaters

The Romans constructed elaborate stone theaters, beginning with Pompey's Theater, which seated seventeen thousand people, in 55 B.C. In a Roman theater, in sharp contrast to a Greek one, the stage was raised, and its back was as high as the auditorium itself, so that audiences would not be distracted by seeing outside. Arched entrances were placed all around the curved exterior, with arches repeated on upper tiers. The arches were flanked by half-columns, a system used in the Theater of Marcellus (13 B.C.) and widely copied thereafter.

The Theater of Marcellus, which seated fourteen thousand, possessed three tiers of arches, the lower featuring Doric columns, the middle Ionic, and the upper Corinthian. (The new Roman columnar orders of Tuscan and Composite had not yet made their appearance.) An awning was spread to shade the audience. (Nevertheless, sudden showers could interrupt a play, forcing theatergoers onto adjacent colonnades.) Despite its semicircular form, the theater clearly presaged the Colosseum. (See photo 3.3.)

The Colosseum and Other Amphitheaters

The 1,900-year-old bricks of the Colosseum (A.D. 70–82) have withstood the ravages of time, and the oval-shaped stadium, with its three tiers of eighty arches, still inspires awe—as well as a certain romanticism that causes people to forget that it was the site of the sacrifice of numerous gladiators, Jews, and Christians. Nevertheless, it was probably constructed by highly specialized Roman construction teams, not by Jews enslaved during the rebellion of 66–73, contrary to the persistent legend.

After opening the gardens of Nero's shockingly ostentatious palace, the Golden House, to the public as a park, the frugal emperor Vespasian drained its lake to form the site of the Flavian Amphitheater, or Colosseum. The

Photo 3.3.　Reconstruction of the Theater of Marcellus. *Scala/Art Resource, NY*

building received its current name in the eighth century in reference either to its size or to the nearly 120-foot statue of Nero, modified by the Flavians to resemble the sun god Sol, that stood nearby. In constructing the Colosseum, Vespasian sought to distinguish himself from Nero as an emperor whose wealth would be spent on the people, albeit in the form of the gory entertainment they loved.

The Colosseum was the largest of all the Roman amphitheaters. Resting on a concrete foundation 25 feet deep, it was 150 feet high and its dimensions were 620 by 513 feet, its arena 287 by 180 feet. It seated fifty thousand spectators and was designed to maximize visibility and audibility. A huge awning, supported by masts maintained by a hundred sailors and hoisted in sections by a thousand men, protected spectators from the sunlight. Occasionally, the pit of the Colosseum was sealed and pumped full of water so that gladiators could fight elaborate and bloody naval battles. The building was cleverly designed with so many entrances and exits that, in the event of an emergency, it could be emptied of its large audience in five minutes. There were seventy-six entrance arches for spectators, two for the emperors and their entourages, and two for the gladiators (one for their procession, the other for the removal of their corpses). Since the entrance arches, landings, and seats were all numbered, and the spectators were issued tickets, they had little trouble finding their seats. Wooden barriers promoted the orderly circulation of spectators. The tiers of passageway arches also served to support the successive tiers of seats. Joined by lateral walls of brick and concrete on the upper floors, tufa on the lower, the building's concentric rings of arches consisted of blocks of travertine, a durable, sedimentary limestone transported from nearby quarries on a special road, clamped together by a total of three hundred tons of iron. The vaults consisted of pumice.

A vast subterranean area contained passageways, chambers for animals, cells for the gladiators, storage rooms, and the machinery that caused scenery and other effects mounted on hinged platforms in the center of the arena to appear and disappear. (See photo 3.4.) Inside each animal cell was a cage attached to a tackle for hauling. The front door of the cell was also the opening to the cage, so that, when the cage was hauled up into the arena, the animal was free to exit up a ramp through a trapdoor into daylight. In a well-managed show thirty-two animals could appear in the arena simultaneously.

The emperor's platform, which contained marble seats protected by a lofty wall, stood at the center of one of the long sides, that of the consuls directly opposite. Gladiators entered from one of the short sides, and their corpses were carried out the opposite end. Places were set aside for priests,

Photo 3.4.   Interior of the Roman Colosseum. *Scala/Art Resource, NY*

Vestals, imperial ladies, and foreign dignitaries. Seating was by class, with the lower orders sitting in the highest seats.

In its final form the Colosseum possessed four stories, each with its own row of arches. The arches rested on piers, to which were attached Doric, Ionic, and Corinthian columns that were purely ornamental. Only the top tier, which was decorated with Corinthian pilasters that alternately flanked quadrangular openings and plain walls decorated with bronze shields, lacked an arcade and contained wooden seats. On the upper levels statues filled the spaces between piers. (See photo 3.5.)

Just as the Theater of Marcellus influenced the design of the Colosseum, so the Colosseum influenced the design of numerous amphitheaters throughout the Roman world and later became a source of inspiration to innumerable poets, novelists, and architects. Unfortunately, beginning in the late imperial period and continuing through the Renaissance, Romans defaced the Colosseum, stealing the iron clamps that held blocks together and looting stone from it. Pope Alexander VI even leased it out as a quarry, collecting one-third of the profits. It was not until 1744 that Pope Bene-

Photo 3.5.   Reconstruction drawing of the Roman Colosseum at the time of Hadrian (A.D. 117–138). *Alinari/Art Resource, NY*

dict XIV forbade the removal of stone from the structure, consecrating the arena to the Christian martyrs who died there and erecting a cross in the center.

Yet the Colosseum still stands, largely impervious to earthquakes, giving rise to a legend recorded by the Venerable Bede in the eighth century and restated by Lord Byron over a millennium later:

> While stands the Coliseum, Rome shall stand.
> When falls the Coliseum, Rome shall fall.
> And when Rome falls, the world.

Other amphitheaters were constructed throughout the Roman world. As early as 80 B.C., Sulla's veterans who had settled at Pompeii financed the construction of a stone amphitheater, at a time when the city of Rome possessed only a wooden one. Unfortunately, the amphitheater, which seated twenty thousand spectators, was the site of a series of brawls between the citizens of Pompeii and a neighboring town that compelled Nero to ban gladiatorial games in the city for ten years. An amphitheater at Fréjus withstood the breach of the Reyran dam in 1959. An amphitheater at Arles, modeled on the Colosseum but better preserved, was the dwelling place of 2,000 people during the Middle Ages, and still hosts soccer matches and bullfights.

These stone amphitheaters constituted a tremendous improvement over their unstable, wooden predecessors. One such amphitheater, at Fidenae, just north of Rome, collapsed in A.D. 27. Many Romans lay buried under rubble, screaming for days. The historian Tacitus later wrote: "Even those whose friends and relations had gone away on other business were alarmed, for while the casualties remained unidentified, uncertainty gave free range for anxieties. When the ruins began to be cleared, people rushed to embrace and kiss the corpses—and even quarreled over them, when features were unrecognizable but similarities of physique or age had caused wrong identifications." Thousands of Romans were mutilated or crushed to death in the collapse. The builder was exiled. Another amphitheater collapsed during the reign of Antonius Pius, killing 1,120 people, and yet another 150 years later.

Circuses

Oval-shaped structures, Roman circuses contained a race track surrounded by banks of seats lining the two long sides and one curved end. At the opposite end stood the chariots' starting bays. A median wall holding water basins, fountains, statues, and columns divided the track in two. Also atop the wall stood four lofty cones to give the charioteers advance notice of when to make their turns. One of the seven bronze dolphins and one of the seven huge, wooden eggs arranged symmetrically along the wall were removed at the end of each lap to indicate the number of laps remaining.

The greatest of the Roman circuses was the Circus Maximus, which seated 150,000 to 250,000 spectators and possessed a track of glistening sand. The circus was 1,800 feet long and 600 feet wide. In the center stood the obelisk of Rameses II brought back from Egypt by Augustus.

Trajan's Market

The growth of the empire necessitated the construction of additional forums, thereby presenting the emperors with the opportunity to glorify their reigns with a profusion of new structures. Trajan's Forum was more than three times the size of Augustus'; in fact, it was almost as large as all the other imperial forums put together. The aesthetic harmony of its design influenced many subsequent town planners.

In designing Trajan's Market, a multilevel, semicircular complex of shops, offices, and storehouses near Trajan's Forum on Quirinal Hill, the Greek architect Apollodorus achieved a significant breakthrough. His large-scale use of cross vaulting (previously used on a smaller scale in the Golden House and in Trajan's Baths) allowed a great deal of light into the complex, since the roof could now be supported by piers placed at intervals rather than by a solid wall running the length of the complex, thereby allowing windows to reach to the top of the vault. (See photo 3.6.)

The three-story market, built of brick-faced concrete, accommodated 150 shops and offices. The second story was lit by twenty-six round-headed windows framed by delicate Tuscan pilasters of brick topped by pediments. The corridor that proceeded around the top floor was probably a promenade gallery from which one could view the forum. As architectural historian Frank Sear has noted, "The creation of Trajan's market was a further step in removing from the old Forum and its surrounding area the commercial and business activity which was traditional to the old Forum and its surrounding area but was inappropriate to its new dignity as the official centre of the Roman Empire."

The Pantheon

Perhaps the greatest marvel of Roman architecture is the Pantheon (118–128), which the emperor Hadrian commissioned to replace a smaller, colum-

Photo 3.6. Interior of Trajan's Market. *Scala/Art Resource, NY*

nar temple built by Agrippa (27 B.C.). Stationed in the heart of the Campus Martius, the Pantheon was originally raised on a podium (the land has since grown around it) and placed at the end of a court surrounded on the other three sides by covered colonnades that obscured the sides of the cylinder, so that the viewer's attention was focused upward at the massive, wide portico of the building.

With its closed interior, circular plan, and domed ceiling, the Pantheon was the antithesis of a Greek temple. It consisted of a large, rectangular, columnar, gable-roofed portico backed by a square-sided block and a huge, domed, cylindrical drum. (See photo 3.7.)

The porch roof originally consisted of gilded bronze tiles supported by a bronze substructure, later looted by Pope Urban VIII and replaced with wood. The portico possessed sixteen unfluted Corinthian columns of tinted Egyptian granite weighing forty-eight tons each, tapering upward, and resting on bases of white marble, a most unorthodox treatment. The eight columns of the façade carried a triangular stone pediment that was taller, in relation to its width, than was common. The eight additional columns of the same type located behind the façade consisted of four rows of two, thereby

Photo 3.7.   Façade of the Pantheon. *Copyright © The Trustees of the British Museum/Art Resource, NY*

dividing the portico into three aisles. While the central aisle led to the bronze doors that served as the entrance, the side aisles terminated in apses in which stood the statues of Augustus and Agrippa. The flank columns were met at the intermediate block, which carried its own pediment, by marble pilasters that continued on the outside of the block, ending at the rotunda. The porch pavement consisted of circles, squares, and oblongs of white marble and dark gray granite.

The height of the rotunda was almost twice that of the portico, the width two-thirds greater. Measuring 142 feet in both height and diameter and composed of five thousand tons of concrete, the rotunda was the largest ever constructed until modern times.

The intermediate block, the rotunda, and the dome were made almost entirely of concrete, which was poured into the low, wide trenches formed by inner and outer brick walls, the trenches rising one upon another until the dome was reached. The concrete of the dome was poured over an immense, hemispheric, wooden form, supported by a forest of timbers and struts, on which the negative wooden molds for coffers were fixed. The architect steadily decreased the thickness of the envelope and steadily lightened the fills in the concrete—from the heavy travertine in the lower part of the wall, to the tufa in the middle, to the brick in the top portion of the wall, and finally, to the light pumice used in the upper reaches of the dome near the oculus—to reduce weight as the dome rose. The oculus rested in an area of almost pure concrete less than five feet thick, fronted by rings of tiles. The reliance on concrete minimized the need for skilled laborers because it did not involve dressing blocks of stone to exact dimensions, as in the Colosseum, though skilled architects, carpenters, and masons were still required.

Striding into the rotunda through the traditional forecourt and the seemingly traditional portico, the viewer was stunned by the new architectural world awaiting him inside—as well as by sudden light after walking through the dark porch. The rotunda was separated into three zones by two cornices that proceeded horizontally around the interior except where the lower cornice dropped back into the vaulted entrance bay and along the base of the concave vault of the apse opposite, both of which broke boldly up into the second zone. The higher cornice surrounded the interior at the base of the dome. In the first zone there were eight large recesses, including the entrance bay and apse, each of which was screened by a pair of Corinthian columns of polychrome marble flanked by a pair of square piers. In contrast to the structural necessity of such columns in Greek architecture, these columns were purely ornamental. Between the symmetrically spaced niches there were eight temple fronts raised on high podia, all alike, except that four had curved pediments, the other four the traditional, triangular ones. The pavement consisted of squares and circles-in-squares, arranged diagonally, of colored granite, marble, and porphyry. In the second zone a band of blue-white marble lay beneath a repeating pattern of pilasters and blind windows. The third zone, the dome, contained five horizontal rows of twenty-eight coffers that diminished in size and depth as they arose, originally decorated with relief stucco moldings and a gilded bronze rosette in the center of each.

At the top of the dome the nearly horizontal surface closed to the ring of an oculus, which was originally surrounded by bronze molding. Although the building was lighted entirely by the twenty-seven-foot oculus in the center of the ceiling, thereby symbolizing the centrality of heavenly light, its polished marble surfaces were designed to reflect light around the enclosure. It was constructed so that, at the summer solstice, light fell first on the walls in the morning, then on the floor at noon, and, finally, later in the day, on the coffers of the dome. (See photo 3.8.)

A temple to "all of the gods," the Pantheon housed statues of Mars, Venus, Julius Caesar, and other gods, arranged in the niches, though the precise arrangement is unknown. Its circular form symbolized universal order

Photo 3.8.   Interior of the Pantheon. *Vanni/Art Resource, NY*

and the harmony and unity that bound the gods with the Roman people and the Roman Empire.

The Pantheon was later Christianized and is now adorned with an altar, as well as with the tomb of the Renaissance master Raphael, whose fans still bring him flowers. While superintendent of antiquities for Pope Leo X, Raphael had made detailed measurements of Roman monuments like the Pantheon and had reported on their condition and on the possibility of their restoration.

The dome of the Pantheon influenced the Baths of Caracalla, as well as temple and tomb design throughout the empire. During the Renaissance, it served as a model for the dome of St. Peter's Basilica. Based on the Pantheon and other Roman structures, Andrea Palladio's *Four Books on Architecture* (1570), then considered the most authoritative work on classical architecture, became one of the most influential architectural books ever written. Among Palladio's numerous devotees was Thomas Jefferson, who preferred Roman architecture to Greek because of its combination of spherical and cubic forms. The library Jefferson designed for his beloved University of Virginia and his Monticello were clearly influenced by the Pantheon, which Jefferson considered the finest example of spherical architecture. The U.S. Capitol, on which Jefferson collaborated with William Thornton and Benjamin H. Latrobe, owed a debt to the Pantheon as well.

Baths

Roman architectural and engineering skills were also on display at various public baths throughout the empire. The earliest baths with heated rooms and running water were the Stabian Baths of Pompeii, built during the second century B.C. Public baths generally included a dressing room, cold room, warm room, hot room, and steam room.

Baths were heated by braziers until the introduction of the hypocaust system in the latter part of the second century B.C. In this system the hot air provided by furnaces passed beneath the concrete floors of the hot and warm rooms, which rested on rows of brick or stone columns, circulating through the empty spaces between the columns. When the heated air reached the walls of the hot rooms, it passed up the hollow tubes that lined them, thereby warming the walls as well as the floor, the rest of the heat escaping through chimneys. (In warm rooms only the floor was heated.) The same furnaces also heated metal water tanks that projected into the hot plunge baths. Hot baths for men and women were located in adjacent rooms so that the same furnace and heating system could serve both. Steam rooms were often circular, with a hole in the dome in which hung a super-heated bronze disc suspended on chains, which could be raised or lowered to regulate the temperature in the room. The sweat baths of Baiae on the Bay of Naples were heated by volcanic steam. Some baths featured water organs, a Roman invention, to provide music.

Roman baths reached their apex in the third century. With vaults as high as 140 feet and featuring hot and cold alabaster pools, an open-air pool, and steam baths, the Baths of Caracalla (A.D. 212–216) accommodated 1,600 bathers. The marble-lined building also contained dressing rooms, exercise facilities, lecture halls, and lounges, while adjacent structures included shops, libraries, and restaurants. The baths' rectangular, circular, and elliptical rooms and open courtyards were all fitted together with consummate skill. Intimate, graceful rooms stood beside huge halls with soaring vaults. Some of the floors possessed softly toned mosaics. The circular hot room projected beyond the line of the building to take advantage of the afternoon sun, its drum pierced by eight windows. Below each window stood a bay containing a hot plunge bath. Small doorways prevented heat from penetrating into the cold rooms or cold into the hot rooms. Cleaning and dyeing establishments in the basement took advantage of the water supply. Open grounds allowed denizens to throw balls, sprint, or perform other exercises. Peddlers, teachers, and poets used the grounds for their own purposes. As usual, bathers were segregated by gender. The Baths of Caracalla now provide a majestic setting for operatic performances.

The even more luxurious Baths of Diocletian (298–306), similar in design but larger, accommodated more than 3,000 bathers. The price of admission was a small copper coin. In this building, as in some others by then, brick ribs were added to the dome, allowing it to become thinner and lighter, so that the walls no longer needed to be as massive and, therefore, could include more windows to admit more light. A portion of the ruins of the building was later converted into the Christian cathedral Santa Maria degli Angeli by Michelangelo.

Apartment Buildings

The Romans also originated the multistoried apartment building. Some Roman apartment buildings (*insulae*, or "islands") reached as high as five stories (though Augustus limited their height to seventy feet), with stairways providing access to the upper stories from the street. Possessing rather severe façades relieved by a doorway of decorative brick or a balcony, these buildings featured large windows that faced the street and inner courtyards with cisterns. Possessing only one lavatory per floor, the buildings were often drafty, noisy, and unconnected to the water system, and a few collapsed or caught fire. Nevertheless, some of the nicer apartment buildings catered to aristocrats—new or temporary residents and men who had lost homes to fire or divorce. The ground floors of the insulae generally consisted of shops. By the fourth century there were 46,000 insulae in Rome, compared with only 1,790 houses, the mark of a great urban center in which real estate was at a premium.

The Triumphal Arch

Like the other Roman structures, triumphal arches were designed to be as huge, grand, and durable as the empire itself. Although honorific arches bearing statues appeared in Rome as early as the second century B.C., the fully developed triumphal arch, with columns, architrave, and attic bearing a dedicatory inscription, dates to the reign of Augustus. Generally dedicated to members of the imperial family, triumphal arches became increasingly elaborate, featuring extensive relief panels depicting the victories and achievements of the emperors and their offspring. They generally spanned a street or path so that victorious armies could march through them.

Early arches, such as the Arch of Titus, contained only a single passageway. Simple and elegant, slightly taller than wide, the arch featured eight half-columns flanking the passageway on a high podium that supported an architrave and a frieze with relief sculptures depicting Titus' triumph over the Jews. (See photo 3.9.) The passageway itself contained the famous relief panels portraying his triumphal procession, including the carrying of the Menorah and the silver trumpets taken from the Great Temple. (See photo 3.10.) Titus rides in triumph, his chariot guided by Roma, as Victory crowns him with a wreath. The relief panel in the middle of the vault showed the deified Titus being carried to heaven by an eagle. Other sculptural groups on the arch portrayed Vespasian and Titus in a *quadriga* (four-horse chariot), as well as a figure of Titus' younger brother Domitian, who commissioned the arch.

The Arch of Trajan at Beneventum (ca. A.D. 114) was used to mark the beginning of the Via Traiana, a road from Beneventum (about 150 miles from Rome) to Brindisi. Similar in design and scale to the Arch of Titus, its panels facing the city depicted Trajan's achievements in Italy, such as the alimenta, while those facing the countryside dealt with his accomplishments in the provinces, such as the founding of colonies. Ordinary Romans are depicted as having easy access to the emperor. As with portrait sculptures, these arches were not erected by the emperors themselves but by supporters, though obviously with the tacit approval of the emperors.

Photo 3.9.   Arch of Titus. *SEF/Art Resource, NY*

The most elaborate arches featured columned plinths adorned with depictions of victories, soldiers, and prisoners, keystones portraying divinities, and a frieze depicting the triumphal procession. In the most richly decorated arches the soffits of the vaulted passageways were coffered and contained a carved panel in the center.

Some later arches had three passageways, the central one being wider and taller than the others. These include the Arch of Septimius Severus (ca. 203), which stands on the opposite end of the Forum from the Arch of Titus and features a bronze quadriga that carries the emperor and his sons above the attic.

Modeled on this arch, the even larger Arch of Constantine (A.D. 315) near the Colosseum depicts the emperor's crucial defeat of Maxentius at the Milvian Bridge in 312, the victory that paved the way for the toleration and

Photo 3.10. Relief from the Arch of Titus, triumphal procession. *Werner Forman/Art Resource, NY*

eventual triumph of Christianity. The soffits of the passageways were uncoffered, and the arch was wide in proportion to its height, giving it a greater sense of solidity than of elegance. (See photo 3.11.) By this point in Roman history, the emperor could no longer find enough skilled sculptors, so he was forced to loot panels from various Flavian and Antonine monuments with which to ornament his arch, his features replacing those of Hadrian, Marcus Aurelius, and others, while some subsidiary figures were updated. The figures sculpted contemporaneously are stumpy, flat, monotonous, and repetitive. All frontal, with a poor depiction of spatial relationships, they are a sad reflection on the decline of the empire.

Photo 3.11.   Arch of Constantine. *Vanni/Art Resource, NY*

CONCLUSION

The old saw, "The Romans are known for their drains, the Greeks for their brains," is misleading. It implies that engineering is a mindless skill, unconnected with creativity. Far from lacking in originality, Roman engineers and architects solved immense problems that had stumped the Greeks and everyone else before them. For this reason they were able to leave a greater number of durable monuments to their civilization than the Greeks or anyone else in Western history.

• *4* •

Epic and Lyric Poetry

$\mathscr{T}$he Romans adopted the poetic forms first established by the Greeks but placed their own indelible mark on them. The poems of Virgil, Horace, and Ovid possessed such beauty and grace that they dominated Western education for almost two millennia.

GREEK PRECURSORS

Homer

Western literature began with the poems of Homer, a blind poet from Chios. The recitation of poetry was a common occupation for the blind of Archaic Greece (ca. 750–500 B.C.). But Homer's descriptions are so vivid it is unlikely that he was born blind. He probably composed the *Iliad* around 730 B.C. and the *Odyssey* about 710 B.C., though both texts were not entirely fixed until about 650 B.C. In both poems Homer wove together previous oral traditions, perhaps even borrowing some traditional lines of verse, to produce unique works of genius.

While the *Iliad* is set during the Trojan War (ca. 1200 B.C.), the *Odyssey* recounts the hero Odysseus' adventures in attempting to return home following the war. The *Iliad* remains the most revered poem in Western literature, the *Odyssey* the most beloved. As the ancient critic Longinus put it, "Homer in the *Odyssey* is like the setting sun; the grandeur remains, but not the intensity." The *Odyssey* presents a more favorable image of the poor and demonstrates a greater concern with ethics than does the *Iliad*. From the *Iliad* to the *Odyssey* the emphasis shifted from the physical prowess of Achilles to the intelligence, patience, self-control, ingenuity, intellectual curiosity, and loyalty of Odysseus. Zeus punishes the monstrous Cyclops for his violation of the cardinal rule, hospitality to strangers, by allowing Odysseus to blind him. The Cyclops had eaten some of Odysseus' men, an act that identified him as a particularly bad host according to Homeric rules of etiquette. This new emphasis on hospitality to strangers was probably a response to the growth of trade, which required more frequent travel. Commoners were no longer mere objects of ridicule, as in the *Iliad*, but potentially worthy of respect. In the *Odyssey* the faithful Eumaeus is presented as a noble and virtuous herdsman who helps Odysseus reclaim his throne. This development was perhaps connected with the rise of a Greek middle class as the result of the expansion of trade during the Archaic Period.

In both the *Iliad* and the *Odyssey* Homer portrays women in an uncommonly favorable light. Though Helen, the unfaithful wife of Menelaus, is depicted as the cause of the Trojan War, Hector's wife Andromache is portrayed as a woman of virtue. In the *Odyssey* Homer's female characters, especially the ingenious and faithful Penelope, possess well-developed personalities.

While the Homeric epics probably contain a few lines added by professional reciters who lived shortly after the time of their composer, the theory that "Homer" was actually a long series of different composers is contradicted by the poems' thematic and stylistic unity. Some modern critics have even argued persuasively that certain passages of the poems once thought to violate thematic unity are actually essential to it.

Just as the Scriptures united the Hebrews, Homer's epics united the Greeks, answering questions about the gods and settling disputes concerning ethics. Despite their quarrels and wars, the Greeks knew that they were bound together by their love and reverence for Homer. Homer was the centerpiece of Greek education, nourishing the imaginations of Greek poets, dramatists, historians, philosophers, sculptors, politicians, and ordinary people for generations. No Greek who lived after Homer could escape his influence, so deeply were his poems embedded in Greek culture. Hence Homer played at least an indirect role in all of the great achievements of classical Greece. When Plato reached dizzying heights of eloquence, it was because he strove unceasingly to equal Homer.

Homer's plots, themes, and dialogue profoundly influenced the development of Greek drama. Aeschylus, one of the greatest of the Greek tragedians, called his own plays "crumbs from the great table of Homer." Aeschylus' *Persians* (472 B.C.), a dramatic account of the Greek victory in the Persian Wars, was thoroughly Homeric, attributing the outcome of the wars to Persian *hubris* (arrogance). Yet, like Homer, Aeschylus depicted the horrors of war even in victory. Also in imitation of Homer, Aeschylus, and other dramatists often utilized their audience's knowledge of Greek myths to great emotional effect, developing a tragic contrast between the audience's knowledge of the characters' impending doom and the characters' blithe ignorance of their own fates.

Hesiod

The son of a merchant-turned-farmer, Hesiod of Ascra (in Boeotia, central Greece) adopted Homer's hexameters and epic themes around 700 B.C. Based partly on preexisting Near Eastern myths, Hesiod's *Theogony* discussed the "origins of the gods," as the title suggests. It remains one of our principal sources concerning Greek mythology.

Hesiod claimed that the universe existed before the gods. The Earth gave birth to Uranus (heaven), who buried alive his own sons out of fear that one would overthrow him. But Uranus' youngest son, Kronos, escaped, overthrew his father, and castrated him with a sickle. Kronos then ate each of his own children in order to prevent any of them from overthrowing him in like manner. But his wife, Rhea, hid their son Zeus and gave Kronos a stone to eat instead. Kronos must not have possessed much of a palate, for he did not notice the difference—a fatal mistake, since Zeus did indeed overthrow his father, banish him to an island, and become ruler of the gods. (Zeus also made his father cough up his brothers and sisters, as well as the stone, which was kept at sacred Delphi as a sort of tourist attraction.)

In *Works and Days*, a forceful and vivid manual of advice to farmers organized as a rebuke to his brother Perses, who had conspired with aristocratic, "bribe-swallowing judges" to defraud Hesiod of part of his father's estate, had wasted his wealth, and had returned begging to Hesiod, the poet redefined *arete* (virtue) so that it was obtainable by commoners like himself. To Hesiod, arete was not the aristocratic, martial qualities of the *Iliad*, but "moderation, justice, and work." Hesiod avenged himself on his brother through relentless heckling, in the form of moral lectures: "A man building evil things for another builds them for himself. . . . Work is no disgrace, but idleness is. . . . Men are wealthy through their deeds, and through their laboring are much dearer to the immortals. . . . Gods and men hate him who lives without work. . . . Possessions are the life of worthless mortals." The tenor of the poem was epitomized in the line: "I mean you well, Perses, you great idiot!" Hesiod was the first Western author to speak directly to the reader about himself, as well as the inventor of the didactic poem.

Hesiod chronicled the decline of humankind and human happiness from the golden age under Kronos, to the silver age, bronze age, and the current iron age, an era of "hard work and pain." His own town he described as "bad in winter, tiresome in summer, and good at no season." The future would be even bleaker, culminating in an age of complete immorality, when even "Decency and Respect" would flee the world.

In contrast to Homer, Hesiod (like most later Greek authors) viewed women as cunning and dangerous creatures who must be controlled. In *Works and Days* he wrote: "He who trusts a woman trusts trickery. . . . Do not let any sweet-talking woman beguile your good sense with the fascination of her shape. It's your barn she's after." Hesiod attributed human suffering to the curiosity of Pandora, who had, against expressed warnings, opened a box of evils, thereby unleashing them on the world. Hesiod claimed: "Hope was the only spirit that stayed there in the unbreakable closure of the jar, under its rim, and could not fly forth abroad, for the lid of the great jar closed down first and contained her. This was by the will of cloud-gathering Zeus of the aegis." Although the story is similar to that of Eve in the Garden of Eden, at least in the Book of Genesis, God creates Eve in order to make Adam happy (though she proves a mixed blessing); Zeus, by contrast, creates Pandora "to be a sorrow to men"—that is, for the expressed purpose of punishing humans for accepting the god Prometheus' illegal gift of fire. Mortal man could not escape the wrath of Zeus, for if he avoided marriage, he came "to a mournful old age, bereft of one to look after him."

Yet there was some good in the world. Hesiod declared: "Upon the prospering earth there are thirty thousand immortal spirits who keep watch for Zeus on all that men do." Zeus' daughter Justice also reported human actions to him, so that he could reward virtue and punish vice. These rewards and punishments were strictly earthly, to be enjoyed and suffered in this life. Hesiod added: "The eye of Zeus sees everything. His mind understands all. He is watching us right now, if he wishes to." This selective omniscience was but a step removed from the continuously omniscient Judeo-Christian God.

The Lyric Poets

One of the innovations of the seventh century B.C. was the development of lyric poetry. Lyric poets sang their poems while playing the lyre, a stringed instrument.

Lyric poets were more concerned with present pleasures than with legends of the heroic past. Their poems did not usually focus on the gods or heroes as Homer and Hesiod had but on the daily experiences of ordinary people—generally the personal loves, hatreds, woes, and adventures of the poets themselves. Lyric poems were much shorter than epic poems and were presented in a variety of meters.

Soldier, sailor, gold miner, vagrant, and satirist (not necessarily in that order), Archilochus of Paros (ca. 650 B.C.) was the first lyric poet whose work was written down and survived in part. His poetry reflected a departure from heroic values in the century after the *Iliad*. He justified what would have been indefensible in Homer's day, a hasty retreat:

> My trusty shield adorns some Thracian foe.
> I left it in a bush—not as I would!
> But I have saved my life; so let it go.
> Soon I will get another just as good.

He even defended drunkenness on duty: "Go take your cup and walk along the timber deck of our roaming ship; drain the hollow casks of all their red wine. How can we stay sober on the watch when all the rest are drunk?" In the same irreverent vein he declared: "I have no love for big, pompous generals, nor those who take pride in their hair or shave their upper lips. I prefer a small one with bowed legs, firmly set on his feet, and full of heart."

After his brother-in-law died, Archilochus expressed the lyric poet's determination to mock death by enjoying life. He declared, "Now I have no desire for poetry or joy, yet I will make nothing better by crying, nor worse by seeking good foods and pleasure." Following an eclipse, he expressed the lyric poet's recognition of the fragility of life: "Nothing in the world can surprise me now. Nothing is impossible or too wonderful, for Zeus, father of the Olympians, has turned midday into black night by shielding light from the blossoming sun, and now dark terror hangs over mankind. Anything may happen."

Embittered by the unwillingness of his father's aristocratic family to accept him as an equal because his mother had been a slave, Archilochus participated in the colonization of Thasos, but became even more bitter there, when his girlfriend's mother refused to allow their marriage. Legend claims that his satire became so relentless and cutting that it finally drove the former girlfriend and her entire family to suicide. Archilochus wrote, "One big thing I understand: I know how to spit back with black venom against the man who wrongs me." Of his own heartache he claimed, "Passionate love relentlessly twists a cord under my heart and spreads deep mist on my eyes, stealing the unguarded brains from my head."

Archilochus finally returned to Paros and died in battle defending the city. He never rejected militarism, only the romanticism of war. He was proud of his reputation as an occasional mercenary: "With my spear I win my bread, and with my spear the Thracian wine, and on my spear I lean to drink."

Sappho of Mytilene on the island of Lesbos (ca. 600 B.C.) was the first and perhaps the greatest of all female poets in Western literature. She was the leader of an informal school of lyric poetry. Although formal education was rare for any Greek, and especially for women, young, aristocratic women of the era were encouraged to learn musical skills prior to marriage.

Described as small and dark featured, Sappho's alleged sexual proclivities inspired a new meaning for the term "lesbian." Her love for her students was passionate, often expressed in delicately sensuous terms, and she was prone to jealousy upon their marriage or study under another teacher. Yet Sappho was married and had a daughter.

Unfortunately, only small remnants of Sappho's poetry remain, including some fragments discovered in the sands of Egypt and others found in the quotations of later authors. But it is obvious from what remains that Sappho was a poet of great skill who employed a concise, vernacular, picturesque style. Plato later declared: "Some say there are nine Muses. How foolishly they speak, for Sappho of Lesbos is the tenth." (The Muses were goddesses who inspired artists of all kinds.)

Sappho's poetry centered on beauty, love, and passion. She sang, "Of all the offspring of the earth and heaven, love is the most precious." After noting that some men considered military processions beautiful, Sappho referred to her student Anaktoria, "the marvel of whose living grace and laughing eyes I'd rather see than chariots all of Lydian race and armored lines of infantry." In language simple and affectionate Sappho captured the outdoor life of the Greeks in a poem concerning children and livestock returning home from the adventures of the day: "Evening star, you bring all that the bright dawn scattered; you bring the lamb and the kid, and the child to its mother."

In love with life Sappho expressed the Greek dread of death. She wrote: "Death is our evil. The gods believe this, or else by now they would be dead." She added, "In all the dominions of the gods only Death allows no place for sweet hope."

Nevertheless, Sappho also expressed the Greek belief in the consolation of fame. She exulted, "The golden Muses gave me true riches: when dead I shall not be forgotten." On her deathbed, she wrote to her daughter, "It is not right for mourning to enter a house of poetry." Her work was greatly admired throughout antiquity.

Anacreon of Teos (ca. 582–485 B.C.) sang playful songs on the pleasures of youth, principally love and wine, and some sad songs regarding the coming of old age and death. He wrote, "Eros, the blacksmith of love, smashed me with a giant hammer and doused me in the cold river." Regarding prostitutes he claimed, "Although we call these women loose, they tighten their thighs around thighs." Concerning drinking parties he wrote, "I do not like the man who sits by his bowl and sobs about the sad wars, but the rake who loves to rave about fine feats in the arts and art of love." On the specter of death he brooded: "The lightless chasm of death is dreadful and the descent appalling. Once cast down into Hades, there is no return."

Anacreon's followers were responsible for the *Anacreontics*, a collection of lyric poems long mistakenly attributed to Anacreon himself. One poem protested: "The dark earth drinks rain, and the trees drink the earth; the sea drinks the rivers, and the sun drinks the sea. Therefore, don't complain, my companions, if I wish to drink also." Another noted: "Nature has endowed bulls with horns, horses with hooves, hares with swift feet, lions with ravenous jaws, fish with the ability to swim, birds with flight, and man with wisdom. But did she neglect woman? No, nature gave her beauty, a match for all the shields and swords in the world—beauty, which is strong enough to conquer steel and fire!"

The Alexandrian Poets

During the Hellenistic Period following Alexander the Great's conquest of the Near East (the fourth to first centuries B.C.), Alexandria in Egypt also became a center for Greek poetry. The decline of democratic politics caused by the rise of the Macedonian kings led to the revival of a poetry concerned with everyday life. Callimachus of Cyrene (ca. 305–240 B.C.), royal tutor and cataloguer at the great Library of Alexandria, wrote poems of every meter, as well as works of prose. Although he crafted hymns to the gods in Homeric hexameters, he claimed that the epic poem was an anachronism, huffing, "A big book is a big evil" (making Callimachus the patron saint of undergraduates?). Versatile and prolific, playful but learned, he wrote for a small, sophisticated, urban audience. His epigrams included this touching epitaph: "Who are you, O shipwrecked stranger? Leontichos found your corpse on the beach, buried you in this grave, and cried, thinking of his own hazardous life. For he knows no rest; he too roams over the sea like a gull." The epitaph he wrote for himself was more whimsical: "'Tis the tomb of Battus' son that you are passing—one who was well skilled in poesy and well skilled in season to laugh over the wine."

In his *Bucolics* (third century B.C.) Theocritus, who had moved from his native Syracuse to Alexandria, advanced the pastoral poem, the ode to the beauty and virtue of the rural lifestyle, beyond its meager beginnings in Hesiod's *Works and Days*. Writing in hexameters, he mingled various dialects and included oppositional elements in his words, sentences, and themes. He had a very precise eye for vegetation, and he was not above having his shepherds abuse one another with coarse jokes. His influence on Virgil and Horace, and through them on Western poetry in general, was considerable.

ROMAN POETRY

The Latin Language

Latin delights in strong contrasts, in ideas logically opposed. It is epigrammatic, condensing wisdom with impressive brevity. It is vigorous and precise. Its majesty contrasts with the dance of the Greek hexameter. Latin was the language of scholarship and diplomacy in the West until the eighteenth century and the language of the Roman Catholic liturgy until the 1960s (it remains the language of official Church documents). It is also the basis for the modern Italian, French, and Spanish languages, and for over a million English words.

Literacy in Ancient Rome

There is evidence of widespread literacy, at least of a rudimentary sort, in ancient Rome. Election posters, shop signs, and public notices were intended primarily for common people. Varro, the agricultural manual writer, recommended posting farm rules where all of the laborers could read them. Pliny the Younger often received written complaints from his tenant farmers. Roman soldiers wrote home, as evidenced by the discovery of hundreds of letters they inscribed on thin pieces of wood while serving on the frontier in northern England. Papyri in the Roman camps at Masada record lines from the *Aeneid* scribbled by soldiers to relieve boredom during the siege. Slingers even wrote words—the names of gods and commanders, as well as obscenities and slurs directed at the enemy—on their ammunition. In fact, the Romans have left us far more letters than the Greeks because their public and private business throughout the vast empire often took them away from home. Household documents have been found as well.

The book trade flourished in Rome. By the late republican and early imperial periods, even political leaders—Cicero, Caesar, Augustus, and Tiberius, for instance—were composing poems in their leisure time.

The Earliest Latin Poets

The earliest surviving Latin texts date from the seventh century B.C., but these are merely brief, formulaic records identifying the occupants of tombs. Around 240 B.C. Lucius Livius Andronicus (ca. 284–204 B.C.), a Greek slave from Tarentum, composed a metrical Latin version of the *Odyssey* and Latin translations of various Greek dramas as primers for his master's children. The first native Latin poet, Gnaeus Naevius, wrote comedies and an epic poem on the First Punic War.

Ennius (ca. 239–169 B.C.)

But the first major Latin poet was Quintus Ennius of Rudiae (in the heel of Italy). Ennius composed the *Annals*, a rough and simple but grand and vigorous prototype of the Latin epic that influenced Virgil. The *Annals* proceeded from the time of Aeneas to Ennius' own day. Ironically, the "Father of Latin Poetry" did not receive Roman citizenship until late in life. When an eighteenth-century Frenchman praised American achievements, John Adams replied modestly, "It is the time of Ennius with us."

Catullus (ca. 84–54 B.C.)

The more polished Gaius Valerius Catullus of Verona in northern Italy is considered the master of Latin lyric verse. Catullus wrote beautiful, earnest, passionate love poems based on the elaborate, refined, and individualistic poetry of Alexandria but whose technical skill surpassed that of its models. Though he experimented with a variety of meters, his favorite poems contained lines of eleven syllables. He often repeated lines for emphasis, especially in closing his poems. His style was direct and often colloquial. Of his older brother's untimely demise and of his own pilgrimage to his brother's gravesite in Asia Minor, Catullus wrote:

> Dear brother, I have come these many miles, through strange lands to
>   this Eastern Continent
> To see your grave, a poor, sad monument of what you were, O brother.
> And I have come too late; you cannot hear me. Alone now I must speak
> To these few ashes that were once your body and expect no answer.
> I shall perform an ancient ritual over your remains, weeping
> (This plate of lentils for dead men to feast upon, wet with my tears).
> O brother, here's my greeting: here's my hand forever welcoming you
> And I forever saying: good-bye, good-bye.

Catullus' love for the unfaithful Lesbia (so named by the author in honor of Sappho of Lesbos) inspired verses of heartbreaking intensity, conveyed in precise and lucid language. In the springtime of the relationship Catullus wrote:

> Come, Lesbia, let us live and love,
> Nor give a damn what sour old men say.
> The sun that sets may rise again,
> But when our light has sunk into the earth,
> It is gone forever.

Lesbia was based on Clodia, the wife of the consul Metellus Celer, whom some accused her of poisoning. Catullus began to see her true colors when she promised to marry him but failed to do so and carried on affairs with many others. Finally, he wrote:

> My Lesbia, that one, that only Lesbia,
> Lesbia whom Catullus loved more than himself and all things
> He ever owned or treasured.
> Now her body's given up in alley-ways,
> Or highroads to fine Roman gentlemen. . . .
> There was a time, O Lesbia, when you said Catullus was the only man on
>   earth who could understand you,
> Who could twine his arms around you, even Jove himself less welcome.
> And when I thought of you, my dear, you were not the mere flesh and
> The means by which a lover finds momentary rapture. . . .
> Your wounds in love's own battle
> Have made me your companion, perhaps a greater lover,
> But O, my dear, I'll never be
> The modest boy who saw you as a lady, delicate and sweet,
> A paragon of virtue. . . .
> No longer I pray
> That she love me again, that her body be chaste, mine forever.
> Cleanse my soul of this sickness of love, give me power to rise, resurrected,
>   to thrust love aside.
> I have given my heart to the gods. O hear me, omnipotent heaven,
> And ease me of love and its pain.

Like the Alexandrian poets, Catullus oscillated between ecstasy and desperation, conveying his torment with the intimacy of poetry intended for an elite circle of like-minded friends. His Lesbia resembles the "dark lady" of Shakespeare's sonnets, another married, aristocratic lady who possesses both physical and intellectual charms and who initially inspires extreme devotion, only to spurn the poet for one of his friends in the end. As the literary historian Karl Harrington put it, "In each case the jilted one came to see that the delicate flower he believed had been stolen from him was after all but a common weed." Catullus' poems about Lesbia may also have influenced Petrarch, the pioneer of the Renaissance, whose sonnets to Laura are marked by the same passion tempered by self-analysis.

By contrast, Catullus' verses against Julius Caesar and numerous others were filled with invective and laced with profanity. He wrote:

> What a pair of pretty boys, Caesar and Mamurra . . .
> Graced with the same learning and the same quick appetite
> For wives of other men. O see them conquering every girl
> In sight and still they're hungry.
> What a pair of pretty boys, Caesar and Mamurra.

He claimed that one of Lesbia's other lovers, Ignatius of Spain, washed his teeth with urine to maintain his bright smile. To Asinius Marrucinus, a rude guest who stole his table linen, he threatened, "I warn you now, 300 hendecasyllables shall follow you forever, or, give me back my napkin." He also wrote: "See that girl, Ameana, the one with the big nostrils? . . . A looking-glass must strike her blind." He claimed that the *Annals* of Volusius of Padua deserved no better use than to serve as wrapping paper for mackerel.

Yet Catullus possessed a self-critical element lacking in many poets. He wrote of his friend Suffenus, who was proud of his bad poetry:

> On that he prides himself, and clearly feels his oats,
> As o'er his fancied, his poetic, gifts he gloats.
> But we too, doubtless, likewise fool ourselves sometimes:
> Each one in turn becomes Suffenus making rhymes;
> Each his hobby, each his sad perversity;
> The ugly hunch upon our back we cannot see.

His longer poems were complex and learned.

A poet of wide range, Catullus was able to achieve dramatic effects by altering his mode of expression in the middle of short works. A planner who weighed words and arranged them precisely, he compelled all later Latin poets to reflect more deeply on matters of style. Of the poems he wrote 116 survive. His poetry influenced Horace, Ovid, and numerous Renaissance poets.

Virgil's tragic, abandoned Dido was based largely on Catullus' Ariadne, abandoned by Theseus after she helped him kill the Minotaur and escape the Labyrinth. Catullus wrote:

> Shaken from dark sleep and dreams that betrayed her, Ariadne
> Gazes, stricken, unbelieving, at this vision of swift oars bearing him,
>   the thoughtless lover, gone from her,
> His promises now mingled with the roaring sea winds rising to the
>   empty skies.
> She stands deserted,
> Helpless on her lonely shore. . . .
> They say that she went mad, her voice a trumpet sound of grief,
>   wordless, issuing from her heart.

In both cases the jilted woman calls down a divine curse on her faithless lover.

The first English madrigal was a translation of one of Catullus' poems. He influenced Philip Sidney, Ben Jonson, Samuel Coleridge, and Alfred Lord Tennyson, who wrote, "I love Catullus for his perfection in form and for his tenderness." Lord Byron's "To Lesbia," written in homage to Catullus, reflects the spirit of many of his lyric poems.

Virgil (70–19 B.C.)

The master of Latin poetry, Virgil (Publius Vergilius Maro) was a large, shy, dark native of Mantua in northern Italy who moved to the Bay of Naples. Virgil's father was a man of low birth who kept bees but acquired some wealth speculating in timber. Virgil studied at Milan and Rome. In 41 B.C. Augustus (Octavian) took possession of Virgil's father's farm as part of the territory he seized for his soldiers. But Virgil's poetry won him favor at Augustus' court; the emperor not only restored the family farm, but also gave him additional land and houses, though Virgil refused an exile's confiscated estate.

Virgil's *Eclogues* (42–37 B.C.) and *Georgics* (37–30 B.C.) reinvigorated the pastoral theme of Hesiod and Theocritus. Alarmed by small farmers' abandonment of their farms and migration to the cities (as we have just seen, in some cases they were forcibly expelled from their farms to make way for the veterans of the civil wars), Virgil portrayed the rural lifestyle as the happiest and most virtuous. Virgil wrote, "Pallas [Athena] can keep her cities, but let the woods beyond all else please you and me."

Inspired by Theocritus' *Bucolics*, but more tender and sentimental, the *Eclogues* consisted of ten brief, melodious, enigmatic, unpretentious poems. The odd-numbered eclogues consisted of dialogues, the even-numbered of monologues. The locale was a composite of Arcadia, Sicily, and northern Italy, but was, above all, Virgil's own imaginative creation, existing nowhere in the real world. Virgil cast a sensuous, enchanted light on rural life, tempered by the good-natured banter of shepherds. Yet there were glimpses of the sorrow caused by love, "such love as holds the heifer, wearied by the search through the woodland glades and tall plantations for her steer, when by a running stream she sinks down in green sedge despairing, and forgets at midnight to go home."

Virgil's fourth eclogue, written while Augustus and Antony were still allies (40 B.C.), expressed the widespread belief that a savior would appear and rescue the world from its many troubles. The theory that Virgil thought the savior would be the child of Antony and Augustus' sister Octavia has been discredited, leaving the matter a mystery. Early Christians, noting Virgil's references to "the virgin," to a divine child who would rule the world in peace, to the "nullification of sin," and to the destruction of "the snake," later believed that the poet had received a vision of Christ from the Holy Spirit. Virgil's *Eclogues* inspired imitations from Dante Alighieri, Petrarch, and Giovanni Boccaccio.

After writing the *Eclogues*, Virgil left Rome for Naples, where he wrote the *Georgics*. Inspired by Hesiod's *Works and Days* but far more elegant, the *Georgics* remains the greatest specimen of didactic poetry ever written. In this masterpiece Virgil celebrated the beauties, labor, and rewards of the farm, a place situated comfortably between the extremes of the savage wilderness and the corrupt city. In this poem, one of the most influential in Western literature, Virgil demonstrated true genius. His problem was a most difficult one: how to write a great poem that was also a manual of practical advice for farmers. Virgil succeeded by virtue of his incredible descriptive power and through his charming ascription of human sentiment to every element of nature. Rather than write, "Don't plant your crops too early," Virgil warns the farmer never to "entrust too early to reluctant soil a whole year's hopes." He ends the second georgic with the pleasing line: "By now we have traversed a course of many leagues; high time to unyoke the steaming necks of our horses." In Virgil's capable hands even a storm seems beautiful. In his vivid imagination rivers feel boats on their backs, ants put aside food for old age, bees engage in "mob violence," "the endive revels in the brook it drinks," green river banks "delight in parsley," and a bull who loses a joust for a heifer anguishes over "lost love" and goes into "exile," quitting "his stable and ancestral kingdom." The poet even manages to inject suspense into an otherwise mundane instruction to keep the pens clean: "Often beneath neglected pens there lurks a dangerous viper, shrinking from the daylight, or an adder, curse of cattle, such as love to creep into the shelter of dark buildings and stab the herd with poison." His description of a fallen ox, the victim of a deadly plague, is strangely moving: "Sadly the plowman goes to unyoke the mate that mourns his brother, and leaves the plow stuck there, its work unfinished. No shade of lofty trees, no luscious meadow, can cheer that beast again." By wrapping the mundane matters of farming in heroic hexameters he endowed them with a dignity that, in lesser hands, might have seemed farcical.

The *Georgics* dispensed advice concerning the cultivation of crops, the growing of trees, the raising of livestock, and the keeping of bees. Some of the advice was quite good. For instance, Virgil, a reader of Greek and Roman agricultural manuals, advised crop rotation over 1,700 years before it sparked the modern agricultural revolution. Nonetheless, Virgil had a poor understanding of bees. Future dead white male and defender of patriarchy that he was, he thought that bees were led by "kings" rather than queens and praised them for their sexual abstinence. He evidently accepted the myth that young bees were not produced by copulation, but were gathered from the flowers that mysteriously generated them. (In other words, Virgil was not the right person to teach children about the birds and the bees.)

In the *Georgics*, Virgil exhorted his fellow Romans to help regenerate the community after a century of civil war by returning to the plow. He wrote:

> How lucky the farmers are—I wish they knew!
> The Earth herself, most just, pours forth for them
> An easy living from the soil, far off
> From clashing weapons. Though the farmer has
> No mansion with proud portals which spits out
> A monster wave of morning visitors
> From every room, nor do his callers gasp
> At inlaid columns, bright with tortoiseshell,
> Or gold-embroidered clothes or bronzes from
> Ephyre, nor in his house is plain white wool
> Dyed with Assyrian poison, nor does he
> Corrupt his olive oil with foreign spice,
> He has untroubled sleep and honest life.
> Rich in all sorts of riches, with a vast
> Estate, he has all the leisure to enjoy
> A cave, a natural pond, a valley where
> The air is cool—the mooing of the cows
> Is ever present, and to sleep beneath
> A tree is sweet. Wild animals abound
> For hunting, and young people grow up strong,
> Hardworking, satisfied with poverty.
> Their gods are holy; their parents are revered.
> Surely, when Justice left the earth she stayed
> Last with these folk, and left some tokens here.

Virgil celebrated the mythic past of the Italian countryside, its olive-laden vines, its perpetual spring, and its freedom from harmful plants and animals. He exulted: "Hail, great mother of harvests, land of Saturn, mighty mother of men; in your honor I tell of the things of that art of husbandry which from ancient times has been your glory; I dare to unseal those sacred springs, and through Roman towns I sing the song which Hesiod sang to the Greeks. . . . I will be the first, if life is granted me, to lead the Muses in triumph from Greek Helicon to my native land."

Virgil also painted a vivid portrait of the high cost and unstoppable momentum of civil war. He wrote: "No due honor attends the plow. The fields, bereft of tillers, are all unkempt and in the forge the curved pruning-hook is made a straight hard sword. . . . Impious War is raging. As on a racecourse, the barriers down, out pour the chariots, gathering speed from lap to lap, and a driver, tugging in vain at the reins, is swept along by the horses and the heedless, uncontrollable car."

A consummate artist, Virgil often wrote a plethora of verses in the morning and then spent the rest of the day polishing them and reducing them to a very small number. His meticulous craftsmanship left only verses of dazzling beauty.

Virgil's greatest masterpiece was the *Aeneid* (29–19 B.C.), an epic poem modeled on Homer's *Iliad* and *Odyssey*. The poem told the story of the Trojan Aeneas, who escaped the Greek destruction of Troy and moved to Italy, where his descendants founded Rome. The *Aeneid* effectively conveyed the Roman mission to conquer and "civilize" the world. The Sibyl of Cumae (the Roman version of the oracle of Delphi) guides Aeneas, newly arrived in Italy, to the underworld, where his father, Anchises, reveals to him the future glory of Rome. Upon his return to the earthly world, Aeneas even visits the site where his descendants, Romulus and Remus, are destined to establish the city. The god Vulcan gives him a shield engraved with designs that convey a further forecast of Rome's grand destiny. A depiction of the Battle of Actium, in which Augustus will defeat Antony and Cleopatra, forms the center of the shield. To Virgil, Augustus' victory represented the triumph of Roman civilization over Eastern barbarism. The last four books of the *Aeneid* concern wars between Aeneas' Trojan émigrés and the Latin tribes, wars ended by Aeneas' marriage to Lavinia, a Latin princess. Thus, the *Aeneid* is an *Odyssey* (a voyage-adventure epic) followed by an *Iliad* (a war epic).

Virgil takes no joy in war, as evidenced by its symbols in his poem: untilled fields, funeral pyres, nameless graves, and despairing parents. Courtly and gracious, Aeneas is a reluctant warrior. His suffering makes him not only stronger but also more humane.

Although Aeneas is a soldier like Achilles and the leader of a traveling band like Odysseus, his dogged dedication to public service contrasts with the individualism of the Greek heroes. He is the prototypical Roman, whose qualities presage Roman greatness. His epithet is "the pious," a title that manifests itself in his devotion to the gods and to family; Aeneas brings both his household gods and his aged father to Italy with him. His travels afford him numerous opportunities to lay aside his arduous destiny for a comfortable life in an existing city. His greatest temptation of this kind occurs in ancient Carthage. The goddess Venus (Aeneas' mother) makes Queen Dido of Carthage fall in love with him and offer him a permanent home. Aeneas stays in Carthage a year, until Jupiter sends Mercury to recall him to his duty. Dutiful Aeneas, though heartbroken, stoically follows the will of fate in opposition to his own desires. Aeneas abandons Dido, who laments, "Had I but borne any offspring of you before your flight, were there but some tiny Aeneas to play in my hall and remind me of you, though but in look, I should not feel utterly captive and forlorn." The desperate queen commits suicide with Aeneas' sword, after calling down a curse of deadly enmity between her descendants and Aeneas'. She cries out to Carthage: "Pursue his seed with your hatred for all ages to come. Let no kindness or truce be between the nations."

Although the myth of Aeneas and Dido could be used to justify the Roman destruction of Carthage by surrounding it with an aura of inevitability, Virgil's poem displays a rare sympathy for most of Aeneas' defeated enemies—tragic figures swimming desperately against the majestic stream of Roman destiny. At the end of the poem Aeneas hesitates before finally killing his Latin rival Turnus, king of the Rutulians; the destiny of a city yet to be born has forced the noble Aeneas to abandon and to destroy those whom he would much prefer to spare. (Historic distance from a defeated foe, be it Troy for the Greeks, Carthage for the Romans, or the England of George III for Americans, often produces a certain magnanimity no less enlightened for its belatedness.) Virgil has Jupiter declare concerning the Romans, "For these I set no limits, world or time, but make the gift of empire without end." He adds that Rome's fate is to "bring the whole world under law's dominion."

Virgil's gods are, in general, more dignified and moral, less drunken and capricious, than Homer's deities. Venus is less cruel and more motherly than Homer's Aphrodite, and Jupiter is less lecherous and more just than Homer's Zeus. A student of philosophy, Virgil's image of the divine was clearly influenced by the Pythagoreans, Platonists, and Stoics who criticized Homer's conception of the gods. Furthermore, like the Stoics, Virgil seems to envision a mysterious Fate as a greater power than even the gods themselves.

Though Virgil had been under intense pressure from Augustus' friend and advisor Maecenas to write an epic about the emperor, the shrewd poet had quickly realized that contemporary history is almost never a suitable subject for an epic. If familiarity does not necessarily breed contempt, at the very least it impedes the aura of grandeur essential to the epic form. Furthermore, the Battle of Actium, the moment of Augustus' triumph, had witnessed very little that might be considered heroic fighting; Augustus himself certainly had not killed hundreds with his own hands like Achilles or Hector. To have made Augustus the central character of such an epic poem would have been to turn the poem into a farce. In addition, if Augustus were made the subject of the epic, there could be no sympathy for his defeated foes—which would remove a large portion of the pathos, the tragic element, that makes the *Aeneid* such a masterpiece. It is precisely because we feel the pain of the abandoned Dido and of the vanquished Latins that we can appreciate the human cost of Rome's fated success. Virgil's brilliant solution to the problem of how to make Augustus a focus of the *Aeneid* without actually making him its central character was perhaps the only solution that could have preserved the poem's grandeur. His solution was to use the stirring story of Aeneas to present Roman history as a progression culminating in Augustus. Virgil shrewdly presents the Battle of Actium as a tableau on a shield rather than as a narrative. The real focus of the *Aeneid* is neither Augustus nor Aeneas. It is Rome.

Finally, the poem serves one other purpose: to reconcile the recently enfranchised Italians with Rome. Jupiter and Juno agree to assuage the Latins' grief over their defeat by making the Italians themselves a source of Rome's future strength: "Italian hardiness will make Rome great." In this way the vanquished Italians join the winning side and reconcile themselves to Roman destiny through participation in it. So wrote the poet from Cisalpine Gaul, the last part of Italy to be enfranchised.

Shortly before his death, Virgil instructed his friends to burn the *Aeneid*, perhaps because he had left some incomplete lines scattered throughout the poem. Fortunately for Western literature, they refused to do so.

One of the most revered poems in Western history, the *Aeneid* influenced Dante, Geoffrey Chaucer, John Milton, Alfred Lord Tennyson, and numerous other poets. Dante's *Divine Comedy* and Milton's *Paradise Lost* were both modeled on the *Aeneid*. Indeed, Dante selected Virgil to represent all that was wise and good in the pagan world, assigning him the task of guiding the narrator through the *Inferno* and the *Purgatorio*, the first two portions of the *Divine Comedy*.

Horace (65–8 B.C.)

The second greatest poet of the Augustan Age was Horace (Quintus Horatius Flaccus), a native of Venusia, a small town in the heel of Italy. Horace's father, a former slave and collector of auction payments, sacrificed much to secure his son a rigorous education in Rome and Athens. While in Rome, Horace's father accompanied him on the walk to his teachers every day in order to keep him from getting into any trouble in the city's rowdy streets. He taught Horace the consequences of good and bad actions, leading Horace to write later, "Thanks to his training, I am free from vices that lead to ruin; the lesser faults I have are, I hope, excusable." Even after he became prosperous and famous, Horace was always proud of his low-born father and appreciative of his sacrifices.

Although Augustus and Antony confiscated Horace's estate in retribution for his fighting in Brutus' army at Philippi, Horace returned to Rome, where he worked in the treasury department. On the recommendation of Virgil, Maecenas made certain that he received the patronage of the magnanimous Augustus, including a famous Sabine farm twenty-eight miles northeast of Rome. Now freed from treasury duties, Horace wrote, "This is what I have been praying for." In fact, Maecenas and Horace became so close that Horace dedicated much of his poetry to him and wrote, "Though your ancestors . . . commanded great legions long ago, yet you, Maecenas, do not, as most men do, turn up your nose at unknown men like myself, a freedman's son." On his deathbed Maecenas begged Augustus, "Be as mindful of Horace as you would of me."

Influenced by Archilochus, Horace's *Epodes* (ca. 41–29 B.C.), seventeen poems consisting of couplets in which a long verse alternated with a short one, introduced various Greek meters that Horace had learned at Athens into Latin. The *Epodes* assaulted social abuses and praised the rural lifestyle, though sometimes with a palpable sense of irony. Horace wrote:

> Happy the man who, free from business worries and free from interest owing, like the men of the old days, tills with his oxen his ancestral fields. . . . He keeps away from the Forum and the proud threshold of the powers that be. . . . He likes to recline now under an ancient oak, now on the thick grass. Meanwhile the brooks flow between the high banks, birds warble in the woods, and springs bubble with running water, a sweet invitation to repose. But when the wintry season of thundering Jove brings back rains and snows, either with his pack of hounds he drives the fierce boars into the traps, or arranges large meshed nets on polished sticks to snare the greedy thrushes. . . . If a modest wife does her part in tending the house and her dear children . . . piles high the sacred hearth with dry firewood, waiting for the return of her tired husband, gathers in a pen made of wattles the fat ewes in order to milk their distended udders, and, drawing from the keg new sweet wine, prepares a meal which she had not to pay for . . . amid such feasts, what joy to see the sheep returning home from pasture, the wearied oxen dragging along the upturned plowshare and the young slaves, industrious swarm of an opulent house, seated around the resplendent Lares.

But the sly poet could not resist adding, "When the moneylender Alfius had uttered these sentiments, he (the would-be farmer) calls in all his loans, and is now trying to put his money out again on usury," leaving the reader in doubt as to the seriousness of the portrait. Thomas Jefferson once planned to inscribe an abbreviated version of this passage near a small, Greek-style temple he hoped to build on his burial ground. Of course, as a fervent supporter of agriculture and the rural lifestyle, Jefferson omitted the poem's ironic ending.

In these early verses, written before the triumph of Augustus, Horace also lamented Rome's disastrous civil wars. He wrote:

> Into what, what, do you wickedly plunge? Why do your hands draw swords from scabbards? Perhaps too little Latin blood has been spilled on battlefields or Neptune's realm? And not that Romans might burn the haughty

towers of emulous Carthage; not that the scatheless Briton might trudge in chains down the Sacred Way; but that in fulfillment of Parthian prayers the city might die by her own right hand. . . . So it goes: a bitter fate pursues the Romans, and the crime of fratricide, since the blood of Remus ran on the earth, the bane of his successors. . . . What Hannibal, whom parents wished away, could not destroy or tame, this impious generation of fated stock will waste and the land belong once more to beasts of prey.

Horace also wrote about the agonies of love. He rebuked the mysterious man who had stolen his lover's affection: "And you, whoever you are, who amble happy and proud in my misfortune, though perhaps you are rich in flocks and land . . . and your beauty surpasses that of Nireus, alas, you shall bewail her favors transferred to another, and I shall laugh last."

Influenced by Alcaeus, Sappho, and the Hellenistic poets, Horace's *Odes* (ca. 23–13 B.C.) were remarkably succinct. Tennyson once called his lines "jewels five words long that on the stretched forefinger of all time sparkle forever." Employing nineteen different meters, Horace painstakingly arranged his words like a mason fitting stones into an arch. Somehow he managed to soften the rugged Latin language into a delicate form.

The theme of more than a third of the poems is friendship. Indeed, many of the verses are addressed to friends, offering advice and encouragement. Another third deal with the joys and tribulations of love, with human nature, and with the countryside. Horace declared, "Thrice happy the couple who are not torn apart by quarrels but are held in a bond of unbroken love which only death dissolves." He resolved to let others write epic poems about heroes while he wrote of the epic struggles between the sexes: "Flippant as ever, whether afire or fancy free, I sing of banquets and 'battles' of eager girls with neatly trimmed nails against the young men."

Although a small group of odes glorified Augustus in gratitude for priceless peace, Horace was no sycophant. He demonstrated genuine respect for Cleopatra, Augustus' fallen foe: "Resolved for death, she was brave indeed. She was no docile woman but truly scorned to be taken away in her enemy's ships, deposed, to an overweening Triumph." Though genuinely appreciative of Augustus' achievements, Horace refused to become Augustus' private secretary, declined to write an epic about him (or anyone else, since he was not an epic poet), and abstained from asking favors. Sounding like Cicero, he wrote:

> The righteous man, tenacious of his purpose,
> Is not shaken in his fixed resolutions
> By the fury of his fellow citizens
> Bidding him do wrong
> Nor by the looks of the threatening tyrant.

He referred to Cato the Younger's suicide to avoid living under the dictator-ship of Julius Caesar, Augustus' adoptive father, as "a noble death."

Painfully aware of the approach of his own death, Horace resolved to live life to the fullest. He wrote: "Pallid Death knocks impartially at the doors of hovels and mansions. . . . One universal night awaits us all. . . . Be wise, decant the wine, prune back your long-term hopes. Life ebbs as I speak—so seize the day [the immortal *carpe diem*], and grant the next no credit. . . . Be glad to take what gifts the passing hour bestows, and leave sad things alone. . . . Happy the man, and happy he alone, who can call today his own; he who secure within, can say, 'Tomorrow, do your worst, for I have lived today.'" Of wine, he wrote, "You bring back hope to troubled hearts; you give courage to the poor man." Horace concluded his third book of odes: "I have built a monument more enduring than bronze. . . . Not all of me shall die."

Horace was buried next to his friend and patron Maecenas on Esquiline Hill in Rome. His poems, like Virgil's, held an honored place in Roman education within less than a century and influenced countless generations of poets thereafter.

Ovid (43 B.C.–A.D. 17)

The third great poet of the Augustan Age was Ovid (Publius Ovidius Naso). Though he was born at Sulmo in the mountains of central Italy ninety miles east of Rome, he lived in the city as a young adult; as a result, his poetry was urbane and sophisticated. His equestrian father, hoping he would pursue a career in politics or law, had him educated by the best professors of rhetoric in Rome. While Ovid benefited from the rhetorical training he received there and in Athens, he found it impossible to confine himself to prose, so great was his natural preference for verse.

Born to the generation that followed that of Virgil and Horace, Ovid composed light, speedy, scintillating verse reflective of a new era. Because he was too young to remember the civil wars, he was also too young to be grate-ful for the Augustan peace.

Ovid's first great work was the *Loves*, fifty elegies written while he was still in his twenties. Ovid began the work with the first word of Virgil's *Ae-neid*, in order to impart a majesty that he could then puncture: "Arms, and the violent deeds of war, I was making ready to send forth—in weighty numbers, with matter suited to the measure." But, Ovid relates, Cupid, "with a laugh, stole one foot." This was a reference to Ovid's elegiac verse, in which six-foot (six-meter) verses, the traditional meter of epic poetry, alternated with five. Ovid continued, addressing Cupid: "My new page of song rose well, with the first verse in lofty strain, when that next one—of your making—changed to slightness the vigor of my work. . . . You iron wars, with your measures, fare ye well!" He later adds: "Of what avail will it be to me to have sung of the swift Achilles? What will the sons of Atreus, the one or the other, do for me? . . . But a tender beloved, at my oft praising of her beauty, has come to the poet as a reward for song. . . . Renowned names of heroes, fare ye well: your favors are not the kind for me!" Playing the part of the great lover, the poet claims: "Often have I made merry through all hours of the night, and reached the morning fit and strong. Happy he whom the mutual strife of Love lays low. Ye gods, let my end come from such a cause!" He then imagines his tearful friends saying over his body, "Yours was a death that accorded with your life."

In the *Loves* Ovid chronicles his relationship with Corinna, the married woman with whom he has a passionate affair. He gains entrance to her house at night by reminding her slave that he once saved him from a scourging, by promising him eventual freedom, and by warning that husbands rarely believe tales of their wives' duplicity told by slaves. At the wife's denial, accompanied by flowing tears, the husband, the slave's master, will beat him: "Though he himself has seen, he will yet believe what he desires. . . . You will lose and get a flogging in the end, while she will look on from the lap of her judge." The poet alleges that he cannot resist women of all kinds, tall and short, blonde and brunette, fair and dark.

Ovid overhears an old, alcoholic hag named Dipsas (Thirsty) counsel Corinna to take on as many lovers as possible and to despoil them all of expensive gifts, as well as "loans that will never be restored." Dipsas intones: "It may be that in Tatius' reign the unadorned Sabines would not be wife to more than one; but now in wars far off Mars tries men's souls, and Venus reigns in the city of her Aeneas. . . . Chaste is she whom no one has asked—or, be she not too rustic, she herself asks first." Dipsas advises against bedding impoverished aristocrats: "Nor let yourself be deluded by ancient masks about the hall. Take your grandfathers and go, poor lover! . . . Let your portal be deaf to prayers, but wide to the giver." Dipsas also counsels her mistress to feign headaches in order to avoid sex and to learn to cry at will.

Ovid later sees Corinna exchanging silent signals with another lover that the poet himself has taught her, as well as French-kissing, a skill learned elsewhere. He writes: "Something new she seemed to have learned. . . . Those kisses must have been lewdly taught. Some master has had a great reward for his teaching." He confesses: "I can live neither with you nor without. . . . Though there was Thebes, though Troy, though Caesar's deeds, Corinna only has stirred my genius."

Ovid's passage on Dawn's separation of lovers influenced an entire genre of medieval verse. In the passage Ovid pleads for Dawn to tarry and accuses her of causing widespread misery by depriving sailors of the guidance of the stars and others of needed rest. Dawn means that farmers have to return to the field, women to the loom, warriors to battle, children to school, and pleaders to court. The poet fails to delay Dawn but does cause her to blush.

Ovid was convinced that the emotional experiences of ordinary people were as worthy of poetic treatment as the fables of the great, human and divine. He wrote slyly, "Either a god is a name without substance whom we fear without reason and who scares the people because of their stupid credulity, or, if any god exists, he loves pretty girls and, more than he should, bids them, and them alone, to get away with everything."

Ovid's *Heroides* consisted of twenty-one imaginative letters, fifteen from mythological heroines to their lovers, six from famous lovers to each other. Ovid used his marvelous descriptive power to counteract the repetitive quality of some of his material, including the recurring theme of wronged and abandoned women, though he was not entirely successful. The pathos of these pleading letters is provided by the reader's knowledge of their ultimate futility. Laodamia writes to her husband Protesilaus, famed as the first Greek killed on the beaches of Troy:

> I warn you to be the last in disembarking;
> It is not the paternal soil to which you hasten.
> But coming home, urge on your boat with both oar and sail
> And swiftly set foot on your own shore!

Medea, who the reader knows will soon kill her own children in revenge for their father Jason's abandonment of her, ends her letter to him ominously: "Something portentous, surely, is working in my soul." While the letters were generally tragic in nature, Ovid sometimes used the reader's foreknowledge for comic effect, as when Paris seduces Helen into running away with him by calming her fears with the question: "Of so many women who have been taken before, tell me, has anyone ever been sought back by arms?"

Ovid's didactic poem *The Art of Love* (2–1 B.C.) instructed the reader on how to seduce women. The first book advised the student on how to find and win a mistress, including the warning against falling for a woman at a banquet where wine and bad lighting might impair judgment, the second on how to keep her. The third provided advice for women. Regarding the romantic combat that occurred at gladiatorial games, he wrote: "Often has Venus' boy fought upon that sand, and he who watched the wounds has himself been wounded. While he was speaking and touching her hand and asking for the program and inquiring who is winning, after placing his bet, he felt the winged weapon and groaned as he was wounded, and was himself part of the show he was watching." Ovid satirized romantic poets who called themselves "soldiers of love" by pretending to take seriously the analogy between love and war: "Tacticians recommend the night attack, use of the spearhead, catching the foe asleep. . . . Lovers use them too—to exploit a sleeping husband, thrusting hard while the enemy snores." He also satirized such poetic clichés as the enslavement of the lover and the divinity of the beloved. Ovid lampooned love poetry by pretending to treat it as a serious science. He had gone from presenting himself as the servant of love, in the *Loves*, to portraying himself as its master: "From practice this book springs; hearken to the experienced bard." While the *Loves* gloried in romantic passion, the *Art of Love* depicted the perfect lover as clearheaded.

Although some of Ovid's advice involved deception—such as making one's mistress believe that it is at her instigation one is freeing a slave or absolving him of punishment, when one has already determined to do so—much of it was tender and good-hearted. He claimed that solicitude and devotion were the best ways to keep a mistress. To be loved one had to become lovable, "and your face and figure are not enough to make you so." Ovid added: "Beauty is not a lasting possession. . . . Mold in time your soul to fit up your beauty; the soul alone remains with you to your last day." Some advice combined tenderness with deception: a man should pretend to find a woman gorgeous, no matter what she wore or how she looked, and a woman should pretend to be under the spell of a man's charm, no matter how dull he was.

Augustus resisted Ovid's own indisputable charm. Ovid's graphic depictions of sex, flippant treatment of adultery, and satire of moralistic literature in *The Art of Love* shocked the emperor. After learning of the emperor's disfavor, Ovid made a halfhearted attempt to recant in *The Cures of Love*, another didactic poem. Ovid cautioned those suffering over lost love to avoid leisure, solitude, and others in love. He advocated pursuits that he had formerly opposed, such as law, politics, and war, as methods by which the despairing lover could distract himself. Ovid contended, "Whoever announces too often: 'I am not in love,' is."

Ovid's greatest work, *The Metamorphoses* (A.D. 1–8), was a complete departure for a poet who had previously written only short pieces concerning real life. Written in hexameters, rather than in Ovid's usual elegiac couplets, the poem interwove more than 250 legends, folk tales, and anecdotes concerning Greco-Roman mythology, organized loosely around the metamorphoses of various figures into animals, plants, and other things. The first metamorphosis was that of the universe from chaos. The theme of metamorphosis allowed Ovid to explore persistence as well as change; the transformed individuals often retained their basic identities, even transforming into something appropriate to their personalities (bloodthirsty Lycaon into a wolf, the bickering Lycians into croaking frogs, and resistant Daphne into a tree). Yet the poem was as much about love, in all of its forms, as about metamorphosis.

A loose collection of often bizarre tales told irreverently, *The Metamorphoses* was so marvelously varied in style, tone, tempo, and subject matter as to serve as a portrait of metamorphosis itself. Ovid spaced out similar stories to avoid monotony and told each differently. He varied concise and energetic narrative with lengthy descriptions of arresting situations. While portions of the *Metamorphoses* are quite serious and genuinely moving, delving into the inner psychology of characters and feeling their losses, Ovid never allowed emotion to run too deep or such moments to become too protracted. He interspersed tragic tales with lighthearted ones. He preferred flowing dactyls (a long syllable followed by two short syllables) to Virgil's majestic spondees (two long syllables).

Largely disinterested in morality, Ovid was as content to recount acts of divine injustice (many of the metamorphoses are produced by vengeful gods) without any attempt to explain them away as he was to recount episodes of divine mercy. Tiresias, the prophet so ubiquitous in Greek drama, is blinded by Juno in punishment for siding with her husband Jupiter in a dispute about which gender enjoys sex more; Tiresias, chosen as judge because of his unique expertise in the matter—he had once been transformed into a woman and had lived that way for seven years—agrees with Jupiter that women enjoy it more. When Mars is caught in the act of adultery with the beautiful Venus, another god wishes "that some day he might be overtaken by such disgrace himself." The other deities roar with laughter.

Ovid liked to thwart readers' expectations by beginning a tale seriously, with talk of crime and punishment, then moving to overly graphic descriptions of the absurd and grotesque. His deaths were sometimes repulsive rather than tragic, and he sometimes exaggerated grief for comic effect. His sarcastic remarks concerning the victims of bizarre deaths oddly resemble those made by the protagonists in modern James Bond or Arnold Schwarzenegger films. But his compassionate reference to sacrificial bulls suggests that, because he did not consider the characters in mythology real in any sense (a fact that separates him from Virgil and most other Romans), he reserved his compassion for real creatures.

The *Metamorphoses* contains sly satire of contemporary poetry. Narcissus' speech to the trees about his love (himself) is a spoof on love poetry of the day, as is his comment, "I wish that he who is loved would outlive me." Another satirical bit is the infatuated Cyclops Polyphemus' song to the resistant Galatea. After combing his "shaggy mop" of hair with a rake, trimming his beard with a sickle, and making faces he considers "more winsome" in a pool of water, the unlikely lover sings a song filled with absurd comparisons of Galatea with various natural features. Mingled with a host of conventional, romantic comparisons are, "You are more obstinate than untrained heifers . . . and more aggressive than a pregnant bear." He then boasts about his collection of livestock, adding the irrelevancy: "I do not know how many; only poor men can count their cows." He sings about making cheese from their milk, about catching two bear cubs to serve as Galatea's pets, and about his own shortcomings ("I have one eye, so what? . . . The great Sun has only one eye"). Since Horace had written, "The man who wishes to vary a single subject in monstrous fashion is like a painter adding a dolphin to the woods, a boar to the waves," Ovid enlivens his discussion of the Great Flood with, what else, dolphins in the woods and boars in the waves (in addition to someone fishing from the top of an elm tree and a wolf swimming with a lamb). He has Mercury slowly put the hundred-eyed monster Argus to sleep, one eye after another, by telling him a dull story that is strikingly similar to one that Ovid has just related, in an exceedingly monotonous fashion, so that the reader feels sleepy as well. While including some genuinely fine rhetoric, the debate between Ajax and Ulysses (Odysseus) over Achilles' armor is a partial spoof of Homer's account of the same debate, and of poetic speeches in general, in which Ajax pokes fun at Ulysses' cowardice, Ulysses at Ajax's stupidity.

The *Metamorphoses* is an egocentric work, constantly drawing the reader's attention back to the author through personal asides, puns, alliteration, and the author's sheer virtuosity in retelling well-known tales. Yet Ovid's egocentrism was not without purpose; the author's own personality provided a unity to the long poem that it might otherwise have lacked. Indeed, the purposely peculiar transitions between some tales, while seeming to detract from the unity of the poem, actually enhance it by reminding the reader that the author's sly personality is the real glue that holds the poem together.

More concerned with the metamorphosis of myth itself than with the mythological metamorphoses he recounted, Ovid infused new life into old tales of the gods, clothing the deities in contemporary personalities. Like his own character the sculptor Pygmalion, who had used his art to bring cold marble to life, Ovid used his own poetic art to revive the lifeless statue of classical myth.

In the final book of the *Metamorphoses*, Ovid made a halfhearted attempt to placate the emperor. Ovid's final metamorphosis was that of Julius Caesar into a god, a transformation he took as an opportunity to praise Augustus, Caesar's heir, as an even greater god. Yet, by questioning, if not denying, the justice of the gods throughout the large poem, the supreme compliment Ovid paid Augustus at the end was seriously devalued. To call Augustus a god at that point was merely to recognize his earthly power, not to applaud his justice. Indeed, Ovid concluded the poem with a prophecy that sounded a note of defiance:

And so I have achieved a work which neither the wrath of Jove, nor fire,
Nor steel, nor gnawing time will be able to undo.
Let come when it will that day which has power over my frame only,
And end my uncertain span of years;
Yet in my better part shall I rise to the vault of the heavens
Perennial, and my name will be safe from oblivion.
Wherever Roman might blankets subject lands, I shall be recited by the
    people;
In the memory of all ages to come, if there be any truth in poets' prophecies,
I shall live.

Ovid's reference to his own fame overcoming even the wrath of Jove, with whom Ovid had just compared Augustus (the one wielding absolute power in the heavens, the other on earth), was clearly aimed at the emperor. Yet it was also an apt conclusion to a poem about transformations, because it asserted that one reality was impervious to change: the poet's own achievement. In so doing, Ovid seemed to be substituting the eternal glory of the creative individual for the eternal glory of not only Augustus but of Rome itself, the usual theme of Roman poets like Virgil.

The most creative and comprehensive mythological work that survived antiquity, the *Metamorphoses* imparted to countless generations of poets, painters, and opera composers not merely a gold mine of information concerning classical mythology but also an imaginative and playful way of regarding it that was worlds apart from the somberness of Hesiod's work, over which it prevailed. It later influenced the troubadours of medieval France, Dante (who classed Ovid with Homer and Horace), Boccaccio, Chaucer, Milton, and Shakespeare. Summaries of classical myth, from Thomas Bulfinch's enormously popular edition in the nineteenth century to Edith Hamilton's in the twentieth, have drawn their stories largely from Ovid.

As Ovid was completing the *Metamorphoses*, the ax fell and Ovid's own fortunes underwent a tragic metamorphosis. Augustus banished the poet to Tomis on the Black Sea (now Constanta, Romania) in A.D. 8, roughly the same time that Augustus exiled his granddaughter Julia, the namesake of his daughter, whom he had exiled for the same offense—adultery—nine years earlier. Augustus had disliked Ovid since the publication of *The Art of Love*, which conflicted with his program of improving public morality, and now accused the poet of having aided his granddaughter in committing adultery. Ovid denied the charge, though unable to deny that he had known of the adultery and had failed to report it. Ironically, Ovid learned of Augustus' banishment order while on the island of Elba, which would be the site of Napoleon's first period of exile in 1814. Despite Ovid's pleading publications (*Lamentations* and *Letters from the Black Sea*) in subsequent years, as well as his laudatory poems in honor of the imperial family, Augustus refused to recall him, as did Augustus' successor Tiberius. Ovid protested: "My life is respectable, though my Muse is full of jesting. A book is not evidence of one's soul." Though homesick and alternating between hope and despair, he continued to write, noting, "My own talent goes with me everywhere and gladdens me; no emperor has any right over that."

CONCLUSION

Rome's greatest poets proved worthy successors to the Greeks. Catullus' poems surpassed their Alexandrian models. If Virgil's *Aeneid* did not surpass its models, the *Iliad* and the *Odyssey*, it proved worthy enough to be spoken of in the same breath with those two masterpieces, a claim that can be made for little or nothing written since the fall of Rome. While Virgil's *Eclogues* were superior to the poems of Theocritus, his *Georgics* far surpassed Hesiod's *Works and Days*. Horace's *Odes* and *Epodes* equaled in quality the works of the Greek lyric poets and were more fortunate in survival and, thus, influence. Ovid's *Metamorphoses* easily surpassed Hesiod's *Theogony* in artistic merit and impact. While Virgil provided an enduring model that glorified a sense of duty to the collective good, Ovid furnished an equally lasting testament to the creativity and freedom of the individual. It was from these Latin poets, rather than from their Greek predecessors, the knowledge of whose language was rare in the medieval and even the modern West, that the Western world learned the beauty and power of verse.

· 5 ·

Speeches, Letters, and Agricultural Manuals

$\mathcal{T}$he Romans excelled in prose as well as poetry. They delivered speeches that have resounded in the minds and hearts of Westerners for two millennia. They exchanged remarkable letters that illuminated the times in which they lived. They wrote agricultural manuals that imparted sound advice to farmers for centuries.

GREEK PRECURSORS

Demosthenes (384–322 B.C.)

The Greeks produced oratorical models that the Romans cherished for generations. By far the most influential Greek speaker was the Athenian Demosthenes. The son of a sword manufacturer, Demosthenes overcame a speech impediment to become one of the greatest orators in Western history. He began studying rhetoric in order to prosecute the inept or corrupt trustees whose mismanagement had cost him his father's estate. Able to recover only a portion of his inheritance, he turned to speechwriting for litigants for his livelihood. He spent months at a time in an underground study, writing and practicing speeches before a full-length mirror, even shaving one cheek so that he would not be tempted to go out of the house and neglect his rhetorical training.

In a series of stirring speeches called the *Philippics* (351–341 B.C.) Demosthenes warned against the growing power of Macedon under the cunning King Philip II, who sought to rule all of Greece. Demosthenes contrasted the apathy and corruption of Athens in the fourth century B.C. with the glorious Athens of the previous century, the Athens that had scorned the bribes and resisted the incursions of another set of barbarians, the Persians. Demosthenes warned of "the restless activity which is a part of Philip's very being and which will not allow him to content himself with his achievements and remain at peace." Demosthenes concluded: "This peace that he speaks of is a peace which you are to observe towards Philip, while he does not observe it towards you. . . . If we will not fight him now in his own country we shall perhaps be obliged to do so in ours. . . . It is by deeds and actions, not by words, that a policy of encroachment must be arrested. . . . The Greeks see these things and endure them, gazing as they would at a hailstorm, each praying that it may not come his way, but no one trying to prevent it. . . . Heaven grant that the time may not come when the truth of my words will be tested with all severity."

Demosthenes' effort to save Greece from Macedonian control failed. Philip conquered Greece, and his son Alexander the Great led the Greeks in the conquest of the Persian Empire. When Alexander died without a clear heir, Athens revolted. Antipater, a Macedonian general, crushed the revolt. Under a threat of execution, Demosthenes killed himself with a poison he had taken to carrying in a hollow bracelet in the event of such a desperate situation.

The Romans considered Demosthenes the greatest of all the Greek orators. Modern republicans considered him a martyr to the cause of freedom. Many centuries later, when facing down yet another cunning tyrant with vast ambitions of conquest and control, Winston Churchill drew solace from the example of Demosthenes.

Xenophon (ca. 431–351 B.C.)

In contrast to their famous speeches, the Greeks published few letters and agricultural manuals, and even fewer have survived, so these literary genres entered the Western canon almost exclusively through the Romans. Famous for his *Memorabilia of Socrates* and for his *Anabasis*, a stirring account of his ill-fated military expedition to Persia, the Athenian Xenophon also published a Socratic dialogue called *Estate Management*. (The original Greek title *Oikonomikos* [literally "on house law"] became the basis for the English word "economics" in modern times since the management of a nation's economy was likened to that of a large estate.)

Though *Estate Management* was widely read by the Roman agriculturalists, sometimes in a Latin translation provided by Cicero, it was very brief and uninformative. Xenophon justified his brevity by arguing that farming was so easy to learn that success was only a matter of diligence—an odd argument for what was supposed to be, at least in part, an agricultural manual—and the information he provided was not always accurate. While the patriarchal Virgil might have learned something from Xenophon's reference to the queen bee, his zoological knowledge would have immediately been set back by Xenophon's attribution of the other bees' loyalty to the queen to "thoughtful acts on her part."

If *Estate Management* imparted anything to the Romans, it was not so much agricultural knowledge as the same doctrine of the moral superiority of the rural lifestyle that was imparted by the Greek pastoral poets. Xenophon had been such an admirer of agricultural Sparta that he had left his own city of Athens to fight with the Spartans. He wrote, "It has been nobly said that agriculture is the mother and nurse of the other arts. . . . [It is] helpful, pleasant, honorable, and dear to gods and men in the highest degree." Agriculture produced "the best citizens and most loyal to the community," men who would defend the soil, in sharp contrast to urbanites, who were not used to "toil and danger." As a gentleman farmer who employed slave labor, Xenophon could add the argument, later used by Thomas Jefferson, that farming also left "to the mind the greatest amount of spare time for attending to the interests of one's friends and city." But the farmer in search of tips on the application of manure had best turn to the more pragmatic Roman writers.

CICERO (106–43 B.C.)

The most influential figure of classical civilization was a Roman statesman, orator, essayist, and philosopher named Cicero. Considered a martyr for republicanism as well as one of the greatest orators in history, Cicero became the role model for many Western statesmen over the centuries.

Cicero's Early Career

The son of an eques from the country town of Arpinum, sixty miles southeast of Rome, Marcus Tullius Cicero was never fully accepted by the snobbish senate elite or by the demagogic leaders of the masses, whom he despised. Cicero is Latin for "chickpea"; it was believed that one of his ancestors had possessed a wart of that shape on the end of his nose. Friends advised Cicero to change his name to something less ridiculous, but he refused.

Despite his odd name and unimpressive lineage, Cicero came to prominence in Rome as an attorney. His first case, in 81 B.C., was a defense of Sextus Roscius on the false charge of murdering his father, an accusation brought by one of Sulla's freedmen in order to seize Roscius' estate. Cicero courageously attacked the dictator's henchman, to thunderous applause. He then took the case of a woman who challenged Sulla's withdrawal of her citizenship. After a tour of the eastern Mediterranean, during which time he studied rhetoric and philosophy, he returned an even more powerful speaker.

In 75 B.C. Cicero was elected quaestor and was sent to Lilybaeum (Marsala) in western Sicily, where he negotiated a fair rate from the grain suppliers of the province and did not take the customary, though illegal, cut for himself. He declared, "The chief thing in all public administration and all public service is to avoid even the slightest suspicion of self-seeking."

Cicero then faced Hortensius, the most renowned attorney of his day, in the prosecution of Verres, the corrupt and ruthless governor of Sicily. Cicero told the jurors:

> Today the eyes of the world are upon you. This man's case will establish whether a jury composed exclusively of senators can possibly convict someone who is very guilty—and very rich. Let me add that because the defendant is the kind of man who is distinguished by nothing except his criminality and his wealth, the only imaginable explanation for an acquittal will be the one that brings the greatest discredit to you. . . . If you are unable to arrive at a correct judgment in this case, the Roman people cannot expect that there will be other senators who can. It will despair of the senatorial order as a whole and look around for some other type of man and some other method of administering justice.

Smelling defeat, Hortensius withdrew from the case. In spite of having been bribed by Verres, the jury fined him three million sesterces.

In 69 B.C. Cicero became an aedile. Although he produced no flamboyant gladiatorial shows, the usual route to popularity for an aedile, his Sicilian friends helped him keep grain prices low. In 66 B.C. he was elected praetor.

Catiline's Conspiracy

In 63 B.C. Cicero became one of the few equites ever elected consul, winning the popular election by a wide margin, without bribery or violence. Almost immediately, while Pompey and his army were away fighting in the eastern Mediterranean, Cicero faced a rebellion led by a corrupt, debt-ridden aristocrat named Catiline (Lucius Sergius Catilina), who had just lost the election for the consulship. Catiline was alleged to have had sex with a Vestal Virgin and to have killed his own son because a woman with whom he was in love did not want a stepson. Catiline now conspired to assassinate the consuls, seize power, and win popular support through the cancellation of debts and the redistribution of land. Cicero discovered the plot through Fulvia, the mistress of one of Catiline's coconspirators.

An ardent defender of the republic, Cicero acted quickly to thwart Catiline's plan. Catiline fled north to Etruria, while Cicero denounced him in a series of famous speeches, and one of Catiline's coconspirators still in Rome plotted to kill all of the senators and to take Pompey's children hostage. Employing a Gallic tribe that pretended to join the conspiracy so that Cicero might obtain documentary proof of it, Cicero located the house in Rome where the conspirators had stockpiled weapons. After the conspirators in Rome were arrested, the irascible Cato the Younger rose in the Senate to argue that they should be executed immediately since they had already confessed to plotting massacres and arson and since he feared the effect of a trial on the volatile city, with Catiline still in the field. Already angered by Julius Caesar's advocacy of a trial, Cato became incensed when a note was delivered to Caesar in the Senate House. Cato accused Caesar of communicating with the conspirators and challenged him to read the message aloud. Caesar passed it across to Cato without comment, at which point Cato discovered that it was a love letter from Cato's own half-sister Servilia to Caesar. Cato then threw it back, saying angrily, "Take it, you drunken idiot!" Nevertheless, the Senate endorsed Cato's motion for execution, and the conspirators were hanged without trial on Cicero's authority as consul. In 62 B.C. a Roman army defeated and killed Catiline at Pistoria.

Cicero and Caesar

Two years later, Caesar, Pompey, and Crassus asked Cicero to join their alliance because they prized his renowned oratorical ability. Though membership in so powerful a collective would have held great financial and political advantages for Cicero, he refused membership in the alliance out of loyalty to the republic. Cicero's decision had the effect of turning what would have been called the First Quartet into the more majestic-sounding First Triumvirate.

Cicero reluctantly sided with Pompey in the civil war a decade later, on the assumption that Pompey was more likely to restore the republic, but was appalled that the talk in Pompey's camp was all about profiting from the war and murdering opponents and even wealthy neutrals for their property. Cicero recalled, "Their conversation was so bloodthirsty that I shuddered at the prospect of victory." When Cicero said he wanted nothing more to do with the war, Pompey's son and friends would have killed him then and there if Cato had not intervened.

Though Cicero's brother and nephew blamed him for their own decision to side with Pompey, the victorious Caesar spared Cicero's life. After Cicero retired from public life, Caesar attached his prestigious name to several of Caesar's own decrees, prompting Cicero to write, "I have had letters delivered to me from monarchs at the other end of the earth thanking me for my motion to give them the royal title, when I for my part was unaware of their existence, let alone of their elevation to royalty."

Cicero was an eyewitness to Caesar's assassination at Pompey's Theater. In fact, immediately after the assassination, Brutus shouted congratulations to Cicero "on the recovery of freedom," a premature declaration to which Cicero responded, like all of the others present, with flight.

Cicero's Death

Cicero was among the most prominent victims of the Second Triumvirate. The triumvirs ordered his execution in 43 B.C. He tried to escape by sea but bad weather and sea sickness forced him back to land near his villa at Formiaea. There he was slain, after commanding his slaves to leave him and save themselves. On hearing the news, Brutus killed Antony's brother Gaius in retribution.

Antony ordered Cicero's head and hands nailed above the rostrum in the Forum, where Cicero had spoken out against him in fourteen speeches, popularly called the *Philippics* after Demosthenes' famous speeches. According to Plutarch, horrified Romans saw in the putrefying remains "not so much the face of Cicero as the soul of Antony." Octavian acquiesced in the murder but later, as the emperor Augustus, called Cicero "an eloquent and learned man and a true lover of his country." Augustus secured a provincial governorship and consulship for Cicero's son Marcus, despite his service in the republican army at Philippi. While consul in 30 B.C., Marcus had the satisfaction of posting the announcement of Antony's death on the same platform where Antony had displayed his father's head and hands. Livy wrote regarding Cicero, "If one weighs his faults against his merits, he was a great man, of high spirit, worthy of remembrance; to sound his praises would require a Cicero for his eulogist."

Cicero's Achievements

Cicero contributed more than any other Roman to making the Latin language a supple and sophisticated tool of expression. For nearly two millennia every educated European and American read Cicero. Cicero astounded both ancients and moderns with the eloquence of his 106 orations (fifty-eight of which survive), his more than 900 letters, and his numerous political and philosophical essays. His majestic style, balanced clauses, and rhythmic cadences so dominated Latin prose that the rhetorician Quintilian said Cicero was "the name, not of a man, but of eloquence itself."

Cicero was the acknowledged master of each of the three types of rhetoric: deliberative, epideictic, and forensic—speeches for the senate building, for the funeral hall, and for the courtroom. In Cicero's rhetorical treatise *The Orator* (55 B.C.) he advocated careful attention to every aspect of public speaking—care of the throat, breath control, tone variation, rhythm, vigor, carriage, expression, eyebrow movement, gestures, toga arrangement, stride, and the production of tears. He advised speakers to modulate their voices, to stand erect, and to avoid exaggerated gestures, pacing about, darting forward, and grimacing. He emphasized the clarity and proper arrangement of words, the use of metaphor and appropriate humor, and the importance of a good memory. The best means of acquiring these skills was by frequent reading of poetry and history and by constant writing: "Write as much as possible. The pen is the best and most eminent author and teacher of eloquence."

Cicero stressed that orators must touch the hearts of their audiences. He contended, "Men decide far more problems by hate, or love, or lust, or rage, or sorrow, or joy, or hope, or fear, or illusion, or some other inward emotion, than by reality, or authority, or any legal standard, or judicial precedent, or statute." He cited the example of a virtuous Roman named Rutilius, who refused to allow his lawyers to play on the jury's emotions and so was condemned to death: "A man of such quality has been lost through his case being conducted as if the trial had been taking place in that ideal republic of Plato. None of his counselors groaned or shrieked, none was pained at anything, or made any complaint, or invoked the State, or humbled himself. In a word, not one of them stamped a foot during those proceedings, for fear, no doubt, of being reported to the Stoics." Attorneys must use emotion to counter the letter of the law when arguing for its spirit, just as politicians must use emotion to arouse a listless nation in some cases and to curb its impetuosity in others. The orator must comprehend the audience's biases in order to lead them where they were already willing to be led and must model the very emotion he wished to evoke. This emotion must be real, not false: "Lest it should seem a mighty miracle for a man so often to be roused to wrath, indignation, and every inward emotion—and that too about other people's business . . . the very quality of the diction employed to stir the feelings of others must stir the speaker himself even more deeply than any of his hearers." After all, even actors who played the same role daily felt genuine emotion. The orator must begin calmly and rationally, yet build emotion through rich, diversified language and an animated delivery as he proceeded. Touches of humor, if not excessive in number and if not involving ridicule of the wretched, obscenity, buffoonery, or "mere mimicking," could win an audience's goodwill, secure its attention, and make the arguments of one's opponent seem absurd.

But Cicero also emphasized the hollowness of eloquence devoid of knowledge and reason. He wrote, "It is from knowledge that oratory must derive its beauty and fullness, and unless there is such knowledge, well-grasped and comprehended by the speaker, there must be something empty and almost childish in the utterance." While the ideal orator's knowledge must include an understanding of human nature and motivation, he must also know law, political and military science, and a host of other subjects. Cicero wrote: "Great indeed are the burden and the task that he undertakes, who puts himself forward, when all are silent, as the one man to be heard concerning the weightiest matters, before a vast assembly of his fellows. For there is hardly a soul present but will turn a keener and more penetrating eye upon defects in the speaker than upon his good points. . . . In an orator we must demand the subtlety of the logician, the thoughts of the philosopher, a diction almost poetic, a lawyer's memory, a tragedian's voice, and the bearing almost of the consummate actor." It was communication that separated humans from animals: "The one point in which we have our very greatest advantage over the brute creation is that we hold converse with one another, and can reproduce our thought in word." It was eloquence that had first formed community, and then civilization. Cicero believed that oratorical skill must be placed at the service of virtue: "By one and the same power of eloquence the deceitful among mankind are brought to destruction and the righteous to deliverance. Who more passionately than the orator can encourage to virtuous conduct, or more zealously than he reclaim from vicious courses? . . . Whose comforting words can soothe grief more tenderly?"

Adopting a middle position between the terse Attic style and the verbose Asianic style, Cicero drafted speeches that were copious without being redundant. Cicero opposed excessive concision in an orator because he believed it hindered the crucial ability to evoke emotion: "Thus, concise or quiet speakers may inform an arbitrator, but cannot excite him, on which excitement everything depends." While varying his vocabulary, he avoided meaningless synonyms, selecting each word for its peculiar force. The rhythm of his sentences was natural, not the artificial product of superfluous words or of unconventional word order. The Roman literary critic Longinus later wrote, "Cicero, like a spreading conflagration, ranges and rolls over the whole field; the fire which burns within him, plentiful and constant, is distributed at his will, now in one part, now in another, and fed with fuel in relays." His speeches were so persuasive that, as consul, he convinced the masses to oppose debt relief and land redistribution.

Like Mark Twain or Winston Churchill in later times, Cicero became so famous for his wit that the witticisms of others were often attributed to him. (Yet, according to Cicero himself, Caesar was shrewd enough, when one of his staff members was collecting Cicero's clever sayings, to distinguish Cicero's witticisms from those falsely accounted to him.) Though Cicero's humor was essential in court, often distracting jurors from the legal weaknesses of a case, his biting wit earned him many enemies. When a snobbish aristocrat sneered, "Who is your father?" Cicero replied, "I can scarcely ask you the same question since your mother has made it rather difficult to answer." When Crassus said that no member of his family had ever lived past sixty, then reversed himself, asking, "What could I have been thinking when I said that?" Cicero replied that he must have been trying to elicit applause. When a young man accused of having given his father a poisoned cake said angrily that he would give Cicero "a piece of his mind," Cicero replied, "I would prefer it to a piece of your cake." When Cicero made an enigmatic remark and Hortensius replied, "I am afraid I am no good at solving riddles," Cicero, remembering that Verres had given Hortensius an ivory sphinx in return for his legal services, retorted, "Oh really, in spite of having a sphinx at home?" When the demagogue Clodius was acquitted of adultery by a jury he had bribed, he told Cicero, who was the prosecutor, that the jury had not believed his evidence. Cicero replied: "You will find that twenty-five of them trusted in my word since they voted against you, and that the other thirty did not trust yours, since they did not vote for your acquittal until they had actually gotten your money in their hands." While tribune, Clodius later had Cicero banished for having executed Catiline's coconspirators without due process of law and had his villas destroyed.

Cicero was also a master of insinuation and invective, two staples of Roman rhetoric. Typical was Cicero's insinuating remark that he would pass over his opponent's robbery of his neighbors and beating of his mother without comment. Concerning Cicero's penchant for invective, it was not without cause that an eighteenth-century American admirer of his claimed that many of his speeches, if delivered in the admirer's own era, would have resulted in a duel.

Cicero's speeches, epistles, and essays, many of which were gathered for posthumous publication by his faithful secretary, freedman, and friend Marcus Tullius Tiro, have shed more light on the stresses and strains of the late Roman republic than any other historical source. They reveal the strengths and weaknesses of the Roman aristocracy, a group who were cultured, proud, patriotic, intensely political, vain, and self-interested. The eloquence displayed in the letters is particularly remarkable considering the fact that Cicero does not appear to have intended them for publication. (Their candor does not always reflect well on the Roman.) Perhaps the greatest compliment Cicero ever received came from his nemesis, Julius Caesar, who declared that

Cicero's achievement was greater than his own: "It is better to have extended the boundaries of the Roman spirit than of the Roman Empire."

Cicero's *On Duties*, written in 44 B.C., after the fall of the republic had driven him from politics, were his last musings on life, proper behavior, and the duties of public office. Cicero wrote: "As a safe voyage is the aim of the pilot, as health is the aim of the physician, as victory is the aim of the general, so the ideal statesman will aim at happiness for the citizens of the state, to give them material security, abundant wealth, ample glory, and untarnished honor. This is the finest of human achievements." But the times were not propitious for such statesmanship, and Cicero's ominous warning foreshadowed the downfall of many future republics: "The armed forces stationed to attack the state are more in number than those which defend it; for it takes only a nod of the head to set in motion the reckless and the desperate—indeed of their own initiative they incite themselves against the state. The sound elements [of society] rouse themselves more slowly. . . . At the last moment [they] are stirred into belated action by the sheer urgencies of the situation." To Cicero, those who attacked the state for selfish ends were fools: "No course which is harmful to the state can possibly benefit any of its individual citizens." Even if one should become a dictator by such means, the end result would be guilt, infamy, "agonies of anxiety, terrors day and night." Cicero saw the horror of tyranny not merely in its destruction of liberty but in its corruption of morals as well. He considered *On Duties* his manifesto and his masterpiece. Voltaire later wrote of the work, "No one will ever write anything more wise, more true, or more useful."

Cicero's only literary failures were his poems, which were so bad they have given joy to countless generations of critics. Tacitus claimed that the verses written by Caesar and Brutus, though no better than Cicero's, were more fortunate since fewer people knew of their existence. The satirist Juvenal wrote that if Cicero's prose had been of the same quality as his poetry, he would never have had to fear the vengeance of Antony.

Cicero's Legacy

So influential was Cicero that the late republican period of Roman history is sometimes referred to as "the Ciceronian age." His writings influenced the early Church Fathers of Christianity. Ambrose used Cicero's *On Duties* as the model for his own influential treatise, *On the Duties of Ecclesiastics.* Jerome read Cicero so much that he thought he heard God ask him once, "What art thou?" When Jerome replied, "A Christian," God answered, "No, thou art not a Christian, but a Ciceronian." In remorse Jerome swore never to read worldly books again. But Jerome's writings continued to show the imprint of Cicero in both style and substance. When taunted with this, Jerome replied that his promise had been for the future; it was impossible for him to forget what he had already learned. In the *Confessions* Augustine claimed that it was Cicero's *Hortensius* that had led him to love virtue.

Early medieval Christians loved Cicero so much that Pope Gregory the Great threatened to burn his writings because their charm diverted young men from the Scriptures. Boethius wrote a commentary on Cicero. Venerable Bede compiled collections of Cicero's famous statements. Alcuin, the leading figure of the Carolingian Renaissance, found time to read from the Roman's works, and Einhard, the famous biographer of Charlemagne, quoted from Cicero's *Tusculan Disputations*. Dante used *On Duties* 1.13 as the basis for his classification of sins in the *Inferno*.

Petrarch, the "Father of the Renaissance," loved the musical quality of Cicero's writings. He began reading Cicero as a small child. His devotion to the Roman so hindered his legal studies that his father burned all of his volumes of Cicero. But, on seeing his son's tears, Petrarch's father rescued one of Cicero's rhetorical works from the flames. As soon as Petrarch was of legal age, he abandoned his legal studies and began collecting and reading Cicero's works again. Indeed, Petrarch's dogged pursuit of all the Ciceronian manuscripts he could find probably saved some of the more obscure works from oblivion. Petrarch was instrumental in the final victory of classical Latin, as exemplified by Cicero, over the less elegant, scholastic Latin that had developed during the Middle Ages.

Indeed, some of the lesser figures of the Italian Renaissance became so zealous on behalf of Ciceronian Latin that they refused to use any word Cicero himself had not employed. Naturally, this absurd prohibition created confusion as new manuscripts were discovered. These zealots evidently forgot Cicero's statement in *On the Nature of the Gods*: "In discussions it is not so much the authorities that are to be sought as the course of reason. In fact, the authority of those who profess to instruct is often a hindrance to their pupils; for they cease to use their own judgment, but accept what they know to be approved by one whom they respect."

Although Desiderius Erasmus, the great Catholic reformer, despised the slavish worship of Cicero, he too admired the Roman. In fact, Erasmus issued his own edition of the *Tusculan Disputations*, writing in the introduction, "Certainly I have never loved Cicero more than I do now."

Erasmus' Protestant counterpart, Martin Luther, agreed, calling Cicero "a wise and industrious man, [who] suffered much and accomplished much." Luther added, "I hope our Lord God will be merciful to him and to those like him."

John Locke recommended the study of Cicero for eloquence, epistolary style, and morals. Frederick the Great, who carried Cicero's works with him on his military campaigns, ordered their translation into German. Cicero's writing style influenced Montesquieu, Samuel Johnson, and Edward Gibbon.

Eighteenth- and nineteenth-century orators ranging in ideology from Edmund Burke to Robespierre studied and admired Cicero's speeches. The "Great Triumvirate" of American antebellum orators, Daniel Webster, Henry Clay, and John C. Calhoun, were all admirers of Cicero.

Cicero's very character or, rather, an idealized version of it, became the model for future Western statesmen. Along with Demosthenes, Cicero became the symbol of the statesman who sacrifices short-term popularity, which can only be purchased by vice, for long-term fame, which can only be secured by virtue.

For instance, John Adams idolized Cicero throughout his whole life. In the autumn of 1758 Adams gloried in the fact that law, his chosen profession, was "A Field in which Demosthenes, Cicero, and others of immortal Fame have exulted before me!" That winter he confessed to his diary the pleasure he derived from reading Cicero's orations aloud: "The Sweetness and Grandeur of his sounds, and the Harmony of his Numbers give Pleasure enough to reward the Reading if one understood none of his meaning. Besides, I find it a noble Exercise. It exercises my Lungs, raises my Spirits, opens my Porrs, quickens the Circulation, and so contributes to [my] Health." Indeed, after a family quarrel a few days later, Adams "quitted the Room, and took up Tully to compose myself." In 1774 Adams urged an aspiring politician to adopt Cicero as his model. He wrote regarding Cicero's term as quaestor at Lilybaeum: "He did not receive this office as Persons do now a days, as a Gift, or a Farm, but as a public Trust, and considered it as a Theatre, in which the Eyes of the World were upon him." Adams added that when Rome was short of grain, Cicero managed to feed the city without treating his own province unfairly.

When Adams, one of the greatest orators of his day, rose before the Continental Congress on July 1, 1776, to rebut John Dickinson's contention that American independence would be premature, the New Englander thought of Cicero. He recorded in his diary: "I began by saying that this was the first time of my Life that I had ever wished for the Talents and Eloquence of the ancient Orators of Greece and Rome, for I was very sure that none of them had ever had before him a question of more importance to his Country and to the World."

Adams' admiration for Cicero outlived the American Revolution. Adams spent the summer of 1796, several months before assuming the presidency, rereading the Roman statesman's essays. In 1803 Adams quoted Cicero regarding the true public servant: "Such a man will devote himself entirely to the republic, nor will he covet power or riches. . . . He will adhere closely to justice and equity, that, provided he can preserve these virtues, although he may give offence and create enemies by them, he will set death itself at defiance, rather than abandon his principles." No one followed this ethic better than Adams. In the 1760s he had refused the lucrative and prestigious position of admiralty court judge because he considered the juryless British courts unconstitutional. In 1770 he had sacrificed his popularity to defend the British soldiers accused of murder in the Boston Massacre. As president, in 1799–1800 he had made peace with Napoleonic France, leaving Jefferson the glory of the Louisiana Purchase three years later, at the expense of his own reelection. While no other founder yearned so much for popularity, none so continually sacrificed it to a strict code of ethics. It is not fanciful to suppose that, when making such painful decisions, Adams found consolation in contemplating the Roman statesman's sacrifices and the eternal glory they had earned him.

Adams continued to express admiration for Cicero in the correspondence of his twilight years. In 1805 Adams wrote: "The period in the history of the world the best understood is that of Rome from the time of Marius to the death of Cicero, and this distinction is entirely owing to Cicero's letters and orations. There we see the true character of the times and the passions of all the actors on the stage. Cicero, Cato, and Brutus were the only three in whom I can discern any real patriotism. . . . Cicero had the most capacity and the most constant, as well as the wisest and most persevering attachment to the republic." In 1809 Adams poured out his heart in another letter:

> Panegyrical romances will never be written, nor flattering orations spoken, to transmit me to posterity in brilliant colors. No, nor in true colors. All but the last I loathe. Yet, I will not die wholly unlamented. Cicero was libeled, slandered, insulted by all parties—by Caesar's party, Catiline's crew, Clodius's myrmidions, aye, and by Pompey and the Senate too. He was persecuted and tormented by turns by all parties and all factions, and that for his most virtuous and glorious actions. In his anguish at times and in the consciousness of his own merit and integrity, he was driven to those assertions of his own actions which have been denominated vanity. Instead of reproaching him with vanity, I think them the most infallible demonstration of his innocence and purity. He declares that all honors are indifferent to him because he knows that it is not in the power of his country to reward him in any proportion to his services.
>
> Pushed and injured and provoked as I am, I blush not to imitate the Roman.

Adams was all too successful in his lifelong attempt to emulate Cicero. Adams' integrity, which found its greatest expression in his unwillingness to endorse party favoritism, led to unpopularity in both parties; and his responses to critics were often marked by the same petulance and vanity as the

Roman's. The only difference between Cicero and Adams was that Cicero, uninfluenced by Christian notions of humility, had found nothing shameful in vanity. Indeed, as a man who had ascended from the equestrian order, a "new man" intruding on the traditional prerogatives of the nobility—not unlike Adams, who was of middle-class origin—Cicero may have considered it necessary to remind the Romans of his accomplishments. Perhaps it is for this reason that Cicero boasted only of his service to Rome, never of his unparalleled eloquence, the attribute for which he was universally admired.

Other Founding Fathers also idolized Cicero. James Wilson cited the Roman statesman more often than any other author in his 1790 lectures to law students at the College of Philadelphia (the University of Pennsylvania). Wilson exulted: "The jurisprudence of Rome was adorned and enriched by the exquisite genius of Cicero, which, like the touch of Midas, converts every object to gold." He called Cicero's *On Duties* "a work which does honour to human understanding and the human heart." Similarly, John Marshall, who patterned his portrayal of George Washington, in his famous five-volume biography of the first president, on Cicero, told his grandsons that *On Duties* was "among the most valuable treatises in the Latin language, a salutary discourse on the duties and qualities proper to a republican gentleman." Benjamin Franklin cited Cicero often on the importance of hard work and virtue.

It was not originality of thought that made Cicero the most influential of all the ancients. Rather, it was originality of expression, combined with a martyr's death, that endeared Cicero to statesmen throughout Western history.

PLINY THE YOUNGER (CA. 61–113 A.D.)

A century later Rome produced another aristocrat with a talent for letter writing. An attorney who specialized in inheritance, Pliny the Younger (Gaius Plinius Caecilius Secundus) held a host of high positions in the Roman government, including service as the emperor Trajan's curator in Bithynia.

Pliny the Younger's 247 personal letters and 74 epistles to the emperor, published in 100–109, embodied the best qualities of the age, its humanity and eloquence. Take, for example, this remarkable letter:

> I am very sad as I write to you, for our friend Fundanus' youngest daughter has died. I never saw anything more jolly than this girl, more lovable, or more deserving not only of long life but almost of immortality. She was not yet fourteen years old, and she had all the sense of an old woman, the dignity of a mother, the shy innocence of maidenhood with the sweetness of a young girl. How she used to cling to her father's embrace, and threw

her arms round the necks of his friends in her affectionate and shy way. She loved her nurses, her teachers and tutors, each in return for what they had done for her. Her reading, how eager and intelligent it was, her play how restrained and circumspect! And think of the self-control, the patience, the courage with which she bore her last illness. She did all that her doctors told her to do; she tried to cheer up her sister and father, and by strength of will she kept her weak body going as its strength slipped away. Her will lasted to the very end, unbroken by her illness or by fear of death, which was to give us all the more urgent cause to miss her and mourn her. Her death was indeed a bitter sorrow; its blow was made even worse by the moment of its coming. She was engaged to an excellent young man; her wedding day had been arranged, the invitations had been sent out. And all that joy was turned to grief. I cannot tell you what a stab it gave me to hear Fundanus—grief discovers such distressing things—giving orders that the money that he was going to spend on bridal clothes and pearls and jewelry should be used on incense and unguents and perfumes needed for the funeral. He is a learned and reflective man, the sort of man who has given all his life to serious study and pursuits; now he rejects with loathing all the counsel he has so often heard and given, and, driving out of his mind every other ideal, he is utterly given up to thoughts of family affection. You will understand him, indeed you will admire him, if you reflect on what he has lost. He has lost a daughter who mirrored no less his character than his features and expression; with a remarkable resemblance she bodied forth her father's very self. If you write to him about this very real grief, be sure you don't write him a letter urging him to pull himself together expressed too vigorously. Write him a gentle and affectionate letter. An interval of time will do much to make him more ready to accept your comfort. A wound that is still raw shrinks from the doctor's touch, then it endures it, and then actually wants it. In the same way grief, when fresh, rejects and shuns attempts at consolation. Soon it desires them and finally acquiesces in them if they are gently made.

With overpowering eloquence and insight into human psychology, Pliny implores his friend Aefulanus Marcellinus not to recite for their mutual friend Minicius Fundanus the usual Stoic platitudes about the need to endure misfortune patiently. However truthful these platitudes, they could hardly assuage the grief of one who had just suffered so devastating a loss. Such grief could not be willed or reasoned away, and a loss of such magnitude should not be trivialized. Only after Fundanus had immersed himself in his grief could his friends begin to lead him back to philosophical truth.

This letter gives an added poignancy to another Pliny wrote to his wife Calpurnia while she was convalescing. Pliny declared:

Even if you were strong, your absence would still disquiet me. For when you love people most passionately, it is a strain and a worry not to know anything about them even for a moment. But, as things are, the thought of your absence, together with your ill-health, terrifies me with vague and mixed anxieties. I imagine everything, my imaginings make me afraid of everything; and, as happens when you are afraid, I picture the very things I pray most may not happen. I beg you therefore all the more earnestly to be kind to my fears and to send me a letter, or even two letters, every day. While I am reading it, I shall worry less. When I have finished it, my fears will at once return.

Yet another letter ends with the words, "Write as often as you can, though the delight of getting your letters is a sheer torment."

Like many of his fellow aristocrats, Pliny was haunted by the long and cruel reign of Domitian, who was preparing to bring Pliny to trial when he died (or so Pliny believed). In a letter noting that Corellius Rufus had just committed suicide after a long bout with a painful illness, Pliny recalled that Corellius had told him during Domitian's reign: "Why do you suppose I endure pain like this so long? So that I can outlive that robber if only by a single day." Pliny decried the fact that his generation had been unable to learn senatorial procedures by observation, as had past generations: "We too were spectators in the Senate, but in a Senate which was apprehensive and dumb since it was dangerous to voice a genuine opinion and pitiable to express a forced one. What could be learned at the time, what profit could there be in learning, when the Senate was summoned to idle away its time or to perpetuate some vile crime, and was kept sitting for a joke or its own humiliation; when it could never pass a serious resolution, though often one with tragic consequences? On becoming senators we took part in these evils and continued to witness and endure them for many years, until our spirits were blunted, broken, and destroyed." The passage is similar to one Pliny's friend Tacitus had written in the *Agricola* a few years earlier.

But Pliny was pleased to report that in the age of Trajan, because of "greater freedom of speech," oratory was "now enjoying a revival after almost dying out." Even the formerly despised literary genre of the panegyric for the emperor was now appreciated due to its greater reflection of reality: "This is yet another tribute to our Emperor: a type of speech which used to be hated for its insincerity has become genuine and consequently popular today."

Pliny combined a strict integrity with a generosity of spirit. He wrote, "One of the most important things in life is to practice justice in private as in public life, in small matters as in great, and apply it to one's own affairs no less than to other people's." He claimed that his goal was to be faultless while forgiving others' faults. He advised a governor setting out for Greece: "Do not allow yourself to be hard or domineering, and have no fear that you will be despised for this. No one who bears the insignia of authority is despised unless his own meanness and ignobility show that he must be the first to despise himself. It is a poor thing if authority can only test its powers by insult to others, and if homage is to be won by terror; affection is far more effective than fear in gaining you your ends. Fear disappears at your departure, affection remains." He contributed vast sums of money to his hometown of Comum, both during his lifetime and in his will. He funded the town's library, paid one-third of its teacher's salary (he would have paid the entire amount but feared a lack of parental involvement if parents contributed nothing), and provided money for children in need. He dined with his slaves and freedmen and worried about them when they were ill. He interceded with a friend on behalf of a wayward freedman, writing, "Mercy wins most praise when there was just cause for anger."

But Pliny's sense of obligation to aid those less fortunate did not in any way lessen his devotion to class distinctions. In fact, he wrote, "Strict equality results in something very different from equity so long as men have the same right to judge but not the same ability to judge wisely." Of class distinctions he claimed, "Once these are thrown into confusion and destroyed, nothing is more unequal than the resultant 'equality.'" Even after declaring that Larcius Macedo, who had just been murdered by his slaves, had been "a cruel and overbearing master," Pliny was so overcome by fear that he could not help but add the illogical postscript, "There you see the dangers, outrages, and insults to which we are exposed. No master can feel safe because he is kind and considerate; for it is their brutality, not their reasoning capacity, that leads slaves to murder masters."

Although Pliny might condescend to dine with his own freedmen, he felt nothing but contempt for those who had erected a monument to Pallas, the emperor Claudius' freedman, who had served as the treasurer of Rome. Pliny was beside himself with indignation at the monument's inscription, a decree by the Senate that honored the freedman. What infuriated Pliny was not so much the Senate's obsequiousness (after all, Pliny himself was extremely obsequious to Trajan, even calling him "that divine hero") as the object of it. Nor was it Pallas' alleged fiscal corruption that so infuriated Pliny, who made no mention of the allegation. What was unforgivable and almost unbearable to Pliny was that the Senate had profoundly degraded the honors and fame that belonged exclusively to the aristocratic class, the honors and fame that were the goal of Pliny's entire existence, by bestowing them on a freedman. Pliny even had the audacity to characterize Pallas' refusal of a vast sum offered him by the Senate, a refusal Pliny would certainly have praised had Pallas been an aristocrat, as a show of contempt. Pliny called the monument "a record in the sight of all, Pallas of his insolence, the Emperor of his complaisance, the Senate of its degradation!"

After recounting the Senate's declaration that it issued the decree "so that by the reward given to Pallas others might be inspired to rival him," Pliny sneered at the very idea that "people of good family could be found who were fired by ambition for distinctions which they saw granted to freedmen and promised to slaves." He added, "How glad I am that my lot did not fall in those days—for which I blush as if I had lived in them." After these uncharacteristic outbursts of anger, Pliny's conclusion is surprising: "Though in some passages I may have let my indignation carry me beyond the bounds of a letter, you will readily believe that I have suppressed my feelings rather than exaggerated them." Unlike Cicero, Pliny published his own letters, or rather, a selection of them.

AGRICULTURAL MANUALS

Cato the Elder (234–146 B.C.)

The Romans also composed manuals of advice for farmers. The most famous of these manuals was Cato the Elder's *On Agriculture* (ca. 160 B.C.), the first work of Latin prose that survives. "Cato," which means "wise" or "shrewd," was an epithet given him by admirers; his actual surname was Priscus.

The estate featured in Cato's text consisted of around one hundred acres (a large estate for that time) and was manned by a few dozen slaves. Especially concerned with the production of olives and viticulture, Cato advised readers, when buying an estate, to count the number of its oil presses and wine vats in order to ascertain its fertility. Cato suggested that rainy days, rather than being spent in idleness, should be devoted to indoor work, such as cleaning wine vats and making and mending harnesses and slaves' clothing. In addition to hard work, Cato advocated frugality, writing, "The master should have the selling habit, not the buying habit." Cato declared that an overseer "must see that the servants are well provided for and that they do not suffer from cold or hunger" and "must express his appreciation for good work, so that others may take pleasure in well-doing." Overseers should receive smaller food rations than field hands since they worked less. But Cato also recommended selling off old or sickly slaves, which he listed with worn-out cattle, blemished sheep, old wagons, "and whatever else is superfluous," when they outlived their usefulness. A quintessential Roman, Cato also included detailed instructions concerning the proper rituals and prayers necessary to appease various gods at various times of the year in order to ensure success.

Varro (116–27 B.C.)

Over a century later Marcus Terentius Varro, the leading scholar of his day, wrote seventy-five works concerning the Latin language and literature, medicine, architecture, history, law, philosophy, music, geography, education, and numerous other subjects. But *On Rustic Things* (37 B.C.), a manual to guide his wife Fundania in the management of a farm she had just purchased, was his only major work that survived.

Remarkably well informed regarding geography and history, Varro knew that "the sun is not visible for six months at a time" in the Arctic Circle, that "navigation in the ocean is not possible in that region because of the frozen sea," and that humans had passed from hunting and gathering into animal husbandry before developing agriculture. He also knew that the illnesses that plagued swamp dwellers were the result of "certain minute creatures which cannot be seen by the eyes . . . [that] enter the body through the mouth and nose," but, like others before and after him, he believed that these microbes were carried exclusively in the air, unaware of the transmission of many by mosquitoes. Varro recommended that villas be placed on an elevation, to avoid flooding and robbers, a recommendation that influenced Thomas Jefferson's placement of Monticello (Italian for "little hill").

Unlike Virgil, who geared his advice to small farmers and hardly mentioned slavery in the *Georgics*, both Cato's and Varro's intended audience were the owners of large estates. (Yet Virgil clearly borrowed some of his information from Varro.) Thus, Varro provided some advice, based on the high monetary value of slaves, that antebellum American slaveholders would often follow: "It is more profitable to work unwholesome lands with hired hands than with slaves; and even in wholesome places it is more profitable thus to carry out the heavier farm operations, such as storing the products of the vintage or harvest." Deceased wage earners were cheaper to replace than dead slaves. Varro instructed concerning overseers, "They are not to be allowed to control their men with whips rather than with words, if only you can achieve the same result." He advised against having "too many slaves of the same nation," not because they would conspire but because they would quarrel. He added: "The hands who excel the others should also be consulted as to the work to be done. When this is done they are less inclined to think that they are looked down upon, and rather think that they are held in some esteem by the master. They are made to take more interest in their work by being treated more liberally in respect either of food, or of more clothing, or of exemption from work, or of permission to graze some cattle of their own on the farm, or other things of this kind; so that, if some unusually heavy task is imposed, or punishment inflicted on them in some way, their loyalty and kindly feeling to the master may be restored by the consolation derived from such measures."

Like Cato, Varro saw animal husbandry as a necessary subfield of agriculture. He recommended one shepherd for every hundred sheep, a common equation that remained popular in Jesus' day more than half a century later (Luke 15:4). He declared that the head herdsman, like the overseer, must be literate and, therefore, able to comprehend written instructions and keep records. Moving beyond the usual passages on sheep and cattle, Varro even presented detailed instructions for the construction and maintenance of aviaries, apiaries, hare warrens, and fish ponds. Thomas Jefferson reproduced one of Varro's fish ponds on his estate.

Columella (First Century A.D.)

Two generations later, building on the works of Xenophon, Virgil, Cato, and Varro, all of whom he cited, Columella (Lucius Junius Moderatus Columella), a Roman citizen from Baetica in Spain, published his own manuscript entitled *On Rustic Things*. The most comprehensive and systematic of all the agricultural manuals, it discussed the cultivation of an enormous variety of crops, vines, and trees and the care of all sorts of animals, including ducks, geese, and peacocks. Disputing Xenophon's contention that farming was easy, Columella insisted that it required "mental keenness." He applauded the global warming he detected in his own time: "The earlier coldness has abated and the weather is becoming more clement," a development he credited with increasing the yield of both olives and grapes. His reference to the Greek saying about the impossibility of making "a rope out of sand" was undoubtedly the source for the classically educated Daniel Webster's famous observation that if the American states were allowed to nullify federal laws, the Union would become a mere rope of sand. Often citing Virgil's *Georgics*, a poem he clearly loved, Columella even wrote the section on gardening in verse, though the results were less than Virgilian ("Let prickly artichokes / Be planted . . .").

After surveying countless pages of sound advice, the reader of Columella's tome is occasionally startled by bizarre superstitions. When referring to the illnesses of oxen, he wrote: "Pain in the belly and intestines is assuaged by the sight of swimming birds, especially a duck. If an ox which has a pain in its intestines sees a duck, it is quickly delivered from its torment. The sight of a duck is even more successful in curing mules and horses."

Columella complained that the Roman aristocrats of his day neglected their farms, handing their management over "to the worst of our slaves." He explained that these aristocrats "think it beneath us to till our lands with our own hands and . . . consider it of no importance to appoint as an overseer a man of very great experience." Warming to his theme, he continued:

Yesterday's morals and strenuous manner of living are out of tune with our present extravagance and devotion to pleasure. . . . All of us who are heads of families have quit the sickle and the plow and have crept within the city-walls, and we ply our hands in the circuses and theaters rather than in the grain fields and vineyards; and we gaze in astonished admiration at the posturings of effeminate males, because they counterfeit by their womanish motions a sex which nature has denied to men, and deceive the eyes of the spectators. . . . We spend our nights in licentiousness and drunkenness, our days in gaming or in sleeping, and account ourselves blessed by fortune that we behold neither the rising of the sun nor its setting. . . . But, by heaven, that true stock of Romulus, practiced in constant hunting and no less in toiling in the fields, was distinguished by the greatest physical strength, and, hardened by the labors of peace, easily endured the hardships of war when occasion demanded, and always esteemed the common people of the country more highly than those of the city.

The aristocratic flight from the countryside was pure folly, because the greatest factor in the success of a farm was close supervision by its owner: "Men who purchase lands at a distance, not to mention across the seas, are making over their inheritances to their slaves, as to their heirs and, worse yet, while they themselves are still alive; for it is certain that slaves are corrupted by reason of the great remoteness of their masters and . . . are more intent on pillage than on farming." By contrast, "land should be purchased nearby, so that the owner may visit it often and announce that his visits will be more frequent than he really intends them to be." Though generally averse to luxury, Columella recommended making the country manor as comfortable as possible in order to induce the owner to visit it as often as possible, especially if his "dainty wife" accompanied him. After all, women had become even more corrupt than men: "Nowadays, when most women so abandon themselves to luxury and idleness that they do not deign to undertake even the superintendence of wool-making, and there is a distaste for home-made garments and their perverse desire can only be satisfied by clothing purchased for large sums and almost the whole of their husband's income, one cannot be surprised that these same ladies are bored by a country estate and the implements of husbandry, and regard a few days' stay at a country house as a most sordid business."

Columella argued that a small estate that was properly tended was much more profitable than a vast estate that was neglected. He criticized "men of enormous wealth who, possessing entire countries of which they cannot even make the rounds," left them barren. He asserted, "No field is tilled without profit if the owner, through much experimentation, causes it to be fitted for the use which it can best serve. . . . Accordingly, there should be no neglect anywhere of experimentation in many forms."

Like Varro, Columella depicted the ethical treatment of slaves as consistent with the interests of the master. He noted that slaves were "more willing to set about a piece of work on which they think that their opinions have been asked and their advice followed." Indeed, labor should be specialized so that slaves would take pride in their work. An overseer "should always cherish the good and diligent and spare those who are not as good as they ought to be, and use such moderation that they may rather respect his strictness than hate his cruelty." He recommended that masters question slaves directly to make certain that they were not being mistreated by overseers and that masters taste the slaves' food and drink to ensure its quality. He advised that the slave mothers of three children be rewarded with exemption from work, those with four or more with manumission, to encourage the reproduction of the slave population.

The Enduring Popularity of the Manuals

Roman agricultural manuals remained popular throughout most of Western history. In the seventeenth century John Milton (*On Education*) proposed that the students of his ideal school spend their evenings reading the manuals of Cato, Varro, and Columella, so that they might learn both farming and Latin. In the following century the Roman agriculturalists inspired the resurrection of the genre of the agricultural manual. Thomas Jefferson and Henry David Thoreau were only two of the many Americans who read the ancient manuals avidly and compared them with their modern successors. Thoreau expressed surprise at how little advice on farming had changed in nearly two millennia.

Classical Pastoralism and Its Influence

Like the pastoral poets, the manual writers encouraged the veneration of the rural, agricultural lifestyle. All of the agricultural manuals reflected classical morality, extolling certain values as both the requisites for, and the products of, farming. Cato wrote of early Romans, "And when they would praise a worthy man their praise took this form: 'good husbandman,' 'good farmer'; one so praised was thought to have received the greatest commendation." Cato added, "It is from the farming class that the bravest men and the sturdiest soldiers come, their calling is most highly respected, their livelihood is most assured and is looked on with the least hostility, and those who are engaged in that pursuit are least inclined to be disaffected." Varro wrote, "It is not without reason that those great men, our ancestors, put the Romans who lived in the country ahead of those who lived in the city. . . . They thought that those who settled in town were more indolent than those who dwelt in the country." For this reason, Varro alleged, early Roman leaders had lived in the country seven days at a time, attending to town affairs only every eighth day. Since their farm work constituted vigorous exercise, they did not need to construct huge, Greek-style gymnasia on their estates to get in shape, Varro added, in a sneering reference to the aristocrats of his own day. Varro concluded: "It was divine nature that gave us the country, and man's skill that built the cities. . . . Not only is the tilling of the fields more ancient—it is more noble." Columella called agriculture one of the few "methods of increasing one's substance that befits a man who is a gentleman and free-born," in contrast to the occupations of merchant, usurer, or attorney, the last of which Columella termed "legal banditry against the innocent and in defense of the guilty."

While the pastoralism of Roman poets and manual writers influenced Thoreau and other Romantics in their idealization of nature, it also contributed to the effort by Jefferson and the Democratic-Republican Party to advance representative democracy in America. In a famous passage in *Notes on the State of Virginia* Jefferson glorified agriculture in a manner strikingly reminiscent of the Roman agriculturalists:

> Those who labor in the earth are the chosen people of God, if ever he had a chosen people, whose breasts He has made His peculiar deposit for genuine and substantial virtue. He keeps alive that sacred fire, which otherwise might escape from the face of the earth. Corruption of morals in the mass of cultivators is a phenomenon of which no age nor nation has furnished an example. It is the mark set on those, who, not looking up to heaven and to their own soil and industry as does the husbandman, for their subsistence, depend for it on casualties and caprices of customers. Dependence begets subservience and venality suffocates the germ of virtue and prepares fit tools for the designs of ambition.

Jefferson believed that the secret of the ancient republics' success was their pastoral virtues. He later wrote: "Cultivators of the earth are the most valuable citizens. They are the most vigorous, the most independent, the most virtuous, and they are tied to their country, and wedded to its liberty by the most lasting bonds. . . . I consider the class of artificers as the panders of vice, and the instruments by which the liberties of a country are overturned." Hence Jefferson predicted: "I think our governments will remain virtuous for many centuries; as long as they are chiefly agricultural; and this will be as long as there shall be vacant lands in any part of America."

Jefferson's passionate embrace of the pastoral tradition colored his perceptions of the world. So determined was he to perpetuate the agricultural character of the United States that he was willing to violate the strict interpretation of the Constitution, one of his core principles, in order to purchase Louisiana. When the absence of a constitutional provision allowing Jefferson to buy foreign territory threatened the future of the republic's agricultural base, and hence its virtue and longevity, Jefferson reluctantly sacrificed constitutional scruples in order to extend the life of the republic. The Virginian frequently compared the British commercialism he detested with that of the Carthaginians, implying an analogy between the United States and the frugal Roman republic.

The ancient and august tradition of classical pastoralism provided the essential service of legitimating the shift from the republican government established by the U.S. Constitution to a more democratic system. The near-unanimous judgment of ancient political theorists and historians against simple majority rule could be overcome only by resorting to an equally revered tradition. Only by arguing that the liberty of the ancient republics had been founded on their agricultural lifestyle, rather than on their balanced governments, could Democratic-Republicans like Jefferson succeed in persuading both themselves and others that a new and unprecedented system of government might be safely adopted. Democratic reforms, such as the linkage of the selection of the Electoral College with the popular vote and the elimination of property qualifications for voting, accomplished by the 1820s, were predicated on this optimism regarding the virtue of the agricultural majority.

CONCLUSION

Throughout most of Western history, the most widely read, admired, and copied of all the ancients was Cicero, who became the image of the ideal statesman. The agricultural manual writers Cato, Varro, and Columella took the bare shell of a genre begun by Xenophon and converted it into an effective means of transmitting a great quantity of sound, useful information on the crucial subject of food production. Along with Virgil and Horace, they also successfully promoted a fervent devotion to the rural, agricultural lifestyle that influenced poets and politicians for many centuries.

· *6* ·

Philosophy

$\mathcal{I}$t was the Romans who preserved and popularized Greek philosophy in the West by presenting it in an aesthetically pleasing yet pragmatic form. Lucretius' elegant poetry immortalized Epicureanism. Cicero's eloquent prose placed the crucial doctrines of popular sovereignty, mixed government, and natural law at the center of Western political theory. Seneca and Marcus Aurelius' direct, colloquial language and emphasis on ethics over metaphysics brought Stoicism down to earth, thereby establishing its profound influence on Western thought.

GREEK PRECURSORS

Plato (ca. 428–347 B.C.)

A champion wrestler, Plato (his real name was Aristocles; "Plato" was a nickname referring to either his "wide" body or "broad" forehead) became a student of Socrates at the age of twenty. In the wake of Socrates' execution Plato left Athens and traveled to southern Italy and Sicily. From the Pythagoreans there, especially Archytas of Tarentum, he learned the importance of mathematics. He then returned to Athens, where he established the Academy in 387 B.C. Located in the groves one mile west of Athens, near the shrine of the local hero Academus, the Academy was a school of higher education that taught philosophy, astronomy, biology, mathematics, and political theory. Above its portal stood the admonition, "Let no one ignorant of geometry enter this building." It operated for nearly a millennium before the Byzantine emperor Justinian closed it in A.D. 524.

Platonism combined the insights of Heraclitus with those of Pythagoras. Plato argued, as had Heraclitus, that the world of the senses was an imperfect world that remained in a constant state of flux. Thus, human knowledge of the material world was limited not only by the imperfection of the senses but also by the fluctuating nature of matter itself. But Plato also believed, as had Pythagoras, in another, perfect world, the "world of the forms," in which ideas like beauty and justice possessed a real and eternal existence. The world of the senses was but a shadow, a pale imitation of the real world, the world of the forms. All human ideas, whether of material objects or of concepts, were intuitive representations of immaterial forms existing on another plane. These forms were derived from the Good, as was the World Soul that continually acted on matter in an effort to replicate the forms within the world of the senses. But matter, by its inherently disorderly nature, passively resisted the order that the World Soul sought to impose on it, so that the material world that resulted, while the best of all possible material worlds, did not conform perfectly to the world of the forms. The human soul, eternal like the Good, the World Soul, the forms, and matter, was a dismembered portion of the World Soul that temporarily occupied a body composed of matter.

Drawing on the Pythagoreans, Plato argued for the existence of natural law, a universal code of ethics divine in origin that remained the same at all times and in all societies and that could be discerned by human intuition. He claimed that there were "unwritten laws" that had been formulated by the gods and that were "uniformly observed in every country." The duty to revere the gods and one's parents were two such laws. He argued that humans were innately good. The understanding of good and evil was imbedded in human nature and accessible through intuition, rather than through reason (logic) acting on sensory experience. The body was actually an "obstacle" to knowledge. He wrote: "And the best sort of thinking occurs when the soul is not disturbed by any of these things—not by hearing, or sight, or pain, or pleasure—when she leaves the body and is alone and, doing her best to avoid any form of contact with it, reaches out to grasp what is truly real." Like the Pythagoreans also, but far less dogmatically, Plato intimated the possibility of reincarnation for some souls. While philosophers enjoyed a blessed state of complete wisdom as companions of the gods in the afterlife, souls virtuous by "habit and custom without philosophy" entered into new human bodies, and impure souls entered into animal bodies or became shadowy apparitions wandering the earth.

Plato's theory of ethics proved as influential as his metaphysics. He identified the four cardinal virtues as prudence, temperance, justice, and courage, a list that would be repeated not only by Platonists but by other philosophical schools for centuries thereafter.

Disillusioned with the democratic government of Athens even before it had executed his mentor, Plato wrote *The Republic* in 374 B.C. In this dialogue Plato presented his ideal polis, a city ruled by an aristocracy of thoroughly educated "guardians" led by a "philosopher-king." Since these wise guardians would be able to distinguish the true good (truth, justice, and virtue, which were accessible only through philosophical understanding) from the false good (wealth, power, and prestige), they would consider their governing function an obligation rather than a source of loot. Plato wrote, "The city where those who are to rule are least anxious to be rulers is of necessity the best managed." The guardians would govern in the best interests of the people, who would be divided into warriors and workers. (Plato believed that war was a fact of human life, writing: "Only the dead have seen the end of war." Indeed, if later writers can be believed, Plato himself had fought valiantly in the Athenian army.) The three groups in Plato's republic corresponded to the three parts of the soul (mind), in descending order of goodness and importance: wisdom, love of honor, and love of pleasure. Plato's Spartan-style system made the citizen a specialist, contrary to the traditional Greek emphasis on versatility.

The guardians would control all aspects of life, including marriage. To prevent selfishness among the guardians, all of their property would be held in common, and their children would be taken from them at birth and raised communally by all of the adults, so that none would even know which child was his own. Once women were past the childbearing age they could have sex with whomever they wished. All illegitimate children, and those "born defective," would be killed at birth. The guardians would make a careful determination of each individual's proper place in society. Those able to grasp the nature of the forms and to apply them to practical situations—that is, the virtuous and the wise—would be placed on the guardian track. They would be taught mathematics and logic, which employed "pure reason" to comprehend the changeless Idea of the Good, and would undergo physical training, to prevent softness. They would be prohibited from studying "anything that is not perfect"—meaning anything associated with the flawed, ever-changing material world. They would be prohibited from drunkenness or idleness. Those who failed the numerous intellectual and physical tests administered to them throughout their lifetimes would be demoted as unfit to share in the rule. Those who passed these tests would participate in the government of the city after age thirty-five. They would be allowed to retire from day-to-day administration at age fifty. The strong and courageous would be placed on the warrior track. Warriors would have no private property and would eat in common mess halls, like the Spartans. They would not be permitted to enslave other Greeks or to burn their property while at war. The rest of the people would be trained in various trades, according to their differing aptitudes.

All citizens, including females, would begin on the same plane and would be educated to the limit of their ability. Plato argued that men and women "differ only in one thing, that the male begets and the female bears the child." He added, "No practice or calling in the life of the city belongs to woman as woman, or man as man, but the various aptitudes are dispersed among both sexes alike." Indeed, Plato himself had admitted a few women of exceptional ability into his Academy.

The guardians would control all artistic expression, since art appealed to the irrational element in the soul, so as to prevent the spread of immorality. While emotion was not in itself bad, it must be shaped and utilized to promote virtue and not vice. To that end, the gods must be portrayed as honest, peace loving, virtuous, and changeless. Children must always be taught that virtue led to happiness, vice to unhappiness. To make guardians and warriors brave, they must be taught that the afterlife was good. Among musical instruments only the simple lyre and harp would be allowed, among songs and poems only hymns to the gods and praise of the good. Painters, architects, and even furniture makers must be monitored so that their works projected a spirit of beauty and harmony. Plato declared, "To hate what one ought to hate and to love what one ought to love: this is true education."

Plato intended his republic to represent the form of "polis." By their very nature, forms could only be approximated in the imperfect world of the senses. Nevertheless, they were essential as models. The role of the statesman, then, was to use the form or ideal of the polis as a painter used his object, as a goal of emulation, though it could never be reproduced completely in the material world. To even approximate his ideal, the statesman, like the painter, must be acutely aware of his materials, including their limitations, and how to use them. Thus, while Plato understood that his ideal republic could not be fully replicated in the world of the senses, he was confident that a wise statesman blessed with auspicious circumstances could at least approximate it. Indeed, Plato ended the *Republic* with this significant conclusion concerning the prospects of creating a republic similar to that which he had just described, "Difficult it is indeed, but possible somehow." Plato explained that a polis similar to his republic could be inaugurated by removing children from their parents at an early age, taking them out to the countryside, and training them in the proper way.

At the urging of friends, Plato accepted the invitation of Dionysius I, dictator of Syracuse, to serve as a tutor to his son, Dionysius II, in 367 B.C. Either because he grew weary of Plato's rebukes concerning the gluttony and sexual promiscuity of the Syracusan court or for political reasons, the dictator sold Plato into slavery. A friend bought the philosopher's freedom, and he returned home.

Plato then composed a series of practical treatises on politics, in the process introducing the influential theory of mixed government. In the *Laws*, a work in which Plato suggested a legal code for a small city to be established in Crete, he stated that there were three simple forms of government: monarchy (rule by the one), aristocracy (rule by the few), and democracy (rule by the many). But each of these forms degenerated over time. Monarchy deteriorated into tyranny, aristocracy into oligarchy, and democracy into ochlocracy ("mob rule"). Plato then suggested that perhaps the best government would be a mixed government, one that balanced the power of the one, the few, and the many. Plato's mixed government theory became one of the most significant theories in Western history.

Nevertheless, though the *Laws* departed from the *Republic* in advocating a mixed government rather than an oligarchy of guardians, it retained much of the rigidity of the *Republic*. Citizens under forty would be prohibited from traveling for fear they would be corrupted by foreign luxury. The sole exception would be Olympic athletes, since their exertions would bring glory to their city. No atheism or ritualistic religion would be permitted; religion would be based solely on belief in the gods and in virtue. While those dissidents amenable to learning would be reformed, the adamant would be imprisoned or killed.

Plato's eloquence was so astonishing that his prose was often compared to Homer's poetry, which was, indeed, his object of emulation. His graceful and versatile style ranged from lighthearted to solemn, often utilizing poetic allegories to convey otherwise inexpressible profundities. His praise for the moral life ("If it should be necessary for me to either do wrong or be wronged, I would choose for myself to be wronged") earned him a central place in Western philosophy. Plato's pupil Aristotle wrote of him: "He was the only man, or at least the first, who showed, through his words and through his life, how a man can become both good and happy at the same time." Cicero later added that if God ever chose to speak in human words, He would write like Plato. Though Plato himself was not an original mathematician, he more than anyone else was responsible for the high favor that the study of mathematics achieved in Western education throughout the ages, a vital factor in the development of modern science. Plato was buried in a garden at his beloved Academy.

Aristotle (384–322 B.C.)

Aristotle, Plato's most brilliant student, moved to Athens from Stagira (in Chalcidice) at the age of seventeen. Aristotle's father had served as physician to the father of Philip II, the future king of Macedon. Aristotle taught at the Academy until Plato died and the Academy passed to Plato's nephew Speusippus. (Some historians believe Aristotle left Athens even before Plato's death due to anti-Macedonian sentiment there.) In 335 B.C. Aristotle returned to Athens and opened the Lyceum, a rival school located in the sacred grove of Apollo Lyceius.

Aristotle presented his philosophy in two great works, the *Metaphysics* and the *Nichomachean Ethics*. Edited by his son Nichomachus, the latter work was the first treatise on ethics ever written. Aristotle envisioned the Prime Mover, or first cause, as a perfect, immortal, immutable unity but not one who intervened in natural processes. In contrast to Plato, he argued that all knowledge was learned: "There is nothing in the intellect that was not first in the senses." He denied the existence of intuition and innate goodness, suggesting that virtue was a product of rational training and habit. Aristotle claimed, "We are not made good or bad by nature."

Aristotle generally defined virtue as the "Golden Mean," the most rational point between behavioral extremes (e.g., the mean between cowardice and rashness, abstinence and indulgence, self-deprecation and vanity), though he noted that some emotions (such as envy) and some actions (such as adultery) were always wrong. Sometimes the "mean" was actually closer to one extreme; for instance, the virtue of courage was closer to rashness than to cowardice. Aristotle conceded: "It is no easy task to find the middle. . . . Wherefore, goodness is rare and laudable and noble."

According to Aristotle, virtue did not generally consist in the rigid application of those absolute moral laws for which Plato searched, but in a difficult daily struggle to discern the probable effects of one's behavior in a given context. An act that might be moral in one instance might be immoral in another. But, though Aristotle was a contextualist, he was not an extreme relativist: he believed that while ethics varied with context, it was still possible to deduce from experience the appropriate behavior for each particular situation. He would not have agreed with the extreme relativist position that one act was as moral or immoral as another.

Aristotle agreed with Plato that the reward for virtue was earthly happiness through self-respect and the respect of others, as surely as the penalty for vice was unhappiness. Aristotle claimed, "Bad men are full of regrets." While Aristotle expressed no opinion on the existence of an afterlife, he clearly viewed earthly happiness as the ultimate prize.

If earthly happiness depended on virtue, and if virtue depended on rational training and habit, as Aristotle contended, it followed that the proper role of both the polis and the friend must be to help the individual in his quest to become virtuous by encouraging him to adopt the appropriate habits. Reflecting centuries of Greek tradition, Aristotle wrote, "Legislators make the citizens good by forming habits in them . . . and it is in this that a good constitution differs from a bad one." Since the attainment of virtue was as difficult as it was essential, it could be achieved only through mutual aid. The polis in which one lived and the company that one kept were crucial to one's chances of becoming virtuous and, hence, happy. This logic explains why ancient political theorists focused so much attention on prohibiting immoral behavior. Immorality was like a cancer that would grow until it corrupted all of society, thereby making it almost impossible for the individual to lead a moral life. It was absurd to pretend that individual immorality had no effect on social virtue, or vice versa. No man was an island. Aristotle claimed, "Man is a social animal and one whose nature is to live with others." Society preceded the individual. The polis was a body, each individual a limb. Virtuous friends were "the greatest of external goods" because they helped one achieve virtue. Aristotle wrote: "If a friend becomes wicked, it is necessary to lead him back into goodness. For it is a better and more loving act to aid him in acquiring character than to aid him in acquiring wealth." Friends were bound together by the closest ties. When asked, "What is a friend?" Aristotle replied, "One soul dwelling in two bodies."

Aristotle immortalized Plato's theory of mixed government by making it the centerpiece of his *Politics*. In the process of analyzing the governments of 158 city-states, Aristotle cited numerous examples of actual mixed systems in the ancient world.

Aristotle also became the first political theorist to argue that a large middle class was essential to republican government. He claimed that those who possessed a golden mean of income lacked the arrogance of the rich and the envy of the poor. Furthermore, having "neither so much property that they are able to enjoy a leisure free from all business cares, nor so little that they depend on the city for support," they would "ask that the law should rule for them" rather than constantly overturning the laws. They were "least prone either to refuse office or to seek it, both of which tendencies are dangerous to poleis." But Aristotle made it clear that the middle class he favored was one composed of farmers, not one formed from the merchants and traders, a class Aristotle despised for their obsession with profit.

Unfortunately, Aristotle's *Politics* also included an influential defense of slavery. Aristotle argued that some were born to lead and others to follow: "The element which is able, by virtue of its intelligence, to exercise forethought is naturally a ruling and master element; the element which is able, by virtue of its bodily power, to do the physical work, is a ruled element, which is naturally in a state of slavery." Just as the mind should rule the body, so those with better minds should rule those with better bodies. Aristotle connected slavery with the universal rule of humans over animals, adults over children, and males over females, power relationships he considered equally natural—though he argued that the rule of male over female should be closer to that of a statesman over fellow citizens than to that of a monarch over his subjects. Slavery was both natural and beneficial to the slave: "Those whose function is to use the body and from whom physical labor is the most that can be expected are by nature slaves, and it is best for them, as it is for all inferior things I have already mentioned, to be ruled." The master was distinguished from his slave not only by his greater intelligence—though Aristotle conceded that in actual practice the slave was sometimes more intelligent than his master—but also by his greater love of liberty. At one point, Aristotle implied that anyone who would allow himself to be enslaved, rather than taking his own life, did not possess the passion for liberty requisite for a citizen in a republic: "For he is by nature a slave who is capable of belonging to another and therefore does belong to another." Aristotle sometimes seemed to suggest, as had Plato, that while it was wrong to enslave fellow Greeks, it was appropriate to enslave "barbarians," who were "natural slaves"—a doctrine useful to Aristotle's pupil, Alexander, in his conquest of the Persian Empire. Slaveholders wielded Aristotle's defense of slavery as a powerful weapon throughout Western history.

Perhaps the most versatile philosopher in human history, Aristotle single-handedly created the Western curriculum, defining its various fields of study. His obsession with, and immense talent for, categorization stemmed from his belief in the divinely ordained order of the universe and its accessibility to human reason. His *Organon* ("Instrument" or "Tool") and his *Rhetoric* became the standard textbooks for the respective studies of logic and oratory for over two millennia. The father of zoology, he analyzed the anatomies, breeding habits, and migrations of 540 animals. He correctly rejected the popular view that acquired characteristics (e.g., large muscles gained through exertion) were inheritable by offspring. He was the first biologist to dissect animals extensively. He wrote treatises concerning mathematics, astronomy, physics, meteorology, geology, chemistry, anatomy, history, and literary criticism. His *Poetics* was the first systematic treatment of aesthetics.

If Aristotle's style is sometimes dry and convoluted, it is partly because most of his surviving works exist in the form of lecture notes. The works that he wrote for the public, his poems and plays, did not survive. His convoluted style also stemmed from his supreme dedication to truth, which caused him to prefer the inconclusive discussion of problems to artificial conclusions. He always clarified issues while doing justice to their complexity, the scholar's most difficult task.

There was hardly a field of study Aristotle did not influence. One ancient commentator reckoned the number of his works at four hundred, another at a thousand, though only forty-seven survive. Medieval theologians like Thomas Aquinas called Aristotle "the Philosopher" and "the master of those who know." Indeed, by the Middle Ages, after Aristotle's works had been translated into Latin, his influence had become too great, so that the quest for truth, to which he had devoted his entire life, had become impeded by the fanatical manner in which his followers clung to his errors in astronomy and physics. (He argued that the earth lay at the center of the universe, that motion required a continuous force, and that heavier objects fell faster than lighter ones.) In contrast to some of his followers, Aristotle himself remained ever humble, writing, "While individually we contribute little or nothing to truth, by the union of all a considerable amount is amassed."

In arguing that the material world was less real than the world of the forms Platonism had emphasized contemplation over observation. In embracing the material world as the ultimate reality, an evolutionary but orderly place whose principles of operation human reason could discover and discern, Aristotle restored the significance of empirical knowledge. Ralph Waldo Emerson once wrote that every man was a follower of either Plato or Aristotle. Both contributed greatly to modern science—Plato to its emphasis on mathematics, Aristotle to its emphasis on empirical observation.

The Stoics

Around 300 B.C. Zeno (ca. 335–263 B.C.), a tall, gaunt Phoenician from Citium in Cyprus who had been shipwrecked in Athens while on a trading expedition a decade earlier, inaugurated the philosophy of Stoicism. The Stoics were so named because Zeno lectured at the city's *Stoa Poikile* (Painted Porch), a public colonnade.

The Stoics believed that all reality was material. But while basic matter was passive, the Logos or World Soul, a finer sort of matter, was the active, animating portion of the universe. Drawing from Plato, Stoics held that human souls were fragments of this common World Soul, a consciousness that diffused itself through space to create and sustain the universe. The World Soul had been called many names over the centuries, including "God," "Fate," and "Zeus." The names of the gods merely represented the World Soul's different attributes (or, as some Stoics would have it, the gods were real but subordinate to the World Soul). The individual soul, which had an intuitive comprehension of the eternal truths of the World Soul, could be fully reintegrated into the World Soul after death if it had been well cared for in life. The World Soul created and destroyed the universe in an eternal cycle; at intervals, the universe was consumed by fire, and an identical universe was formed in which the same events were repeated.

The Stoics were fatalists. They believed that the universe was an endless chain of causation, like a river destined to flow in a certain direction. Since it was futile to battle the inexorable current of the universe, the Stoics emphasized the need to endure such hardships as pain, sorrow, and death patiently.

The Stoics believed in the spiritual equality of all humans. While most contemporary religions and philosophies were hierarchical in nature, the Stoics considered women and slaves spiritually equal to free men.

Like Plato and Aristotle, the Stoics believed that earthly happiness was the reward of virtue. An individual who put himself at odds with the natural flow of the universe through wicked acts could not truly be at peace with himself and with others. The fruits of virtue were self-respect and the respect of others, both of which were necessary to human happiness.

Building on the work of Pythagoras and Plato, the Stoics were the first to fully develop and emphasize the concept of natural law. Cleanthes of Assus (ca. 331–232 B.C.), a disciple of Zeno and an ex-boxer who made his living watering gardens and milling grain at night, taught that virtue lay in "living agreeably to nature in the exercise of right reason."

The Stoics assumed a middle position between Plato and Aristotle concerning the mechanics of natural law. Although the Stoics agreed with Plato that humans possessed an innate predisposition to virtue, they denied that natural law could be grasped solely through intuition, which required the help of reason acting on sensory information. As Maryanne Cline Horowitz once aptly summarized this aspect of Stoic philosophy: "They believed that the mind is born predisposed to certain ideas which are not yet consciously held. These ideas are evoked and developed through the stimulus of sense impressions and the development of reason." Zeno portrayed the human soul as a spark from the "Great Flame" (the World Soul) that could be extinguished by a bad upbringing.

Epicurus

Born of Athenian parents, Epicurus (341–270 B.C.) moved from Samos to Athens around 307 B.C. There he began a school, popularly known as "the Garden," that rivaled the Academy and the Lyceum. He agreed with the guiding principle of the Platonic, Aristotelian, and Stoic philosophies: that earthly happiness was the reward of virtue. In one of his three surviving essays, written in the form of a letter, he declared: "The virtues go hand in hand with pleasant living, and the good life cannot be divorced from them. . . . The just man enjoys the greatest peace of mind, while the unjust is full of the utmost disquietude."

Epicurus denied the existence of anything other than matter and void. The universe was infinite and eternal, though it possessed numerous perishable worlds, some of which were hospitable to life and some of which were not. Epicurus believed that the gods were material beings, though consisting of a type of matter superior to that which composed humans, and that they did not interfere in the affairs of humans. He claimed, "What is happy and indestructible neither is troubled itself nor causes trouble to others." Furthermore, there was no such thing as intuition, spirit, or a separable soul. Epicurus wrote, "It is upon sensation that reason must rely when it attempts to infer the unknown from the known." Humans must use reason, acting upon information provided by the senses, to deduce from nature those moral laws essential to earthly happiness and must test them through experience.

Epicurus' emphasis on testing moral principles to determine their consequences did not lead him to moral relativism. Since the universe was orderly, Epicurus assumed that human experience naturally favored some qualities and actions over others. Hence through reason and experience, trial and error, humans would inevitably be led in the same direction—toward the four cardinal virtues that Plato had identified.

Epicurus agreed with the Stoics that happiness could be attained through an untroubled state neither agitated by excessive pleasure nor subject to avoidable discomfort and pain, a state he termed *ataraxia*. Ataraxia, in turn, could be achieved only by freeing the body from pain through a moderate lifestyle and by freeing the mind from fear of the supernatural and of death. While the Stoics sought to diminish the fear of death by focusing on its inevitability (why worry about something one could do nothing about?) and on its benevolence (death simply involved reintegration into the World Soul), Epicurus sought to achieve the same objective by preaching that death was nothingness and, hence, not to be feared: "Death, [considered] the most horrible of all evils, is nothing to us; for when we are alive it doesn't exist for us, and when it is present we no longer exist." The knowledge of this simple truth transformed life, removing its terrors: "There is nothing terrifying in living to one who has genuinely grasped the fact that there is nothing terrifying in not being alive."

Epicurus also preached withdrawal from moneymaking, politics, and romantic love, each of which was likely to trouble the mind. Epicurus wrote, "You must free yourself from the prison of politics." (Although equally concerned with preserving serenity, the Stoics retorted that it could not be preserved by flouting one's responsibility to participate in public affairs.) Like the Stoics, Epicurus also denounced luxury, since dependence on it would lead to unhappiness if misfortune took it away, and espoused a belief in moral equality. In fact, Epicurus admitted women and one of his slaves into his school.

Epicurus rejected Stoic fatalism. All was not planned; there was an element of chance in the universe. Atoms sometimes deviated slightly from their normal trajectories without cause. Epicurus rebelled against the Stoic conception of Fate: "What is the use of ridding ourselves of the fear of heaven if we are to bow to natural law? Better were our former masters [the gods]; for, tyrants though they were, they were at least capable of being propitiated, whereas physical fate is inexorable, blind, uniform."

Epicurus was convinced that by adopting his philosophy, man, though mortal, could become godlike in a sense. He wrote that a true Epicurean "will never suffer disturbance, whether sleeping or waking, but you will live as a god among men; for one who lives amid eternal gods is not like a mortal creature."

Critics of Epicureanism managed to stigmatize it as mere hedonism, the advocacy of sensual pleasure. Although nothing could have been farther from Epicurus' meaning, his use of the word *hedone*, which could mean either "happiness" or "pleasure," gave fodder to his slanderers. Epicurus himself complained of this calumny:

> When we say, then, that pleasure is the greatest good, we are not referring to the pleasure of debauchery or those that consist of sensual gratification, as some people claim because of their ignorance, disagreement with our views, or deliberate falsification of our teachings; what we mean, rather, is the freedom of the body from pain [through moderate living] and the mind from torment. It is not a string of drinking-bouts and revelries, not sexual love, not the enjoyment of the fish and other delicacies of a luxurious table, which produce a pleasant life; it is sober reasoning, searching out the grounds of every choice and avoidance, and banishing those beliefs through which the greatest tumults take possession of the soul. . . . It is not possible to live pleasurably without living sensibly and nobly and justly.

ROMAN PHILOSOPHY

Lucretius (ca. 95–55 B.C.)

Roman authors explored many of the issues raised by the Greek philosophers. Indeed, most of what the modern world knows about Epicureanism comes not from Epicurus himself but from a Roman named Lucretius (Titus Lucretius Carus).

In the only surviving philosophical poem of the ancient world, *On the Nature of Things* (50s B.C.), Lucretius synthesized the teachings of Epicurus and applied them to the fields of anthropology, history, and physics in order to demythologize the universe. In explaining his selection of the poetic form he noted that just as children could be persuaded to take foul-tasting medicine by putting honey on the rim of the cup, so readers would receive philosophical wisdom more readily if it was couched in graceful verse. Influenced by Hesiod and the Alexandrian poets but surpassing them in elegance of expression, Lucretius' mastery of the didactic poem directly influenced Virgil's *Georgics*. It was an interesting choice of format for Lucretius, considering that his idol Epicurus had rejected poetry and the other arts as opposed to happiness and considering that from the very beginning of philosophy in the sixth century B.C., nearly all of the Greek philosophers had chosen to write prose, which they thought more appropriate for rational discourse than verse.

While adopting the doctrines of Epicurus, Lucretius eschewed his dry philosophical prose for rich poetic imagery that embodied Roman concreteness about the practical realities of life. His willingness to explore deeply, rather than cavalierly dismiss, the physical and emotional pain of a lingering death stood in stark contrast to Epicurus' cerebral approach. While Epicurus intellectualized death in order to rob it of its capacity to induce fear, Lucretius acknowledged and explored its genuinely fearful aspects while simultaneously delving into the unnecessary agony humans added to their suffering through irrational fears. His conclusion of the poem with a discussion of a plague in fifth-century B.C. Athens, a story originally reported by Thucydides, demonstrated that even the great city of philosophers, of Epicurus himself, had not only been impotent in the face of sudden and unforeseeable death but had made the calamity far worse through irrational superstition, as in the case of violent quarreling over the burial of corpses.

According to Lucretius, the gods were material, though composed of a superior, indestructible kind of matter. Since they existed in the empty spaces between worlds, their atoms could not collide with others. The gods had not created the universe, which was the product of the accidental collisions and conjunctions of atoms, nor did they intervene in human affairs, but allowed the universe to operate according to natural laws that human reason could discern through the aid of the senses. Lucretius was convinced that the senses were reliable, writing, "What can be a surer guide to the distinction of true from false than our own senses?" He blamed optical illusions not on the senses, but on misinterpretation by the mind. He believed that there was an element of chance in the universe; atoms sometimes veered "a little from their track." Nevertheless, like many of his modern, materialist heirs, Lucretius often fell into the trap of personifying the same Nature on whose cold impersonality his philosophy insisted. He wrote, "Nature is free and uncontrolled by proud masters and runs the universe by herself without the aid of the gods."

Lucretius asserted that the key to earthly happiness, which was the ultimate goal of human existence since there was no afterlife, was a virtuous lifestyle. One should enjoy the long-term pleasure of contemplating the beauty and order of the universe, rather than wallowing in the fleeting pleasures of the body, which often ruined one's health, or pursuing political ambitions. Romantic love was a type of mania that produced unhappiness as well. The only antidote was to "concentrate on all the faults of mind or body of her whom you pursue and lust after" (a suggestion later pursued by Ovid in *The Cures of Love*). Wealth and power did not produce happiness either, since they did nothing to reduce the superstitious fears of death that walked "unabashed among princes and potentates."

Lucretius claimed that there were numerous other worlds and beings. Considering the limitless size of the universe and the large number of atoms flowing through it, he argued:

> It is in the highest degree unlikely that this earth and sky are the only ones to have come into existence and that all those particles of matter outside are accomplishing nothing. This follows from the fact that our world has been made by nature through the spontaneous and casual collision and the multifarious, accidental, random and purposeless congregation and coalescence of atoms whose suddenly formed combinations could serve on each occasion as the starting-point of substantial fabrics—earth and sea and sky and the race of living creatures. On every ground, therefore, you must admit that there exist elsewhere other clusters of matter similar to this one which the ether clasps in ardent embrace. . . . You are bound therefore to acknowledge that in other regions there are other earths and various tribes of men and breeds of beasts.

Although worlds, like humans, were destructible, the atoms that composed them were indestructible and combined into new worlds. Thus, humans might draw some comfort from the indestructibility of the universe. Their participation in the great relay race of life could be beneficial only if they died and returned their atoms to the earth to nurture future generations: "In a short span of time the generations of animals are changed and, like runners, hand on the torch of life."

Lucretius won some converts to Epicureanism in Rome during the late republican era, a time of unspeakable chaos and violence, by emphasizing its value in emancipating humans from fear of death. At a time when many suffered through torturous lives, it was comforting to believe that no torturous afterlife awaited. Lucretius assured people that they had nothing to fear from death, since the spirit, like the body, consisted of decaying atoms. Mind and spirit were "so conjoined as to constitute a single substance," and mind could not "exist apart from body." Disembodied spirits could have no senses. Lucretius ridiculed the Pythagorean and Platonic belief in reincarnation, writing: "It is surely ludicrous to suppose that spirits are standing by at the mating and birth of animals—a numberless number of immortals on the look-out for mortal frames, jostling and squabbling to get in first and establish themselves most firmly. Or is there perhaps an established compact that first come shall be first served, without any trial of strength between spirit and spirit?" Lucretius went further, attacking the very idea of a separable soul: "It is surely crazy to couple a mortal object with an eternal and suppose that they can work in harmony and mutually interact." Lucretius added: "What has the bugbear Death to frighten men, if souls can die as well as bodies? So, when our mortal frame shall be disjoined, the lifeless lump uncoupled from the mind, from sense of grief and pain we shall be free. We will not feel, because we shall not be." But religious superstition filled this, our only life, with needless terrors: "The life of fools in the end becomes a hell on earth." The gods should be treated as models of serenity, not objects of fear.

Many Roman aristocrats agreed. According to the historian Sallust, Julius Caesar declared in a speech to the Senate that death could be a relief to some, for in it "there is no place for either tears or rejoicing." (Cato the Younger, a statesman famed for his Stoicism, responded to Caesar's Epicurean conception of death as nothingness with his belief that "the wicked go a different way from the good, and inhabit a place of horror, fear, and noisome desolation." While this conception of the afterlife owed more to popular belief than to Stoicism, it was viewed favorably by Stoics since it at least upheld the doctrine of an afterlife.)

It is a measure of the horrors of the late republican era (and an insight into the rise of the emperors) that the absence of an afterlife should have constituted the prime attraction of a philosophy. Other Romans valued Epicureanism as a justification for their retreat from politics, a field of endeavor that had become increasingly dangerous. Indeed, the Epicureans favored monarchy precisely because it required the least involvement of the citizen in politics. Thus, although Caesar's political career rendered him at best an imperfect Epicurean, it served the needs of his more fully Epicurean brethren.

Another cause of the considerable influence of Lucretius' philosophy in late republican Rome was his paradoxical passion on behalf of reason. This passion, exhibited in a profusion of creative imagery and metaphors, rendered Epicureanism less austere and forbidding. Consider this ironic passage in which Lucretius deifies Epicurus for his rejection of religion, keeping in mind that Lucretius' original Latin employed the hexameter, the meter of epic poetry:

> When before the eyes of men Human Life lay still upon the ground,
> prostrate in foul dejection, crushed and burdened with the dead weight

of Religion, which put forth her head from the heavenly places and with the terror of her countenance lowered upon mortal men and brooded over them—then it was that a man of Greece first had the courage to lift up his eyes—the eyes of a mortal—to meet her eyes and to be the first to withstand her to the face. This man neither stories about the gods nor the gods' lightning nor heaven with its threats and its thunder could keep within bounds: they only spurred the more his mind's searching courage to long to be the first to splinter the bars that lock the gates of Nature's world. Therefore his mind's violent energy carried through to victory; he passed far beyond the flaming ramparts of the universe and ranged in mind and spirit through the unmeasured whole. Thence bringing his spoils in triumph he comes back to tell us what things can come into being, what things cannot—in short, what is the principle by which each thing's potentialities are marked out, its boundary stone set deep within itself. That is how Religion is overthrown and trampled down underfoot; this man's victory puts us on a level with heaven. . . . You are my leader, O glory of the Grecian race. . . . It is from love alone that I long to imitate you, not from emulous ambition. Shall the swallow contend in song with the swan? . . . You are our father, illustrious discoverer of truth.

Here Lucretius worships Epicurus for his refusal to worship. Nor is this the only paradox generated by Lucretius' employment of the tropes of epic poetry. He begins the poem with a prayer to Venus, the mother of life, "Endow my verse with everlasting charm," as well as with a request that she persuade Mars to stop "this brutal business of war." While the prayer for inspiration forms a fairly typical prologue of an epic poem (unlike the pacifistic request), both the prayer and the request contradict one of the central theses that follow, the claim that the gods never intervene in human affairs.

Some critics have suggested that Lucretius' obsession with conquering the fear of death is itself proof that he himself was unable to conquer it. He has Nature say concerning the human desire for an afterlife: "Because you long for what you don't have and disregard what you have, your life has slipped away from you unfulfilled and unenjoyed. . . . Now give up things unsuited to your years and make way for younger men; for there is no escape." Why the word "escape," if, as Lucretius continually assures us, there is nothing to fear in death? The cracks in Lucretius' bravado are sometimes visible as he versifies past the graveyard. Similarly, his argument that the infinite oblivion before one's birth, which was not regretted because one was not in existence to regret it, is no different from the infinite oblivion after one's death and, therefore, no cause for regret, is flawed because it compares the loss of a good (a life) with the nonexistence of a good (a life before it came into being). While it is true that if a deceased person is insentient, he cannot regret his own death, it does not follow that a sentient being has no cause to regret his impending insentience. Indeed, unlike most Greco-Roman poets, Lucretius cannot even offer himself the consolation of eternal fame since Epicureanism posits the eventual death of the world (though not of the universe).

It has sometimes been suggested that Lucretius was successful in promoting Epicurean philosophy because what inhabitants of the Greco-Roman world feared most was to have their eternal fates left to the mercy of their capricious gods, whereas modern humans fear death because they fear eternal nothingness, the very "comfort" Lucretius offers his readers. But Lucretius' contemporaries were hardly oblivious to the latter fear either. Why else did Lucretius himself often succumb to that temptation so common among those who reject the existence of an afterlife, the temptation to make death more bearable by granting it a measure of sentience, thereby undermining his chief argument that death was not to be feared precisely because it was an insentient state? For instance, Lucretius wrote that the living should say to the dead, "You are at peace now in the sleep of death"—as though a pile of decaying atoms could in any way sense the "peace" of "sleep." Elsewhere he referred to death as "restful." Sleep is not an insentient state but, at its best, a state of "peace" and "rest" that can be enjoyed only by a sentient being; therefore, to liken death to sleep is to grant death a measure of sentience. In any case, in 55 B.C., Lucretius was able to make a direct test of his theory of death.

Since most of the writings of Epicurus himself were lost, and since Latin, not Greek, became the universal language of the medieval West and the common focus of the Western educational system until the twentieth century, it was through Lucretius that Epicureanism came to exert a significant influence in modern thought, beginning with the influential writings of Pierre Gassendi in the seventeenth century. Eighteenth-century deists clearly derived their belief in the nonintervention of the deity from Lucretius, and other proponents of the scientific materialism of the Enlightenment, including Thomas Jefferson, paid homage to the Roman Epicurean. In the nineteenth century John Stuart Mill claimed that his own philosophy, utilitarianism, merely represented the rebirth of Lucretius' Epicureanism.

The Eclecticism of Cicero

A philosopher as well as a statesman and political theorist, Cicero's elegant prose placed the Greek doctrines of popular sovereignty, mixed government, and natural law at the center of Western political thought. Although Cicero did not discuss the theory of popular sovereignty explicitly, all of his political writings assumed that no form of government—whether monarchy, aristocracy, democracy, or mixed government—was legitimate unless the people consented to it.

Cicero's *Republic* (51 B.C.) attributed Roman success to the republic's allegedly mixed government. Cicero wrote: "Just as in the music of harps and flutes or in the voices of singers a certain harmony of the different tones must be maintained . . . so also a state is made harmonious by agreement among dissimilar elements. This is brought about by a fair and reasonable blending of the upper, middle, and lower classes, just as if they were musical tones. What musicians call harmony in song is concord in a state." Cicero considered it an advantage that the Roman constitution's balance between the consuls, the Senate, and the popular assemblies had evolved over time. He noted that Cato the Elder "used to say that no genius of such magnitude had ever existed that he could be sure of overlooking nothing; and that no collection of able people at a single point of time could have sufficient foresight to take account of everything; there had to be practical experience over a long period of history." Ironically, at one such assemblage, the U.S. Constitutional Convention, Alexander Hamilton and other Founding Fathers cited Cicero on the need to establish a mixed government. As a result, the founders balanced the power of the federal government between the one (the president), the representatives of the few (the Senate), and the representatives of the many (the House of Representatives).

Though entertaining an eclectic mixture of opinions on various philosophical issues, Cicero was largely Stoic on the question of natural law. He conceived of the universe as "one commonwealth of which both gods and men are members." Natural law was not handed down by the gods, but was the glue that connected them to humans in the one great organism of the universe. Concerning natural law Cicero wrote:

> This law, my lords, is not a written but an innate law. We have not been taught it by the learned; we have not received it from our ancestors; we have not taken it from books; it is derived from nature and stamped in invisible characters upon our very frame. It was not conveyed by instruction but wrought into our constitution. It is the dictate of instinct. . . . There cannot be one law now, and another hereafter; but the same eternal immutable law comprehends all nations, at all times, under one common master and governor of all.

Yet Cicero also joined the Stoics in arguing that the human understanding of natural law was not entirely innate but required ethical training as well. Humans discerned natural law through a combination of reason and intuition. He wrote regarding Nature and Man:

> It is true that she gave him a mind capable of receiving virtue, and implanted at birth and without instruction some small intimations of the

greatest truths, and thus, as it were, laid the foundation for education and instilled into those faculties which the mind already had what may be called the germs of virtue. But of virtue itself she merely furnished the rudiments, nothing more. Therefore, it is our task (and when I say "our" I mean that it is the task of art) to supplement those mere beginnings by searching out the further developments which are implicit in them, until what we seek is fully realized.

Cicero used the two analogies of sparks and seeds to clarify his position. At one point, in the manner of Zeno, he stated that humans were all sparks temporarily separated from the Great Flame (the World Soul), but a spark might be extinguished by a bad upbringing. On another occasion he argued that the seeds of virtue were manifested in the social nature of humans, in their "gregarious impulses." The two analogies differed somewhat: nurturing a seed into a full-grown plant generally requires more conscious effort than keeping a flame lit.

Like most of the classical philosophers, Cicero possessed an optimistic conception of nature and, hence, of human nature. He claimed: "Great-heartedness and heroism, and courtesy, and justice, and generosity are far more in conformity with nature than self-indulgence. . . . Our nature impels us to seek what is morally right." Those who violated natural law were punished, not by the "penalties established by law, for these they often escape," but by "their own degradation." The reward of virtue was self-respect and the respect of others: "The reputation and the glory of being a good man are too precious to be sacrificed in favor of anything at all."

Cicero assaulted the Epicureans. He wrote, "Brave he surely cannot possibly be that counts pain the supreme evil, nor temperate he that holds pleasure to be the supreme good." Regarding the Epicurean doctrine that virtue was whatever contributed most to happiness, Cicero wrote, "No fixed, invariable natural rules of duty can be posited except by those who say that moral goodness is worth seeking solely or chiefly for its own sake." He quoted Plato, "We are not born for ourselves alone." He considered the Epicurean retreat from civic life and its obligations immoral: "Our country did not give us life and nurture us without expecting to receive in return, as it were, some maintenance from us. . . . No, it reserved the largest and most numerous portions of our loyalty, ability, and sagacity, leaving to us for our private use only what might be surplus to its needs." The statesman was horrified by the notion that the virtuous should leave politics to the wicked.

Cicero's philosophical treatises, written late in life as he grieved over the deaths of both his beloved daughter Tullia and the Roman republic itself, noted the need to endure old age patiently and expressed confidence in the existence of an afterlife. He noted, "Everyone hopes to attain an advanced age; yet when it comes, they all complain!" Of Nature he wrote: "I follow and obey her as a divine being. Now since she has planned all the earlier divisions excellently, she is not likely to make a bad playwright's mistake of skimping on the last act. And a last act was inevitable. There had to be a time of withering, of readiness to fall, like the ripeness which comes to the fruits of the trees and of the earth. But a wise man will face this prospect with resignation, for resistance against Nature is as pointless as the battles of the giants against the gods." The trouble with some old men was not their age but their character: "If a man controls himself and avoids bad temper and churlishness, then he can endure being old. But if he is irritable and churlish, then any and every period of his life will seem to him tiresome." He added: "Great deeds are not done by strength or speed or physique; they are the products of thought, and character, and judgment. And far from diminishing, such qualities actually increase with age. . . . Spring, the season of youth, gives promise of fruits to come, but the later seasons are those that reap the harvests. . . . If some god granted me the power to cancel my advanced years and return to boyhood, and wail once more in the cradle, I should firmly refuse. Now that my race is run, I have no desire to be called back from the finish to the starting point!"

The marvelous nature of the human mind convinced Cicero that it "cannot be mortal." He added: "It is only after liberation from all bodily admixture has made them pure and undefiled that souls enter upon true wisdom. . . . I look forward to meeting the personages of whom I have heard, read, and written. . . . I am leaving a hostel rather than a home. . . . As I approach death I feel like a man nearing harbor after a long voyage: I seem to be catching sight of land. . . . Once we have arrived at the other place, and only then, shall we live. For this life is truly death, and I could, if I would, weep for it." He hypothesized that individual souls both originated and concluded in the Milky Way in a type of World Soul, where they enjoyed a blissful existence before being joined to a human body and after departing it, except for the wicked, whose souls swirled "around close to the earth itself, buffeted about for many years," after leaving their bodies, before finally being allowed to return to the World Soul.

Yet Cicero had disagreements with Stoicism as well. He rejected Stoic asceticism and fatalism. In a legal case he conducted while consul he ridiculed the asceticism of Cato the Younger, a Stoic who even went about without shoes. Sounding like the Athenian Pericles, with whose Funeral Oration (recounted by Thucydides) he was quite familiar, Cicero declared that Romans "who set aside time for pleasure as well as time for work" had maintained their constitution and power better than the ascetic Spartans. Cato's rigid Stoicism rendered him almost incapable of compromise, a great liability for a politician. Cicero once remarked, "He speaks in the Senate as if he were living in Plato's Republic instead of Romulus's cesspool."

Like most other Roman philosophers, Cicero was a pragmatist who emphasized ethics over metaphysics. For this reason he granted a primacy to politics, which he considered a branch of ethics. While both Plato and Aristotle, quintessential Greeks and philosophers, had argued that philosophy was superior to politics because it concerned higher thought, which was closer to that of the gods, Cicero, the Roman and the politician, countered that politics affected more lives than philosophy—though he conceded that philosophers could be valuable in training politicians. While he considered the passion for knowledge innate, he warned his son Marcus against devoting "too much industry and too deep study to matters that are obscure and difficult and useless as well." Philosophers could be engaged in passive injustice if their immersion in study prevented them from shielding others from wrong. He added, "The whole glory of virtue is in activity," and called justice "the crowning glory of the virtues."

A man with few military achievements, Cicero was most un-Roman in giving politics primacy over war, claiming that the only legitimate goal of war was a more perfect peace, that courage in an unjust war was no virtue, and that lawmakers were superior to warriors. He declared, "Arms are of little value in the field unless there is wise counsel at home."

Although Cicero's philosophical ideas were hardly original—he once conceded, "I supply only the words, and I don't lack those!"—"supplying the words" is at least as crucial to the popularity of a philosophy as supplying the ideas. Indeed, in Cicero's case supplying the words involved inventing a whole new Latin vocabulary that corresponded to technical terms in Greek philosophy.

Though he was not a philosopher or political theorist by profession, Cicero's essays on these subjects exerted a profound influence on Western history. The poet Dante found consolation for the death of Beatrice in Cicero's essay *On Friendship*, which presented arguments for an afterlife. Eighteenth-century deists used Cicero's two rational arguments for the existence of God—humans' intuitive connection to Him and the order of the universe—as the basis for their rejection of the need for divine revelation. Voltaire especially liked Cicero's essay *On Divination*, which was directed against superstitious belief in magic and augury.

Cicero's influence on modern republicans was vast. They deduced from Cicero's exposition of the theory of natural law the concept of natural rights that forms the basis of those bills of rights that now distinguish democratic nations from the rest of the world. Cicero's condemnation of "party strife," which had destroyed the Roman republic, contributed greatly to the Founding Fathers' denunciation of political parties, including George Washington's warning against the evils of faction in his Farewell Address. Cicero also reinforced their pastoralism by his glorification of the agricultural lifestyle: "But of all the occupations by which gain is secured, none is better than agriculture, none more profitable, none more delightful, none more becoming to a freeman."

Seneca (4 B.C.–A.D. 65)

Just as Epicureanism became known to the modern West through Lucretius, in part because of his superior eloquence and passion and in part because so few of Epicurus' writings survived, Stoicism was introduced to the medieval and modern West largely through the pragmatic works of Seneca and Marcus Aurelius, since the writings of Zeno, Cleanthes, and the other Greek Stoics perished as well. In the end, Epicureanism was unable to win as many Roman converts as Stoicism, which accorded much better with Roman culture. In fact, after the Greek general Pyrrhus explained Epicurean doctrines concerning the primacy of pleasure, the gods' indifference toward humanity, and the necessity of an individual's withdrawal from politics to Gaius Fabricius, Fabricius allegedly exclaimed, "Grant that Pyrrhus and the Samnites continue to take these doctrines seriously so long as they are at war with us!" The Stoic emphasis on piety, perseverance, and public service harmonized much better with traditional Roman values.

The most influential Stoic was Seneca (Lucius Annaeus Seneca) of Carduba, an old Roman colony in Spain. Seneca's failure to transform his pupil Nero into a virtuous and benevolent ruler led, ultimately, to Seneca's own suicide in order to escape execution for treason in A.D. 65. Seneca called in his secretaries to dictate to them one final dissertation before he died. (He was publishing and perishing at the same time.) But the pupil survived his teacher by only three years. Nero disregarded Seneca's soundest advice at his own peril: "A ruler's greatness is stable and secure when all men know that he is *for* them as much as *above* them." Some considered Nero a living refutation of the Stoics' optimistic view of human nature.

Seneca promoted Stoicism in Rome through a series of epistles and essays, written in a colloquial Latin that avoided the irritating hairsplitting of some of his Greek predecessors. As with Cicero, most, if not all, of Seneca's works were penned during his years in political exile. Seneca wrote: "God [the World Soul] is near you, he is with you, he is within you. This is what I mean, Lucilius: a holy spirit dwells within us, one who marks our good and bad deeds, and is our guardian. . . . No man can be good without the help of God. . . . The totality in which we are contained is one, and it is God; and we are his partners and his members. Our spirit is capacious, and its direction is toward God, if vices do not press it down. . . . Our soul, which may reach outward at will, was fashioned by Nature to desire equality with the gods." Seneca defined God as a "creative reason" that was the active portion of the universe, diffused throughout it, from which the passive portion, a lesser form of matter, proceeded. He saw proof of God's existence in the alleged consensus in that belief among all peoples, as well as in the orderliness of the universe. Lucretius' doctrine that the universal order consisted of "a property of matter moving at random" was nonsense, Seneca explained: "So mighty a structure does not persist without some caretaker."

Seneca believed that the divine source of every human soul rendered humans spiritual equals. He refuted Aristotle's belief in "natural slaves," considering enslavement the work of Fortune rather than the product of inferiority. He called slaves "men," "comrades," "humble friends," and "fellow slaves, if you remember that Fortune holds equal sway over both" the free and the slave. He wrote: "The man you call slave sprang from the same seed, enjoys the same daylight, breathes like you, lives like you, dies like you. . . . Treat your inferior as you would wish your superior to treat you. . . . Treat your slave with compassion, even with courtesy. . . . A man is a fool if he looks only at the saddle and bridle and not at the horse itself when he is going to buy one; he is a greater fool if he values a man by his clothing and condition, which only swathes us like clothing. . . . Slaves ought to respect rather than fear you." Seneca argued that slaves should not be insulted, much less physically abused. Their advice should be sought, and they should be invited to share the master's table regularly. Nevertheless, Seneca was hardly an abolitionist (there was no real abolitionist movement in the ancient world), calling only for masters to treat their slaves humanely and to retain fewer of them since they decreased a master's self-sufficiency.

Seneca considered the lawful and orderly universe similar to a river that flowed in a fated path. He wrote: "Cause is linked with cause, and a long chain of events governs all matters public and private. Everything must therefore be borne with fortitude, because events do not, as we suppose, happen but arrive by appointment. . . . What is the duty of the good man? To offer himself to Fate. It is a great consolation that our rapid course is one with the universe's." Hardship was necessary to greatness. What mattered was not what befell an individual but how he bore it: "If a great man falls and keeps his greatness where he lies, he is no more scorned than are the ruins of sacred edifices trodden upon; the pious revere them as much as when they were standing."

Seneca considered reason the only sure antidote to sorrow. He wrote: "No situation is so harsh that a dispassionate mind cannot find some consolation in it. . . . The mind must be recalled from externals and focus on itself. . . . A grief beguiled and distracted by pleasures or amusements rises again, and the respite refreshes its energy for savage attack. But a grief which has submitted to reason is appeased forever." For instance, a sudden loss of wealth could be borne when taken in context: "What you regard as disastrous is the daily life of many races. . . . How absurd it is to suppose that it is the financial balance, not the mind's, that matters! . . . For greed nothing is enough; Nature is satisfied with little." Part of the work of reason must be done before tragedy struck, in preparation for it: "A great part of mankind never think of storms when they contemplate a voyage. . . . The pang of disappointed wishes is necessarily less distressing to the mind if you have not promised it sure fulfillment. . . . Never have I trusted Fortune, even when she seemed to be at peace; all her generous bounties—money, office, influence—I deposited where she could ask them back without disturbing me." In the end Fate was just. Seneca wrote of the famous Cornelia: "When her friends were weeping around her and cursing her fate, she forbade them to make any indictment of Fortune, since it was Fortune who had allowed the Gracchi to be her sons."

Seneca agreed with the other Stoics that humans understood natural law through intuition combined with rational training. He claimed, "At our birth, nature made us teachable, and gave us reason, not perfect, yet capable of being perfected." He added, "Every living thing possessed of reason is inactive if not first stirred by some external impression; then the impulse comes, and finally assent confirms the impulse." Regarding virtue he wrote, "Nature could not teach us this directly; she has given us the seeds of knowledge, but not knowledge itself." He added: "Virtue can occur only in a soul trained and taught and raised to its height by assiduous exercise. For this, but not with it, were we born, and even in the best of men you will find, before they are educated, the raw materials of virtue, not virtue itself. . . . Reason is shared by gods and men; in them it is perfected, in us it is perfectible." When seeing virtue represented in present and past examples, children instinctively recognized its inherent beauty and sought to reproduce it. But children who rarely experienced virtuous behavior could not develop their intuitive sense of morality to its full potential.

Reason and experience were as necessary to the production of virtue as intuition was. For this reason, Seneca inveighed against the corrupting influence of gory gladiatorial contests—"man killing man, not in anger or fear, but to provide a spectacle!" To the spectator of such shows, Seneca declared, concerning the gladiator, "Because he killed a man he deserves his fate, but what did you do, poor man, to deserve having to look on?" Indeed, it has been suggested that it was Seneca's influence that caused Nero, early in his reign, to make the unusual call for a gladiatorial show in which no one was to be killed to celebrate the opening of a new amphitheater. Whatever may be said against him, Seneca's retirement in 62 appears to have been a turning point for the worse in Nero's reign, the year that the emperor's trials of senators began.

Seneca believed in an afterlife consisting of reabsorption into the World Soul. He wrote, "What hardship is there in returning whence you came?" The body was "the prison and fetter of the soul" but the soul (which Seneca equated with the mind) was "sacred and everlasting." He claimed: "We are ripening for another birth. Another beginning awaits us, another status."

Some of Seneca's ideas were similar enough to Christian thought that a series of fictitious letters between Seneca and the apostle Paul later circulated. But, whatever their similarities concerning the divine origin of humankind and the equality of souls, the Christian and Stoic theories of human nature were diametrically opposed. While the Stoics, the heirs to Platonic philosophy, believed human nature to be good, the Christian doctrine of original sin held that humans were innately selfish (hence the need for Christ's atoning sacrifice for humanity's incorrigible sin).

Seneca has often been accused of hypocrisy. The most common and just criticism is that he failed to exhibit the Stoic ideal of courage and dignity in the face of danger that he himself extolled. In an essay published soon after Nero's murder of his brother Britannicus, an essay intended to reassure the public that the assassination was not the precursor to further purges, Seneca engaged in gross adulation of the emperor, even touting his mercy and advancing the dubious claim that Nero wept when forced to sign death warrants. To curry favor with the new emperor, Seneca also wrote a satire about Nero's predecessor Claudius—whom Seneca had also flattered while Claudius was still alive. In the satire Seneca has Apollo say of Nero, "He is like me in the beauty of his looks and not inferior in his singing voice." Not only was the second point a howler, but the whole analogy encouraged Nero to see himself as a second Apollo who towered above mere mortals. (It is no accident that many of Nero's pastimes—poetry, lyre playing, and chariot racing—were pastimes of Apollo.) Furthermore, as Nero's principal speechwriter, Seneca probably assisted the emperor in writing the letter to the Senate that justified his execution of his mother, Agrippina, the patroness who had secured Claudius' recall of Seneca from exile (on a probably false charge of adultery) and who had appointed him Nero's tutor. Yet, in the end, Seneca did face his own forced suicide courageously.

The criticism that Seneca's practice of lending money at "usurious rates" and his acceptance from Nero of estates and villas that Seneca then adorned lavishly contradicted his teachings is less just. Seneca never preached hostility to wealth, only indifference to it. Prevailing interest rates were much higher then due to the much higher risks involved in lending money. Seneca was quite generous with his clients and others. He could hardly have rejected the emperor's gifts without giving offense. His diet remained very simple, and if he adorned his villas, it was partly because, as the emperor's advisor, he was obliged to entertain many guests. As soon as Nero allowed him, he retired to a simple life devoted to philosophy, and he contributed some of his wealth to the restoration of Rome after the Great Fire.

Seneca's emphasis on morality over metaphysics, as well as his tempering of Stoic austerity with an urbane humanitarianism, made his works irresistible to contemporary Romans and to countless other readers in the millennia that followed. Better versed in Latin than in Greek, the founders of the United States read Seneca's works far more often than the surviving fragments of the Greek Stoics. Even George Washington, who never learned Latin, read an English translation of Seneca's dialogues as a seventeen-year-old; they became one of his lodestars, teaching him frugality, simplicity, temperance, fortitude, love of liberty, selflessness, and honor. As the historian Samuel Eliot Morison noted, "The mere chapter headings are the moral axioms that Washington followed through life." Morison even suggested that Washington's Stoicism was a source of solace to him in his dealings with Sally Fairfax, the wife of his best friend, a woman whom he loved but could not have, a Stoicism that enabled him to exercise restraint and to follow the practical solution of marriage to Martha Custis. Seneca's *Essays* rested on Thomas Jefferson's reading table when he died. Though Jefferson preferred Epicureanism, he borrowed from Seneca and the other Stoics the un-Epicurean belief in intuition ("the moral sense" in the terminology of the Scottish moral philosophers, who were also heavily influenced by the Stoics). The Stoics even comforted the founders in dealing with the premature deaths so common in premodern society. Montesquieu, another fan of Seneca, declared that if he were not a Christian, he would be a Stoic.

Marcus Aurelius (121–180)

The popularity of Stoicism in Western thought can also be traced to *Meditations*, a philosophical diary of the Roman emperor Marcus Aurelius. Marcus' style was dignified, earnest, and direct, yet his touching humility and humanity tempered the austerity of his message of strict discipline and self-scrutiny.

Like the other Roman philosophers, Marcus viewed philosophy, first and foremost, as a guide to moral action. He wrote, "What then can direct our actions? One thing and one thing alone, philosophy, which is to keep the deity within inviolate." He sought to practice simplicity, goodness, sincerity, earnestness, humility, justice, piety, thoughtfulness, affection, and devotion to duty. A committed Stoic, his personal goal was "not to look at anything but Reason even for a moment; to be the same man always, when in great pain, at the loss of a child, or during a long illness . . . to show no trace of anger or any other passion." He argued, "What happens alike to good and bad men can be in itself neither bad nor good." He instructed himself, "You should look upon things on earth as one who looks from above on things below." A person's only fortress was his own soul: "Nowhere can a man withdraw to a more untroubled quietude than in his own soul. . . . If you are distressed by something outside yourself, it is not the thing which troubles you but what you think about it, and this it is within your power to obliterate at once." Hardship and death should not trouble a person:

> Journey through this moment of time in accord with nature, and graciously depart, as a ripened olive might fall, praising the earth which produced it, grateful to the tree that made it grow. Be like a rock against which the waves of the sea break unceasingly. . . . [Hardship] can in no way prevent you from being just, great-hearted, chaste, wise, steadfast, truthful, self-respecting, and free, or prevent you from possessing those other qualities in the presence of which man's nature finds its fulfillment. . . . See the abyss of past time behind you and another infinity of time in front. In that context, what difference is there between one who lives three days and a Nestor who lives for three generations? . . . Alexander the Great and his groom are reduced to the same state in death. . . . No one can hurt a man but himself. . . . Things material cannot touch the Soul in any way whatever, nor find entrance there, nor have power to sway or move it.

In fact, Marcus' scorn for material things sometimes created a conflict with his pantheism. Since the World Soul was not only the author of material things, but actually embedded in them as a higher form of matter, contempt for them, while necessary to Stoic ethical teaching as the psychological underpinning for the exhortation to bear misfortune patiently, could become problematic to Stoic metaphysics. One biographer of Marcus sarcastically called Stoicism a system in which "the sum of despised particulars becomes somehow Divine."

Like most Stoics, Marcus leaned toward the belief in an afterlife consisting of the reintegration of the individual soul with the World Soul. Drawing on Cicero, he compared life to a voyage and marveled at the reluctance of the passengers to disembark on arriving at the destination. Nevertheless, since the emperor's point was to show that the efficacy of morality did not depend on any external reward, including a good afterlife, he was far from dogmatic on this question.

The emperor urged against vengeance. He wrote:

> The best method of defense is not to become like your enemy. . . . Take care that you do not have toward the inhuman the same feelings as they have toward mankind. . . . Whenever anyone wrongs you, consider what view of good or evil prompted his action. Realizing this, you will pity him. . . . Someone despises me. That is his concern. My concern is that I not

be found to do or say anything which deserves to be despised. . . . The gods, who are immortal, are not vexed that through such a length of time they must always endure so many and such inferior creatures; moreover, they care for them in all sorts of ways. Do you then, who are almost on the point of death, refuse to do so, even though you are one of the inferior creatures yourself? . . . How much harder to bear are the consequences of our anger and vexation at such actions than the actions themselves which provoked our anger and vexation.

His credo was: "If someone can show me and prove to me that I am wrong in what I am thinking or doing, I shall gladly change it, for I seek the truth, by which no one was ever harmed."

Like his fellow Stoics, Marcus possessed an optimistic view of both nature and human nature, which he portrayed as complementary. He wrote, "Nothing that is according to nature is evil." Lacking Aristotle's emphasis on the importance of habit, much less a Judeo-Christian conception of original sin, the emperor believed that reformation of character was a simple matter of the individual choosing to turn back to the good. Unlike the Platonists, whose hypothesis of reincarnation presented the likelihood that souls already possessed divergent experiences at birth, Marcus and his fellow Stoics' belief in identical souls emanating from the same World Soul left them without resource to explain why a few individuals chose to live virtuously ("in accord with nature") but most did not. (The Stoics, while optimistic about the individual in theory, were almost uniformly pessimistic about people in practice.) There was occasionally the suggestion of a limited free will—the belief that while humans could not help what befell them, they had complete freedom of choice concerning how to respond to it ("soul is self-swayed, self-moved")—but even this suggestion was logically problematic because it conflicted with Stoic fatalism. Would not the individual's choice of response to experience affect the outer world, thereby creating havoc in the otherwise orderly constructions of the World Soul, from whose very order the Stoics drew such comfort? It would seem so, yet Marcus was insistent that the design of the World Soul could not be harmed or hindered; the sole casualty of rebellion against it was the rebel.

Marcus exhorted himself to maintain his ethics. He wrote: "Return to, and find repose in, philosophy, which also makes the life of the palace bearable to you, and you bearable in it. . . . See to it that you do not become Caesarized." His political ideal was "a Commonwealth with the same laws for all, governed on the basis of equality and free speech, also the idea of a monarchy which prizes the liberty of its subjects above all things."

Marcus expressed a skepticism concerning the value of fame that was exceedingly uncommon in the classical world. He wrote:

I have often marveled that every man loves himself above all others, yet that he attaches less importance to his own idea of himself than to what his neighbors think about him. . . . Even the greatest of posthumous fame is small, and it too depends upon a succession of short-lived men who will die very soon, who do not know even themselves, let alone one who died long ago. . . . Nothing becomes better or worse by being praised. . . . Those who pursue posthumous fame do not take into account that posterity will be the same kind of men as those whom they now dislike. Posterity too will be mortal. What is it to you, anyway, what words they will utter about you or how they may think of you?

Unlike the Greek philosophers Zeno and Cleanthes who founded Stoicism, men who avoided political involvement even as they called it a duty, the most famous Roman proponents of the philosophy were practical, political men who gave it a moral emphasis that brought it down to earth, thereby increasing its influence both in Rome and in the Western world at large thereafter. While statesmen like Cato the Younger and Brutus became famous as Stoic martyrs for republicanism, and others like Thrasea and Helvidius (the victims of Nero and Vespasian, respectively) as opponents of imperial tyranny, Seneca and Marcus Aurelius—one the chief advisor to an emperor, the other an emperor himself—penned the works that immortalized Stoicism. In this they were aided by Cicero, another practical politician and republican martyr, whose eclectic philosophy contained a large element of Stoicism.

CONCLUSION

The Western world learned Greek philosophy largely through Roman works. It was the elegant and passionate poem of Lucretius, not the prosaic writings of Epicurus (few of which survived) that influenced Western intellectuals. It was Cicero's essays on philosophy and political theory more than those of Plato and Aristotle that enshrined the theories of popular sovereignty, mixed government, and natural law as the core principles of modern democracy. (Indeed, even Plato and Aristotle owed their survival in the medieval West to their works' translation into Latin, and even when the Greek language was again studied widely, most Westerners still preferred to read the Latin and vernacular translations.) It was Seneca and Marcus Aurelius, not Zeno or Cleanthes, whose eloquent yet direct and colloquial writings popularized a quintessentially Roman form of Stoicism that emphasized ethics over metaphysics.

Historical Writing

$\mathscr{I}$n Sallust, Livy, and Tacitus the Romans produced historians who equaled the Greeks. Their works became required reading for Western statesmen for centuries to come, and their various styles influenced historical writing well into the nineteenth century. Suetonius, who exerted a tremendous influence on early medieval historiography, remains the most complete source for the lives of the early Roman emperors, as well as the lives of Virgil and Horace.

GREEK PRECURSORS

Herodotus (ca. 484–425 B.C.)

Herodotus of Halicarnassus (in southwestern Asia Minor), spent four life-transforming years in Athens (447–443 B.C.), where the city's great minds influenced him deeply. Justly called the Father of History, it was Herodotus who first used the term *historia* (research or inquiry) to refer to study of the past.

Herodotus differed from the mythologists of previous eras in several ways. First, although Herodotus did not banish the supernatural completely from his *Histories*, an account of the Persian Wars, he attributed most past events to natural causes, especially to the actions of prominent individuals. Thus, Greco-Roman historians began the focus on "great men" that dominated Western historiography until the late nineteenth century, when Marxism and other ideologies inaugurated an equally strong emphasis on social and economic forces. Herodotus' belief that the wisdom of the Athenian leader Themistocles and the courage of free men had won the Persian Wars contrasted sharply with the constant meddling of the gods in Homer's

Iliad and other Greek poems. Herodotus even related those occasions when prophecies of the oracle of Delphi had proven inaccurate or when the oracle had been bribed to favor a side in a dispute.

Second, unlike the mythologists, Herodotus based his history on real research. Herodotus did a remarkable job of gathering evidence throughout the eastern Mediterranean world and weaving it together into a plausible narrative. His accuracy was astonishing considering that some of the events he recounted had occurred centuries before his time and that he had to rely mostly on oral sources even for more recent events. While he did exaggerate the size of the Persian army, that error was due partly to the unreliability of his Persian sources.

Third, unlike the mythologists, Herodotus always identified his sources, even when he doubted their veracity. He wrote, "For myself, my duty is to report all that is said; but I am not obliged to believe it all alike—a remark which may be understood to apply to my whole history." Indeed, after Herodotus related the popular story of a diver who swam eleven miles underwater without ascending for air, he deadpanned, "My own opinion is that on this occasion he took a boat."

Fourth, the difference between history and mythology was further expressed in the decision of Herodotus and his successors to write prose, not poetry—significantly, the same decision previously made by the Greek philosophers of Asia Minor. Though Herodotus' work was often amusing, sometimes dramatic, his principal purpose was to inform, only secondarily to entertain.

Exiled from Halicarnassus in 457 B.C. for his opposition to Persian rule, Herodotus traveled through much of the known world—Egypt, Tyre, Mesopotamia, Arabia, the Black Sea, and the north Aegean—gathering material for a geographical work. He then landed at Athens, where the city's leader Pericles and the playwright Sophocles befriended him. The city itself, as well as Athenian stories of the Persian Wars, so impressed Herodotus that he decided to change his topic of study. The first part of Herodotus' *Histories* concerned the rise of the Persian Empire, the second portion the resulting wars with Greece.

Herodotus was not only the first historian but also one of the most entertaining historians who has ever written. His hilarious digressions on Near Eastern cultures, the products of a passionate curiosity and love of life, represent a gold mine of anthropological research. Indeed, Herodotus has also been called the first anthropologist, sociologist, and archaeologist. No subject was too small or inconsequential to evoke Herodotus' interest, none too dull for his fertile imagination to enliven. A typical example was Herodotus' discussion of the theory that Egyptian skulls were harder than Persian skulls. A true empiricist, Herodotus felt compelled to test the hypothesis. So he journeyed to a battlefield where the Egyptians and Persians had recently fought and began smashing the heads of corpses with rocks. He found that while Egyptian skulls could barely be cracked with huge stones, Persian skulls could be crushed using small rocks. Having validated the hypothesis, Herodotus then developed a typically imaginative theory to explain the phenomenon. Because Egyptians shaved their heads and walked about without any head covering, while the Persians wore their hair long and wrapped in a turban, the Egyptians required thicker skulls to withstand the heat of the sun. This was almost a theory of natural selection.

Another tale typical of Herodotus is that of Darius I's accession to the Persian throne. When the previous emperor, Cambyses II, died without heir, the seven leading noblemen of Persia met to determine who should replace him. The seven decided to allow the gods to decide. (The ancients often employed what modern people would call games of chance to allow the gods to participate in important decisions.) The seven Persian aristocrats decided to ride their favorite horses to a certain spot before dawn the next day. The owner of the first horse to neigh after sunrise would become the new emperor. Darius' lowly groomsman found a way to fix the contest. Before dawn, he rubbed the genitalia of the favorite mare of his master's horse and stuffed his hands in his cloak to preserve the smell. Then, as the sun rose at the designated location, the groomsman pretended to fasten the horse's bit. The horse smelled his hands and neighed. That is how Darius became emperor of Persia, the most powerful man in the world. This story is typical of Herodotus because it demystifies an important event, attributing its outcome to a clever human, rather than to the gods. (In reality, it was not quite as easy as that; Darius had to win a brief but bloody civil war to secure his throne.) Herodotus is like a favorite uncle—brilliant, endearingly eccentric, and, above all, always fun.

Unfortunately, Herodotus died at the Athenian colony of Thurii in 425 B.C. before he had quite completed the *Histories*. Ironically, the very man who immortalized Athens at the height of its glory was barred from becoming an Athenian citizen by his friend Pericles' recent restrictions on naturalization.

Thucydides (ca. 460–400 B.C.)

An Athenian of aristocratic lineage whose family owned rich mines, Thucydides has been called the first scientific historian. By this it is meant that he was the first to remove supernatural causation from history altogether. He also began the association of history with political and military affairs, an equation that dominated Western historiography until the 1960s, when Herodotean social history was resurrected—though even Herodotus had felt compelled to justify his lengthy, anthropological digressions on the dubious grounds of establishing the background for his central concern, the Persian Wars. For millennia the association of history with political and military matters made it the exclusive study of adult male aristocrats, leaving little place for a discussion of the lives of lower-class males, women, children, and slaves.

Thucydides began his *History of the Peloponnesian War*, an account of the bloody war between Athens and Sparta, by remarking that although his work would not be as entertaining as that of some unnamed but obvious predecessor, he hoped it would be "a possession for all time." Thucydides succeeded. A masterpiece of concision and precision, Thucydides' history is filled with insights that are so universal in application that it continues to be read and cited by the best historians, political scientists, and military strategists. Thucydides' distinction between the underlying and immediate causes of war still dominates that field of inquiry. His grave and intense language effectively conveys the drama of history. His concision, expressed in such lines as the one in which he summarized Athens' calamitous Sicilian campaign, "Having done what men could, they suffered what men must," influenced the writing styles of numerous Greek and Roman authors, including Sallust and Tacitus.

Thucydides believed that history was cyclical. If one selected an important set of events that included many variables and closely investigated that historical sequence, one would find a pattern that could be used to predict future events. Although Thucydides believed that human development proceeded in cycles, his belief in the utility of history implied that knowledge of the past might allow humans to break these cycles.

Thucydides believed that historians should write only about recent events, since he doubted the accuracy of oral accounts of the distant past. Because of this, some have called Thucydides a journalist rather than a historian, though in several instances he did recount the events of past centuries—largely to show that past wars had been inferior to the Peloponnesian War in size and significance.

Like Herodotus, Thucydides had a habit of creating fictitious speeches for historical figures as a means of conveying their personalities and ideas, though he assured the reader that he did his best to reflect faithfully the content, if not always the wording, of what had actually been said. While this practice, followed by nearly all of the ancient historians, would be considered scandalous if practiced by a historian today, it was expected by contemporary readers and, hence, was not deceptive in any sense.

In 424 B.C., Thucydides was exiled from Athens for arriving too late to defend the Athenian colony of Amphipolis against a Spartan attack. Located in Thrace, Amphipolis, the "city surrounded" by the looping Strymon River, was a vital source of metals and timber and an essential base for protecting grain shipments from the Black Sea region.

Thucydides' period of exile left him with plenty of time to write a history. His banishment probably increased his bitterness toward Athenian democracy, which he portrayed, at least in the later stages of the war, as the severest form of mob rule. Indeed, Thucydides' writings bolstered an antidemocratic tradition that dominated Western literature until the rise of representative democracy in the nineteenth century. Even Thucydides' reverential treatment of Pericles was perhaps a way of contrasting him with the "demagogues" who succeeded him, one of whom (Cleon) had played a leading role in Thucydides' banishment.

Yet Thucydides retained an obvious love for his former polis and displayed great pity at its suffering. Furthermore, however colored by his own experience, much of what Thucydides wrote about Athenian democracy was probably true. Although he fell short of his impossible goal of complete objectivity, Thucydides was perhaps the greatest of all the ancient historians.

Thucydides returned to Athens after the war ended in 404 B.C. but died about four years later, before he could complete his *History of the Peloponnesian War*. It ends in midsentence in the year 411 B.C.

Polybius (200–118 B.C.)

Polybius of Megalopolis chose as the subject of his *Histories* Rome's rise to power from the beginning of the First Punic War to the end of the third (264–146 B.C.). Polybius' audience consisted largely of fellow Greeks who were confused by the Romans' unprecedented success in conquering the Mediterranean world. Having befriended Roman leaders while held hostage in Rome for sixteen years (as a cavalry officer for the vanquished Achaean League) and serving as a tutor for the children of one of the city's leading citizens, Polybius contended that the Roman conquest of the Mediterranean was the product of *Tyche* (Fortune), a vague entity similar to Stoic Fate. Polybius wrote: "From this point onwards history becomes an organic whole. . . . Fortune has steered almost all the affairs of the world in one direction and forced them to converge upon one and the same goal." Through Rome, Tyche sought to unify "almost the whole of the inhabited world."

According to Polybius, the chief instrument through which Tyche had achieved this worthy goal was the alleged mixed government of Rome. Polybius agreed with Aristotle that the best constitution assigned approximately equal amounts of power to the three orders of society. Polybius explained that only a mixed government could circumvent the cycle of discord that was the inevitable product of the simple forms. Hence, only a mixed government could provide a state with the internal harmony necessary for prosperity and for the defeat of external enemies. Polybius claimed that the cycle began when primitive man, suffering from chaos and violence, consented to be ruled by a strong and brave leader. Then, as men began to conceive of justice (by developing the habit of imagining themselves in others' positions), they replaced the strong and brave leader with the just leader and chose his son to succeed him. This last move was a mistake. They expected that the son's lineage and education would lead him to emulate his father. But, having been accustomed to a special status from birth, the son did not possess any sense of duty toward the public, and, soon after acquiring power, sought to distinguish himself from the rest of the people. Monarchy had deteriorated into tyranny. But when the bravest and noblest of the aristocrats (for who else would risk their lives in such an endeavor?) overturned the tyranny, the people naturally selected them to succeed the king as rulers. The result was aristocracy, "rule by the best." Unfortunately, the aristocrats' children were not the best but the most spoiled and, like the king's son, soon placed their own welfare above that of the people. Aristocracy had deteriorated into oligarchy. The oppressed people rebelled against the oligarchy and established a democracy. But the wealthy, seeking to raise themselves above the common level, soon corrupted the people with bribes and created factions. The result was the chaos and violence that always accompany mob rule. When these reached epic proportions, sentiment grew for a dictatorship. Monarchy reappeared. This cycle, Polybius contended, would repeat itself indefinitely until a society had the wisdom to balance the power of the three orders of society.

Polybius believed that the Roman republic was the most outstanding example of mixed government. He claimed that the Roman system of government, which had been constructed slowly through trial and error and had reached perfection at the time of the Second Punic War, was the chief cause of Roman success. Its balance between the consuls, the Senate, and the popular assemblies produced compromise and internal harmony.

By contrast, mob rule, the inevitable result of democracy, was the worst form of government. Polybius compared democracy with the crew of a ship who bicker most of the time, only coming together to obey the captain's orders during a storm or enemy attack. Polybius claimed, "The result has often been that, after escaping the dangers of the widest seas and the most violent storms, they wreck their ship in harbor and close to shore." Consistent with his advocacy of mixed government, Polybius placed the zenith of the Athenian constitution during the days of Themistocles, before the reforms of Ephialtes and Pericles had converted the polis into a full-fledged democracy. Since the statesman-warrior defined history in the traditional fashion, as politics and war, it is not surprising that he ignored the fact that it was during the age of Pericles that Athens reached its artistic and literary summit. More surprising, since he seemed to measure the success of a constitution at least partly by its ability to build an empire, was his failure to acknowledge that it was also under Pericles, not Themistocles, that Athens amassed most of its empire in the Aegean. Perhaps he considered such distinctions inconsequential given his general conclusion regarding the Athenian and Theban democracies: "Their growth was abnormal, the period of their zenith brief, and the changes they experienced unusually violent."

As we have seen, the Roman republic, even at its height, was never really balanced. The Senate possessed far more power than the consuls or the masses. But it was only natural that Polybius, in his anxiety to explain a momentous and baffling phenomenon—the Roman conquest of what Polybius called "almost the whole of the inhabited world" (the Mediterranean basin)—should turn to a Greek theory proposed by one of the most respected philosophers, however poorly Greek theories might fit Roman realities. Indeed, the analyses of Aristotle and Polybius were so impressive that they convinced some Roman intellectuals, like Cicero, that Rome possessed a mixed government and that it was the secret of Roman success.

Yet Polybius concluded that the same mysterious Fortune that had built Rome might well destroy it. Polybius believed that, although the Roman system was in many ways superior to the Spartan, it was inferior in one respect: it had failed to deal with the corrupting effects of wealth. Thus, Polybius became the first of many historians to suggest that the debilitating effects of Rome's tremendous prosperity might cause its fall. Hence, despite occasional intimations of Rome's historical transcendence, Polybius' broader view of history was as cyclical as that of the other classical historians and of the Stoic philosophers. Humanity, like the universe itself, passed through cycles of unity and division, order and chaos.

Polybius believed that the historian's task was "first and foremost, to record with fidelity what actually happened and was said, however commonplace this may be." He added, "It is not the historian's business to show off his ability to his readers, but rather to devote his whole energy to finding out and setting down what was really and truly said, and even of this only the vital and most effective parts." While Polybius' claim to having written only "what was really and truly said" should not be taken too literally—like nearly all other ancient historians, he seems to have composed partially fictitious speeches for his historical figures—he probably meant that he agreed with Thucydides that such speeches should not be wholly fictitious, but should at least follow as closely as possible the actual arguments the speakers employed.

Polybius considered it essential that a historian possess political and military experience, travel to historical sites to obtain geographical knowledge, and examine documents. He also wrote: "A good man ought to love his friends and his country, and should share both their hatreds and their loyalties. But once a man takes up the role of the historian he must discard all considerations of this kind. . . . We must therefore detach ourselves from the actors in our story, and apply to them only such statements and judgments as their conduct deserves." It must be so if the study of history was to serve its purpose, the learning of lessons: "There are two ways by which all men may reform themselves, either by learning from their own errors or from those of others; the former makes a more striking demonstration, the latter a less painful one. . . . From this I conclude that the best education for the situations of actual life consists of the experience we acquire from the study of serious history. For it is history alone which, without causing us harm, enables us to judge what is the best course in any situation or circumstance."

Polybius' discussion of the Achaean League, a federation of Greek cities in the Peloponnesus in which voting was proportional to population, informed the ruminations of James Madison and Alexander Hamilton concerning federal systems at the U.S. Constitutional Convention and in their *Federalist* essays. His analysis of mixed government was also highly influential at the Constitutional Convention.

ROMAN HISTORIANS

Quintus Fabius Pictor wrote the first Roman history (in Greek) in the 190s B.C. He began the Roman tradition of an annalistic presentation of events, based on the annual terms of most Roman magistrates and on the manner in which public records were kept. Half a century later Cato the Elder wrote the first prose history in Latin, *Origins*. Yet Cicero contrasted these early Roman historians, whom he termed "chroniclers and nothing more," with their Greek precursors, whom he admired. He attributed the superiority of the Greek achievement in historical writing to the fact that while the most eloquent Greeks wrote history, the most eloquent Romans were men of action, lawyers and politicians like himself, who lacked adequate time for extensive historical research.

Julius Caesar (100–44 B.C.)

Yet Roman men of action often found the time to publish memoirs that explored contemporary history. The most famous memoirs were the two autobiographical histories of Julius Caesar, works that were elegant but highly subjective.

In preparation for a campaign for the consulship Caesar kept his name before the Roman public by publishing his *Commentaries on the Gallic War*, a memoir of Caesar's conquest of Gaul in which he wrote of himself in the third person in order to present the illusion of objectivity. Caesar's *Commentaries*, one of modern historians' most important sources concerning the early Gallic and Germanic tribes, was written so well that it is still used as a Latin primer. Its simple but nonrepetitive prose is as free of colloquialisms as it is of pedantic terminology.

As dictator, Caesar also published an account of his defeat of Pompey called *The Civil War*. Even Cicero, whose style was far more florid, admired Caesar's lucid, graceful writing, remarking of his sentences, "They are like nude figures, upright and beautiful, stripped of all ornament and style as if they had removed a garment."

Sallust (ca. 86–35 B.C.)

Sallust (Gaius Sallustius Crispus), a native of Amiternum in the Sabine country, was the first great Roman historian, as well as one of the few ancient historians who sided with the popular party rather than with the aristocratic faction. In 50 B.C. the censors expelled Sallust from the Senate for sexual immorality, though the charges against him were probably false and certainly politically motivated. More likely true was the accusation brought against Sallust after he served as proconsul of Africa Nova (Numidia) that he had plundered his province. Sallust escaped prosecution only because of an enormous bribe to Julius Caesar. The scandal effectively ended Sallust's political career in 45 B.C.

Despising the triumvirs Antony, Octavian, and Lepidus, who followed Caesar in dictatorial power but seemed to lack his wisdom and magnanimity, Sallust remained in retirement from politics after Caesar's death, when he decided to write history. Sallust wrote *Catiline's War* (43–42 B.C.) and *The Jugurthine War* (41–40 B.C.) concerning two episodes of the late second and first centuries B.C. that he depicted as epitomizing severe moral decline in Rome. In *Catiline's War*, Sallust claimed the common motive of classical historians, the desire for fame and glory. He wrote: "Since only a short span of life has been vouchsafed us, we must make ourselves remembered as long as may be by those who come after us. Wealth and beauty can give only a fleeting and perishable fame, but intellectual excellence is a glorious and everlasting possession." In *The Jugurthine War*, Sallust went further, stating that politics had become futile and that it was better to write history than to offer vain resistance to tyranny or, worse, to support it. The prospect was dark; the Roman world would either collapse in ruin or hold together in bondage.

Though both works were subject to chronological errors, Sallust's histories were uncommonly balanced. In *Catiline's War* he managed to give his former leader Caesar his due while also praising Caesar's nemeses, Cato the

Younger and Cicero. Sallust showed that, despite mistaken suspicions that Caesar had been an accomplice in Catiline's conspiracy to overthrow the government, Cicero had refused to trump up false evidence against Caesar. Sallust also gave Cicero credit for forcing Catiline to leave Rome by confronting him in a speech in the Senate. Sallust claimed that both Caesar and Cato were "men of striking worth" who possessed "nobility of soul," and that while Caesar was famous for his generosity and mercy, Cato was revered for his morality and austerity. Indeed, Sallust's positive portrayal of Cato and Cicero was both courageous and seditious, considering that he was writing at a time when the triumvirs were castigating the memory of both men. After all, Cato had committed suicide rather than live under Caesar's rule, and Cicero had been executed by Antony. Indeed, Sallust slyly used Caesar against his alleged followers by having him speak against unconstitutional murders in his history. Furthermore, Sallust was as balanced in his treatment of the poor as in his treatment of Cato and Caesar. Though criticizing the poor for their tendency to support "unprincipled characters" like Catiline, Sallust added the empathetic line, "Poverty has nothing to lose."

But Sallust adopted no balanced position on Catiline, whom he portrayed as a bloodthirsty, crafty demagogue with "a vicious and depraved nature." According to Sallust, Catiline gathered around him "all who were in disgrace or afflicted by poverty or consciousness of guilt." He preyed on the young and impressionable, procuring mistresses for them. After killing his own son to please a woman, Catiline's "unclean mind, hating god and fellow man alike, could find rest neither waking nor asleep, so cruelly did remorse torture his frenzied soul." He kept his cohorts at work, doing evil: "Rather than allow his pupils to lose their skill or nerve through lack of practice, he would have them commit needless outrages." Yet, not trusting popular stories to the effect that Catiline had killed his own brother and married his own daughter, Sallust left these rumors out of his own account.

Nor was Sallust kind to Catiline's followers. He wrote of Sempronia, a highly educated and intelligent woman who served as one of Catiline's chief lieutenants: "There was nothing that she set smaller value on than seemliness and chastity, and she was as careless of her reputation as she was of her money. Her passions were so ardent that she more often made advances at men than they did at her." Yet Sallust added, "She could write poetry, crack a joke . . . she was in fact a woman of ready wit and considerable charm."

Sallust was one of the first historians to address the eternal question of republicanism: what is the proper balance between security and liberty? In a remarkably evenhanded fashion, Sallust presented the senate debate between Cato the Younger and Julius Caesar concerning what to do with some captured coconspirators of Catiline. The coconspirators had revealed Catiline's plan to use acts of terror in Rome (widespread arson and the assassination of senators) to wreak havoc in the city in order to soften it for conquest by his rebel army. Departing from his usual role as the spokesman for the Roman legal tradition, Cato spoke for security, emphasizing that no one knew how many other terrorists remained at large in the city. To merely hold the captured coconspirators in a makeshift jail was to invite attempts by their colleagues to free them and begin their reign of terror: "Other crimes can be punished when they have been committed; but with a crime like this, unless you take measures to prevent its being committed, it is too late. . . . Catiline and his army are ready to grip us by the throat, and there are foes within the walls, in the very heart of our city." Therefore, Cato argued that the terrorists, as confessed plotters of murder and arson, should be killed immediately, just as though they had been caught in the act.

Ironically in light of later events, Caesar was the spokesman for liberty and law on this occasion. While he expressed nothing but contempt for the coconspirators, claiming that "any torture would be less than these men's crimes deserve," he reminded the Senate that they were Roman citizens and, hence, possessed the right to a trial by jury. Therefore, they should be held until trial. The Senate voted a recommendation of execution to the consul Cicero, who carried it out on his own authority.

The eloquent and dramatic speeches of both Cato and Caesar were prophetic. Cato predicted correctly that the immediate execution of the coconspirators would take the wind out of Catiline's sails, leading to desertions from his rebel army. But Caesar predicted correctly that once the danger had passed, many Romans would blame the government for its unconstitutional action: "Most people remember only what happens last; when criminals are brought to justice, they forget their guilt and talk only of their punishment, if it is of unusual severity." Indeed, Cicero paid the price of a temporary exile for his unconstitutional action. In this age of terrorism and prison camps for suspected terrorists, Sallust's straightforward but powerful account of the senate deliberation regarding the proper balance between security and liberty seems as up-to-date as the morning newspaper.

Sallust's treatment of the Jugurthine War was also fairly balanced. He gave ample credit for the defeat of Jugurtha to the aristocratic generals Metellus and Sulla, though he despised the latter for his later atrocities and though he correctly noted that it was the popular general Marius whose energetic policy of pressing Jugurtha at all points brought the war to a successful conclusion by leaving Jugurtha no refuge except the treacherous Bocchus, who turned him over to the Romans. Nor did he depict Marius as faultless. On the contrary, he portrayed Marius conspiring against his commander Metellus and violating custom by enrolling men without property into the army, one of the first steps that led to the fall of the republic, since such soldiers were more likely to be loyal to the commander than to the republic. Nevertheless, Sallust was overly harsh in attributing the Senate's slowness to deal with the threat posed by Jugurtha exclusively to bribery, dismissing the consideration that the German threat to the north caused some senators to oppose sending too many soldiers southward, and Sallust failed to note the self-interested nature of equestrian calls for war in Africa. (Equestrians often benefited from war contracts.)

It was Sallust, in *The Jugurthine War*, who popularized the theory of the "Punic Curse," the belief that the fall of the Roman republic had been caused by unprecedented wealth that had resulted from Rome's defeat of its nemesis, Carthage. Sallust wrote: "To the men who had so easily endured toil and peril, anxiety and adversity, the leisure and riches which are generally regarded as so desirable proved a burden and a curse. Growing love of money, and the lust for power which followed it, engendered every kind of evil. . . . Nothing [was] too sacred to sell. . . . When the disease had spread like a plague, Rome changed: her government, once so just and admirable, became harsh and unendurable. . . . Rome was like a sewer." The aristocratic class lost the virtues that had made their ancestors aristocrats in the first place. Sallust claimed that love of money "knows no bounds and can never be satisfied: he that has not wants, and he that has wants more." It was Sallust who put into the mouth of Jugurtha the famous line about Rome: "Easy to be bought if there were but a purchaser." Of early Romans, Sallust wrote: "When they conquered a foe, they took nothing from him save his power to harm. But their base successors stuck at no crime to rob subject peoples of all that those brave conquerors had left them, as though oppression were the only possible method of ruling an empire." Sallust's condemnation of province looters is especially ironic considering his own behavior in North Africa. But this theme had apparently grown so popular as to be employed by all factions: in Sallust's account, even Catiline, whom Sallust presents as the very personification of vice produced by luxury, tells his followers that they will prevail because it is their opponents who have been softened by luxury.

Taking Thucydides and Cato the Elder as his rhetorical models, Sallust adopted a style that was concise, austere, dramatic, passionate, vigorous, and majestic. Like Thucydides, his tone was somber and disillusioned, the natural effect of writing about the decline of their respective republics from positions of political exile. Like Thucydides also, Sallust crafted a unique verbal style involving the use of archaic or invented words. Like Thucydides, he emphasized natural causes almost completely to the exclusion of the supernatural, generally avoiding the catalog of dreams, omens, and other supernatural portents that fill the works of most Roman historians. Indeed, his exclusion of the supernatural has led some to speculate that he was an Epicurean, a theory made more plausible by his inclusion of an exchange between Caesar (representing the Epicurean position) and Cato (representing the Stoic position) on the existence of an afterlife, a discourse that would seem out of place in a debate about what to do with captured conspirators.

Sallust's moralistic prose earned him tremendous popularity both in his own day and in the medieval and modern eras that followed. His epigrammatic style influenced Tacitus and several of the early Church Fathers, including Jerome and Augustine. His work also influenced Virgil, whose shield of Aeneas depicted Catiline suffering eternal torment and Cato among the blessed. (That the shield failed to reveal Caesar's eternal fate should have been no surprise; the Senate had already deified the man its members had murdered, in spite of that man's disbelief in an afterlife, and perhaps Virgil did not wish to rush in where the Senate had already treaded.)

Livy (ca. 59 B.C.–17 A.D.)

One of the greatest of the Roman historians, Livy (Titus Livius) wrote the *History of Rome* over a period of about forty years, beginning in 26 B.C. A prose epic of 142 books (a classical book was roughly equivalent to one of our chapters), the *History* charted the Roman past from the foundation of Rome to 9 B.C. Unfortunately, only thirty-five of these books survive, none of which cover the period after 167 B.C. Legend claimed that Livy's history was so popular in his own day that a man walked from Gades (Cadiz) in Spain to Rome just to meet the historian. One of Livy's harshest critics claimed that the pilgrim died of his disappointment.

Livy's *History* was extremely patriotic. He boasted, "If any nation deserves the privilege of claiming a divine ancestry that nation is our own." Indeed, while Polybius had attributed Rome's success largely to its mixed government, Livy attributed it mostly to its traditional values. He wrote, "I hope my passion for Rome's past has not impaired by judgment; for I do honestly believe that no country has ever been greater or purer than ours or richer in good citizens and noble deeds; none has been free for so many centuries from the vices of avarice and luxury; nowhere have thrift and plain living been for so long held in such esteem." He insisted that the Romans of Alexander the Great's day could have defeated the Macedonian in battle since their own generals had been just as good, their soldiers and javelins superior.

Though Livy's patriotism was generally sober, restrained, and tempered by a willingness to praise virtuous non-Romans and to condemn vicious Romans, it occasionally burst forth in peculiar claims. For instance, he wrote, "No other race has been more gentle in its punishments," a statement made at a time of crucifixion. Similarly, Livy betrays no hint of irony when he records the sentiments expressed by Greeks after Flaminius announced the Roman intention to leave them their freedom after the Battle of Cynoscephalae in 197 B.C., "There was upon the earth a race which waged war at its own expense, toil, and danger for the freedom of others," sentiments invalidated by the Roman conquest of Greece and the burning of Corinth in the following decades.

Though not blind to Roman faults, Livy tended to ascribe them to individuals rather than to Rome itself. He also tended to engage in ethnic stereotyping: the Carthaginians were cruel and treacherous, the Numidians oversexed, the Gauls lazy, the Greeks verbose and immoderate, the Samnites fierce, and the Sabines incorruptible.

Livy's belief that Rome had been fated by Fortuna, the Roman equivalent of Polybius' Tyche, to conquer the world and establish the pax Romana was a direct product of Stoicism. Like many Stoics, Livy believed in the gods but saw them as subordinate to "fate, by whose law the unchangeable order of human affairs is arranged," a universal force to which all beings must submit. He validated traditional Roman beliefs in omens, dreams, and augury by depicting them as ways in which the fated future could be foreseen to a limited extent. Livy's first ten books suggested that Rome had to undergo a protracted military and civic testing at the hands of Fortuna in order to become physically and morally capable of world rule. In fact, Livy was more Stoic than Polybius, eschewing Polybius' occasional portrayals of Tyche as capricious and vindictive and offering instead a Fortuna that consistently rewarded virtue and punished vice. As Livy put it, "I ask that each individual should keenly direct his glance at the kind of lives and manners of ancient times, and observe through what men and by what attributes in war and at home the empire was acquired and increased."

Although those parts of the *History* that concern Livy's own time have been lost, he made it clear in other passages that, although he admired the republican age above all, he was grateful to Augustus for restoring peace and order. (In Augustan Rome praise for the republic was not only permissible but encouraged, since Augustus claimed to have restored it.) Though Livy called the Senate "the fountain-head of true government," he also wrote, "Augustus Caesar brought peace to the world by land and sea."

Yet Livy was no sycophant. He criticized Caesar, Augustus' granduncle and adoptive father, and praised Caesar's rival Pompey and his assassins Brutus and Cassius.

Livy shared Augustus' religious and moral concerns. He wrote: "The might of an imperial people is beginning to work its own ruin. . . . Of late years, wealth has made us greedy, and self-indulgence has brought us, through every form of sensual excess, to be, if I may so put it, in love with death both individual and collective." (In modern times Pope John Paul II referred to the prosperous, modern West as a society "in love with death." Did he borrow the phrase from Livy?) Livy referred to "the sinking of the foundations of morality as the old teaching was allowed to lapse, then the final collapse of the whole edifice, and the dark dawning of our modern day when we can neither endure our vices nor face the remedies needed to cure them." In fact, it is more likely that Livy's popular writings on the piety and virtue of the early Romans influenced Augustus' religious and moral reforms than the reverse.

Livy tended to exaggerate both the morality of early Romans and the immorality of his own day. He asked, "Where nowadays could you find in a single person the moderation, the fairness, the magnanimity which then possessed the whole community?" He tended to overlook his Roman heroes' faults, as reported by Polybius and his other sources.

It has been aptly noted that the real heroes of Livy's history are piety, fidelity, integrity, harmony, self-discipline, obedience, prudence, reason, mercy, chastity, courage, dignity, and frugality. Indeed, Livy's whole conception of the purpose of history was moralistic: "The study of history is the best medicine for a sick mind; for in history you have a record of the infinite variety of human experience plainly set out for all to see; and in that record you can find for yourself and your country both examples and warnings, fine things to take as models, base things, rotten through and through, to avoid." Livy's upbringing in Patavium (Padua), a country town known for its conservatism and moral rectitude, no doubt influenced his judgment.

Livy had several deficiencies as a historian. Because he lacked most classical historians' experience as a soldier, statesman, and traveler, his understanding of military tactics, partisan politics, and geography was limited at best. When confused by dissimilar accounts of the same battle, he sometimes made the mistake of portraying them as separate battles. He generally preferred to read the works of other historians than to consult original documents, though this was somewhat understandable given the scattered nature of Roman priestly, senatorial, and family records and the enormity of his undertaking. By its very nature, his comprehensive history of Rome was bound to be more of a synthesis than a work of original research.

Indeed, given the vastness of his forty-year task, Livy generally achieved a commendable degree of accuracy. Most modern historians have judged Livy's work solid and dependable, aside from the first ten books, which began with Aeneas and which were, by Livy's own admission, more mythological than historical. Even in these early books he not only related legends but also presented naturalistic interpretations of them and used both propatrician and proplebeian sources, thereby giving his crucial and indispensable account of the rise of the Roman republic a rare balance. Though his view of the Senate was somewhat idealized, he provided posterity with useful information on its workings.

Livy wrote with astonishing skill and charm, in a style famously fluent and colorful. His style, especially in relating speeches, was largely Ciceronian, not Sallustian, confining archaisms to the orations of early Romans. Livy's speeches, which often concluded with emotional appeals to past Roman examples of whatever behavior was sought, were so popular that later Romans separated them from the rest of his text and studied them as oratorical models. (True, Livy's love of rhetoric sometimes caused him to add lengthy speeches where they were inappropriate, such as in one passage in which a commander gives a long address to his soldiers before leading a surprise attack on an adjacent hill.) The rhythm of Livy's prose (especially in the early, more mythological books) sometimes resembled that of the dactylic hexameter, and he employed other poetic effects, such as repetition and alliteration of key words, contrasting clauses of equal syllables, and the juxtaposition of words possessing similar sounds but dissimilar meanings.

Eschewing Polybius' deliberately dry, analytical style, Livy successfully conveyed the dramatic qualities of past events without descending into melodrama. Despite Livy's reputation as a romantic, he was quite willing to depict the barbarism of war along with its glory, as when he related the story of a Numidian dragged from beneath a dead Roman the day after the battle at Cannae; the Numidian was still alive, but his ears and nose had been gnawed beyond recognition by the Roman, who had been unable to grasp his weapon but had stubbornly refused to quit fighting before death.

Much of the power of Livy's narrative stems from the keenness of his psychological insight. In fact, his deficiencies as a relater of battlefield tactics are as much the result of his psychological and moral focus as of his lack of military experience. He often depicted battles from the viewpoint of the defeated, showing great sympathy for them. Livy's emphasis on morality, which might have been oppressive had he expressed it principally through overt preaching, acquired great charm when expressed through the contrasting speech and actions of his subjects and the responses of their contemporaries.

Livy acquired fame and adulation throughout the ages because he conveyed eloquently the ideal of Rome. The fact that reality fell short of this ideal (as reality invariably falls short of all ideals) did not detract from its beauty and power. As the historian R. H. Barrow once put it: "[In Livy] Rome is the heroine inspiring Romans to heroic deeds to fulfill her destiny. Virgil and Livy perfected the language for showing the Roman at his noblest in action and character." To the considerable extent that Livy inspired future generations of both Romans and non-Romans with this powerful ideal, he himself became a historical actor on a par with the heroes he presented. Furthermore, he powerfully influenced the style of historical prose writing well into the nineteenth century.

Tacitus (ca. A.D. 56–120)

Considered by many the greatest of all the Roman historians in both style and substance, Tacitus (Publius Cornelius Tacitus) was also the most fervent in denunciation of the emperors. An eques from thoroughly Romanized southern France, Tacitus served as a quaestor under Titus, as a praetor under Domitian, and as consul and governor of the province of Asia (in western Asia Minor) under Trajan.

Tacitus' *Agricola* (ca. A.D. 98) was an eloquent account of the life and military career of his father-in-law Gnaeus Julius Agricola. More than a typical eulogy, it contained common elements of Roman historical writing, including speeches and an ethnographic account of Britain, where Agricola had won many battles.

Tacitus insinuated that Agricola had been poisoned by a jealous and paranoid Domitian, the first of Tacitus' many judgments against the emperors that have been questioned by some modern historians. Tacitus referred to the age of Domitian as "savage and hostile to merit," since the emperor removed anyone whose merit might make him a rival. Tacitus contended: "Rome of old explored the utmost limits of freedom; we have plumbed the depths of slavery, robbed as we are by informers even of the right to exchange ideas in conversation. . . . Think of it. Fifteen whole years [under Domitian]—no small part of a man's life—taken from us. . . . The few of us that survive are no longer what we once were, since so many of our best years have been taken from us. . . . The worst of our torments under Domitian was to see him with his eyes fixed upon us. Every sigh was registered against us."

Yet Tacitus was grateful for the freedom of speech he possessed under the emperors Nerva and Trajan. He wrote: "Now at long last our spirit revives. In the first dawn of this blessed age, Nerva harmonized the old discord between autocracy and freedom; day by day Trajan is enhancing the happiness of our times. . . . Modern times are indeed happy, as few others have been, for we can think as we please, and speak as we think." Nevertheless, pessimistic by nature as well as by experience, Tacitus added, "Cure operates more slowly than disease."

Tacitus' closing encomium to the just and humble Agricola remains one of the greatest in history. He wrote:

> Your daughter and I have suffered more than the pang of a father's loss: we grieve that we could not sit by your sick-bed, sustain your failing strength,

and satisfy our yearning for your fond looks and embraces. We should surely have received some last commands, some words to be engraved forever on our hearts. It was our own special sorrow and pain that through the accident of our long absence we lost you four years before your death. All, more than all, dear father, was assuredly done to honor you by the devoted wife at your side. Yet some tears that should have been shed over you were not shed; and, at the last, there was something for which your dying eyes looked in vain.

If there is any mansion for the spirits of the just, if, as philosophers hold, great souls do not perish with the body, may you rest in peace. May you call us, your family, from feeble regrets and unmanly mourning to contemplate your virtues, for which it were a sin to mourn or lament. May we honor you in better ways—by our admiration and our praise, and if our powers permit, by following your example. That is the true honor, the true affection of souls knit close to yours. To your daughter and widow I would suggest that they revere the memory of a father and a husband by continually pondering his deeds and sayings, and by treasuring in their hearts the form and features of his mind, rather than those of his body. Not that I would forbid likenesses of marble or of bronze. But representations of the human face, like that face itself, are subject to decay and dissolution, whereas the essence of man's mind is something everlasting, which you cannot preserve or express in material wrought by another's skill, but only in your own character. All that we loved and admired in Agricola abides and shall abide in the hearts of men through the endless procession of the ages; for his achievements are of great renown. With many it will be as with men who had no name or fame: they will be buried in oblivion. But Agricola's story is set on record for posterity, and he will live.

This was a self-fulfilling prophecy, for Agricola's memory lives almost exclusively through his son-in-law's powerful eulogy. Indeed, through it Tacitus won immortality not only for his beloved father-in-law but for himself as well.

In Tacitus' *Germania* (ca. A.D. 98), the only purely ethnographic study that survives from antiquity, his discussion of the frugality, chastity, and love of freedom he perceived among the primitive Germanic tribes of western Europe constituted an implicit attack on the corruption of imperial Rome. He wrote concerning the Germans: "They live uncorrupted by the temptations of public shows or the excitements of banquets. . . . No one in Germany finds vice amusing, or calls it 'up-to-date' to seduce and be seduced. . . . Good morality is more effective in Germany than good laws are elsewhere." For instance, the Suebians, unlike the foppish youth of imperial Rome, decked themselves out for battle, not seduction. German mothers nursed their own babies; they did not hand them over to servants as Roman aristocrats did.

Tacitus equated the Germans with the early Romans. Yet Tacitus did not shrink from criticizing German drunkenness and quarrelsomeness, and his later references to the Germans were less positive.

Many modern republicans, both in Britain and in the United States, cited Tacitus' *Germania* as proof that the Anglo-Saxons who later settled England had possessed a republican form of government. Unfortunately, Tacitus had misunderstood the Germanic tribes' political systems, presenting them as far more republican than they actually were. The *Germania* also fanned the flames of German nationalism in the nineteenth and twentieth centuries, establishing Herman, the destroyer of Varus' army at the Teutoburg Forest, as the prototypical German hero.

Nevertheless, Tacitus showed great foresight in perceiving the Germanic tribes as a potential threat to Rome. His *Germania* shed some rare light on the tribes that were to destroy the empire three centuries later.

In Tacitus' masterpieces, the *Annals of Rome* (ca. 117), a haunting, tortured history of Rome from the death of Augustus to that of Nero (A.D. 14–68), and the *Histories* (ca. 108), the history of Rome from the death of Nero to that of Domitian (A.D. 69–96), only one-third of which survives, Tacitus vividly depicted the degeneration of Roman morals, which he believed had begun in the late republican period and had accelerated under the emperors. Tacitus contended, "Traditional morality, gradually slipping away, was entirely undermined by imported luxury so that whatever corrupts or can be corrupted would be seen in Rome, and foreign taste would reduce our youth to a bunch of gymnasts, loafers, and perverts." Roman moral decline had produced the emperors, who had, in turn, degraded morality further.

Tacitus identified the emperors' corruption of language as their greatest contribution to moral decline. Cicero and the other heroes of the republic had used rhetoric for the public good, to persuade their fellow citizens to adopt wise measures. But under the empire, old republican labels were used to camouflage new autocratic realities and traditional rhetorical methods were prostituted to flatter emperors, to condemn innocent people to death for the sake of tyrants or personal vendettas, and to rationalize imperial incest. Tacitus wrote: "The greatest figures had to protect their positions by subservience; and, in addition to them, all ex-consuls, most ex-praetors, even many junior senators competed with one another's offensively sycophantic proposals. There is a tradition that whenever Tiberius left the senate-house he exclaimed in Greek, 'Men fit to be slaves!' Even he, freedom's enemy, became impatient of such abject servility."

Parts of Tacitus' *Annals* bear an eerie resemblance to George Orwell's famous novel *1984*, in which history is continually rewritten to coincide with the government's latest policy. By the end of Tiberius' reign, it had become a capital crime to have been a friend of Sejanus, the former leader of the Prae-torian Guard and Tiberius' own former companion, who had been executed for conspiring against the emperor. Those charged with this crime of friend-ship with Sejanus wrote pathetic letters to the emperor asking how they could be found guilty of treason against the emperor for mirroring the emperor's own conduct. Autocracy bred such absurdities, Tacitus seemed to suggest. The ultimate end was the silence of a police state. Tacitus wrote concerning the height of Tiberius' treason trials: "Never had there been more anxiety and terror in Rome. People were secretive to their own families, and they avoided meetings, conversations, and the ears of friends and strangers alike; even the inanimate walls and ceiling were looked on with suspicion." Such paranoia was not entirely irrational since paid informers sometimes hid behind walls with writing implements to record subversive statements and even family members betrayed one another to collect imperial rewards.

Following in the stylistic tradition of Sallust while discarding his archa-isms, Tacitus' style was somber, concise, and caustic. While eschewing the rotund periods of Cicero as unsuited to his own era and topic, he also rejected Seneca's colloquialisms as lacking the dignity and dramatic power requisite in historical writing. His descriptions were vivid, his command of language impressive. Taking full advantage of the remarkable economy of Latin and his own genius at selecting the precisely appropriate word, he composed sen-tences that are impossible to translate into English with equal concision. It was a style that assumed and rewarded the intelligent and careful reader.

Tacitus was a master of irony and the deflating postscript. His humor was dark. Following Tacitus' report of Otho's and Vitellius' mutual accusations of debauchery, we find the typical Tacitean line: "Neither was lying." After Sen-eca ends a conversation with Nero by thanking him, Tacitus quips, "So end all conversations with tyrants." Tacitus loved contrasts: the virtue of Germanicus versus the vice of Tiberius and the idyllic setting of Capri versus the terrible depravity Tiberius practiced there, for instance. When presented with varying accounts of the emperors' motivations and behavior, he almost always stated the more sinister account last, so that it lingered in the mind of the reader.

Despite Tacitus' expressions of contempt for the theater, his books often began and ended like the acts of a play. He used rumors as a kind of Greek chorus to comment on events, and he sought to inspire pity and fear like the ancient tragedians.

So impressive were Tacitus' plot devices and quips that they were copied for centuries. Shakespeare lifted the device of having Henry V walking among his men in disguise to determine their mood on the eve of the Battle of Agincourt from Tacitus' account of Germanicus. Tacitus' comment that British chieftains "fight separately and are conquered together" inspired Benjamin Franklin to remark to his colleagues on July 4, 1776, "We must all hang together, or, most assuredly, we shall all hang separately." Lord John Russell derived the phrase "conspicuous by its absence" from Tacitus' statement regarding the shockingly absent effigies of Brutus and Cassius at a family funeral, "But Brutus and Cassius were most conspicuous precisely because their portraits were not seen." (Family members, terrified by the prospect of Tiberius' wrath if they displayed effigies of the tyrant killers, violated the most sacred of Roman traditions in failing to display images of their most prominent ancestors.)

Tacitus sifted through eyewitness accounts and consulted a wide range of primary and secondary sources. The former category included senate records, speeches, letters, and memoirs. He often cited his sources for specific information. His methodology was impeccable: "When the sources are unanimous, I will follow them; when they provide different versions, I will record them with attribution." The degree of detail he provided concerning the reign of Tiberius and the Civil Wars of 68–69 was unique. He was more accurate than Livy (though imperfect) concerning chronology, geography, and military tactics; modern archaeology, where applicable, has generally supported his conclusions.

Underlying Tacitus' meticulous attention to detail was a sense of the malevolence of destiny, a theme reinforced by his serious treatment of divine omens, rewards, and wrath. Though Tacitus expressed some skepticism about omens, he consistently followed Roman historical tradition by including them, and not just for dramatic purposes; a flurry of dark omens almost always precedes disaster in Tacitus' histories. He wrote, "The gods are indifferent to our tranquility, but eager for our punishment," and referred to "heaven's impartiality between good and evil." Tacitus seemed to embrace Stoic fatalism but without the Stoic belief in Fate's benevolence. He recognized that his history was a far cry from Livy's: "My chronicle is quite a different matter from histories of early Rome." While such accounts spoke of great heroes, "Mine, on the other hand, is a circumscribed, inglorious field. . . . My themes concern cruel rulers, unremitting accusations, treacherous friendships, innocent men ruined—a conspicuously monotonous glut of downfalls and their monotonous causes. . . . This torrent of wasted bloodshed far from active service, wearies, depresses, and paralyzes the mind."

Yet, however dark, Tacitus' passionate portrayal of tyranny was anything but monotonous. His flexible mind could surprise the reader on occasion, as when he wrote, "Everything was not better in the past; our own age has also produced many examples of honor and virtue that deserve future imitation." Tacitus was quite willing to present these examples in his histories. The difference between his world and Livy's was that in Livy's, courageous acts produced positive consequences for Rome, whereas in Tacitus', such actions, however admirable and worthy of relation, were ultimately futile.

Although the most common criticism of Tacitus is that his treatment of Tiberius was excessively harsh, the facts largely confirm his analysis. It is certainly true that some of Tacitus' snide remarks and dark suspicions—perhaps the result of his hatred of Domitian, who had emulated Tiberius' reliance on a system of paid informers and who had read Tiberius' journals as a pastime—were unwarranted. Particularly pernicious was Tacitus' habit of introducing vile rumors, only to discount them, like a prosecutor who lets slip innuendo against the defendant, knowing that the judge will rule it inadmissible but the jurors will be unable to forget it. Indeed, Tacitus had been a highly successful attorney.

But it is also true that the contemporary historian Suetonius, who is generally considered to have been more dispassionate than Tacitus, not only corroborated many of Tacitus' allegations against Tiberius but added lurid tales of his own. He not only joined Tacitus in implicating Tiberius in numerous murders but also went into greater detail concerning the emperor's molestation of both children and adults and, unlike Tacitus, attributed the emperor's atrocities to an absolute "lust for seeing people suffer." Suetonius wrote: "A detailed list of Tiberius' barbarities would take a long time to compile. . . . Not a day, however holy, passed without an execution. . . . An informer's word was always believed. Every crime became a capital one, even the utterance of a few careless words." Suetonius emphasized that Tiberius' numerous victims included women and children. This suggests that the number of trials exceeded those noted by Tacitus, who presented a representative sample of famous victims, not an exhaustive list. The fact that some of the executions occurred at the order of Sejanus, while Tiberius lived in self-imposed exile at Capri, does not exonerate the emperor, since the treason trials started a full decade before Sejanus' administration of the empire, since Tiberius certainly knew Sejanus' character when he abdicated his own responsibility and relinquished the empire to him, and since Tiberius fully supported the system of informers that drove the treason trials. In fact, Tiberius' cowardly decision to live in seclusion for over a decade on an unusually defensible island was itself a product of the very paranoia that inspired the executions—executions that only accelerated after Sejanus' death. As Suetonius wrote regarding Tiberius, "With Sejanus out of the way, his savageries increased, which proved that Sejanus had not, as some thought, been inciting him to commit them, but merely provided the opportunities that he demanded." In reality, what most distinguishes Tacitus' account from Suetonius' is that Tacitus includes fairly lengthy discussions of Tiberius' virtues—his financial generosity, his concern for the provinces, his rejection of flattery, and his refusal to be worshipped as a god—so that a rather complex, tragic portrait of the emperor emerges from the *Annals*.

In short, based on the available evidence, one must conclude that Tacitus was far closer to the truth concerning Tiberius than some of Tacitus' modern critics. While Tacitus can be faulted for failing to fulfill his promise to avoid writing "with indignation," the real fault lies in the promise rather than in his inability to fulfill it, since some facts demand indignation from any moral being—or perhaps it lies in our interpretation of the phrase "without indignation," which Tacitus may have intended to mean simply that he would refrain from the use of invective, a rhetorical device that was common in the orations of his day.

From a modern point of view, Tacitus' chief flaw as a historian was not his exaggeration of the depravity of the emperors but his single-minded focus on the effect of imperial rule on the senatorial elite. Even the worst emperors largely confined their murders and depredations to the aristocratic class of the city of Rome, from whose ambition they had most to fear. It was precisely for this reason that aristocratic historians like Tacitus so despised the emperors, whom he also criticized for elevating freedmen and others he regarded as inferiors to high positions he considered reserved for his own class and for other measures that modern historians now celebrate as social reforms. The ordinary provincial saw little difference between the administrations of a "good emperor" and a "bad emperor," since the imperial system remained largely the same regardless of who stood at the helm. In short, Tacitus' histories, however brilliantly written and instructive concerning the effects of autocratic rule, were insular accounts directed at a small, urban, aristocratic audience. Although it would be anachronistic to criticize him for a perspective he could not avoid—a definition of history as politics and war that was as old as historical writing itself—it would be equally foolish to pretend that his histories offer a comprehensive account of the early Roman Empire.

Nor can Tacitus' condemnation of the worst emperors be confused with a denunciation of the imperial system. Although Tacitus' heart was republican, his mind told him that the Rome of his day could not avoid monarchy. On the one hand, he believed that the republican era had been a more heroic age involving great wars of expansion that had made Romans rugged and self-disciplined. On the other hand, he claimed that by the late republic, "morality and law were nonexistent, criminality went unpunished, [and] decency was often fatal." He also contended that mixed government theory, the central theory on which the republic was based, was a fiction: "A mixture of the three [forms of government] is easier to applaud than to achieve, and besides, even when achieved, it cannot last long."

Consequently, Tacitus believed that autocracy had become a necessary evil, so that the most prudent and virtuous course of action lay in the middle ground between futile rebellion against the tyrant and complicity in his crimes ("a path . . . between abrasive obstinacy and disgusting groveling"). His heroes were men who quietly devoted themselves to their public duties and maintained their own morality even under the worst tyrants. Since this was also a description of Tacitus himself under Domitian, there was more than a hint of defensiveness in his remarks. Tacitus wrote in the *Agricola*: "Let all those whose habit is to admire acts of civil disobedience realize that great men can exist even under bad emperors, and that compliance and an unassuming demeanor, if backed by energy and hard work, can attain a pitch of glory which the majority reach, without benefiting their country, through an ostentatious and untimely death." Tacitus mingled admiration for the courage of Stoic martyrs like Thrasea and Helvidius with contempt for their stubborn self-righteousness. He considered more laudable men like Agricola, whose endurance and integrity had allowed him to serve Rome honorably without any philosophical grandstanding. Since rebellion against tyrants could not produce a better form of government, given the moral decline of Rome and the resultant impracticality of republican government there, the wisest and most virtuous course for the individual was to wait them out. Tyrants, like storms, came and went, but Rome remained. The individual must serve Rome while avoiding both "perilous insubordination and degrading servility."

The sole glimmer of hope lay in the office of historian. Since rebellion could not produce a better form of government, the proper way to check tyrants was by appealing to their fear of posterity's judgment. Tacitus claimed, "It seems to me a historian's foremost duty to ensure that merit is recorded and to confront evil deeds and words with the fear of posterity's denunciation." In the *Annals* Cremutius Cordius, the historian whose works were burned by Tiberius because they praised Brutus and Cassius, declares, just before leaving the Senate to commit suicide in anticipation of his execution, "If I am condemned, there are those who will recall not only Brutus and Cassius, but me as well." Tacitus follows this with the observation that Cremutius' books were hidden and republished later, causing him to add: "It makes me laugh at the stupidity of those who believe that today's tyranny can also obliterate the memory of a future generation. On the contrary, the suppression of genius increases its authority; kings and those who imitate their cruelty achieve nothing but glory for their victims and their own infamy."

Influenced by Tacitus and the other classical historians, the founders of the United States had the same conception of "History" as judge. While in retirement, Thomas Jefferson wrote: "[I] turn from the contemplation [of King George III and Napoleon] with loathing, and take refuge in the history of other times, where, if they also furnish their Tarquins, their Catilines, and their Caligulas, their stories are handed to us under the brand of a Livy, a Sallust, and a Tacitus, and we are confronted with the reflection that the condemnation of all succeeding generations has confirmed the censures of the historian, and consigned their memories to everlasting infamy, a solace which we cannot have with the Georges and Napoleons but by anticipation." If twenty-first-century people are less sanguine about the deterrent power of "History" as judge, it is because we are no longer certain that tyrants can be deterred by such considerations (they were rarely deterred by the fear of infamy even in Tacitus' day, when a desire for lasting fame was arguably stronger) and because we know that "History" is but the product of subjective historians and, therefore, cannot serve as a judge because it does not speak with a single voice.

Like many of the best Greek and Roman historians before him, Tacitus had the remarkable ability to combine a fervent patriotism with a willingness to explore the arguments of his nation's enemies in a fair-minded manner. Recall that it was Tacitus, the Roman patriot, the same man who glorified the expansionist heroes of the past and who faulted Tiberius for being "uninterested in expanding the empire," who placed in the mouth of the Briton Calgacus the famous criticism of Roman imperialism: "They make a desert and call it peace." He also had a Caledonian chieftain call Scotland "the last inch of liberty" and eulogized Herman as "unmistakably the liberator of Germany." Indeed, Tacitus composed stirring speeches against Roman tyranny not only for Herman, but also for the British Boudicca (a woman), and the Gallic Sacrovir, while portraying most Roman senators as cowardly sycophants of the emperors. (But note that each of these foreign leaders and their tribes were Western; Tacitus possessed a general contempt for easterners and their bizarre religions, and he certainly did not depict the rebellious Jews, or even the more submissive Christians, in a favorable light.) As in the *Germania*, Tacitus' positive depiction of the resisting tribes was, at least in part, a mechanism for demonstrating the shameful condition of the Romans. But it was clearly more than that. Tacitus' love of Rome and appreciation of the benefits of Roman civilization were tempered by regret at the loss of freedom and even virtue they entailed in the conquered territories as well as at home.

Tacitus displayed ambivalence about women as well. On the one hand, he seemed to think that one of imperial Rome's greatest problems was the prominence of women whose desire for political power he termed "masculine" and considered unnatural. He accused Augustus' wife Livia of a long string of poisonings designed to gain the throne for her son Tiberius. Ironically, both Livia and Agrippina the Younger, to whom Tacitus attributed a similar campaign on behalf of her son Nero, were eventually brushed aside by their sons, who were no more inclined to be ruled by women than Tacitus was. Yet, oddly enough, Tacitus also commented, in both instances, that these mothers had somehow acted as checks on the depravity of their respective sons. Even when discussing these allegedly masculine, ambitious, ruthless women, Tacitus could not escape the stereotype of mothers as moderating influences. Tacitus was contemptuous of Claudius, despite his conquest of southern Britain and other achievements, precisely because he was controlled by women, first by the nymphomaniac Messalina and then by his niece-wife, Agrippina the Younger. While Agrippina used sex to gain power, Augustus' daughter, Julia, and Messalina both allowed sexual passion to destroy their power. Regarding the Sitones, a Germanic tribe allegedly ruled by women, Tacitus wrote, "To this extent they have fallen lower not merely than freemen but even than slaves." Yet Tacitus referred affectionately to his own wife at the time of their betrothal as "already a girl of great promise" and added regarding the success of a husband, "A good wife deserves more than half the praise, just as a bad one deserves more than half the blame."

After a long period in which Tacitus' works were neglected, Niccolò Machiavelli, Francesco Guicciardini, and other Italians revived interest in him during the Renaissance. His perceived antimonarchical fervor, moralistic tone, and remarkable eloquence earned him the admiration of most modern republicans, who faced the revival of absolutism in seventeenth-century Europe. John Milton, who gave Satan characteristics of Tiberius in *Paradise Lost*, called Tacitus "of all others the greatest Enemy of tyrants." Francis Bacon admired his moral instruction, Michel de Montaigne his political analysis. Bacon also popularized an epigrammatic style of English based on Tacitus' Latin. Thomas Jefferson called Tacitus "the strongest writer in the world." Baron Charles de Montesquieu wrote, "Tacitus summarized everything because he saw everything." In his vastly influential book *The Spirit of the Laws* (1748) Montesquieu cited Tacitus more than any other author. Jean-Jacques Rousseau and Denis Diderot translated him into French, and he was cited frequently in the *Encyclopedia*. Diderot wrote, "Of all the Latin writers it is he whom intellectuals esteem most highly." Madame Roland read the *Annals* while awaiting the guillotine and remarked ruefully that the reign of Tiberius and his informers had returned.

Tacitus influenced historians and philosophers of history even more profoundly. The influential eighteenth-century philosopher of history Giambattista Vico cited Tacitus over sixty times in his *New Science*. Vico wrote, "With an incomparable metaphysical mind, Tacitus contemplates man as he is, Plato as he should be." Edward Gibbon called Tacitus "the most philosophical of historians." Although Gibbon generally displayed a more luxuriant style, he praised Tacitus' "expressive conciseness" and attempted to copy it on occasion. He gave Tacitus the greatest compliment one historian can give another when he started his *Decline and Fall of the Roman Empire* where Tacitus had left off. (Perhaps the only compliment Tacitus would have relished more was the rage of Napoleon, that worshiper and imitator of the Roman emperors, who once shouted, "Tacitus!? Don't speak to me about that pamphleteer! He has slandered the emperors!" Or perhaps the compliment of being banned from eastern Europe by communist regimes that sensed danger in his prescient discussions of tyranny and corruption.) The philosopher and historian David Hume called Tacitus "a penetrating genius." Thomas Macaulay wrote, "In the delineation of character, Tacitus is unrivaled among historians, and has few superiors among dramatists and novelists."

While English Puritans praised the *Annals*, comparing the Stuarts to the Julio-Claudians, the Catholic Thomas More's *History of Richard III* portrayed Richard as a latter-day Tiberius, in the process influencing Shakespeare's portrayal of Richard. Shakespeare acted in Ben Jonson's *Sejanus* (1603), which was also based heavily on the *Annals*, as was Jean Racine's play *Britannicus* and, three centuries later, Robert Graves' best-selling historical novel *I, Claudius*.

Suetonius (ca. A.D. 69–130)

After serving as the director of the imperial library under Trajan and as Hadrian's secretary until he was dismissed for improper behavior with the empress, Suetonius (Gaius Suetonius Tranquillus) of Hippo Regius (Annaba, Algeria) wrote *The Lives of the Caesars* (ca. A.D. 121), a collection of biographies of Julius Caesar and the Julio-Claudian and Flavian emperors. Because Suetonius loved anecdotes, his work is a mine of information on the early Roman emperors, especially those, like Caligula, Titus, and Domitian, whose reigns are absent from the surviving portions of Tacitus' histories.

Lacking Tacitus' moralistic focus, Suetonius provided information regarding the physical peculiarities of the emperors (baldness, acne, warts, body odor, etc.) and concerning their reputed sexual deviancies that Tacitus considered beneath the dignity of a historian to relate. Unlike other ancient biographers, who wrote in chronological order, Suetonius organized his material according to themes, including the characteristics of his subjects. His work was more balanced and varied but less orderly and harmonious than that of Tacitus.

Yet Suetonius could make harsh judgments when warranted. While he wrote that some actions of Nero were "deserving of no small praise," a concession Tacitus did not make in Nero's case, Suetonius also declared, "Although his first acts of wantonness, lust, extravagance, avarice, and cruelty were gradual and secret, and might be condoned as follies of youth, yet even their nature was such that no one doubted that they were defects of his character and not due to his time of life." While Tacitus insinuated that Nero burned Rome but left it an open question, Suetonius stated baldly that Nero "set fire to the city."

Suetonius also wrote *Concerning Illustrious Men,* which consisted of short biographies of literary figures. It is the source of much of what we know about the lives of Virgil and Horace. This departure of biography from politics and war, the traditional subjects of history, was highly unusual.

Until the Renaissance, Suetonius' *Lives of the Caesars* was the principal model for biographies, including Einhard's *Life of Charlemagne.* Suetonius was less popular among modern republicans than Tacitus because his prose was far less dignified, moralistic, and bitter toward the emperors.

CONCLUSION

Although it is often said that the victors write the history, this is true only when the victors write history. Despite the fact that Sparta defeated Athens in the Peloponnesian War, everything we know of Spartan history comes to us from Athenians and other Greeks, because the Spartans did not write history. Similarly, although Germanic tribes conquered the western half of the Roman Empire, what little we know of these tribes and their culture comes to us from a Roman historian named Tacitus. In contrast to the Spartans and Germans, the Romans not only wrote history but wrote it superbly. As a result, they left accounts of themselves and their empire that soon enthralled even their conquerors and their descendants, who made them fixtures of a Western educational system that was later exported to distant continents like North America and Australia.

Until the philhellenic movement of the mid-nineteenth century, Westerners were more apt to read Sallust, Livy, and Tacitus in their original language than Herodotus and Thucydides because the Western educational system emphasized Latin over Greek. From these historians they learned to revere the Roman republic and to condemn the tyranny of the emperors. Westerners' very conception of history as a narrative of political and military affairs written in a dramatic style, whether with the concision and directness of a Sallust or Tacitus or with the floridity of a Livy, derived largely from the Roman historians.

This was especially true of the founders of the United States, whose education consisted largely of Latin and who read these historians in colonial grammar schools and colleges. John Dickinson ended his *Letters from a Pennsylvania Farmer* (1768), the most influential pamphlet of the Revolutionary era, with Memmius' declaration, as recounted by Sallust, "I shall certainly aim at the freedom handed down from my forebears; whether I am successful or not in doing so is in your control, my fellow countrymen." John Adams transcribed sizable passages from *Catiline's War* into his Harvard commonplace book. (Commonplace books were notebooks in which eighteenth-century students copied their favorite passages from literary works.) In 1782 Adams wrote, "My boy should translate Sallust and write to his papa." He wrote to his son John Quincy: "In company with Sallust, Cicero, Tacitus, and Livy you will learn Wisdom and Virtue. You will see them represented with all the Charms which Language and Imagination can exhibit, and Vice and Folly painted in all their Deformity and Horror. You will ever remember that all the End of study is to make you a good Man and a useful Citizen." Benjamin Franklin hoped that the proceedings of the U.S. Congress would "furnish materials for a future Sallust." Having read Livy in the original Latin at age fifteen, Patrick Henry made it a rule to read a translation of the historian through every year. Thomas Jefferson even rebuked his daughter Martha for not keeping up with her Livy, though her gender entitled her to read the Roman historian in Italian translation. Jefferson considered the speeches contained in the works of Sallust, Livy, and Tacitus models of simplicity, rationality, and brevity—the three ideal qualities of republican oratory. He was so immersed in these historians that they profoundly influenced his writing style, helping to produce the clarity and concision that stand as his trademark. James Madison and Benjamin Rush copied extracts from Tacitus' *Annals* into their commonplace books. In short, the Roman historians taught the founders to idealize the Roman republic and to fear autocratic rule. Is it any wonder that the founders constructed the U.S. Capitol (a Roman term in itself) on the Roman model, employed words like "Senate" for some of their governing institutions, and adopted the theory of mixed government, the theory that had allegedly undergirded the glorious Roman republic, as the foundation of their own system of government?

· 8 ·

Comedy and Satire

$\mathscr{L}$ike the Greeks, the Romans wrote comedies for the stage. Plautus and Terence, who improved the Greek New Comedy by lampooning its conventions and enriching its characters, became the Western world's most influential comic playwrights, partly because their plays survived, while most of the Greek comedies did not. The Romans also inaugurated the genre of satire. Written in both poetry and prose, Roman satire influenced the epigram and the novel, two other genres pursued successfully by Roman authors that influenced subsequent Western literature profoundly.

GREEK PRECURSORS ON THE COMIC STAGE

Aristophanes (ca. 450–385 B.C.) and the Old Comedy

Greece's greatest comic playwright, Aristophanes of Athens, satirized everyone—other playwrights, public officials, philosophers, generals, wars, and the people themselves. His approximately forty plays, eleven of which survive, combined poetry, fantasy, buffoonery, indecency, puns, and parody. They traversed a remarkable range, from the most sophisticated humor to the most scatological brand of comedy. His actors wore ludicrous masks and padded clothes, the male characters often displaying exaggerated leather penises. The masks were sometimes caricatures of the famous people he lampooned. Yet his plays often included beautiful and serious verse. While *The Babylonians* (426 B.C.) depicted the cities of the Athenian (Delian) League as slaves grinding at Athens' mill, *Knights* (424 B.C.) portrayed the demagogue Cleon as the slave of the fickle Demos (the people).

The Clouds (423 B.C.), which won third prize at a festival, so ridiculed Socrates that the philosopher later complained at his trial that the play had prejudiced the people against him. (Nevertheless, according to Plato, the playwright and the philosopher remained friends years after the play was produced.) In the play Strepsiades sends his son Pheidipides to Socrates' "thinking shop" to learn how "to win any case, however bad," so that Strepsiades can avoid paying his debts if taken to court. An eccentric Socrates sits suspended in a basket so that he can have "lofty thoughts." He declares that thunder is not caused by the gods, but by the collision of dense clouds—which he compares to the flatulence of a man who has just eaten a large meal. He scoffs at those who believe in the gods. But Strepsiades' plan backfires. Pheidipides learns at Socrates' school that it is acceptable to strike his father. Now shameless, Pheidipides tells the horrified Strepsiades: "It's delightful to be acquainted with the wisdom of today, and to be able to look down on convention. . . . What is law, anyway? It must have been made at some time, and made by a man just like you and me." Furious, Strepsiades burns down Socrates' thinking shop. Aristophanes slandered Socrates in this play, attributing to him the atheism and moral relativism of the more extreme Sophists, with which Socrates strongly disagreed. Aristophanes chose Socrates to represent the sophistry he detested due to Socrates' fame as a philosopher—every Athenian would recognize the name—either not bothering to learn Socrates' actual beliefs, or not caring to present them accurately.

The Wasps (422 B.C.) satirized the epidemic of litigation in Athenian society. The chorus consisted of old, idiotic jurors who carried skewers as their stingers. One character, a son, has to shut his father up in the house, guarded by slaves, to keep him out of the law courts.

Women were as often the butt of Aristophanes' jokes as men, though he displayed an uncommon belief in the intelligence of at least some women. In *Lysistrata* (411 B.C.) the women of Greece take an oath to withhold sex from their husbands until the men agree to end the Peloponnesian War. After the male leader of the chorus coins a famous phrase, "We can't live with you, and we can't live without you," Lysistrata, the leader of the striking women, asks the men, "Is it right that we shall not be allowed to make the least little suggestion to you, no matter how much you mismanage the City's affairs? . . . I am a woman, but I am not brainless." The wise Lysistrata soon has the Athenian and Spartan ambassadors compromising—marking out the geographical territory they want, using a nude female as their map, and singing songs about the Persian Wars, when Athenians and Spartans had fought together to save Greece. *Thesmophoriazusae* (411 B.C.) concerns women who hatch a plot against the playwright Euripides because of his alleged misogyny, a vehicle that allows Aristophanes to ridicule the tragedian.

Indeed, even death could not shield Euripides from Aristophanes' barbs. In *The Frogs* (405 B.C.) the god Dionysus, patron of drama, descends into Hades determined to set Athenian theater back on track by returning with whomever he determines to be the greatest tragedian. Sophocles is too peaceable to participate in a contest, so Aeschylus and Euripides are left to vie with each other for the honor by ridiculing each other's lines. Aeschylus wins the contest.

In the whimsical *Assemblywomen* (393 B.C.) the Athenians decide to turn the government over to women, who institute socialism. In *Wealth* (388 B.C.), Wealth is blind and gives his benefits to the wrong people. As a result, Chremylus consults the oracle at Delphi to learn how he can turn his son into "a scoundrel, wicked, rotten through and through," so that the poor youth can achieve success in Athens. Apollo then shows Wealth that the god Asclepius can cure blindness. When Wealth regains his eyesight, a rich woman loses her gigolo, who now has his own money. Wealth is then enthroned in his home of the good old days, the Athenian treasury.

Combining a love of solid, old-fashioned, country people with a remarkable energy and exuberance, Aristophanes displayed a rare humanity and an irresistible charm. At a party that served as the setting for Plato's *Symposium*, Aristophanes explained the origin of romantic love with the following fable. There once were hermaphroditic creatures that had two heads, four arms, and four legs. The gods feared them but wanted their sacrifices, so Zeus cleaved them in two with bolts of lightning. Aristophanes explained: "When the original body was cut through, each half wanted the other and hugged it; they threw their arms around each other, desiring to grow together in the embrace. . . . So you see how ancient is the mutual love implanted in mankind, bringing together the parts of the original body, and trying to make one out of two, and to heal the natural structure of man. . . . Each one seeks his other half. . . . The way to make our race happy is to make love perfect, and each to get his very own beloved and go back to our original nature."

Fortunately for Aristophanes, there were no libel laws in Athens. Enraged when *The Babylonians* was performed before an audience containing foreign dignitaries, Cleon prosecuted the young playwright for slandering the city in the presence of foreigners. But no one could touch the clown prince of Athens. The next year he returned with an even harsher attack on Cleon (in *The Acharnians*), calling him "a coward" and "a cheat," whose lips "spewed out a torrent of sewage." Though Aristophanes penned the play under a pseudonym, the identity of the author must have been obvious. Referring to the absence of foreigners in the audience on that occasion, a character in the play remarks slyly, "Now we are by ourselves."

Aristophanes lampooned everyone from the gods to the audience itself. Even in the midst of the Peloponnesian War, a struggle to the death against Athens' hated enemy, Sparta, Aristophanes repeatedly produced plays attacking both the war itself and the Athenian people's general penchant for war. He even made a character who clearly represented the playwright himself declare that the Spartans "have a good many legitimate grievances against us."

The leader of the chorus in Aristophanes' *The Acharnians* spoke truly when he instructed the audience regarding the playwright: "Hold on to him. He'll carry on impeaching every abuse he sees, and give you much valuable teaching, making you wiser, happier men. . . . Nor will you drown in fulsome praises, such as all the rest bestow on you. He thinks his job is to teach you what is best."

Menander (ca. 342–291 B.C.) and the New Comedy

Writers of the New Comedy like Menander of Athens abandoned the political satire favored by Aristophanes for the parody of everyday life. (The transition actually began with some of Aristophanes' later plays.) The typical New Comedy plot involved an aristocratic young man who had fallen in love with a courtesan but was unable to pursue his affair because his father opposed it and refused to pay the expenses. The young man would then call on his clever slave, who would hatch an elaborate scheme to bilk the father out of the money. The courtesan almost invariably turned out to be the long-lost daughter of a nobleman, thus clearing the way for marriage. Plots revolved around comical misunderstandings.

Stock characters were as common as stock plots. The clever slave, the strict father, and the love-struck youth were often joined by the shrewish wife, the troublesome mother-in-law, and the villainous slave trader–pimp, with occasional appearances by the boastful soldier, the pretentious cook, and the incompetent doctor. In fact, these characters were such staples of the New Comedy that they often even shared the same names from one play to the next, and actors wore the same masks and clothes so that audience members could identify each stock character at a distance.

The New Comedy featured more scenery and more realistic masks and clothing than the old. Like the Old Comedy, it employed verse, but the verse was now only slightly more elevated than common speech.

The most popular of the New Comedians, Menander displayed a rare compassion for his characters, even while spoofing their eccentricities. Although only fragments from ten of Menander's more than one hundred plays survive, they are a gold mine of epigrams: "He whom the gods love dies young"; "He who runs away will fight again"; "A man rises higher so that he may fall faster"; "If someone has a beautiful body and an ugly soul, he has a good ship and a poor steersman"; "To make the same mistake twice is not the act of a wise man"; "Peace feeds the farmer well, though he lives on rocky soil, but war feeds him poorly, though he lives on the plains"; "The gods see men and are near to them, and are pleased with the just and not with the unjust"; "Time is the physician of all evils"; and "Whenever you intend to criticize your neighbor in some way, examine your own evils first."

In Menander's play *The Arbitration* a woman considers abandoning a baby out of shame because it is the product of illicit sex with an unknown man in the dark at an evening festival four months before her marriage. But the father of the baby turns out to be her own husband. In a sly wink to the audience Menander has one character tell another: "I'm sure you've been to the theater and remember lots of situations like this."

ROMAN COMEDY

Plautus (ca. 254–184 B.C.)

The first great Roman comedian, Titus Maccius Plautus, wrote more than a hundred plays; the twenty-one that survive are among the earliest surviving works in Latin. Although Plautus was clearly influenced by Menander and the other New Comedians of Greece, whose plots he borrowed, an even greater source of inspiration for him was a southern Italian dramatic tradition known as the Atellan farce. This genre was highly improvisational, involving a standard plot provided in advance but with the rest improvised by the actors. The improvisational spirit of the Atellan farce not only exhibited itself in Plautus' radical reworking of the Greek plays, including the combination of different plots from various plays and the revamping of dialogue into much more complex metrical patterns, but also inspired him to convert the heroes of his plays, the clever slaves, into masters of improvisation themselves. Constantly improvising new schemes to stave off disaster for himself and his master, the clever slave is generally the most intelligent, imaginative, eloquent, and self-aware character of Plautus' plays, coaching and rehearsing the other characters in speech and action in execution of his schemes, which often involve securing a mistress for his infatuated young master against his father's wishes. Thus, as the director of the players within a web of schemes, the slave becomes the master.

In one such play, *Epidicus*, the title character's reluctance to accept freedom from his master as a reward for a successful scheme is really an acknowledgment that he is already not only free but, in fact, the real master of the household who can bend the other members to his own will through knowledge of their stock character traits. Similarly, in *Pseudolus*, the title character, despite having devised no scheme yet, is so confident of his power to bilk his master that he bets him that he can get money from him: "I swear you'll give me cash; I'll certainly relieve you of it yet." He adds humorously, "Make me your slave if I fail," thereby accentuating the truth of the real power relationship. Needless to say, Pseudolus wins the wager in the end. By suckering his master into another bet that he can steal a slave girl his master's son loves from a slave trader and winning that bet, he succeeds in getting money from his master, thereby winning the previous bet.

Rather than copying Greek plays, Plautus lampooned their conventions. While Menander parodied life, Plautus satirized Menander himself, and the play itself. Though employing the same stock characters and the same masks to denote them as the New Comedians, he routinely subverted the audience's expectations, to their own delight. In *Persa* the clever slave Troxilus schemes to secure his own mistress rather than his young master's. In *Asinaria* the mother of the mistress of the young aristocrat Argyrippus scolds him for failing to properly play his stock-character role of the passionate lover who spends money recklessly on his mistress. In *Casina* the wife of the young master's father abandons her usual role as the nag and unexpectedly seizes the role of the schemer from the clever slave in order to thwart her husband's planned infidelity. (Her husband has an unpleasant surprise when a male slave impersonates his would-be mistress in the bedroom.) In Plautus' plays the standard roles are often taken up only to be dropped, transferred to others, or subverted.

Plautus' characters, especially his clever slaves, speak as though aware of their involvement in the play itself. In *Persa*, Toxilus tells a fellow slave concerning the costumes required for his latest scheme, "Get them from the producer—that's his job. The aediles assigned him to provide them." Troxilus even tells another character to project his voice when reading a letter. He holds a sort of cast party onstage for his fellow schemers after their scheme has succeeded. In another play Pseudolus refuses to relate a scheme to his master, saying, "I don't want to repeat it twice; plays are long enough as it is." When the slave trader Ballio is asked what Pseudolus said to him, he replies, "Theatrical nonsense, the usual things said to a pimp in comedies." In the *Bacchides*, Chrysalus boasts that he is cleverer than other slaves, including Syrus, the slave character from a play by Menander on whom he is based. When Chrysalus triumphs, he tells the audience, which is expecting the clever slave to deliver the standard, grandiose, satirical speech employing the language of a conquering general, that he refuses to do so because this comic bit has been overdone and abruptly leaves the stage.

While Greek New Comedy had generally striven to maintain a wall of illusion between the audience and the stage, Plautus, as part of his effort to lampoon the conventions of comedy itself and in an attempt to attract and maintain audience interest, liked to have his characters speak directly to the audience. Pseudolus warns the audience not to trust him. In the prologue to the *Amphitruo*, Mercury tells the audience: "I'll explain the plot of this tragedy. What? You're frowning because I said this was going to be a tragedy? I'm a god, I'll change it. If you wish, I'll make this into a comedy from a tragedy, with all the lines the same." In another play the crafty slave Gripus tells the audience: "I've often seen actors in a play deliver themselves of gems of wisdom of this sort—and seen them get a round of applause for having mouthed for the audience all these rules of good behavior. Then, when the audience left and everybody was back in his own home, there wasn't a one who behaved the way he had been told to." Sometimes the characters maintain the theatergoers' interest by singling out individual audience members, as when the miser Euclio asks several audience members to watch his pot of gold for him.

While it was common for Roman comedies to include a brief epilogue requesting applause, Plautus took this convention in unexpected directions as well. In *Asinaria* the audience is told regarding a character whose wife has caught him with his son's mistress: "Now if you want to save this old man from a beating, we think you can, if you applaud long enough." When his master's father suggests that Pseudolus invite the audience to go drinking with him in celebration of his victory, Pseudolus replies, "By heaven, they don't usually invite me, so I won't invite them. Though if you want to applaud and acclaim the troupe, I'll invite you to another play tomorrow." The epilogue of the *Mercator* calls for a law against old men running after young girls (an element of the plot), adding that young men in the audience should applaud because such a law will benefit them by reducing the competition.

Since comedies were often performed at festivals, it is not surprising that Plautus' comedies were often bawdy, focusing on explosive, quick-fire buffoonery. In the spirit of the festival the plays' sexual morality was rather loose. But it was not nonexistent; in *Casina*, the old master's lechery, which takes the form of attempted homosexual rape and improper advances on his son's mistress, is condemned as excessive and animalistic and leads to his downfall.

Plautus emphasized jokes, puns, music, and dancing over consistency of characters and plot development. When Pseudolus is confronted with poor handwriting in a letter conveying bad news, he quips, "It is tragically written." The humor sometimes involved threats of violence, as when Mercury, disguised as a slave, says to the slave Sosia: "I'm going to make you into a real aristocrat. . . . Once I get my hands on a club, you won't walk away from here, you'll be carried." Plautus employed the aside, the soliloquy, eavesdropping, and role-playing by characters (as part of various schemes) cleverly. In the *Bacchides*, Chrysalus dictates a letter to his master (a comic inversion of roles), in the process trying different salutations, abandoning them all, and, after getting little beyond that, requests that the few words he has dictated be read back to him—the beginning of a bit that has been repeated countless times over the centuries.

By mocking himself, his fellow comedians, and their conventions, Plautus breathed new vitality into what had become a stale, formulaic art involving stock plots and characters. Ironic self-awareness became a vital element of comedy.

Plautus' comedies greatly influenced William Shakespeare's *The Comedy of Errors*, Molière's *The Miser*, and, more recently, *A Funny Thing Happened on the Way to the Forum*, which even borrowed the name of one of Plautus' clever slaves (Pseudolus) for its principal character.

Terence (ca. 190–159 B.C.)

The six surviving comedies of Terence (Terentius Afer), a North African freedman who had served as the slave of a Roman senator, all produced in the 160s B.C., are more gentle and contemplative. Terence's well-constructed plays were comedies of character, smooth and precise in language, filled with psychological insight and moral musings. They were more polished, graceful, and touching and less boisterous than those of Plautus. In fact, in the prologue to *The Self-Tormenter*, the play's actor-producer, Lucius Ambivius, slyly calls the play one of "quiet action," in contrast to those requiring him "to act everlastingly at the top of my voice and with extreme exertion." He adds, "Nowadays, writers of new plays have no mercy on an old man. A fatiguing plot, and it's me they run to." Terence followed Aristotle's dramatic rules, which required unity of action (all subplots must assist the main plot), unity of time (all action must occur in a single day), and unity of place (all action must occur at the same location). Terence's plays often featured double plots that interwove two love affairs, in which the happy resolution of one was dependent on the outcome of the other.

While Plautus was famous for his dialogue, Terence was known for his expertise in characterization. His characters, especially fathers and sons, often possessed genuine affection for one another, though hindered by misunderstandings caused by poor communication. He often depicted a character's traits in sharp relief against the background of a counterpart; this was one reason he liked to use pairs (of fathers, sons, etc.). In *The Girl from Andros*,

Terence's first play, young Pamphilus, unlike nearly all stock characters of the New Comedy, actually matures over the course of the play. In *The Self-Tormenter*, Chremes, a genuinely caring but rather self-righteous busybody who is always ready to proffer unsought advice on parenting, and who justifies meddling with philosophical platitudes ("I am a man; what affects another man affects me"), learns that he has been mistaken about his own son for years. Parenting was clearly a concern of Terence, for in *The Brothers*, Terence presents two brothers, one who is too lenient with his son, the other too strict, and depicts the advantages and defects of each practice. While Demea's strictness and moral lectures lead his son to hide his schemes from his father, giving Demea a false sense of his son's true character until it is devastatingly revealed, Micio takes to absurd lengths his attempts to act as "a friend" to his son by indulging all of his wishes.

In *The Mother-in-Law* characters learn the dangers of stereotyping, a lesson as much directed at the typical New Comedy as at the audience. In this play two mothers-in-law are wrongly accused by their husbands of breaking up a marriage. One of the wronged mothers-in-law, Sostrata, diagnoses the problem, "They have made themselves believe that all mothers-in-law are harsh." Meanwhile, Phidippus declares concerning courtesans, "Such women have no fear of God, and God, I think, has no regard for them." Likewise, the courtesan Syra generalizes concerning men, "There's not one of them, you may be sure, comes to you except with the intention of coaxing you into sating his love of pleasure as cheaply as ever he can." Another courtesan says of wives, "We are natural enemies." Each of these generalizations and stereotypes is proven false in the course of the play.

Terence often displayed compassion for lowly courtesans and poor women. In *The Self-Tormenter* he has Bacchis justify the notoriously mercenary traits of courtesans: "It is our beauty that attracts lovers to court us. When that's faded, they switch off their inclinations, and if we have made no provision in the meantime, we live in neglect." In *Phormio* the slave Geta notes, "When a poor girl is given to a rich husband, it's slavery, not matrimony." Yet, in two different plays, Terence trivialized rape, even of free women, as a matter easily rectified by the rapist's marriage to the victim.

Terence often used his prologues to respond to critics (rival playwrights) rather than to advance the play. This meant that his opening scenes required more exposition than those of other playwrights. Terence's unusual use of the prologue for self-defense may have been justified, at least in part, by the misbehavior of his rivals, who may have been responsible for rumors that caused the cancellation of *The Mother-in-Law* twice. During the premiere, many audience members visited the neighboring circus during the intermission when they heard false rumors of a tightrope act and never returned, causing the cancellation of the rest of the play; on the second showing, the equally false rumor of an impending gladiatorial contest sent a crowd pushing and shoving into the theater, causing another cancellation. Terence also used the prologue of two different plays to beg audience members for silence and attention, since Roman audiences sometimes created such a commotion that only the people seated in the front rows could hear the play.

Terence based most of his plots on those of Menander, though, like Plautus, he often combined elements of more than one Greek play in his own. In fact, Terence died in a shipwreck while returning from a voyage to Greece, where he had found additional plays by Menander to adapt.

Within a century of his death Terence's plays had become standard texts in Roman schools. Both Cicero and Julius Caesar praised the purity of their language. Nor was this a passing judgment. Schools used Terence's plays as a Latin model for centuries. At the age of eighty-one John Adams excerpted approximately 140 passages from them for his grandchildren.

Terence provided an important model for playwrights searching for a sophisticated and urbane alternative to Plautus' broader humor yet one possessing moral value. Terence was popular with the Christian playwrights of the Middle Ages, who eschewed the vulgarities of Aristophanes and Plautus. (Yet Terence required some adaptation too. His indulgent depiction of young men's dalliances with concubines—"it's a thing young men do"—would hardly have endeared him to devout Christians.) He influenced Renaissance comedy, the plays of Molière, and other seventeenth- and eighteenth-century English comedies of manners. Richard Steele's *The Conscious Lovers* (1722) was based on *The Girl from Andros*. Denis Diderot wrote: "What man of letters has not read his Terence more than once and does not know him almost by heart? Who has not been struck by the truth of his characters and the elegance of his diction?" Oscar Wilde's *The Importance of Being Earnest* (1895), with its two interconnected love affairs and its improbable recognition scene, was clearly a debtor to Terence.

SATIRE

A literary genre of Roman origin, though influenced by the social criticism of Greek comedy and the informality, personal revelations, and invective of Greek lyric poetry, satire began as a form of poetry that later included prose as well. The word *saturae* was first used in a literary sense by Ennius, though his satires, only 31 lines of which survive, seem to have been very different from what the genre soon became. In addition to his more famous and more highly esteemed epic poetry, Ennius published a collection of short poems on various topics that employed different meters, which he called the *Saturae*. While the term is mysterious, it seems to have derived either from a dish containing many diverse ingredients presented to gods at religious festivals or a kind of sausage made from many different ingredients—in either case, a satisfying meal composed of diverse components. (The popular belief that the word "satire" derives from the satyrs of Greek mythology and the "satyr play," a comedy added to a trilogy of Greek tragedies for comic relief, is understandable but mistaken.) Ennius' *Satires* included a dialogue between Life and Death, a fable of Aesop, and the surviving line, "the monkey—how similar to us is that most disgusting beast."

Lucilius (ca. 180–102 B.C.)

Although it was Ennius who first used saturae as a literary term, it was Gaius Lucilius who pioneered the actual genre of satire and was regarded as its founder by later practitioners. The incisive and irreverent Lucilius, a wealthy aristocrat who was Pompey's granduncle, employed invective, anecdotes, dialogues, the letter format, and fables, swathed in a colloquial style similar to that of his contemporary Plautus, in poems of varying length. After experimenting with various meters in the manner of Ennius, Lucilius settled on the dactylic hexameter, the meter of epic poetry, as the preferred meter for his lampoons; it soon became the standard meter for verse satire.

Lucilius assaulted both the extravagance of the rich and the frugality of country bumpkins. He sneered at Tronginus, an auxiliary of Celtic origin, for his dinner parties, characterized by rickety furniture, bad food, and the company of "lousy old bags with teeth like razors . . . the greedy, stupid bitches."

Lucilius was often criticized for attacking individuals by name. For instance, he wrote:

> Mycilla dyes her locks, 'tis said,
> But 'tis a foul aspersion.
> She buys them black; they therefore need
> No subsequent immersion.

Yet Lucilius apparently had no sense of humor where his own name was concerned; he once sued a comic playwright for lampooning him.

Cicero admired Lucilius' satires, which may have contributed to the former's propensity for invective in his own speeches. Horace wrote, "Lucilius first had the courage to write this kind of poetry and remove the glossy skin in which people were parading before the world and concealing their ugliness."

Horace (65–8 B.C.)

In addition to his other poetry, Horace published his own collection of *Satires* (35–30 B.C.), ten poems that rejected wealth and power and emphasized the need for serenity. They mocked familiar social types in a general and genial manner and displayed the remarkable variety of theme and tone that was to become one of Horace's trademarks. For instance, while some characters, such as Horace's slave, speak in informal meters, others, like the pretentious town mouse, use grandiose forms, with comic effect.

Though acknowledging Lucilius' status as the pioneer of the satiric genre, Horace refused to follow his practice of attacking people by name, employing pseudonyms instead, and employed less vulgarity. Criticizing Lucilius' verbosity, he also adopted a more succinct style.

Horace claimed that the wise man preferred the riches of friendship to monetary wealth. He wrote (1.1): "All these men say they labor and risk danger to lay by enough wealth for old age; nevertheless, they never stop so long as they see another man richer than themselves. What good does it do them? . . . No man can eat but so much. . . . Why does a man always compare himself with the few richer . . . instead of the far greater number of the poorer?" He added (1.6): "So long as I am of sound mind I shall never rate anything so high as the company of a delightful friend."

In another satire (1.9) Horace is pursued through the streets of Rome by a relentless bore who desires an introduction to the patron Maecenas. When the bore remarks that his relatives are all deceased, Horace thinks, "O lucky creatures! But I survive! Oh, finish me!" Seeing a common acquaintance, Horace "nodded my head and rolled my eyes as signs for him to come to my rescue." But the gambit fails: "The mean fellow, with a laugh, pretended not to understand me." Horace refers to Homer and uses military language to portray the incident as a battle. This satire captures Horace's nature perfectly: intelligent enough to find the bore insufferable but kind enough to be unable to dismiss him.

Yet another satire (2.7) epitomizes the poet's willingness to poke fun at himself. One of Horace's slaves makes use of the traditional freedom of the Saturnalia to repeat for his master a Stoic sermon that he has heard second-hand from the porter to the effect that only the wise are free. In the process the slave berates his master for his hypocrisy. The slave notes that Horace lauds pristine simplicity while avidly accepting invitations to lavish dinner parties at Maecenas' mansion and denounces the slave's use of prostitutes while engaging in extramarital affairs of his own. Horace finally loses his patience and his temper. The poet often exaggerated his own defects for humorous effect—not only his impatience, but his talkativeness and laziness as well. He referred to his own method as "laughingly to tell the truth." When he explored some fault, his target was always the fault itself rather than the person who exemplified it.

Both Horace's own testimony and other evidence indicate that his *Epistles* (ca. 20–19 B.C.) were intended as a continuation of the *Satires*. The epistolary form was commonly used in satire, and the content and tone of the *Epistles* are similar to those of the *Satires*. Written in hexameters, the *Epistles* continued the author's persona as a kindly, tolerant, humane, realistic, and self-deprecating man who was suspicious of wealth without being ascetic. He warned readers, "Your money, piled up, is your master or your servant." Wealth should contribute to the good life, not substitute for it. Nevertheless, Horace called himself "a porker from Epicurus' herd" who disliked extreme Stoicism, which could be rigid and inhuman in its complete rejection of pleasure and emotion.

The *Epistles* included influential literary criticism, especially in *The Art of Poetry* (2.3). Against the literary critics who favored only archaic verse Horace argued: "Suppose the Greeks had resented newness as much as we do, what would now be old? And what would the people have to read and thumb with enjoyment, each man to his taste?" Nevertheless, he acknowledged his own debt to the archaic Greek lyric poets (while criticizing the pedantic Alexandrians). He defined a literary critic as "a grindstone which sharpens steel but has no part in the cutting." A good poem required unity, harmony, proportion, good diction, subject matter suited to the author's powers, and a meter appropriate to the subject matter. The poet's qualifications included common sense, an understanding of human nature, adherence to high ideals, and a willingness to profit from constructive criticism. Of the true poet Horace wrote: "[He] will remove objectionable words, he will bring out picturesque phrases used by famous writers of old and also employ new words that have come into general usage. He will aim at strength and clarity, he will prune luxuriant expressions, and he will smooth what is rough, and conceal the effort." This is a fine description of Horace's own art. The *Art of Poetry* dispensed literary advice equal in value to that contained in Aristotle's *Poetics*.

Persius (A.D. 34–62)

A wealthy eques from Tuscany who died of a stomach disease shortly before his twenty-eighth birthday, Persius (Aulus Persius Flaccus) was the only major satirist who was also a strict Stoic, having studied under Seneca's freedman Cornutus. (Most Roman satirists were skeptical of philosophy and doubly so of philosophers; to the extent that their attitudes reflected any philosophy at all, it was generally a mild form of Epicureanism.) Although Persius' extant work consists of only about 650 lines in six satires published posthumously, it created the enduring persona of the angry and alienated young man.

Persius used the humorous juxtaposition of vivid images to express abstract thought in a concrete way and used graphic language to deglamorize his targets. He rebelled against the superfluous words employed by the poets of Nero's court to create a sensual feel, opting instead for a style so compact that it is occasionally obscure, a problem exacerbated by abrupt transitions. In contrast to the frivolous court poets, Persius labored over every word. His style was concise and colloquial, marked by arresting turns of phrase.

Persius combined Lucilius' harsh tone with Horace's refusal to attack specific individuals (a dangerous practice in an age of public recitations). Instead, Persius assaulted all Roman classes (sometimes using names borrowed from the comic stage or from Horace to personify them), comparing their moral sickness with a physical illness that required harsh and unstinting treatment. His insistence that all men were fools except for the Stoics was not one calculated to convert many, but he doubted the possibility of conversion for most, anyway. In his first satire he claimed that "at most one or two" Romans would be interested in his poem about "mortal ambition" and the "towering emptiness of human enterprise." Persius concedes the point of his imaginary interlocutor (whom he slyly calls "whoever you are whom I've made up to argue with") that all poets prefer fame to having their poems "wrapping mackerel" but adds that much trash is called "exquisite" by Romans. After citing examples of bad poetry from the Neronian age, he asks, "Do you think stuff like that would get written if our generation hadn't been born without balls?" He adds, "No sign there of table pummeled for the one word, and nails bitten to the quick." When the interlocutor warns that if the poet adopts so harsh a tone, "You're likely to find the doorsteps of the great chilly and—listen—there's the snarl of the dog," Persius pretends to comply with his wishes, saying sarcastically, "Everybody's nice, everybody's incomparably wonderful!" Persius then identifies his models, "And yet Lucilius took the skin off this city. . . . And sly Horace could tease his way into the guts of his laughing friend and touch the fault there. . . . And I mustn't utter a word? Not to myself? Not into a ditch? Not anywhere? Well, I will. I'll bury it here. Little book, I've seen this, seen it." Persius declared that his intended audience consisted of the few discriminating readers who loved the plays of Aristophanes, not the sort of person who "nearly splits with the humor of shouting, 'Hey, One Eye!' at one-eyed men." He concluded, "Let them go spell out the playbills plastered up in the Forum for their morning reading."

In his second satire Persius lashed out at the multitudes who uttered materialistic prayers, even including secret prayers for the death of an uncle from whom they hoped to inherit. How could one who uttered such prayers escape divine judgment? he asked. "Do you think that Jupiter will allow you to pluck out his insensitive beard in handfuls? And what have you bestowed upon the gods that they're so willing to indulge you? Those little favors of greasy offal?" People prayed for good health, then ate "mountainous platters" of food. Other half-wits slaughtered large numbers of their livestock as sacrifices as a prelude to asking the gods to multiply their herds. Human temples were filled with gold, including golden images of the gods, based on a false projection of human greed onto the deities: "Oh souls hunched low, with thoughts empty of heaven, what point is there in filling the temples, too, with our ways and from our iniquitous flesh deducing what would please the gods?" It was better to bring to the altar "a soul in harmony with the dictates of heaven, a mind pure in its secret places, a generous and honest heart."

In the third satire Persius referred to a man "sunk so deep [in vice] that he doesn't even send up a bubble." He exclaimed, "Oh wretches, come learn the causes of things—what we are, what manner of life we were born for." Yet Persius anticipated the jeering reaction of "some goat-adorned centurion." In the fourth satire he decided, "No one tries the descent into himself, no, not one," and writes regarding the extremely wealthy man, "The gods loathe him; his own soul can't stand him."

In the fifth satire Persius returned to his refusal to write flowery court poetry and expressed his determination to seek true freedom. He tells himself that it is not "your custom to caw to yourself, like a crow, a lot of grave drivel. . . . You employ the language of common speech. . . . I don't want to cram my page full of ceremonious nothings." He adds: "We desire liberty, though not the kind which any slob can acquire. . . . You don't imagine that the only master is the one from whom the praetor's wand can release you? . . . If masters spring up within you, there in your feeble guts, do you think you'll get off lightly, any more than that lash-harried slave with the scrapers?" Avarice, luxury, ambition, and superstition were four such masters. Regarding political ambition, Persius wrote, "That smooth candidate gaping for office like a fish at a fly, would you consider him his own master?" No more so than the superstitious, whose "lips twitch in silence and turn pale at the sabbath of the circumcised" and who worry about black ghosts, broken eggs, and demons. Persius imagines that his discourse causes "a varicose centurion" to emit "a horse-laugh" and declare that "he'd not give a clipped coin for a hundred of your highbrow Greeks [Stoics]."

In his last satire Persius declared his adherence to the golden mean concerning spending. On the one hand, he avoided "being so lavish as to feed my freedmen on turbot nor being of so sophisticated a palate that I can tell hen thrush from cock thrush by the taste." He exhorted, "Live on your own harvest, mill your own grain; that's as it should be." On the other hand, one should not live as a miser, a practice whose only beneficiaries were greedy heirs. One should not deny charity to a wretched, shipwrecked friend out of fear that one's heir would "stuff your bones unperfumed into the urn," muttering, "Thought you could shave bits off your estate and get away with it, did you?" while another friend would grouse against the Stoic sages of Greece, saying, "That's how it goes, ever since that neutered brand of philosophy was imported into this city along with the dates and pepper." Persius asks, "Why should you worry about this sort of thing once you're on the other side of the fire?" He then taunts his own (imaginary) greedy heir, threatening to deprive him of his estate by treating the public to expensive games "with a hundred pairs of gladiators" in honor of Caligula's imaginary victory over the Germans. Relishing the heir's discomfort, he continues, "Who would dare say I shouldn't? God help you if you don't play along! Oh, and I'm having a largesse of bread and meat and oil distributed to the populace. Any objections? Speak up. 'Oh, no,' you say, 'Not with that field full of stones within easy range.'" Persius then threatens to select a new heir from among the beggars. After all, doesn't every family tree go back to some "son of the soil," anyway? "Besides, you've got nerve, when you're ahead of me, grabbing for my torch before I've finished my race." Finally, Persius tells the heir that he will not stint his own lifestyle, reducing himself to eating "smoked cheek of pork and split pig's ear garnished with nettles," so that a successor may "eat goose livers," and will not "abstain till I'm diaphanous so that his paunch can jiggle like a priest's."

By the late second century Persius' *Satires* had become a school text. (Ironically, in his very first satire Persius had sneered at the imaginary interlocutor who asked, "To have a hundred unkempt schoolboys worrying over your text, really, wouldn't you like it?") Jerome borrowed from him, and Augustine admired him as a moralist. As such, he was popular in the Middle Ages.

Petronius (First Century A.D.)

In the early 60s Petronius (Gaius Petronius Niger), a capable governor of Bithynia and consul for Nero but also a pleasure seeker who advised the emperor on the hosting of luxurious parties (Nero's chief concern), composed a mock epic called the *Satyricon*, which blended artfully the sensibility and verse of traditional satire with the narrative prose of the Greek romance novel and short story. Petronius' models for such a blend were few and inferior to his own creation: some satires by Varro now lost to us and Seneca's lampoon of Claudius' deification.

The *Satyricon*'s antihero Encolpius is a student, thief, and pervert who is afflicted by Priapus, the god of sexual potency, with the curse of impotence, just as Poseidon had persecuted Odysseus with numerous hardships. Spoofing heroic dialogue, Encolpius intones: "So now, upon me too Priapus' wrath falls, hounding me on, over land and sea, on and on, relentlessly on."

The *Satyricon* also poked fun at the melodramatic orations of self-important rhetoricians, the tasteless, conspicuous consumption of the nouveau riche, and the schemes of inheritance seekers. Satirizing a theme commonly employed by rhetoricians, Encolpius blasts the florid Asiatic style of rhetoric and urges imitation of the good, old-fashioned simplicity of Demosthenes and Cicero . . . in a verbose, Asiatic speech.

The tasteless freedman Trimalchio, who has compiled a fortune as a wine merchant and banker, attempts to host a stylish party, with disastrous results. He empties his bladder into a chamber pot made of solid silver in front of his guests, picks at his teeth with silver toothpicks, discusses his constipation, invites his guests to test his fine cutlery on their beard stubble, and makes vulgar exclamations. He washes his hands with wine, wipes them on the locks of an Alexandrian slave boy, and pours from a gravy boat shaped like a satyr with a phallus for a spout. He serves ludicrous dishes, such as a hare adorned with feathers that is intended to represent Pegasus. He tells his guests to feel free to pass wind at the table. He mangles the story of the *Iliad*, then serves a boiled calf wearing a helmet, which is carved up by a cook impersonating mad Ajax. He has his secretary read aloud reports from his vast estates. He speaks of buying Sicily so that he can journey from Italy "to Africa without ever stepping off my own property."

At the end of his party Trimalchio gets into a drunken quarrel with his wife in which he remarks on her past as a prostitute, reads his own epitaph, bursts into tears, puts on dazzling funeral clothes, lies on a heap of cushions, and says, "Pretend I'm dead. Say something nice." The false lamentation of his slaves at his pretended death is so loud that it summons firemen, who break down the door and throw water everywhere. The intellectual pretender Encolpius snickers at Trimalchio's lack of refinement behind his back while hypocritically guzzling his wine and pocketing his fruit. When a slave boy who has been forced to dance on a ladder falls on Trimalchio, injuring him, Encolpius remarks coldly: "We were not, of course, in the least concerned about the boy, whose neck we would have been delighted to see broken; but we dreaded the thought of possibly having to go into mourning for a man [Trimalchio] who meant nothing to us at all."

Throughout this vignette Nero's "arbiter of elegance" gives us a singular portrait of wretched taste. In addition, the banal conversation that pervades the feast is perhaps meant to contrast with the philosophical discourse of Plato's *Symposium* (Greek for "Drinking Party") and the heroic tales of the dignified royal feasts of the *Odyssey* and the *Aeneid*.

Encolpius and his comrades then journey to a town that is obsessed with inheritance hunting. This gives his friend Eumolpus the opportunity to pose as a wealthy but childless aristocrat in order to bilk the greedy townsmen, who hope to be added to his will, of expensive gifts.

Nearly every character is both a deceiver and a self-deceiver. However capable Eumolpus may be of deceiving others for his own personal gain, he is also quite capable of deceiving himself as well. He is such a bad poet that he gets stoned by the people or evicted from the bath every time he attempts to recite some of his verse yet considers himself a second Homer.

In the end Encolpius bribes a priestess of Priapus to restore his sexual function. The moral, if it can be called such, is clearly stated, "Whoever has money shall always sail with a favoring wind and control fortune at his will."

While the *Satyricon* consists mostly of narrative prose, occasional snippets of verse are used to parody moralistic sermons, prayers, and other epic tropes. At one point Encolpius addresses his defective member in grandiose verse. Skillful narration keeps the action moving at a rapid pace, and Petronius achieves a naturalistic reproduction of common speech. In fact, the Trimalchio vignette is one of the most valuable surviving documents for the study of common Latin, whose grammatical and syntactical forms later formed the foundation of the modern Romance languages of Italy, France, and Spain.

Charged with treason against Nero, Petronius was forced to commit suicide in A.D. 66. But before he took his own life, rather than discoursing on philosophy like Socrates or like Nero's numerous Stoic victims, Petronius broke his signet ring so that it could not be used to falsely incriminate others, smashed a very expensive wine dipper just to deprive Nero of it, and then dispatched to the emperor a sarcastic letter detailing Nero's perversions and affairs with both men and women. The emperor was shocked by the extent of the knowledge it displayed.

Later Roman grammarians considered Petronius a master of Latin prose and his *Satyricon* a guide to word usage. The sixth-century philosopher Boethius used him as a model for his own satire. Ironically, because the *Satyricon* was long preserved in small fragments, many of which were moral maxims hypocritically spoken by Encolpius and the other antiheroes of the work and, therefore, intended to be satirical, Petronius was valued as a great moralist during the Middle Ages. His observation that "the whole world can be seen to be indulging in a mime" was the ancestor of Shakespeare's "all the world's a stage." Ben Jonson admired him. The poet John Dryden later called Petronius "the greatest wit perhaps of all the Romans" and "the most elegant and one of the most judicious authors of the Latin tongue." Frederick the Great even reenacted Trimalchio's feast. Alexander Pope wrote:

> Fancy and art in gay Petronius please,
> The scholar's learning, with the courtier's ease.

Juvenal (ca. A.D. 55–130)

Influenced by the rhetorical style of his day, Juvenal (Decius Junius Juvenalis) composed sixteen biting verse satires of urban life in Rome in the urgent, vehement style of a declaimer. We know little of Juvenal's life. Despite the legend of a later date that he was embittered by exile and loss of property, a sentence supposedly imposed by Domitian on the basis of a false charge, the fact that his satires were not dedicated to any patron may indicate that he was wealthy.

In the first six satires Juvenal's tone was as caustic as that of his contemporary Tacitus. He created the hilarious persona of a grouchy old man who exaggerates contemporary greed and sexual depravity, who claims to be the voice of reason yet quickly loses control of his emotions and engages in lengthy, unstructured diatribes, and who displays rank prejudice. In short, his comic persona was essentially that of a Roman Archie Bunker.

In the opening lines of the first satire Juvenal immediately reveals the impatient nature of his persona, whose tendency is to be outraged by trivialities. He asks, "Must I be always a listener only, never hit back . . . never obtain revenge when X has read me his comedies, Y his elegies?" Yet the reader, while amused by the persona's exaggerations, is clearly not supposed to dismiss him completely but to recognize at least a small measure of truth in his distorted claims.

Like all previous satirists, Juvenal was forced to defend his choice of satire, a genre of lesser prestige than epic or lyric poetry, in his first poem. He explained, "It's hard to look about and not write satire." Having been warned that he might be destroyed if he attacked the powerful, Juvenal facetiously promises to attack the deceased alone.

Juvenal claimed that his introduction to life in the capital was to be "naturalized"—that is, to have a chamber pot dumped on his head as he walked beneath a window. In the third satire Juvenal painted an even direr picture of city life. A friend explains why he is leaving Rome: "Hurry as I may, I am blocked by a surging crowd in front, while a vast mass of people crushes onto me from behind. One with his elbow punches me, another with a hard litter-pole. One bangs a beam against my head, someone else a wine cask. With mud my legs are splattered. From all sides huge feet trample upon me, and a soldier's hobnails are firmly planted on my toes." There is also a complaint that easterners, especially Jews and Greeks, are displacing native Romans. But the reader's suspicion that the speaker is engaging in gross exaggeration is validated by the fact that the poet himself remains in the city after the friend departs.

While the first five satires focused on the follies and crimes of men, the sixth focused on those of women. In this poem the persona advises the young man Postumus against marriage, declaring: "All chance of domestic harmony is lost while your wife's mother is living. She gets her to rejoice in despoiling her husband, stripping him naked. She gets her to write back politely and with sophistication when her seducer sends letters. She tricks your spies or bribes them. . . . Maybe you think that her mother will teach her virtuous ways—ones different from her own? It's much more productive for a dirty old lady to bring up a dirty little girl." He portrayed Roman wives as beside themselves at the sight of an actor in the theater and their children as likely to have the features of a performer. He added a shot at wives who used drugs to cover up their adulteries: "Virtually no gilded bed is laid out for childbirth—so great is her skill, so easily can she produce drugs that make her sterile or induce her to kill human beings in her womb. You fool, enjoy it, and give her the potion to drink, whatever it's going to be, because, if she wants to get bloated and trouble her womb with a live baby's kicking, you might end up being the father of an Ethiopian—soon a wrong-colored heir will complete your accounts, a person whom it's bad luck to see first thing in the morning." Rather than being a genuine example of racism, which was rare among the ancients, who tended to be ethnocentric but not racist, this last flourish was clearly designed for comic effect. At any rate, as usual, Juvenal undermines the persona at the end of the poem by having Postumus ignore his advice against marriage, which had been the whole point of the diatribe.

Beginning with the seventh satire, Juvenal, having milked the grouchy old man persona to its utmost extent, changed his tone. Rather than start the satire with the usual angry question or mark of indignation, he began the formation of a new persona who was still pessimistic but more detached, restrained, and rational. In the seventh satire Juvenal complained about the poverty of even successful writers, lawyers, and teachers when compared with the prosperity of lowly entertainers.

In the eighth satire Juvenal advised against reliance on one's ancestry. He wrote: "However far back you care to go in tracing your name, the fact remains that your clan began in a haven for outlaws. The first of all your line, whatever his name may have been, was either a shepherd—or else a thing I'd rather not mention."

In the ninth satire a client complains about his former duties of sexually servicing both his patron and his patron's wife and fathering his children. The angry tone is undermined by another speaker who insults the oblivious client.

The tenth satire exposed the vanity and absurdity of human aspirations by addressing the folly of most prayers, including those for eloquence, military success, long life, and beauty. Juvenal noted that Cicero's eloquence cost him his life—whereas if his speeches against Antony had been as bad as his poetry, he would have been safe. Regarding the common prayer for military success, he noted that the sole success of mighty Hannibal, killed by the self-administration of a "little ring" full of poison, was to "become a subject for declamation"—such as Juvenal's own speech. He finally suggested praying only "for a healthy mind and a healthy body . . . that you may have something to ask for—some reason to offer the holy sausages and innards of a little white pig in a chapel." The ironic ending was typical of the satirist.

In the eleventh satire Juvenal compared the sad expressions of chariot race spectators whose team had just lost to that of the vanquished Romans after the calamitous Battle of Cannae. In the twelfth he compared a friend's willingness to jettison his cargo during a violent storm to the stratagem of the beaver that escaped destruction by biting off the testicles for which he was being hunted. In the fourteenth he complained that greed was the only vice parents actually commended to their children as virtue.

While bewailing the overcrowded, dangerous conditions of Rome, Juvenal also took aim at its lawyers, inheritance seekers, sexual deviants, and corrupt Greeks. Indeed, he blamed the corrupting influence of Greek culture for the luxury and effeminacy of modern Rome, writing: "Now we suffer the evils of a long peace; now wanton excess ravages us more fiercely than war and revenges the conquest of the world. No crime, no deed of lust, is missing since Rome lost her poverty." Like many affluent Roman contemporaries, such as Pliny the Younger and Tacitus, he felt contempt for easterners, whom he saw as both luxurious and superstitious, for freedmen, and for women who sought to transcend gender roles. Concerning a female gladiator, he wrote:

> What a great honor it is for a husband to see, at an auction
> Where his wife's effects are up for sale, belts, shin-guards,
> Arm-protectors and plumes!
> Hear her grunt as she works at it, parrying, thrusting;
> See her neck bent down under the weight of her helmet.
> Look at the rolls of bandage and tape, so her legs look like tree-trunks,
> Then have a laugh for yourself, after the practice is over,
> Armor and weapons put down, and she squats as she uses the vessel.

Referring to the nonenforcement of an old Roman law against sodomy, he wrote: "We've sunk this low, though our spears arc the sea. . . . What we do here lewd savages disdain."

Infused with a profound sense of the failure of the Roman dream, Juvenal's hexameters possessed the force of hammer blows. His relentless caricatures depicted an aristocracy who cared more about noble lineage than virtue and tiresome old ladies who insisted upon discussing literature and law at dinner and on correcting other people's grammar.

The gap between human ambitions and human fate elicited tears from other poets, laughter from Juvenal. Reversing the epic poets' tendency to build to a climax, he often started with a dignified, dramatic subject and worked down to something commonplace or absurd.

Juvenal's biting satire influenced John Donne, John Dryden, Jonathan Swift, Alexander Pope, and Samuel Johnson. Donne adopted Juvenal's aggressive style of verse satire. Johnson adapted the third satire into "London," the tenth into "The Vanity of Human Wishes." In his *Imitations of Horace*, Alexander Pope used not merely the satires of Horace and Juvenal but the full range of the ancient tradition to write a political, social, and literary satire suited to his own day.

RELATED GENRES

Roman satire influenced other genres, such as the epigram and the satirical novel. The writers of epigrams shared themes and even some phrases with satirists.

Martial (ca. A.D. 40–104)

Martial (Marcus Valerius Martialis) of Bilbilis in northeastern Spain became the ancient world's greatest writer of satirical epigrams (*Epigrams*, ca. 86–102). After moving to Rome in his twenties, he lived in relative poverty on the third floor of an apartment building, despite receiving honors from the emperors Titus and Domitian. His keen eye for the ridiculous punctured Roman social pretensions. His variety of theme and tone, his polish, and his ingenuity were impressive. He accosted the reader of romantic poetry: "You who read of Oedipus and Thyestes . . . why does the empty nonsense of a wretched sheet please you? Read this, of which life can say, 'It is mine!' You will not find Centaurs, Gorgons, or Harpies here; my page smells of men."

Martial's humor could be cruel. He wrote:

> For girlishness is what you lack,
> Maxine, and your three teeth are black.
> So, trust your looking glass and me,
> And be as much afraid of glee
> As Spanius dreads a breeze that may
> Blow off his elegant toupee. . . .
> Avoid Philistion's funny cracks,
> And parties where behavior's lax.
> Don't let inelegant guffaws
> Unhinge the portals of your jaws.

He also wrote:

> Paula, it comes to me as no surprise
> You want to marry Priscus; you are wise.
> But Priscus doesn't want to marry you,
> Which goes to prove, I'd say, that he's wise, too.

Concerning those who sought inclusion in the wills of wealthy old men, he claimed:

> He who gives presents to a rich old man,
> Like you, for instance, Gaurus—never doubt it
> Is telling you as plainly as he can,
> "Kindly drop dead, and hurry up about it!"

Of a quarrelsome drunkard he wrote:

> Thraso picks quarrels when he's drunk at night,
> When sober in the morning, dares not fight.
> Thraso, to shun those ills that may ensue,
> Drink not at night, or drink at morning too.

Martial assailed quack doctors, whose chilly-handed interns left him sicker than before, and verbose lawyers, "who sound off about Hannibal and Carthage, days that will live in infamy forever, our heroic Mariuses and Sullas" in cases involving the theft of three goats. He urged a tiresome attorney who paused for a drink of water:

> End your thirst and your speech alike.
> Drink from the water clock!

To the noisy teacher who lectured early in the morning he pleaded:

> We next door wish to doze during some of the night hours.
> Entire lack of sleep makes us ill.
> Let 'em out. What they pay you for bawling,
> We'll pay, if you only keep still.

To a former doctor, he wrote:

> Though a soldier at present, a doctor of yore,
> You but do with a sword what your pills did before.

When the wretched writer Theodorus asked why Martial did not send him a copy of his latest book, Martial replied, "I feared you would send me your own." To the plagiarist Fidentius, Martial declared:

I wrote that book you read us, as can readily be shown;
You read it, though, so vilely it begins to be your own.

Martial found humor in marriages as well. Of one couple he wrote:

Alike in temper and in life
The crossest husband, the crossest wife:
It looks exceedingly odd to me
This well-matched pair can disagree.

Of two notorious spouse killers he claimed:

Chrestilla has buried her husbands,
While Fabius has buried his wives.
Since they both make every wedding into a wake,
Please, Venus, unite their lives.

But perhaps Martial's most wounding shots were reserved for literary critics. At one he fired this self-contradictory arrow:

You fear, Ligurra, that I'll write
A poem on you, out of spite,
A fierce and stinging epigram.
What makes you think I give a damn? . . .
A Libyan lion's charge applies
To bulls, but not to butterflies. . . .
You understand, I'm sure, by now;
My brand will never mark your brow.

He challenged the critic Laelius:

You damn every poem I write,
Yet publish not one of your own.
Now kindly let yours see the light,
Or else leave my damned ones alone.

To a third critic Martial spoke defiantly:

Readers and listeners enjoy my books,
But poet Whozis thinks I'm pretty crude.
I don't much care. I'd rather have my food
Appeal to hungry feasters than to cooks.

Yet Martial could be tender and touching too. Concerning the death of a little girl, he wrote: "Let the turf be not hard that covers her soft bones; earth, be not heavy upon her—she was not heavy upon you." Celebrating a friend's happy marriage, he wrote:

> Those other years as nothing were:
> You count your life these years with her.

Regarding people who sought attention by grieving publicly, he noted sadly, "He grieves most truly who grieves alone."

He loved his friends. He wrote charming verses inviting them to dinner, including obvious exaggerations of the menu and promises to allow his guests to recite large poems. He teased one of his wealthier friends:

> I am broke, my dear Regulus. All I can do
> Is dispose of your gifts. May I sell some to you?

After thirty-four years spent enjoying the libraries and theaters of Rome, as well as conversations with some of its most learned men, Martial at last returned to his quiet village in Spain, with the financial help of his friend Pliny the Younger. Martial characteristically committed his motive to satirical verse:

> In Rome a poor man cannot find
> A place to think, or peace of mind. . . .
> How many rapes my sleep endures
> In this metropolis of yours. . . .
> But as for me, the noisy, shrill
> Ha-ha-ing mob goes cackling by
> Within three feet of where I lie.
> In fact, I seem to have all Rome
> Around my bed when I'm at home,
> Until exhausted, sick with worry
> To my Nomentan hut I hurry.

Martial's name soon became synonymous with the epigram, and his influence far outlasted his own day. Venerable Bede cited him. His verses appeared in medieval anthologies. In the fifteenth century there began a long line of scholar-poets who spent the next two centuries producing Latin epigrams largely inspired by, and imitative of, his poems. The epigrams of Thomas More and John Donne were based on Martial's. Ben Jonson, Jonathan Swift, Joseph Addison, Richard Steele, Samuel Johnson, and Lord Chesterfield all quoted and adapted the Latin poet's work. Addison called one of his epigrams "the best transmitted to us from antiquity." Samuel Coleridge and Lord Byron sometimes imitated him. Martial's influence even transcended the genres of humor: his beautiful lines on the joys of country life influenced pastoralists, and his tributes to friends, playful but sincere, influenced subsequent encomiums.

Apuleius (ca. A.D. 125–171)

A lawyer, orator, and philosopher as well as a novelist, Apuleius of Madaura, a Roman colony in North Africa, traveled widely and received a thorough education in Carthage, Athens, and Rome. At Carthage, he was so renowned for his eloquence in both Greek and Latin that statues were erected in his honor and he was made a priest of Aesculapius, the Roman god of healing.

Apuleius wrote his *Metamorphoses*, or *Golden Ass* as it was more popularly known (ca. 158), in a crisp, colloquial, yet vivid style, employing the tale-within-a-tale motif. The descendant of Greek romance novels and ribald short stories (the Milesian tales, first popularized by Aristides in the second century B.C.), *The Golden Ass* was the first Roman novel, or at least the first that has survived. It is the story of a Corinthian named Lucius whose foolish desire for magical powers leads to his accidental conversion into a jackass, a beast of burden who must carry "the heavy pack of Fate." Lucius' ordeals at the hands of various masters, which include hard labor, beatings, and brushes with death and gelding, teach him wisdom.

As with much of Roman satire, the humor is sometimes grotesque and even cruel. Lucius abandons a boy who has abused him pitilessly to a rampaging bear, rejoices at the boy's death, and defecates on the boy's mother when she shoves a hot coal between his legs as punishment for his cowardice.

Among Lucius' many owners during his year as a jackass are a band of Syrian eunuchs, whom Apuleius portrays as greedy, conniving, sexually perverted, self-flagellating, religious fanatics. One of them, we are told, "acted the part of a raving lunatic—as though the presence of the gods did not raise man above himself but depressed him into disease and disorder."

Lucius is finally rescued by the tender goddess Isis, whom he terms "the natural mother of all life" and whose devoted priest he becomes. The discontented hedonist becomes a happy ascetic.

The lesson seems to be that real happiness comes not from dark, occult practices, which rob their devotees of all humanity, but from true religion, which can restore an individual to his full humanity through the habits of obedience, devotion, and chastity. Apuleius himself had been initiated into the mysteries of Isis and possessed a deep interest in Platonic philosophy, which eventuated in some philosophical writings.

In *The Golden Ass*, Apuleius displays a remarkable range in theme and tone. The novel ranges from the magic spells of filthy witches to mystic visions of deity, from the vulgarity of rank obscenity to the rapture of spiritual trance.

The Golden Ass exerted a considerable influence on Western literature. Apuleius' prose influenced the diction and phraseology of Tertullian, the late second- and early third-century North African Christian. Augustine, another North African Christian, later wrote long discussions of Apuleius' work. A statue was erected to him in Byzantium in the sixth century.

But it was during the Renaissance that Apuleius found numerous kindred spirits. Among the greatest of these was Giovanni Boccaccio. After making his own copy of *The Golden Ass* from an old manuscript, Boccaccio was soon retelling two of Apuleius' stories in Italian in the *Decameron*, a novel in which ten Florentines pass the time at a country villa during the Black Plague by telling tales. The lively spirit of the novel, as well as its use of the story-within-a-story motif, clearly owed much to *The Golden Ass*. Possessing the same characteristics, Geoffrey Chaucer's *Canterbury Tales* was, in turn, influenced by the *Decameron*.

From the Renaissance to the nineteenth century numerous short stories, plays, and operas were adapted from *The Golden Ass* in various languages. Edmund Spenser briefly related its story in *The Faerie Queene*. In *A Midsummer Night's Dream* Shakespeare was content to have only Bottom's head transformed into that of an ass, but the debt to Apuleius was clear. Molière wrote a play based on *The Golden Ass*, which he produced for Louis XIV. Bernard de Fontenelle wrote a poem, a play, and a novel based on it. Miguel Cervantes adapted Lucius' encounter with the three wineskins, which he mistook for robbers, into Don Quixote's battle with wineskins. Elizabeth Barrett Browning later wrote a verse translation of various passages of the novel.

The touching story of Cupid and Psyche, which appears nowhere in classical literature before *The Golden Ass*, was enormously influential, inspiring numerous artists, poets, and storytellers for centuries. In the novel an old hag distracts a kidnapped bride from her troubles by telling the story (which she calls "an old wives' tale") of how the lovers Cupid and Psyche overcame the jealousy of Venus, Cupid's mother, and of the numerous hardships the goddess imposed on her would-be daughter-in-law, to enjoy wedded bliss in the end. From the second to the fourth century Christian tombs portrayed the pair of lovers, in the belief that they represented an allegory of the Soul's (*psyche* is Greek for "soul") final securing of Love (Cupid) in the afterlife after enduring the many hardships of this life. Raphael painted the entire story of Cupid and Psyche as a breathtaking mural. Titian, Caravaggio, Rubens, Van Dyck, and Canova all tackled the subject. Rodin even crafted an impressionistic, impassioned sculpture of the lovers. Boccaccio retold the story in his *Genealogy of the Gods*. John Keats referred to the tale at length in a tender ode.

CONCLUSION

Plautus and Terence reshaped and revitalized Western comedy in radically different but equally important ways. Plautus did so by ridiculing the conventions that had turned it into a stale, lifeless genre and by inviting the audience to join in the joke. Terence approached the problem from a different angle but offered an equally viable solution, a more sophisticated brand of comedy that relied heavily on well-drawn characters and character development. In so doing, each became the progenitor of a style of comedy that thrives even today. While the works of nearly all of their Greek predecessors became extinct, the plays of Plautus and Terence survived through the ages, influencing, either directly or indirectly, numerous purveyors of laughter.

Meanwhile, Lucilius and Horace established a new genre of literature called satire that proved equally influential, whether executed in the harsh style of the former or the more genial mode of the latter. While verse satire influenced the epigram, a genre popular in both ancient and modern times, Petronius pioneered a new form of satire that mingled prose with poetry, a style that influenced the satirical novel of Apuleius, which, in turn, impacted a long line of storytellers, culminating in the modern novel.

· 9 ·

Greek and Jewish Contributions in the Roman Era

$\mathscr{G}$ reeks and Jews continued to contribute to Western civilization in the Roman era, especially in the fields of art, historical writing, philosophy, and science. But even these contributions were dependent on the wealth and stability afforded by the Roman Empire. Indeed, the Romans saved many classical Greek artistic masterpieces from oblivion by purchasing large numbers of copies, thereby dramatically increasing the chances of their survival. Greek and Jewish historians rifled Roman history as much as their own for their topics and themes. Greek philosophers and scientists received crucial patronage from Roman emperors and aristocrats.

ART

Much of what is called "Roman art" was produced by Greek artists according to Greek artistic models. Virgil was clearly referring to the Greeks when he wrote in the *Aeneid*, "Others will beat out more subtly lifelike figures in bronze, I have no doubt, and draw living faces from marble."

The Roman Market for Greek Art

But the artistic skill of the Greeks would not have translated into large numbers of dazzling sculptures, reliefs, and paintings without the vast market provided by the Romans' unprecedented wealth and durable roads and without the stability afforded by the Roman peace. The Greek artists of the Roman Empire matched or exceeded the technical skill of their Hellenistic forebears while pursuing themes that appealed to their Roman clients. Beginning in the early second century B.C., the burgeoning wealth of Italy produced an ever-increasing demand for Greek art with which to line the marketplaces, gardens, and baths of prosperous cities. The Campus Martius in Rome was filled with the workshops of stonemasons and sculptors. Aediles sometimes borrowed works of art from private citizens to display in the Forum. When, under Augustus, Asinius Pollio established the first public library in Rome, he made it a museum of sculpture and painting as well as a repository for manuscripts, a precedent that was widely followed.

The demand for art was satisfied by an early form of mass production centered in Italy, Athens, and Caria. The results were not always edifying; sculptors sometimes placed the individualized heads of their middle-aged clients atop mass-produced, athletic bodies. Yet even here one has to admire the cleverness with which joints were hidden.

On the other hand, some sculptures of the Roman era were superb copies or adaptations of Greek masterpieces, made through the use of plaster casts or simple sketches. Indeed, since much of the Greek art of previous centuries survives only in copies and adaptations purchased by wealthy Romans, Rome can be credited with rescuing nearly all of classical art from oblivion. The copy of the *Laocoön* that graced Nero's palace revolutionized art, influencing Michelangelo and many others. The *Laocoön* depicted a Trojan priest of Apollo and his two sons inextricably enwrapped by giant sea serpents sent by the deity, in vengeance either for the priest's violations of his vow of celibacy or for warning the Trojans not to accept the Greeks' wooden horse (there are various versions of the myth). The intricacy of the sculpture and the agony of the three men epitomize Hellenistic artists' radical departure from the simplicity and idealization of fifth-century B.C. Athenian art, as characterized by the figures that graced the Parthenon. (See photo 9.1.)

Other crucial Roman copies include those of Myron's *Discus-Thrower* (ca. 450 B.C.), the first sculpture to combine the mastery of movement with harmonious composition, Polyclitus' *Spear-Bearer* (ca. 440 B.C.), with its counterbalance between tensed and relaxed body parts, and Praxiteles' *Aphrodite of Cnidus* (ca. 370–330 B.C.), which Pliny the Elder considered the greatest statue in the world. The four surviving busts of Pericles are all copies that date from the Roman period, as do the surviving copies of Polyeuctus' famous statue of Demosthenes with his hands clasped.

The artists of the Roman era were not unique in copying (earlier Greeks had copied one another's statues too), were selective in doing so, and were as apt to copy contemporary statues as ancient ones. Furthermore, it is sometimes difficult to determine the extent to which an original work that is no

Photo 9.1.   *Laocoön.* Alinari/Art Resource, NY

longer extant was modified by the "copier," so that what are often called "copies" may, in fact, be more original than presumed.

The large public and private markets for images of the emperors provided Greek sculptors with an opportunity to explore the human form. Throughout the empire statues of Augustus represented him variously as the simple citizen, the philosopher, the man of religion, the Hellenistic monarch, and the conqueror. The most famous of these statues, the *Prima Porta Augustus*, a marble copy of a bronze original, depicted the emperor as a handsome young general in the field (though barefooted like a Homeric hero), his raised hand commanding silence before addressing the troops, as tiny Cupid clings to his cloak. (Since Augustus' family traced their ancestry to the goddess Venus, her son Cupid would have been a relative of the emperor.) Exquisitely carved on Augustus' breastplate was a scene depicting the Parthian return of standards captured from the Romans, his diplomatic triumph of 20 B.C. Gods and goddesses surround the exchange. (See photo 9.2.) Such officially sanctioned images of the emperor appear to have been manufactured in Rome and copied elsewhere. When Augustus died in A.D. 14, he was seventy-six years old yet was still universally portrayed as a fresh-faced youth. This is an indication that Augustus preferred the idealized art of classical Athens to the more popular Hellenistic sculptures, in sharp contrast to Roman aristocrats of the republican era, who had gloried in the realistic depiction of their grizzled features, characteristics they believed connoted gravity and dignity.

The Altar of the Augustan Peace (13–9 B.C.)

Other indications of Augustus' preference for fifth-century Athenian artistic models are the grace and fine sense of proportion that characterized the reliefs Augustus commissioned for the monumental *Ara Pacis Augustae* (the *Altar of the Augustan Peace*). This altar was situated on a stepped platform surrounded by high marble walls broken by entrances on the east and west—a form inspired by the Altar of the Twelve Gods in the Athenian agora. (See photo 9.3.) Decorations on the altar itself include a frieze depicting the altar's dedication ceremony (9 B.C.), attended by the emperor, his family, various priests, and the Vestal Virgins. On the outer side of the wall are scrolls of fantastic, varied vegetation that climb the Corinthian pilasters at the corners. Small animals, such as frogs, birds, and insects, appear in the vegetation. Above this decorative zone on the side walls is a frieze depicting two views of the same ceremonial procession, that which preceded the consecration of the site in 13 B.C. The frieze is marked by calm faces but animated gestures, as Augustus performs sacrifices, accompanied

Photo 9.2. *Augustus of Prima Porta.* Vanni/Art Resource, NY

Photo 9.3. *Ara Pacis (Altar of the Augustan Peace).* Nimatallah/Art Resource, NY

by magistrates, priests, his son-in-law Agrippa, family members, senators, and ordinary Romans. The solemnity of the occasion is relieved by restless children in small togas (see photo 9.4). (This frieze was clearly based on the processional frieze of the Parthenon, in which the gods await the participants of a procession, who are likewise calm in face but animated in action, and Cupid provides the smile.) Relief panels flank the doors on either end. On one panel at the western end Romulus and Remus are suckled by a wolf as Mars, their father, looks on; on another, Aeneas sacrifices a sow following his arrival in Italy, thus connecting his piety to that of Augustus, who is conducting his own sacrifice nearby. At the eastern end a panel portrays Tellus (Earth) offering her bounty to the Romans—fruit, flowers, livestock, and suckling children—all of the blessings of the Augustan peace. Another finds Roma, flanked by Honor and Courage, sitting on the spoils of war.

After the altar was completed by Greek sculptors, it was placed in Augustus' new forum, in which caryatids like those that graced the Erechtheum on the Athenian Acropolis adorned the surrounding colonnades. The altar was located next to a giant sundial whose pointer was an Egyptian obelisk, another symbol of Augustan conquest.

Photo 9.4. Detail from the *Ara Pacis*, procession of the imperial family. *Alinari/Art Resource, NY*

Trajan's Column (A.D. 113)

Equally impressive is the 670-foot frieze that encircles Trajan's Column, designed by Apollodorus, a Greek from Damascus, to commemorate the emperor's victories in Dacia (101–106). An engineer and architect as well as a sculptor, Apollodorus had already proven his genius to Trajan by constructing a bridge across the Danube (at three-quarters of a mile, the longest in the ancient world), the stone piers of which survived until fairly recent times, and by designing Trajan's Market.

Consisting of 155 scenes and 2,500 figures arranged in a three-foot band that spirals around the column twenty-three times (see photo 9.5), the frieze portrays self-confident Roman soldiers crossing the Danube, first on a pontoon bridge (see photo 9.6) and later on Apollodorus' great bridge, foraging, building camps, and slaughtering bearded Dacians from a variety of perspectives, while a calm and larger-than-life Trajan sacrifices to the gods, addresses his troops, consults with his generals, supervises military operations, receives envoys, and offers clemency to the defeated. The largely

Photo 9.5.   Trajan's Column. *Scala/Art Resource, NY*

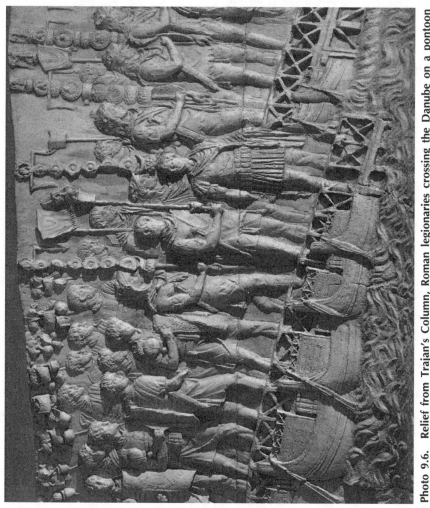

Photo 9.6. Relief from Trajan's Column, Roman legionaries crossing the Danube on a pontoon bridge. *Erich Lessing/Art Resource, NY*

realistic frieze, which serves as a continuous, scrolling narrative, also depicts Roman military surgeons (mostly Greeks) tending to the suffering wounded and Dacian women torturing Roman prisoners. Two tall trees serve to divide Dacians felling trees for their defenses from Romans doing the same, just as buildings sometimes separate one scene from another. The sculptors also portrayed the Romans cutting an impressive road into the cliffs along the Danube, a road widened by planks supported on wooden beams inserted into holes in the cliffs.

Indeed, the column frieze reveals more pride in achievements of intelligence and craftsmanship than in feats of courage: while the auxiliaries (foreigners fighting for Rome) are given more than their share of credit for battlefield victories, appearing in nineteen of twenty battle scenes, only legionaries (Roman citizens) are depicted engaged in military engineering, though this is almost certainly an inaccurate representation of reality. (Another difference is that auxiliaries are sometimes presented decapitating the enemy, something Romans are never shown doing.)

The battle scenes portray the order and unity of the Romans and their allies in contrast to the disorder and disunity of the Dacian "barbarians" and their Scythian allies from the Ukraine, though the courage and self-sacrifice of the foe are also memorialized. The Romans felt understandable pride in their conquest of the Dacians, who had raided Roman provinces, had destroyed an entire legion sent by Domitian to punish them, and had even forced that emperor to pay tribute and to give them Roman military engineers, whose services they then used against the Romans. Some Dacian warriors are depicted killing one another to avoid capture when all is lost; the Dacian leader himself, Decabulus, cuts his own throat. One of the final scenes of the frieze depicts a group of men wearing civilian clothes but military boots marching into the land vacated by the Dacians, whom the Romans deported to other parts of the empire to make way for veterans and other Roman colonists who would stabilize the province for Rome. (These colonists were the ancestors of latter-day Romanians, whose language is a descendant of Latin.) The natives are shown driving their cattle forward, but looking back wistfully at their lost homeland.

Despite the empathy displayed for the defeated, the overall theme of the frieze is that of Roman triumph. As the spiral grows narrow at its end, sheep graze around young trees, sprouting from the new Roman province as symbols of peace, fertility, and renewal, directly beneath a platform on which originally rested a gilded bronze statue of Trajan at the column's summit. (In Christian times the statue was replaced with one of the apostle Peter.) The frieze constitutes a spiral of glory, in which the actions of Trajan's soldiers, under his wise and benevolent leadership, raise the emperor to godhood, as represented by the colossal statue at the top. Despite the many hands that must have carved these numerous figures under Apollodorus' supervision, the style and technique are remarkably uniform and excellent.

The one-hundred-foot, marble Doric column—a height meant to represent the amount of earth that had to be removed from Quirinal Hill to make way for Trajan's Forum—consists of seventeen drums. The column rests on a cubic pedestal, seventeen feet on each side, in which golden urns containing the ashes of Trajan and his wife Plotina were eventually deposited, and which is decorated by a relief depicting Dacian spoils. Inside the column a spiral staircase was lit by forty-three evenly spaced, small, rectangular windows. The roofs of the libraries on either side of the column allowed the viewing of the frieze on the upper part of the column, which was only faintly visible from below. Erected nearby, the Column of Marcus Aurelius, completed under Marcus' son Commodus in the 180s to celebrate Marcus' defeat of the Germans, had a higher base and possessed clearer, simpler, more repetitive reliefs designed for better viewing from below.

Equestrian Statues

Although the Greeks had sculpted equestrian statues for centuries, the greatest surviving example from antiquity is the impressive statue of Marcus Aurelius (ca. A.D. 164). (See photo 9.7.) The gilded bronze figure was spared the fate of so many others that were melted down by medieval Christians because it was falsely believed to be a statue of Constantine, the first Christian emperor. Indeed, the head and one hand of Constantine's own colossal statue (ca. 313), designed in a seated posture like Phidias' *Zeus*, have survived as well.

Funerary Art

Roman art was not confined to the affluent. For instance, most surviving funerary art memorializes middle-class Romans, including artisans and tradesmen. In the late first century B.C. the tombs of prosperous freedmen often featured portrait reliefs set into the walls. The reliefs sometimes depicted the tools of the freedman's trade as well. The heads of some freedwomen of the late first century A.D. were depicted resting on nude, standardized, Venus bodies. In the early second century, when burial began replacing cremation as the predominant funerary practice, mass-produced sarcophagus reliefs portrayed soldiers in battle, intellectuals grasping scrolls, and spouses holding hands.

Photo 9.7.   Equestrian statue of Marcus Aurelius. *Alinari/Art Resource, NY*

Wall Paintings

Wall paintings at Pompeii, perhaps based on Hellenistic stage scenery, often depicted imaginary vistas through imaginary windows. The vistas included elaborate buildings with columns, pediments, and accompanying sculptures. They created a consistent and convincing illusion of depth and demonstrated an understanding of perspective that remained unsurpassed until the Renaissance fifteen centuries later. Although these frescoes sometimes constituted a way for patrons to impress their clients, who were regular visitors at their homes, small houses and shops in the city were similarly decorated, and even private rooms were lavishly painted.

Mosaics

Greek artists working for Romans also achieved a mastery of mosaics. Developed by the Greeks in the fifth or fourth century B.C., mosaics consisted of cubes of colored stone, glass, tile, or shell sometimes as small as a millimeter or two in width, closely set in mortar in order to decorate floors with patterns or scenes. While some mosaic floors were decorated with black and white geometric designs, others portrayed battles, exotic animals, and other vivid imagery. In fact, the most famous depiction of Alexander the Great in battle is a mosaic from a house in Pompeii. Some Roman dining rooms possessed mosaics that cleverly imitated a floor strewn with bits of discarded food after a banquet; highlights and gray shading gave the pieces of litter a three-dimensional appearance. In another case a dog was presented as if rising from the floor, with the inscription, "Beware of the dog!" written beneath him; the shadows cast by the dog's legs and the chain dangling from his neck helped create the illusion of depth. In the public bath at Ostia, Rome's chief port, a mosaic portrayed Neptune driving a team of sea horses. The entrances of shops at Ostia sometimes featured mosaics related to the trades conducted there.

HISTORICAL WRITING

Josephus (ca. A.D. 37–100)

Born Joseph ben Matthias, an orthodox Jew of the priest class, Josephus allegedly attempted to prevent the Jewish insurrection of A.D. 66–73 but was given command of Galilee by the rebel leaders nonetheless. After his army dissolved following the appearance of a large Roman force, he was captured at the siege of Jotapata. Vespasian's son Titus persuaded Vespasian not to kill Josephus after he prophesied that Vespasian would soon become emperor. As Vespasian was marching on Jerusalem, he learned of Nero's death, and, believing that Josephus' prophecy was coming true, freed him. While Vespasian went to Rome to seize the throne, Titus was left behind to conquer Jerusalem. He sent Josephus to the walls of the city to urge his fellow Jews to surrender; instead, they fired arrows at him. After the Romans captured the city, Josephus intervened to save his friends from slavery or crucifixion. He went to Rome, became a citizen, and received an imperial pension. As a common token of gratitude, he assumed the family name of the new emperor, Flavius.

Josephus wrote *The Jewish War* (ca. 80s), an account of the Jewish rebellion against Rome, in Aramaic but later translated it into Greek, the literary language of the eastern empire. Since the history portrayed both Vespasian and his son Titus in a positive light, it is not surprising that both men certified its accuracy. Josephus' most controversial claim was that it was a Jew who had set fire to the Great Temple when Roman soldiers burst into the city and approached it, though Josephus conceded that angry Roman soldiers had added firebrands of their own and that Titus had subsequently ordered the entire city razed as a warning to future rebels.

Nevertheless, Josephus depicted Titus as a benign general who, far from delighting in slaughter, had offered the rebels many opportunities to surrender out of a desire to save both the city and the temple. Josephus called the temple "the most wonderful edifice ever seen or heard of."

Josephus portrayed the revolutionaries as a small minority of thugs who forced the Jews to fight the Romans against their will, a claim his own narrative belied. Nonetheless, he also placed some blame at the feet of two Roman governors, Albinus and Florus. Josephus claimed that he sought "less to eulogize the Romans than to console their defeated enemies and to deter any who may be thinking of revolt."

Josephus claimed that the reason he had sought to squelch the Jewish revolt was that God had given him dreams "of the calamities coming to the Jews and of the fortunes of the Roman emperors." Josephus concluded: "It was God who condemned the whole nation. . . . God was indeed on the side of the Romans." Josephus seemed to think that God had used a foreign army to chastise His people for their corruption and gross violations of the Mosaic Law, just as He had used the Babylonians over six centuries earlier. Like Caesar, Josephus wrote of himself in the third person.

Josephus also wrote *Jewish Antiquities* (A.D. 93–94), a history of the Jewish people and a defense of Jewish religion, law, and culture. In contrast to his earlier history, he now placed some of the blame for the Jewish revolt on malfeasance by Nero, King Herod Agrippa II, the Jewish high priests, and anti-Semitic pagans (Greeks and Samaritans) who had attacked the Jews without cause. Josephus wrote: "The misfortunes of all other races since the beginning of history, compared with those of the Jews, seem small; and for our own misfortunes we have only ourselves to blame." The first half of this statement is more defensible than the second.

The Christian Eusebius later wrote concerning Josephus, "He was by far the most famous Jew of that time, not only among his compatriots but also among the Romans, so that he was honored by the erection of a statue in Rome." His two works are the most important sources for the political history of the Jews in Greco-Roman antiquity.

Plutarch (ca. A.D. 46–120)

The greatest biographer of antiquity, the prolific Plutarch of Chaeronea in Greece was also a priest at Delphi and a Neoplatonic philosopher. His greatest work was *Parallel Lives*, forty-six biographies of famous Greeks and Romans arranged in pairs for comparison (e.g., Alexander the Great is paired with Julius Caesar). In each case he began with the subject's family and childhood, then proceeded to his introduction to public life (all were statesmen or warriors), his career, his death, and his posthumous reputation. Though Plutarch was a Roman citizen honored by Trajan, he hoped to demonstrate that the Greeks had produced men as great as the greatest Romans, as well as to extract moral lessons from history.

Plutarch was quite aware of the difficulties involved in uncovering historical truth. He noted: "How thickly the truth is hedged around with obstacles and how hard it is to track down by historical research. Writers who live after the events they describe find that their view of them is obscured by the lapse of time, while those who investigate the deeds and lives of their contemporaries are equally apt to corrupt and distort the truth."

Plutarch emphasized natural causes but maintained that they were the principal means the gods employed to shape events. He wrote: "Those who say that to discover the cause of a phenomenon disposes of its meaning fail to notice that the same reasoning which explains away divine portents would also dispense with the artificial symbols created by mankind. The beating of gongs, the blaze of beacons, and the shadows on sun-dials all have their particular causes, but have also been contrived to signify something else."

A classic of Greek literature whose engaging style and numerous anecdotes maintain the reader's interest, Plutarch's *Lives* is also a mine of information for modern historians of Greece and Rome. Plutarch demonstrated a remarkable gift for recognizing and relating the telling detail that would uncover the true nature of a historical figure's character. He noted: "The most brilliant exploits often tell us nothing of the virtues or vices of the men who performed them, while on the other hand a chance remark or a joke may reveal far more of a man's character than the mere feat of winning battles. . . . It is my task to dwell upon those actions which illuminate the workings of the soul." Yet, despite Plutarch's uncommon attention to the private lives of his subjects as a means of disclosing their true character, a method that yielded a wealth of fascinating and significant details generally absent from the works of traditional historians, it is also important to note that all forty-six of his subjects were statesmen and warriors. Like nearly all other classical historians, Plutarch held to the traditional understanding of history as politics and war.

Republican in spirit, *Parallel Lives* nevertheless accepted the necessity of the imperial system, given the moral decline in Rome that had begun during the late republican era. While it was the Greek Plutarch, as much as the Roman Livy, who immortalized the heroes of the Roman republic, about half of his Roman biographies were drawn from the last century of the republic, a tragic time when the republic gave way to a monarchy. Plutarch was no imperial lackey; he characterized Augustus' early career as ruthless and bloodthirsty and his republican opponents as heroes. Yet Plutarch clearly valued the peace

Augustus had restored to the devastated Roman world after a century of civil war and appreciated his skillful administration of the empire.

Nor did Plutarch bewail the Greeks' loss of freedom to Rome, despite his nostalgia for the eras of Greek greatness. Like Polybius and Josephus, two other foreign subjects of Rome who wrote histories of Roman conquest, Plutarch considered the Roman Empire the product of a divine will that was irresistible.

Plutarch's nostalgia for Greece's historic greatness did not render him oblivious to the faults of past Greeks or to the weaknesses of their regimes. Although he admired the culture and learning of fifth-century B.C. Athens, he portrayed its democracy as both unstable and corrupt, even suggesting that its leader Pericles had prosecuted the Peloponnesian War, a war that ended in the destruction of the city's empire, to cover up financial mismanagement (a charge absent from Thucydides' equally critical discussion of Athenian democracy). Similarly, while Plutarch was largely responsible for immortalizing Spartan courage, discipline, frugality, and patriotism, he was also aware of the glaring weaknesses of the polis's rigid, totalitarian system, and, as a philosopher trained in Athens, he could hardly approve of Spartan anti-intellectualism. Plutarch portrayed the Roman republic as having achieved a marvelous blend of the strengths of Athens and Sparta, until it too fell to corruption, a tragic but unavoidable development that paved the way for a more peaceful and prosperous though less noble and heroic empire.

Plutarch also wrote *Moralia*, a collection of more than eighty essays on moral philosophy imbued with a humane spirit. Plutarch advised couples, "Married people should have what they want from each other through persuasion and not by quarreling and fighting with each other." Just as children were common to both parents, spouses "should put everything they have in a common fund; neither of the two should think of one part as belonging to him and the other as not belonging." Plutarch added that a husband should educate his wife in philosophy. A Neoplatonist, Plutarch rejected Stoic fatalism and pantheism and also opposed Epicureanism, which he considered a godless philosophy. Unlike Epicurus, he did not believe that the fear of death was rooted in the dread of a bad afterlife but in the fear of eternal oblivion, which is precisely what Epicurus offered, so that Epicureanism seemed to him not only false but useless. Plutarch interpreted traditional Greek myths as symbols of truth corrupted by spirit beings ("daemons") into immoral tales. *Moralia* influenced Montaigne, Ralph Waldo Emerson, and numerous others.

Plutarch was the most influential of all the ancient historians and perhaps the most influential historian in Western history. He was the favorite author of the Renaissance and of the eighteenth century. Shakespeare used Thomas North's translation of Plutarch's biographies as the basis for *Julius Caesar* and *Antony and Cleopatra*, even borrowing dialogue from them. Nearly every home in the American colonies possessed two works, the Bible and an English translation of Plutarch's *Lives*. From his biographies, modern Westerners learned to idolize Greek and Roman heroes and to idealize classical republicanism. It is no exaggeration to state that the American Revolution might not have occurred without Plutarch's influence.

Diogenes Laertius (Early Third Century)

Much of what we know regarding the history of ancient Greek philosophy comes from Diogenes Laertius, a Greek of mysterious origins who wrote *The Lives and Opinions of Eminent Philosophers*. While this collection of biographies was poorly organized, contained some factual errors, and was sometimes marred by excessive credulity, it was clearly the product of a person given to multifarious reading, amazing industry, and insatiable curiosity. It was a gold mine of anecdotes, witty sayings, decrees, epitaphs, and wills that have survived in no other form. Particularly valuable are the letters and fragments of Epicurus, quoted verbatim, that, together with the writings of Lucretius, constitute our only knowledge of Epicureanism derived from a sympathetic source.

Though Diogenes Laertius' biographies were hardly equal to those of Plutarch, their focus on philosophers, rather than on warriors and statesmen, was highly unusual for an ancient historian and, thus, constitute a unique contribution to Western knowledge. Diogenes Laertius was a favorite of Montaigne and of the influential Epicurean Pierre Gassendi, who coined the term "blank slate" (often falsely attributed to John Locke, who used a similar image in referring to an infant's mind as "a white paper, void of all characters, without any ideas") in connection with Epicurus' famous theory concerning the absence of a human nature.

PHILOSOPHY

Epictetus (ca. A.D. 55–135)

The freedman and Stoic philosopher Epictetus, a Greek from Asia Minor, served in important offices under Nero and Domitian, before Domitian evicted him and other philosophers from Rome. He then lectured at Epirus, where some of his notes were preserved and published by his student Arrian, and he became a friend of Hadrian.

Like other Stoics, Epictetus claimed that the individual human soul originated in the World Soul. He wrote: "If Caesar adopted you, who could stand your intolerable pride? But if you know that you are the son of God, are you not proud?" Epictetus tended to personalize the World Soul, portraying it more as a loving father than as a vague, all-encompassing entity. Nevertheless, even a loving father sometimes had to use stern measures for the good of his child: "When in the future some special crisis befalls you, remember that God, as some stern master in wrestling, has set you to fight a stout and vigorous rival that you may become an Olympian victor; and this does not come to pass without sweat."

Epictetus argued that inner peace was the true path to freedom. Employing the Socratic method, Epictetus fired searching questions at his audience. Some of his sayings include:

> How shall I free myself? Have you not heard many times that you ought to eradicate desire utterly? . . . The eyes of the dead are picked out by ravens only when the dead no longer need them; flatterers, on the other hand, injure the soul of the living and blind the soul's eyes. . . . Man has been endowed by Nature with two ears but only one tongue, so that he may listen to others twice before speaking once. . . . Free is the man who is a master of himself. . . . Control your passions, or they will avenge themselves upon you. . . . Strengthen yourself with self-satisfaction, for that is an unconquerable defense. . . . As the Sun needs no prayers and songs to rise in the sky, but sends forth its warmth and brightness and is beloved by all, so you should not need applause and loud praise to perform your duty. Do good of your own volition and you will be loved like the Sun.

Although Epictetus' fiery language helped popularize Stoicism, and he exerted a profound influence on the Stoic philosophy of Marcus Aurelius, he differed from most other Stoics in important ways. He doubted the existence of an afterlife, he argued for a limited free will (influencing Marcus here), he sometimes suggested that humans could understand natural law through intuition alone, and he condemned suicide. (Zeno, the founder of Stoicism, and Cleanthes, one of its earliest and most influential proponents, had both committed suicide due to ill health, and Seneca, who had committed suicide to avoid execution, considered it justifiable on numerous grounds.)

Plotinus (ca. A.D. 205–270)

The latter part of the imperial period witnessed a revival of Platonism. The most influential of the Neoplatonists was Plotinus, a Greek raised and educated in Egypt who moved to Rome. His student Porphyry, who published his notes as the *Enneads*, claimed that Plotinus spoke little about his own background because he was "ashamed of being in a body." Yet, like Plato himself, Plotinus did not consider matter evil, merely inferior to the perfect, immaterial world of forms (ideas) it represented. He allegedly declined to have his portrait painted on the Platonic ground that the painting would be the mere image of a mere image.

Whereas Plato envisioned the supreme deity ("the Good") as a formless but finite being whose product, the World Soul, used forms to organize preexisting matter, Plotinus viewed "the One" as an infinite being that originated all things. The Mind (*Nous*) emanated from the One, the World Soul (which included human souls) from the Mind, and the material world from the World Soul; each product, while inferior to its producer, resembled it in some ways. Reason (*Logos*) was that part of the World Soul that did not ascend to contemplate its progenitor, Mind, but descended to create, order, and maintain the material world by combining qualitative forms with quantitative matter. While Mind contemplated the One and produced the World Soul, the World Soul contemplated Mind and produced matter.

As parts of the World Soul, human souls simultaneously soared to the level of Mind and stooped to administer the material world. Possessing a sort of free will (Plotinus rejected both Stoic and astrological fatalism), the individual soul could choose to ascend to the level of Mind through contemplation or to descend to base servitude to its material inferiors, a descent that not only constituted a punishment in itself but was also punished by the transmigration of the soul from body to body after the death of each until it completed its expiation. Plotinus suggested that this was probably the fate of most souls, since individual souls seemed to possess a weakness, a propensity for self-centeredness, completely uncharacteristic of their source, the World Soul, caused by their envelopment in matter. (This raised the unanswered question of why individual souls must descend rather than remain out of harm's way like the rest of the World Soul, which managed to create and administer matter through the mysterious power of Reason without sullying its hands through actual, debilitating physical contact with it.) Thus, Plotinus rejected Stoic materialism and pantheism completely; while the Stoic World Soul was a material entity at one with the universe, Plotinus not only insulated his own version of it from so direct and sordid a connection with the material world, setting up Reason as an intermediary, but also guarded the purity of the ultimate source of existence, the One, behind yet another intellectual barrier, Mind.

Despite Plotinus' insistence that matter was not evil, it is difficult not to see a visceral disgust for it behind his manic erection of a cumbersome series of abstractions—Mind, the World Soul, and Reason—intellectual chastity belts clearly designed to protect the One's virginal innocence. Never has there been conceived (no pun intended) a being with so many offspring yet so little direct involvement or interest in the messy process of procreation as Plotinus' One.

Though engaged fully and perpetually in self-contemplation, the One was inherently fruitful. Plotinus compared the One to a spring of water that never runs dry but stays the same despite the stream of creative power that flows from it continuously. Just as a person walking on a beach leaves footprints, so the infinite One left a finite trace, Mind. The trace was separate from the tracer, though reflective of it. Mind then left its own trace, the World Soul, whose own trace was the material world.

The material world was even more inferior to the World Soul than the World Soul was to Mind, or Mind to the One, because it lacked the power of contemplation, and only the contemplative were fully real. There was a steep declension from the unity of the One to the multiplicity of matter. Matter was the final, sterile stage in which the productive force that proceeded from the One petered out.

Possessing an indescribable type of consciousness, the One engaged in eternal, serene self-contemplation. The One was what it willed and willed what it was. Will and accomplishment were contemporaneous in an eternal being. The One was higher than will itself, which was one of its products.

Plotinus counseled his followers to abandon material interests for intellectual meditation in order to lift themselves to an intuition of Mind and, ultimately, to a complete, ecstatic union with the One. Plotinus claimed to have experienced such a union a few times during his life, an achievement secured by stripping away from one's mind everything of a lower nature and becoming simple and harmonious like the One. Even in such a union, the One remained a separate being, though qualitatively the same as the ascending soul.

Plotinus' emphasis on contemplation over action, metaphysical doctrines over moral concerns, epitomized a general, very un-Roman movement directed toward the inner life that would culminate with the triumph of Christianity and the fall of the empire. Lacking any interest in politics, he suggested that it was unreasonable to expect good men to give up the higher, contemplative life, which was far superior to the wielding of earthly authority, to take over the reins of government. Even Plato, who had agreed that the life of the philosopher was superior to that of the politician, had not gone so far in the rejection of the political life; on the contrary, like his student Aristotle, he had written treatises on political theory for the statesmen of his day. By the third century A.D., the traditional Greco-Roman emphasis on civic virtue, which had been ratified by an army of Platonic, Aristotelian, and Stoic philosophers over the centuries, was giving way to a contemplative spiritualism.

Elements of Plotinus' Neoplatonic philosophy influenced numerous thinkers throughout Western history. His characterization of matter as the good product of a good God, though not the highest good and though productive of weakness, and his definition of evil as the absence of good rather than as an active principle in its own right, exerted a powerful influence on Augustine and, through him, on Christian theology in general. Seventeenth-century Puritans, centered at Cambridge University, later became part of a widespread movement to restore Christianity to its Augustinian Platonism after its flirtation with Aristotelian Scholasticism in the Middle Ages. As rejecters of orthodox Christianity, nineteenth-century Neoplatonists, including many of the Romantic writers who created the first national literature of the United States, were able to make even greater use of Plotinus by stripping away the Christian admixtures.

Greek Philosophy in the Streets

It would be a mistake to view Greek philosophy in the Roman era as merely a matter of competing abstractions. While the leading philosophers occupied their time disputing the intricacies of their metaphysical theories, the students who filled their schools were generally partying and brawling. In Athens of the late fourth century A.D., a university town if ever there was one, it was not uncommon for the students of competing philosophical schools (or even of different teachers of the same philosophy) to assault one another with clubs, stones, and knives. Nor was it uncommon for them to kidnap new students landing at Athens' port of Piraeus, in order to force them to join their own particular school, a peculiar but highly effective method of recruitment.

SCIENCE

Science is one area in which the Romans contributed very little to Western civilization. Fervent utilitarians, the Romans were engineers, not scientists. Perhaps their greatest failing—one that may have destined their empire for destruction—was their relative disinterest in any research whose immediate utility could not be demonstrated. The few contributions to science made during the days of the Roman Empire were made largely by Greeks, not Romans.

Indeed, the relative poverty of early medieval knowledge of science was largely the result of the loss of Greek texts and their replacement by simplistic and inaccurate manuals like the *Natural History* (A.D. 77) of Pliny the Elder (A.D. 23–79). A chaotic work filled with sensational tales, this thirty-seven-volume encyclopedia discussed astronomy, geography, ethnology, anthropology, physiology, zoology, botany, horticulture, pharmacology, mineralogy, and met-allurgy (as well as the fine arts and art history). While the sections on mineralogy and metallurgy contained some valuable information, and Pliny's productivity was little short of astonishing (the encyclopedia was compiled while he served three emperors as a general and administrator), the work was riddled with misconceptions based on the misreading and oversimplification of Greek texts. Pliny often failed to distinguish reliable from unreliable sources or trustworthy from worthless information.

Pliny himself conceded that the Romans had done a poor job of build-ing on Greek achievements in science. He blamed this failure on greed: "Now that every sea has been opened up . . . an immense multitude goes on voyages—but their object is profit, not knowledge." Pliny was asphyxiated by poisonous vapors while studying the eruption of Mount Vesuvius and at-tempting to rescue others.

Strabo (ca. 64 B.C.–A.D. 24)

A Greek from Pontus (northern Asia Minor), Strabo compiled a new map of the known world based on his own extensive travels. His was the first map to reflect the importance of projection, the distortions that occur when one reproduces a round object on a flat surface.

Dioscorides (ca. A.D. 40–90)

A Greek physician, botanist, and pharmacologist, Pedanius Dioscorides of Anazarbus in southeastern Asia Minor compiled an encyclopedia of more than a thousand drugs and the plants, animals, and minerals from which they were made. The scale and thoroughness of his work, *On Medical Materials*, far surpassed that of all previous texts. (The whole Hippocratic corpus of the fifth century B.C. had listed only 130 drugs.)

While Dioscorides was not the first to discover most of the remedies contained in his text, he collected them from various lands both within and outside of the Roman Empire, including Arabia and India, codified the data, organized them in a rational fashion, and presented them in a clear, concise style. He combined his own experience as a physician with previous tradition and the reliable testimony of others.

Most of Dioscorides' remedies came from plants. He organized his plants based on the physiological effects of the drugs derived from them. In so doing, without any knowledge of chemistry, he pursued a method whose results were similar to that of modern chemical classification. An astute ob-server, he repeatedly noted the similar effects of similar drugs, even when the plants from which they were derived did not appear related. He supplied the name(s) of each plant, an excellent description and detailed drawing of it, its habitat, the properties of the drugs it provided, the medicinal uses of these drugs, their harmful side effects, impeccable instructions for the harvesting, preparation, and storage of the plants, methods of detecting the adulteration of the drugs, and their veterinary usages.

Some of Dioscorides' remedies were quite sensible and effective. Some treatments involving moldy bread seem to have derived their effectiveness from the power of penicillin; others involved plants now known to contain other natural antibiotics. His recommendation of the consumption of autumn crocus leaves soaked in wine for dissolving cancerous lumps is especially intriguing in light of the fact that modern chemotherapy began in 1938 when it was discovered that autumn crocus produced an alkaloid that disrupted cell division in cancerous cells. Dioscorides also employed squirting cucumber against malignant skin cancer, another remedy rediscovered in modern times. He recommended the use of zinc oxide and copper for skin ailments; they are now components of most dermatological powders, ointments, and lotions. Like many modern physicians, he recommended the moderate use of alcohol while warning against the health problems caused by excessive drinking. Cautious by nature, he generally employed weak terminology like "is good for" and "is useful for," reserving verbs like "cures" and "heals" for well-attested remedies. When he referred to popular traditions of magical cures involving various plants, as all ancient pharmacologists were expected to do, he never validated them by his own authority as he did with natural remedies.

Dioscorides was acutely aware that many drugs have harmful side effects. He included some plants in his text not because they provided real remedies but in order to warn of the side effects of the medicines obtained from them, and he included some drugs because they were useful in counteracting the side effects of others. He warned against breathing the vapor when smelting lead; in fact, not only did he decline to prescribe any internal uses for lead but pointedly failed to include the popular wine sweetener and preservative *sapa*, which contained a lead compound, as one of his recommended wine additives. (X-ray analysis of skeletons has led some modern observers to conclude that the Roman use of sapa and lead cooking utensils exposed them to lead poisoning.)

Dioscorides also understood the crucial connection between the proper harvesting and storage of plants and drug effectiveness. In fact, he was reluctant to prescribe precise dosages of drugs because he recognized that drug potency varied with the time of harvest. He knew that the plants that provided drugs needed to be dried and kept out of the sunlight and was aware that the type of container and length of storage affected drug potency.

A staunch empiricist, Dioscorides confined himself to cataloguing drugs and their observed effects, eschewing involvement in the heated disputes between contemporary dogmatists over their competing, elaborate theories of medicine, theories that were often equally fallacious. If his emphasis on the cure rather than the cause of ailments failed to advance medical theory, it greatly enhanced medical practice while avoiding the tragic errors of his contemporaries that impeded the advancement of medical theory.

For centuries subsequent writers on pharmacology made their contributions within the form and context established by Dioscorides. Unlike many other Greek manuscripts, *On Medical Materials* did not have to be rediscovered by the Western world during the Renaissance because it never left circulation. Translated into Latin and Arabic, it was considered the greatest authority on medicines from Britain to India, from the ancient world until the nineteenth century.

Dioscorides' contributions to botany were nearly as great as his contributions to pharmacology. Many plant names were first known to succeeding generations through Dioscorides' authority. His observations about plants were so acute that even some modern, highly specialized botanists and phytochemists have been amazed at the depth of his insight.

Galen (ca. A.D. 129–216)

Galen, a Greek from Pergamum, the site of a hospital and temple to Asclepius, the Greek god of healing, studied under a series of renowned anatomists before becoming the physician for a school of gladiators, a military surgeon, and, ultimately, the emperor Commodus' personal physician. Galen avoided membership in any of the contemporary schools of medical thought because he considered them all too dogmatic. He preferred to learn from experience, whether by tending the gaping wounds of gladiators and soldiers, by dissecting goats, pigs, and monkeys (human autopsy was frowned upon), or by examining human skeletons.

Galen carried anatomy to a point unsurpassed for another eleven centuries. In *Anatomical Procedures* he charted the bones, muscles, and tendons of the shoulder. In other works he explained the mechanism of respiration, demonstrated that veins and arteries carried blood, showed that an excised heart would continue to beat outside the body, and proved that injuries to one side of the brain produced disorders in the opposite side of the body. He noted the functions of the bladder and the kidney and identified seven pairs of cranial nerves. He discovered the roles played by the brain and larynx in voice production and described the heart valves. He proved that paralysis was caused by damage to the spinal cord. Galen was also aware of the influence of the mind on the body. His writing revealed an abundant knowledge of diseases, and he was skilled in the use of unguents for the healing of wounds. Using opium for anesthesia, his successful surgeries included the removal of nasal polyps, goiters, and tumors. Like his Hippocratic forebears, he emphasized the importance of diet, exercise, and hygiene.

Galen believed that the wonderful unity of the human body produced by incredibly varied and complex organs was conclusive evidence for the existence of a Creator. He wrote concerning the hand and foot: "In explaining these things, I esteem myself as composing a solemn hymn to the great architect of our bodily frame, in which I think there is more true piety than in sacrificing hecatombs of oxen or burning the most costly perfumes, for I first endeavor from His works to know Him myself and afterwards by the same means to show Him to others, to inform them how great is His wisdom, His goodness, and His power."

Galen believed that the Creator, a deity served by the traditional gods of the Greco-Roman pantheon, worked purely through natural causes. For instance, he wrote, "Drugs act like the hands of the gods." Galen believed that natural causes included dreams. Tradition held that Asclepius often healed through dreams, either directly or by suggesting remedies. Galen believed that Asclepius had suggested successful treatments to him in dreams and had even appeared to Galen's father in a dream, urging him to direct his son into medicine rather than politics, as his father had originally planned.

Galen wrote so many books, including medical dictionaries, philosophical works, and histories of science, that his own summary of them, which has been termed the first autobibliography in history, was forty-four pages long. Unfortunately, Galen's biological and medical encyclopedia, one of the most widely used medical books in history in its abridged form (*The Art of Medicine*), helped enshrine the Hippocratic doctrine of the four body humors, the theory that illness was the result of an imbalance between the body's four liquids (blood, phlegm, black bile, and yellow bile). From this theory Galen developed an elaborate theory of four temperaments whose designations (sanguine, choleric, melancholic, and phlegmatic) still influence our language today. As a result of his adoption of the theory of humors (the humorous theory of Hippocratic oafs?), Galen recommended the use of leeches, in some instances, to drain "excess blood." Ironically, modern historians of medicine believe that Galen's recommendation may have actually cured some Romans, including himself, during one bout of plague. Since the Roman diet was iron poor, the withdrawal of moderate amounts of blood may have starved some disease-causing bacteria without killing the patient. Other patients, especially in the medieval and early modern periods, when Galen's encyclopedia became the standard medical authority and leeching was carried to extremes, were not so fortunate. Furthermore, by elaborating and popularizing the pneumatic theory, the traditional theory that the body was regulated by three spirits emanating from the liver, brain, and heart, his authority blocked the discovery of pulmonary circulation until the seventeenth century.

Nevertheless, Galen's works formed the basis for Byzantine, Arabic, and Western medicine until modern times. While his expertise cannot compare with that of modern doctors, who have the benefit of information and technology vastly beyond anything Galen could have imagined, his ingenuity and common sense compare favorably with most of the Western physicians who succeeded him for centuries, though most considered themselves his followers.

Greek physicians like Galen contributed greatly to the success of Roman legions by advancing Roman military medicine. Their emphases on nutrition and sanitary conditions gave Roman soldiers an average life span longer than that of civilians, despite the inherently dangerous nature of their occupation. Greek surgeons developed a special device that could remove arrows without tearing the tissue in which they were embedded and created a surgical clamp that helped prevent gangrene. Military doctors were positioned so as to be able to get to wounded soldiers quickly, at least when the Romans were victorious.

Claudius Ptolemy (ca. A.D. 100–170)

An Alexandrian Greek, Claudius Ptolemy attempted to chart the earth and the heavens. His map of the Roman world was extremely accurate and well projected, employing lines of latitude and longitude. Nevertheless, his underestimation of the size of the planet and overestimation of the size of Asia later led Christopher Columbus to believe that he could reach India in only six weeks by traveling westward across the Atlantic Ocean.

But Ptolemy's most famous error was his support for the geocentric theory, the traditional hypothesis that the earth lay at the center of the universe and that the sun, moon, other planets, and stars all revolved around it, which became the basis of medieval astronomy. Ptolemy also championed the epicycle, a fictitious orbit within an orbit, in order to make discordant planetary observations fit the geocentric theory.

These significant mistakes aside, Ptolemy contributed much to ancient mathematics and science. He developed and improved trigonometry. He constructed astrolabes, devices that determined latitude through the positions of the stars (often used by ships), and sundials. His *Optics* explored the refraction and reflection of light.

It is a tragic irony that the medical and astronomical theories of Galen and Ptolemy, theories their creators intended as a basis for further investigation, were later used to stifle it. As the historian A. R. Burn put it: "It was not the fault of these two great observers and thinkers that later centuries chose them to represent ancient and unquestionable authority. If their work had not existed, something, probably less good, would have been found. For when they died, almost everywhere, for social reasons, the lights of ancient Greece were going out." Indeed, with the exception of pharmacology, Western science during the early Middle Ages was dominated by Pliny's inferior writings; it was not until the twelfth century that most Greek scientific works, including those of Galen and Ptolemy, were rediscovered by the West and translated into Latin.

Both the Greeks and the Romans possessed cultural traits that inhibited the growth of applied science. Most Greek scientists detested what the modern world calls applied science, the attempt to put scientific theories to practical use. Considering all manual labor degrading, these aristocratic scientists rarely built machines of any kind. They believed that men were most divine when they contemplated the universe, most debased when they worked with their hands (except for the sake of art). To use scientific theories for such tawdry purposes as making money was to debase divine truths. Xenophon wrote, "What are called the mechanic arts carry a social stigma and are rightly dishonored in our cities." Even Archimedes, whose ingenious contraptions demoralized the Romans who attacked his native Syracuse in the third century B.C., was not proud of these devices. Although he wrote much about his scientific theories, he wrote nothing about any of these mechanical inventions. The first-century Alexandrian Greek Hero envisioned no use for his primitive steam engine beyond the powering of a child's toy (a hollow ball made to revolve on a pivot by steam raised in a cauldron). As noted previously, Roman utilitarianism was as extreme as Greek disdain for applied science.

Yet the combination of Greek and Roman traits provided the basis for modern science. The modern scientist combines the Greek love of speculation and research concerning the fundamental traits of nature with the Roman focus on the practical employment of knowledge. As a result, modern science and its by-product, modern technology, have revolutionized life in a short time.

CONCLUSION

Even the contributions to the Roman world made by Greeks and Jews were heavily dependent on the patronage, roads, and stability afforded by the

Roman Empire. Greek artists produced large numbers of sculptures and paintings that catered to the tastes of a huge Roman market; in the process they preserved (and perhaps adapted) art of the Greek classical period that would otherwise have been lost. Showered with awards and granted citizenship by Roman emperors, Greek and Jewish historians wrote history that placed the pasts of their own homelands within the context of Roman history and sought to reconcile them to Roman rule. The emperors also patronized the Greek philosophers and scientists whose ideas provided some of the intellectual foundations of the medieval West.

· *10* ·

The Rise and Romanization of Christianity

$\mathscr{I}$t was a Roman citizen named Paul of Tarsus who saved Christianity from extinction. Through the doctrine of justification by faith, Paul was able to appeal to the Gentile multitudes of the Roman Empire. Almost three centuries later a Roman emperor named Constantine set the new religion on a path to even greater expansion by showering the Church with favor. At the same time, by transforming the Church from a victim of persecution into an integral part of the Roman establishment, Constantine set Christianity on a course of increasing Romanization. When the Church rapidly integrated large numbers of new converts who were only partially converted, the inevitable result was the incorporation of various traits of Roman religion. Yet another century later, another Roman citizen named Augustine again saved Christianity from destruction by refuting the charge that the religion was responsible for the collapse of the Roman Empire and by furnishing it with an influential theology.

JUDAIC ROOTS: THE HEBREW PROPHETS (CA. 850–500 B.C.)

The diverse religions of the ancient Near East possessed four common elements. First, they were polytheistic. Second, their gods generally appeared and behaved like human aristocrats, differing only in their possession of greater power and of immortality. Far from omniscient, the gods could be manipulated and fooled. Third, ancient Near Eastern religions were ritualistic. Humans won the favor of the gods through animal sacrifices and other rituals, rather than through adherence to a moral code. The gods cared little about human welfare. Fourth, a class of priests regulated each religion thoroughly.

By contrast, the Hebrew religion involved the worship of Yahweh, an omniscient, omnipotent, and inscrutable but loving and creative God who appeared in various forms (e.g., as a burning bush) and whose name could not be uttered. Thus began the Judaic paradox: a God whose omniscience and omnipotence placed Him far above humans but whose immense love for humans brought Him emotionally close to them. For instance, while both the Babylonian and Hebrew traditions included the story of a great flood and of the salvation of land creatures through the building of an ark, the differences between the two stories are more revealing than the similarities. While the Babylonian gods are moved to destroy humankind by mere annoyance (the noisy humans are disturbing their sleep), the Hebrew God is angered by humans' unethical treatment of one another. The Judaic emphasis on ethical behavior fostered an uncommon belief in spiritual equality, which allowed lay prophets to arise repeatedly and rebuke the priestly class for its deadening preoccupation with ritual.

The Hebrews' great contribution to the Western world was ethical monotheism, the belief that the universe was governed by a single, just God who had created the universe and who demanded that humans behave justly toward one another. The Hebrews had to struggle to preserve their unique religion in the face of the universal polytheism of the region.

It was the prophets who succeeded in placing ethical monotheism at the core of Hebrew religion. The very existence of prophets, often laymen unassociated with any court or sanctuary who presumed to challenge the authority of the priest class, was extraordinary, stemming from the Hebrews' uncommon aversion to absolute rule of any kind. The prophets arose in the period following the death of King Solomon, when the decline of royal power increased the ability of the Hebrew nobility to exploit the poor. The prophets were social, as well as religious, reformers who broached the radical concept of spiritual equality.

Yahweh was a jealous God who demanded that His "chosen people" worship no other. Most ancient peoples could not comprehend this exclusiveness. The Romans, who were always ready enough to add a new god to their pantheon, including Yahweh, considered the Jews (and the Christians) exasperatingly stubborn and singularly narrow-minded for refusing to reciprocate by adding Roman gods to their religion. Since the Romans, like the Near Easterners, did not believe that the gods were omniscient, they cared little about their subject peoples' inner beliefs, demanding only that they placate the gods with outward signs of fidelity.

Yet the prophets' insistence on isolation from Gentiles in order to maintain the purity of Judaism did not arise from a belief in the superiority of the Hebrew people. On the contrary, the prophets made a nuisance of themselves by repeatedly reminding the Hebrews that God had not chosen them because of their superior morality but, rather, in spite of their stubborn tendency to immorality.

The prophets waged an uphill battle against the universal polytheism of the region. In the ninth century B.C. Elijah rebuked King Ahab of Israel for erecting a temple to Baal, equipped with an image of the mother goddess Asherah. Ahab's wife Jezebel, a Phoenician princess from Sidon, was so fervent a worshiper of Baal that she ordered the execution of a hundred Hebrew prophets. According to 1 Kings 17:1, Yahweh then sent a drought to show that Baal had no power in his own alleged sphere, that of fertility. A century later Hosea excoriated the Israelites for continuing to believe that their prosperity came from Baal. Isaiah also castigated them for their idolatry.

The prophets had as great a difficulty persuading the Hebrews to live according to the high ethical standards of the Mosaic Law. Isaiah, Amos, Micah, and Jeremiah each rebuked the Hebrews for thinking they could placate God with sacrificial offerings while continuing to oppress the poor. According to Isaiah (1:11–12, 17), God proclaimed: "I have had enough of burnt offerings of rams and the fat of fed beasts. . . . Who asked this from your hand? . . . Learn to do good; seek justice, rescue the oppressed, defend the orphan, plead for the widow, and help the poor, the fatherless, and widows." Isaiah lambasted the Hebrews for their injustice, taking particular aim at kings (1:23; 3:12–14): "Your princes are rebels and companions of thieves. Everyone loves a bribe and runs after gifts. They do not defend the orphan, and the widow's cause does not come before them. . . . Your leaders mislead you." Amos blasted the rich, who sold "the righteous for silver and the needy for a pair of sandals" (2:6). In the Book of Amos, God scorns sacrifices and songs in His honor, demanding righteousness instead. Amos considered the Hebrews more worthy of criticism than other peoples because they knew God but continued to sin. Micah also spoke for poor farmers who suffered at the hands of rich landlords. He decried the common emphasis on sacrifices (6:7–8): "Will the Lord be pleased with thousands of rams, with ten thousands of rivers of oil? . . . He has told you, O mortal, what is good; and what does the Lord require of you but to do justice, and to love kindness, and to walk humbly with your God?" Micah quoted God (9:23–24): "I am the Lord; I act with steadfast love, justice, and righteousness in the earth, for in these things I delight."

Of course, the prophets also prophesied. Isaiah predicted the Assyrian destruction of the northern kingdom of Israel, saying that God would tear out his vine of Israel since it now yielded bad grapes. Hosea predicted the same calamity as punishment for the worship of Phoenician idols. But the purpose of God's wrath was redemptive: it was intended to shock Israel into liberating itself from its enslavement to false things. Indeed, Hosea was the first prophet to use the analogy of marriage: Israel was the bride of Yahweh. Jeremiah predicted the destruction of Jerusalem by the Chaldeans for its idolatry and other sins. He smashed a clay pot at the Valley of Hinnom, where human sacrifice was practiced, in order to symbolize the coming destruction of Jerusalem. Jeremiah claimed that the impending destruction was not so much an intervention by God as a withdrawal of His saving power (as in Eden), leaving rebellious people to suffer the consequences of their own folly.

The Hebrew prophets also spoke often of the coming of a Messiah, who would lead the world into a golden age of peace and prosperity. In the late sixth century B.C. Isaiah predicted (11:1–2, 4, 6, 10; 28:16):

> A shoot shall come out from the stump of Jesse [King David's father], and a branch shall grow out of his roots. The spirit of the Lord shall rest on Him, the spirit of wisdom and understanding. . . . With righteousness He shall judge the poor and with equity the meek of the earth. . . . The wolf shall live with the lamb, the leopard shall lie down with the kid. . . . On that day the root of Jesse shall stand as a signal to the peoples; the nations shall inquire of him, and His dwelling place shall be glorious. . . . Thus says the Lord God, "See, I am laying in Zion a foundation stone, a tested stone, a precious cornerstone."

In a more famous phrase, now inscribed near the United Nations building, Micah prophesied concerning the golden age the Messiah would produce (4:3): "They shall beat their swords into plowshares and their spears into pruning hooks; nation shall not lift up sword against nation, neither shall they learn war any more." Micah further predicted that the Messiah would be born in Bethlehem.

But perhaps the most influential of the messianic passages was Isaiah's discussion of the "Servant" in chapter 53. Referring to God's promise to Abraham (Genesis 12:3), "In you all the families of the earth shall be blessed," Isaiah foretold the arrival of a "Servant" who would suffer for the sins of others. The work of the Servant would go far beyond Israel. Though imprisoned, tried, and killed as an innocent man, He would not cry out in bitterness or self-pity, but would voluntarily take the sins of others upon Himself and go to the slaughter as willingly as a lamb. Isaiah even implied that the Servant would be resurrected, an idea then alien to Judaic theology. Over five centuries later Jesus began his ministry in Nazareth by reading these passages and announcing, to scandalized gasps: "Today this scripture has been fulfilled in your hearing" (Luke 4:21).

Equally significant to the development of Christianity was Jeremiah's prophecy of a "new covenant" between God and the Hebrew people (31:31–34) involving the forgiveness of sins and based more on a reformation of the heart than on an empty adherence to the laws found on the stone tablets in the Great Temple. Paul and other Christians later wrote that the new covenant had been fulfilled in Jesus, based on Jesus' statement at the Last Supper (Matthew 26:27): "This is my blood of the new covenant." Jeremiah claimed that the new covenant must replace the Sinai Covenant between God and the Hebrew people, which had, in turn, replaced the original, private covenant between God and Abraham.

Christians would later claim that the Jews had rejected Jesus as their Messiah because they had failed to realize that the powerful Messiah and the suffering Servant were one and the same and that there would be *two* comings of the Messiah. Jesus the Messiah had come first as a humble, suffering Servant who died for humanity's sins, but would also come again as an all-powerful king to judge and to rule the world.

THE RISE OF CHRISTIANITY

Jesus (ca. 3 B.C.–A.D. 32)

Jesus of Nazareth was probably born in about what our medieval dating system inaccurately terms 3 B.C. The Gospel of Luke (3:1, 23) states that Jesus began his ministry at the age of thirty "in the fifteenth year of the reign of Tiberius Caesar," which would have begun in A.D. 28. From the biblical description of the shepherds out watching over their flocks, it is doubtful that Jesus was born in the winter. December 25, which was the birthday of the rival god Mithras, was not celebrated as Christmas until the fourth century. The title "Christ" derives from the Greek *Christos*, meaning the "Anointed One," a rough translation of the Hebrew "Messiah."

After a three-and-a-half-year ministry, Jesus was crucified around A.D. 32. The moneylenders and the Pharisees, a sect of devout Jews whom Jesus had criticized, persuaded the Sanhedrin, the council responsible for local government, to arrest Him. Shocked by the blasphemy they perceived in Jesus' claim to divinity but lacking the authority to execute Him, the Sanhedrin turned Jesus over to the Roman procurator Pontius Pilate for crucifixion. The Sanhedrin claimed that Jesus had proclaimed Himself King of the Jews, a treasonable offense. Pilate reluctantly ordered the crucifixion.

Jesus' followers claimed that He rose from the dead and appeared to them before ascending into heaven. One reason this claim was accepted by a sizable group was that, according to a centuries-old Roman policy, those soldiers who failed to keep watch were beaten to death with cudgels and stones by their comrades. For this reason, Polybius had written, "In the Roman army the night watches are faultlessly kept." It seemed inconceivable to many that the guards ordered to watch over Jesus' tomb would have forfeited their own lives by being derelict in their duty. In any case, the disciples declared that Jesus promised to return one day, to judge humanity and to reign in peace and justice, first for a thousand-year period, and then for all eternity.

Paul (ca. A.D. 10–67)

Christianity probably would have perished if not for the apostle Paul, whose original Jewish name was Saul. His family, which was prosperous enough to have acquired Roman citizenship, had originated in the town of Gischala in Galilee but had moved to Tarsus in southeastern Asia Minor. After learning the family trade of tent-making from his father, Paul, an intelligent and spirited boy, had begun training under Gamaliel, one of the greatest rabbis of the day. A second-century account described Paul as having been short and bald, with crooked legs and a hooked nose, but also as having possessed "the face of an angel."

Like most Jews and nearly all of his fellow Pharisees, Paul initially considered the Christians blasphemers. In fact, he became a leading persecutor of them. Paul began imprisoning Christians on the authority of the chief priest and voting for their execution. The Jews who stoned Stephen, the first Christian martyr, laid their coats at Paul's feet for safekeeping, while he nodded approvingly. Interestingly, Paul's mentor, Gamaliel, opposed persecution of the Christians, arguing that if they were not of God, nothing would come of their teaching, and if they were of God, they should not be opposed.

On the road to Damascus, where Paul intended to help Jewish authorities uncover and arrest Christians, Paul saw a vision of Jesus, asking him, "Why do you persecute me?" Paul then continued to Damascus, where he created a stir with his Christian preaching. His old allies among the Jews now wanted to kill him. They watched the gates daily to catch him in his attempt to escape the city. But one night his former enemies among the Christians, who were now his comrades, lowered him down in a large basket through an opening in the city wall.

After living in the desert for three years, praying, reflecting on the implications of his vision, and reaching a new theological perspective based on a reinterpretation of Old Testament scriptures, Paul journeyed to Jerusalem, where his preaching was received with equal violence from the Jewish leaders there. He returned to Tarsus, where he made tents for five or six years. He then spent a year as pastor of a growing Christian church in Antioch.

Against the outraged pleas of some Jewish Christians, who believed that Jesus' teachings were intended for Jews alone, Paul began preaching to the Gentiles of Asia Minor and Greece. Roman peace and roads greatly facilitated Paul's mission.

Paul's decision to carry Christianity to the Gentiles was crucial, since the religion never flourished in Judea. Vital to Paul's success in converting Gentiles was his emphasis on the doctrine of justification (salvation) by faith rather than through adherence to Mosaic Law. Had Gentiles been forced to submit to painful adult circumcision and to the various Jewish dietary restrictions, few would have converted to Christianity.

Paul argued that Christ's death, by paying the penalty for humanity's sins, had freed humankind from the yoke of the Mosaic Law and had placed new importance on simple faith. The contract between God and humans had changed. God no longer demanded adherence to a complex and trying set of regulations and rituals. He now demanded only faith in Jesus. The Law of Moses had served its purpose as a tutor, not only in providing an ethical ideal but also in demonstrating the innate sinfulness of humans through their inability to keep it, thereby also proving the need for a Redeemer. In His crucifixion, Christ, who was without sin, became sin itself, offering Himself up as a sacrifice, so that whoever accepted Him might be held blameless before God. Through Adam's disobedience, sin had come into the world, bringing death in its train; through Christ's obedience, grace had come into the world, bringing with it the free gift of eternal life. While it was perfectly acceptable for Jewish Christians to continue to observe the Mosaic Law, as Paul himself did, Gentiles were certainly not obliged to do so. Their faith in Christ would result in an indwelling of the Holy Spirit, a spiritual rebirth that would inspire them to follow the ethical teachings of Jesus, which were more than sufficient, surpassing the Ten Commandments' admonitions against harming others by adding the duty to help others.

Peter, Jesus' chief apostle, agreed that Gentiles should be admitted into the Church so long as they abstained from eating the meat of animals sacrificed in pagan rites and avoided fornication. He persuaded a synod of Christian leaders to endorse this viewpoint.

From about A.D. 46 to 58 Paul toured the eastern Mediterranean, preaching the gospel. In all Paul traveled over thirteen thousand miles, much of it on foot through rugged terrain, sometimes at night. On his first missionary voyage Paul was stoned nearly to death by a Jewish mob in Lystra. Though left for dead in a garbage heap, the determined evangelist reentered the city that evening. On his second journey Paul was beaten with rods at Philippi. In his later years he contracted malaria or some similar disease and lost much of his eyesight. Paul responded to all of these tribulations cheerfully, writing (Romans 8:18), "I consider that the sufferings of this present time are not worth comparing with the glory about to be revealed in us."

In every city Paul began by preaching at the local synagogue but was generally harassed by Jewish leaders, even to the point of being beaten, stoned, or imprisoned. Paul would then reach out to the local Gentiles, with whom he was generally more successful. Indeed, on his first missionary journey, Paul converted Sergius Paulus, the Roman proconsul of Cyprus. It was then that Saul, encouraged by his success among the Gentiles, began to use his Latin name Paul (*paulus* essentially means "small"). Nevertheless, some Gentiles, such as the idol salesmen of Ephesus, were as hostile to his mission as were the Jewish leaders.

About A.D. 58 Roman soldiers arrested Paul while he was in Jerusalem, after a group of irate Jews spotted him at the Great Temple. During the riot, Paul was beaten severely and nearly lynched. He was imprisoned in Caesarea for two years by the procurator Felix, Pontius Pilate's successor, who refused to release Paul because he feared the Jewish reaction. Felix's own successor, Festus, delayed Paul's release for the same reason.

Realizing that he was not going to be released, Paul demanded a hearing before the emperor's court at Rome, a privilege guaranteed by his Roman citizenship. No doubt relieved to have the matter taken out of his hands, Festus replied, "You have appealed to Caesar; to Caesar you shall go."

After an arduous journey, during which he was shipwrecked on the island of Malta for three months, Paul was placed under house arrest in Rome for another two years. During this time he was manacled to a Roman soldier but allowed to receive visitors. This opportunity allowed him to build up the church in Rome. After his release, Paul preached in the capital and elsewhere.

About A.D. 67, perhaps as part of Nero's campaign against the Christians, Paul was again arrested. This time he slept alone on the cold, dark floor of the Mamertine Prison. Spared crucifixion because of his Roman citizenship, Paul was beheaded. While awaiting execution, he wrote (2 Timothy 4:6–8, 16–18): "I am already on the point of being sacrificed; the time of my departure has come. I have fought the good fight, I have finished the race, I have kept the faith. Henceforth there is laid up for me the crown of righteousness, which the Lord, the righteous judge, will award to me on that day, and not only to me but to all who have loved His appearing. . . . No one stood with me in court, everyone abandoned me; I pray that God will not hold it against them. But the Lord stood with me and strengthened me. . . . To Him be the glory forever and ever. Amen."

Lacking the benefit of Roman citizenship, Peter was crucified shortly thereafter. Tradition holds that Peter, feeling unworthy to die in the same manner as Jesus, was crucified upside down.

The Triumph of Christianity: Constantine and Theodosius

The work begun by Paul bore fruit. By the middle of the third century A.D. Christianity was the fastest growing religion in the Roman Empire. It had spread from its original home in Judea to Syria, Asia Minor, Greece, Italy, France, Britain, North Africa, and Spain, and even beyond the bounds of the empire into Armenia and Ethiopia. Yet it was still a minority religion.

In 313 Constantine's Edict of Milan reversed two and a half centuries of imperial policy, granting toleration to Christians throughout the Roman world. Constantine was the first openly Christian emperor. According to the church historian Eusebius, Constantine claimed that he and his soldiers had seen a cross in the noonday sun, inscribed with the words, "By this, conquer." That night he dreamed that Christ visited him, bearing the same symbol, and commanded him to use its likeness in his engagement with Maxentius, his pagan rival for the throne. (Perhaps Eusebius was confused because the actual symbol used by Constantine was the chiro, a symbol of his own creation, which consisted of a *rho* superimposed over a *chi*, the first two letters of *Christos* in Greek.) In any case, the next day, after Maxentius left the bastion of Rome, Constantine caught his army in a pincer movement. Maxentius' soldiers fled in panic back over Milvian Bridge; Maxentius himself was pushed over the side and died.

Constantine's victory (312) changed history. The Christian emperor lavished subsidies and land grants on the Church and exempted it from taxes. He built magnificent churches filled with gold crosses and chalices and with paintings and statues, made Sunday (the Christian Sabbath, the day of Jesus' resurrection) a holiday, exempted the Christian clergy from taxes, military duty, and (briefly) service in municipal councils, repealed Augustus' laws penalizing the unmarried and childless (to the benefit of Christian celibates), granted citizens the right to appeal the decisions of civil and military courts to Christian bishops, prohibited husbands from divorcing their wives except for adultery (a position based on the words of Jesus in Matthew 5:32), and gave funds to Christian churches to support widows and orphans. He employed Christian bishops in his army units, the first known instance of the use of military chaplains. He forbade the use of his own image in pagan temples, and medals depicted him in a posture of Christian devotion. He prohibited crucifixion and gladiatorial contests, two methods by which Christians had been executed, though the latter continued to reappear for nearly another century. Also in accord with Christian values, he decreed that slave families must be sold together to avoid separation.

In 392 the emperor Theodosius I proclaimed Christianity the state religion of Rome. Considering paganism the worship of demons, Theodosius prohibited pagan sacrifices and the worship of idols, closed some pagan temples, and allowed others to be converted to Christian use. The emperor also discontinued the Olympics, which had always served as a festival for the Greco-Roman gods and whose nudity offended some Christians. Although the emperor did not remove pagans from schools, the army, the Senate, or even the palace, the elimination of pagan public worship doomed an already feeble religion. Within three decades of Theodosius' death the pagan religions were virtually extinct in the empire.

Other Reasons for the Success of Christianity

While Paul's message to the Gentiles of justification by faith in Christ was essential, and Constantine's support for the Church was important, to the survival and eventual triumph of Christianity, there were several other crucial reasons for the success of Christianity. Both Christianity's similarities and its differences with its competitors contributed to its eventual triumph.

Christianity struck a resonant chord with the increasing numbers of Roman subjects who gave credence to some of the doctrines of classical philosophy, especially Stoicism and Neoplatonism. Unlike traditional Greco-Roman religion but like Stoicism and Neoplatonism, Christianity concentrated divinity into a single, powerful entity, a reassuring concept in an era increasingly characterized by division, uncertainty, and powerlessness. (In Stoicism the unifying divinity was the World Soul, in Neoplatonism the One.) By the second century even most followers of traditional Greco-Roman religion had come to believe that the gods were nothing more than the mediating spirits of a universal organizing principle.

Christians, Stoics, and Neoplatonists (as well as the followers of the Persian Mithras and the Egyptian Isis) also shared a belief in the immortality of the soul. This was a great consolation during the late imperial period, when barbarian invasions, bloody civil wars, despotism, and recurrent epidemics severely limited life expectancy.

Homer had portrayed Hades, the Greek afterlife, as a dismal, shadowy realm of reduced consciousness and some pain. Achilles, by then a resident of the place, informs the visiting Odysseus that it is better to be a slave on earth than the king of Hades. As a result, the Greek poets and playwrights often brooded over death. In Euripides' *Iphigenia in Aulis*, Iphigenia pleads with her father, Agamemnon, who is about to sacrifice her to appease the gods: "Oh, my father, do not kill me. Life is so sweet, the grave is so black. . . . Death is nothingness. The most wretched life is better than the most glorious death."

Before the mid to late imperial period, the Romans had possessed the same view of death. Catullus called Hades "a sad place from which no one returns," adding, "My hatred rises against your power, you that devours all things beautiful." To his dead brother he wrote: "Never shall I hear the story of your life, speak to you again, nor see you; more than my soul I loved you, brother." Even Virgil, who was not generally a brooder, referred to "Death's unpitying harness," which carried all away without exception. His Eurydice tells her husband Orpheus: "Goodbye forever. I am borne away, wrapped in endless night, stretching to you, no longer yours, these hands, these helpless hands." This view of Hades as "endless night" was reflected in numerous epitaphs, such as that of Eucharis in first-century B.C. Rome: "Now I observe

my fourteenth birthday here among the shadows of Death's ageless home."
While Hades was not a place of extreme torture, it was dismal enough for the
Gospel writers to feel comfortable using it as their Greek name for hell.

But Christianity taught not only that Hades was a place easy to escape
through simple faith in Christ, but also that a far better place awaited the
faithful. By contrast, the Stoic and Neoplatonic conception of the afterlife
as reintegration into the World Soul was abstract and involved the loss of
individuality, deficiencies that led the Stoics and Neoplatonists, like nearly
all other classical philosophers, to a fatal emphasis on earthly happiness as
the ultimate good—fatal because however much classical philosophers might
emphasize the insignificance of external, alienable goods to earthly happiness,
their exhortations inevitably rang a little hollow. Plotinus was compelled by
his exclusive emphasis on earthly happiness to the absurd claim that even a
man who was being tortured had a part of him that was happy, the part of
his soul that contemplated the One continually—even though the rest of the
poor, tortured man had no consciousness that this was even occurring. It was
far easier for Christians to justify suffering by claiming that earthly existence
was but a fleeting condition easily trumped by the eternal afterlife.

Like the Stoics, Christians emphasized spiritual equality, at a time
when crippling taxation and hyperinflation were impoverishing the empire
and destroying the middle class, and when the courts increasingly favored
the wealthy over the poor. While most contemporary religions reflected the
social hierarchy, aristocrats sat as equals with manual laborers, slaves, former
criminals, and other outcasts in Christian churches. Jesus Himself had been
the son of a carpenter, and Paul had written (Galatians 3:28): "There is no
longer Jew or Greek, there is no longer slave or free, there is no longer male
or female; for all of you are one in Christ Jesus." Although a hierarchical
clergy gradually developed within the early Church, the talented poor could
rise within it.

The Christian belief in spiritual equality increased the religion's appeal
to the rootless multitudes of great cities like Rome, Antioch, and Alexandria—that is, to those people most alienated from Roman society and most
open to new ideas. Christianity was especially popular among the lower
middle class and the free poor—those with something to lose and in the
process of losing it.

Christianity was also popular among women, who constituted a solid
majority of early church members. Aristocratic Christian women gladly introduced the religion to their influential husbands since it taught the revolutionary doctrines that women were equal to men in God's eyes, that husbands
should treat their wives with consideration, and that adultery was as serious a
sin in a husband as in a wife. In sharp contrast to classical biographers, who

focused almost exclusively on political and military affairs, areas of life from which women were excluded, Christian authors included female saints in their hagiography.

Slaves were also drawn to Christianity by its egalitarianism. The treasuries of Christian churches were often used to finance the manumission of a considerable number of slaves who were prisoners of war. Several emancipated slaves became bishops. The Church contradicted Roman law in recognizing marriages between free and slave. Though Aelius Aristides' accusation that Christians "show their impiety as you would expect them to, by having no respect for their betters" was more than a bit exaggerated, it expressed the outrage of aristocratic pagans at the greater degree of egalitarianism among early Christians.

But although Christianity's similarities to classical philosophy were important to its success, its differences were equally crucial. First, the Christian faith was based upon a historical figure. While Stoicism, Neoplatonism, and the other philosophies of the day were too abstract for most people, Christianity was based on a real man who had walked the earth, who had loved, and who had suffered and died. Christian theologians like Justin Martyr portrayed Jesus as the bridge that joined Plato's world of the forms with his world of the senses, the spiritual with the material.

Of course, the dual nature of Jesus as both man and God created theological problems as well. To some, the Holy Trinity of God, Jesus, and the Holy Spirit conflicted with Hebrew monotheism. In 325 a council of bishops at Nicaea in Asia Minor upheld the Trinity over the doctrine of Arius that both Jesus and the Holy Spirit were creations of God, different in substance from Him—a doctrine that contradicted the apostle John's statement concerning Jesus (1:1, 14), "In the beginning was the Word, and the Word was with God, and the Word was God. . . . And the Word became flesh and dwelt among us." The council declared Jesus and the Holy Spirit equal members of the Trinity and of the same substance as God. In 381 another council, at Constantinople, reaffirmed and strengthened the Nicene Creed. Although the Arian doctrine was banned as heresy, it made repeated appearances throughout Western history. Others, including many Gnostics, attacked the Trinity from the other side, slighting or denying many of Jesus' human traits, a heresy that was condemned by the Council of Chalcedon in 451.

But many early converts were attracted to Christianity by the combination of humanity and divinity joined in Jesus. The Trinity seemed to represent the three greatest manifestations of God's love for humanity: creation, redemption, and inspiration. While Christ had made God visible to the world during His lifetime, the Holy Spirit, dwelling in the hearts of individual believers, made God visible in the centuries after Christ's death and resurrection.

Second, early Christians evoked both sympathy and fascination by their willingness, even eagerness, to suffer persecution and death for their faith, a trait that originated in the conviction that a far better and more permanent world awaited them. Viewing Christians as dangerous traitors whose attack on Roman religion constituted a masked assault on the Roman state itself, Nero charged Christians with the burning of Rome in 64, executing women and children as well as men. While the "Five Good Emperors" of the second century ordered their provincial governors not to seek out Christians for arrest, they instructed them to execute those charged and convicted of being Christians. Even the magnanimous Pliny the Younger ordered the execution of Christians while serving as the emperor's curator in Bithynia, insisting that the Christians' "stubbornness and unshakable obstinacy" in refusing to repudiate Christ and make offerings to the emperor's statue "ought not to go unpunished." In 177 the entire Christian communities of Lyons and Vienne were tortured to death by mobs. The emperors Decius (249–251), Valerian (257–258), Diocletian (303–305), Galerius (305–311), and Maximin (311–313) launched even more vigorous campaigns of persecution. Soldiers burned an entire Christian town in Phrygia. Churches were destroyed, copies of Scripture were burned, and Christians were imprisoned, mutilated, beaten, drowned, branded, decapitated, tortured, hanged, and starved to death. Searching out, arresting, and killing all of the Christians he could, Diocletian declared his intention to end Christianity. Maximin even offered tax exemptions to cities that demonstrated a willingness to persecute Christians. This intense persecution of Christians was especially remarkable considering the Romans' usual tolerance of other religions. The historian Edward Gibbon once wrote: "The various modes of worship which prevailed in the Roman world were all considered by the people as equally true, by the philosopher as equally false, and by the magistrate as equally useful." Yet Roman magistrates exempted Christianity from this judgment.

Christian courage amidst persecution transformed pagan opinion of them. Initially, most pagans feared and despised Christians, considering them an upstart cult of bizarre and rebellious Jews, slaves, and other rabble who worshipped a crucified criminal, plotted treason (at secret meetings where they preached the fall of the Roman Empire and the rise of a new king), practiced black magic and cannibalism (a misunderstanding of the Eucharist), engaged in orgies and infanticide (why else did meetings occur secretly and in the evening?), and endangered the unity and safety of the state by dividing families and by refusing to worship the gods, who responded by sending droughts. Others denounced Christians to get their property. Nevertheless, accustomed to broad latitude in religious matters, many Romans were horrified by the persecution of Christians. Even Tacitus, who detested the Christians, denounced Nero's treatment of them. He noted that the emperor's scapegoating of the Christians had backfired: "Their deaths were made farcical. Dressed in wild animal skins, they were torn to pieces by dogs, or crucified, or made into torches to be ignited after dark. . . . Nero provided his Gardens for the spectacle, and exhibited displays in the Circus. . . . Despite their guilt as Christians, and the ruthless punishment it deserved, the victims were pitied. For it was felt they were being sacrificed to one man's brutality rather than to the national interest." Even leading Stoic and Neo-platonic critics of Christianity, like Epictetus, Marcus Aurelius, Galen, and Celsus, were impressed by the courage of Christians. Though he had heard that Christians were cannibals, the pagan Justin Martyr nevertheless became so convinced by their courage that they possessed supernatural power that he converted to the religion and became one of its leaders. Tertullian, a converted North African, summarized the effect of persecution: "The more we are mowed down by you, the more we will multiply. The blood of Christians is seed!" As the historian E. R. Dodds aptly put it: "Christianity . . . was judged to be worth living for because it was seen to be worth dying for. . . . We know from modern experience of political martyrdoms that the blood of the martyrs really is the seed of the Church, always provided that the seed falls on suitable ground and is not sown too thickly. But pagan martyrs under Christian rule were relatively few—not because Christianity was more tolerant, but because paganism was by then too poor a thing to be worth a life."

Third, Christianity was based on a profoundly eloquent written work. The books of the New Testament were written from approximately 50 to 100 A.D. By the end of the second century the New Testament canon had gradually coalesced from among various rival works, a selection process based on the age of the books and on the degree to which they conformed to what were considered the teachings of Jesus' first followers. The Gospels of Matthew and John were selected because they had been two of Jesus' apostles, the Gospels of Mark and Luke because they had worked under Paul. As the historian Henry Chadwick put it, "The truly astonishing thing is that so great a measure of agreement was reached so quickly." In 367 Athanasius, the bishop of Alexandria, commanded the acceptance of twenty-seven books of the New Testament and no others. Ecclesiastical councils endorsed his list in 393 and 397. Against modern speculations to the contrary, the historian Paul K. Conkin concludes: "It now seems almost certain (on none of these issues can anyone be fully certain) that three and possibly all four canonical gospels were written before 100 C.E., that the churches early accepted them as genuine, that the received and critically compared texts are very close to the originals, that the authors were probably directly influenced by the apostles . . . and that other early, competing, largely Gnostic-influenced gospels had much weaker credentials on strict scholarly grounds."

The New Testament was simple yet profound. Written in plain but powerful Greek, it was one of the few works not written by aristocrats for aristocrats. The New Testament was written simply enough that the illiterate members of a congregation could readily understand it when read by the literate members. Yet its wisdom was profound enough to dazzle intellectuals like Augustine, who wrote concerning it: "While readily available to all men, it yet kept the grandeur of its mystery under a more profound sense; by clear language and simple style making itself available to all men, yet exercising the intent study of those who are not light-minded." One of the most intriguing passages of Augustine's *Confessions* is his account of his initial dismissal of the Scriptures as inferior to the works of Cicero and other classical philosophers, an attitude he claimed revealed more concerning his own previous arrogance and folly—his unwillingness to learn from the humble Jesus—than concerning the Bible. Like most proud intellectuals, Augustine had assumed that works were profound precisely to the extent that their style rendered them inaccessible to the masses. But, on closer inspection, he had found that the Scriptures contained all the truths of the classical philosophers without any of their errors—and with the added benefit of the salvation conferred only by Jesus. Augustine concluded regarding classical works: "Those pages do not show the countenance of piety, the tears of confession, Thy sacrifice, a troubled spirit, a contrite and humble heart, the salvation of a people, the promised city, the promise of the Holy Spirit, or the chalice of our redemption. . . . It is one thing to see from a wooded mountain top the land of peace, and not to find the way to it, and to push in vain over tractless country . . . and it is quite another thing to keep the way which leads there, which is made safe by the care of the heavenly Commander." Classical works had shown Augustine the beauty of virtue and a vision of peace, but, in so doing, had only left him frustrated at his inability to attain these goods. It was the simple yet profound Scriptures, so denigrated by foolish intellectuals, that had shown him the path to salvation.

Jesus' well-chosen metaphors were particularly effective in conveying the full meaning of God's love to the ancient world's multitude of farmers and shepherds. In explaining the need for His own death Jesus said (John 12:24), "Unless a grain of wheat falls into the earth and dies, it remains just a single grain; but if it dies, it bears much fruit." In depicting His love for humankind He declared (John 10:11): "I am the good shepherd. The good shepherd lays down his life for the sheep." In portraying the love of God for lost sinners Jesus said (Luke 15:4–7): "Which one of you, having one hundred sheep and losing one of them, does not leave the ninety-nine in the wilderness and go after the one he lost until he finds it? When he has found it, he lays it on his shoulders and rejoices. And when he comes home, he calls together his friends and neighbors, saying to them, 'Rejoice with me, for I have found my sheep that was lost.' Just so, I tell you, there will be more joy in heaven over one sinner who repents than over ninety-nine righteous persons who need no repentance." Filled with such treasures, the New Testament conquered the Roman Empire.

Perhaps most important, Christianity was the first religion to place love at its center. While previous religions had certainly included love in their theology, no other religion had made it the chief obligation of its adherents. Jesus (Matthew 22:37–39) claimed that the Ten Commandments could be summarized in two statements: love God with your whole heart, soul, and mind, and love your neighbor as yourself.

Love is the only theme that runs through every book of the New Testament. In a famous passage (John 3:16) Jesus declared, "For God so loved the world He gave his only Son, so that everyone who believes in Him may not perish but may have eternal life." John also wrote (1 John 4:8, 11): "Whoever does not love does not know God, for God is love. . . . Beloved, since God loved us so much, we also ought to love one another." Paul wrote (Romans 8:38): "What can separate us from the love of God? I am convinced that neither death, nor life, nor angels, nor rulers, nor things present, nor things to come, nor powers, nor height, nor depth, nor anything else in all creation will be able to separate us from the love of God in Christ Jesus our Lord." Paul also declared (1 Corinthians 13:1–3, 13):

> If I speak in the tongues of mortals and angels, but do not have love, I am a noisy gong or clanging cymbal. And if I have prophetic powers, or understand all mysteries and all knowledge, and if I have all faith, so as to remove mountains, but do not have love, I am nothing. If I give away all my possessions, and if I hand over my body to be burned, but do not have love, I gain nothing. Love is patient; love is kind; love is not envious or boastful or arrogant or rude. It does not insist on its way; it is not irritable or resentful; it does not rejoice in wrongdoing, but rejoices in the truth. . . . There remain but three things: faith, hope, and love; and the greatest of these is love.

Augustine wrote: "Let them all mark themselves with the sign of the cross, let them all say Amen, sing Hallelujah, let them all be baptized, go to church and build basilicas—there is nothing which distinguishes the children of God from the children of the devil but only love." A pleasant and universal emotion, love has proved an excellent basis for religion—and not just in the brutal days of the late Roman Empire.

Christianity possessed a sense of warmth and benevolence absent from the cold duties of Stoicism, Neoplatonism, and the other classical philosophies. Although the Christian duty to love his neighbor was far more difficult to obey than the classical obligation to merely avoid injuring him, the former duty was far more emotionally fulfilling. Paragons of classical virtue were admirable fellows in many ways: honest, hardworking, self-disciplined—men of iron integrity, near gods by the standards of their day. But there was little in them to touch the heart. The classical ethic was justice, not love or mercy. Men like Cato the Elder would not fail to give others their due. But they would not smile while doing so and would not give an ounce more. And one could be certain that they would insist on their own, and would defend it with a righteous violence if necessary. In contrast to Hesiod's dictum, "Invite your friend to dinner; have nothing to do with your enemy," Jesus instructed (Matthew 5:44), "Love your enemies; bless those who curse you."

Converting to Christianity meant joining a family that offered physical, economic, and emotional support in an exceedingly troubled time. Early Christians shared their wealth freely with widows, orphans, the elderly, the unemployed, the disabled, and the ill. They placed their lives at grave risk caring for victims of the plague and other natural disasters, while pagans fled. They ransomed one another from barbarian captors, distributed bread during famines, and visited prisoners and miners, the most wretched of all slaves. One group of Christians in Rome even sold themselves into slavery to raise the money to ransom their brethren from prison. Other Christians provided for the burial of the poor and were hospitable to travelers. Even the hostile emperor whom the Christians called "Julian the Apostate" complained, "These godless Galileans feed not only their own poor but others, while we neglect our own." The Christian sense of community, reinforced by common rites, a common way of life, and the common threat of persecution, gave its members a sense of belonging that was probably more important than the material security it afforded. Tertullian said, "We hold everything in common but our spouses"—the reverse of the rest of Roman society, he joked, where most people shared nothing else.

While the ethical codes of Christianity and classical philosophy were similar, they differed in a few significant respects, and the Christian and classical conceptions of the purpose of ethical behavior differed markedly. The historian Forrest McDonald once explained the difference between a "man of religion" and a "man of honor" (in this context, an orthodox Christian and a classical philosopher): "The one considers vice as offensive to the Divine Being, the other as something beneath him." To the classical philosopher (the "man of honor"), virtue was rewarded in this life through self-respect and the respect of others. By contrast, the Christian (the "man of religion") sought his reward exclusively in the next life, expecting only persecution for his virtue in this sinful world, in imitation of Christ, and considering the love of praise a vice. In Christianity the quest for heaven replaced the classical quest for honor and fame. The former quest was more attractive since the latter was more problematic: as even Marcus Aurelius noted, how could one be assured that future generations would honor one's contributions, and even if they did, one would no longer be around to acknowledge, much less enjoy, this fame. Throughout history most people have shared Woody Allen's sentiment, "I don't want immortality through my work; I want immortality through not dying." The doctrine of the immortality of the soul answers this desire.

Christians differed from classical philosophers even more markedly in praising humility. While the Greeks and Romans never considered vanity a vice (classical heroes like Achilles and Odysseus were an exceedingly vain lot), Christians considered pride the greatest sin, constituting a form of blasphemy. Vanity also conflicted with the Christian emphasis on the insignificance of worldly success when set against the tremendous importance of the eternal afterlife. Christianity taught that God had not only lowered Himself to become a man, but had even adopted the humble status of a carpenter's son. What right to vanity had any mere human then? In the Sermon on the Mount, Jesus declared (Matthew 5:5), "Blessed are the meek, for they will inherit the earth." Paul commanded (Romans 11:20), "Do not become proud, but stand in awe." Augustine concluded: "And therefore it is that humility is specifically recommended to the city of God as it sojourns in this world and is specially exhibited in the person of Christ its King, while the contrary vice of pride, according to the testimony of the sacred writings, specifically rules its adversary the devil." Augustine argued that classical virtue, through its impious substitution of self-admiration and the applause of others for a recognition of one's sinfulness and a plea for divine help, could itself become a vice, a proud form of self-love.

Like Jews, Christians were scandalized by the classical notion that the gods differed from mortals only in their greater powers and in their immortality. Lacking any doctrine of original sin and raised on the traditional stories of self-centered, petty gods, pagans claimed, "Man is a mortal god, and god an immortal man." While the Judeo-Christian tradition proposed a much larger gap between the nature of God and that of humans than the classical tradition, it proposed a much smaller gap in sentiment, claiming that the Judeo-Christian God, unlike the selfish Greek gods or the emotionless, self-absorbed, noninterventionist One of the Neoplatonists, Aristotelian Prime Mover, Stoic World Soul, and Epicurean deities, loved and aided humanity.

But orthodox Christians (such as this author, in the interest of full disclosure) would be far from satisfied with an exclusive emphasis on these purely natural causes of the rise of Christianity. Rather, orthodox Christians insist that this great movement was primarily the work of the Holy Spirit touching human hearts. Christians believe that from the time of the Holy

Spirit's first appearance to the apostles at Pentecost (Acts 2), when individuals from different nations each heard the apostles speaking eloquently in his own language, the Holy Spirit began acting as the guardian of the Christian Church until the Second Coming of Christ.

THE ROMANIZATION OF CHRISTIANITY

After Constantine transformed the Church from a victim of the Roman establishment into an integral part of it, it became Romanized. In the century following Constantine's conversion, the number of those who called themselves Christians rose from approximately five million to thirty million. As large numbers of pagans joined the Church and even the Christian clergy for unspiritual reasons—to be on the winning side, to secure goodwill, money, and even political offices from an emperor who was notoriously credulous where professing Christians were concerned, to avoid onerous service in the army or on town councils, or, by the fifth century, to avoid the wrath of Christianized Germanic tribes—rather than for the spiritual reasons of the persecuted early converts, the Church was as much influenced by the tidal wave of partial converts as the partial converts were by the Church.

The result was the transformation of Christianity by a new syncretism with Roman paganism. The setting for worship became more elaborate, the liturgy became more ritualistic, the language of Scripture changed from Hebrew and Greek to Latin, scriptural interpretation became more allegorical, church polity became more hierarchical, the Church became deeply involved in the workings of the State, Roman anti-Semitism seeped into the Church, and new doctrines, such as the intercession of Mary and the saints, salvation by a combination of faith and works, purgatory, and the efficacy of relics were introduced, along with new practices, such as pilgrimages to holy sites.

Enormous, ornate churches, often funded by the emperors and modeled on Roman basilicas, replaced private homes and catacombs as places of worship. An awestricken Spanish visitor to the Church of the Holy Sepulcher in Jerusalem remarked: "The decorations really are too marvelous for words. All you can see is gold and jewels and silk. . . . You simply cannot imagine the number and the sheer weight of all the candles, tapers, lamps, and everything else they use for the services. . . . They are beyond description, and so is the magnificent building itself. It was built by Constantine and . . . was decorated with gold, mosaic, and precious marble, as much as his empire could provide."

These basilicas were filled with art inspired by pagan models. While early Christians had avoided depicting Jesus out of a Judaic fear of encouraging idolatry, Roman artists now depicted Him either with the long, unkempt hair, beard, and extensive robes of an itinerant Greek philosopher, or seated on a throne in the posture of a Roman emperor. Representations of His childhood resembled those of the god Dionysus.

At the same time, an early form of the Latin Mass replaced the simple gatherings of early Christians. In the second century Pliny the Younger had discovered that the Christians of Bithynia met before dawn "on a fixed day to chant verses alternately amongst themselves in honor of Christ as if to a god," after which they took an oath "to abstain from theft, robbery, and adultery," meeting only once more for a communal meal (the *agape*), a simple mode of worship consistent with the New Testament accounts of the previous century. The increased ritualism of the liturgy in the fourth century was an expression of the traditional Roman preoccupation with ritual, rather than a recurrence of Judaic ritualism. To cite one example, the historian Dionysius of Halicarnassus had described a Roman festival procession in the first century in which men "carried censers in which perfume and frankincense were burned along the entire route," an element of Roman paganism now inherited by the Church.

The Bible was now read in Latin rather than in the original Hebrew and Greek in the West. The core of the Vulgate Bible, the standard Scripture in the West for over a millennium, as well as an essential tool in attracting Roman converts, was provided by Jerome of Dalmatia (ca. 347–420), who translated the Book of Psalms and the Gospels into Latin. The product of eighteen years in isolation in Bethlehem, Jerome's translation was as elegant as previous Latin translations had been wretched. Latin became not only the language of the Mass and of the Bible in the West but also the official language of the Church itself.

Another aspect of the Romanization of Christianity was the development of a hierarchical clergy. In the beginning church polity had been rather simple and democratic. By the 50s A.D. some local churches were organized under deacons ("those who serve"), who collected and redistributed alms, and presbyters ("elders," the forerunners of priests), who provided religious instruction and discipline. Congregations were joined together in dioceses under bishops (*episkopoi*). Initially, the laity of each diocese elected their own bishop, though at least three bishops from neighboring dioceses had to agree to consecrate them.

But by the fourth century the life-tenured bishops had taken control of the selection process. Considered successors to the apostles, they had the power to deny the Eucharist to the ethically or doctrinally impure. They could appoint and suspend deacons and elders and could excommunicate members of their congregations, which was considered to be the equivalent of a sentence of damnation. Their councils, whose decisions were increasingly regarded as infallible products of the Holy Spirit, followed procedures modeled on those of the Roman Senate and of Roman municipal councils. They began to take a larger role in examining sinners and assigning days of fasting to them, the beginnings of the sacrament of confession.

Meanwhile, the bishop of Rome increased in importance. As early as 100 A.D., one such bishop, Clement, had advanced the Petrine theory, the claim that the leadership of the Church rightfully belonged to the bishop of Rome, who was the heir of Peter, whom Jesus had called "the rock on which I will build my church" and who had possessed the power to "loose or bind" sins (Matthew 16:18–19). The doctrine gained momentum during the fourth century, when some Christians believed the Arian controversy revealed the need for greater standardization of church doctrine through the centralization of authority. The theory received further support in the fifth century, when the need for centralization amid the collapse of the western empire encouraged Pope Leo I (440–461) to endorse the doctrine. Though other bishops remained largely independent of the formal authority, if not the considerable influence, of the bishop of Rome until the eleventh century, the Petrine theory was well on its way to acceptance. By the fourth century popes were living in such opulence that the proud pagan aristocrat Vettius Agorius Praetextatus quipped, "Make me a bishop of Rome, and I will at once become a Christian!"

The Church became as deeply involved in the affairs of state as pagan religion had been. By the end of the fourth century state power was being used to punish pagans and heretics, and Christian bishops held key posts in Roman civil and military administrations.

Though the Church had been founded by Jewish Christians, it was now increasingly pervaded by Roman anti-Semitism. Jesus and all twelve of His apostles had been Jews; in fact, all of the authors of the New Testament, with the possible exception of Luke (who may have been a Jewish convert before he converted to Christianity), were Jews. The apostles had not only been ethnically Jewish but had continued to live according to Mosaic Law their whole lives, though not requiring it of Gentile converts. Nor had the New Testament confined the Judaic nature of Christianity to the past: the Book of Revelation looked forward to the day when Jesus, as Messiah and king, would be recognized universally as "The Lion of Judah, the Root of David" (5:5) and labeled the eternal, heavenly city "the New Jerusalem" (3:12; 21:2), its twelve gates inscribed with the names of the twelve tribes of Israel (21:12). Nevertheless, Gentile Christians now began to justify the persecution of Jews on the grounds that they had been responsible for the crucifixion of Jesus, forgetting that their own scripture emphasized the crucial fact that Jesus had been a sacrificial lamb, "slain from the foundation of the world" (Revelation 13:8), for the sins of all humankind.

Constantine himself, though relatively tolerant in practice, had imbibed traditional Roman anti-Semitism and was not shy about expressing it in Christianized form. For instance, he objected to calculating the proper date of Easter according to the Jewish calendar: "It seems unworthy to calculate this most holy feast according to the customs of the Jews, who, having stained their hands with lawless crime, are naturally, in their foulness, blind in soul. . . . What right opinions can they have who, after the murder of the Lord, went out of their minds and are led not by reason but by uncontrolled passion." He added that the main object of Christians should be to "sever all communication with the perjury of the Jews."

Like many of the new Gentile Christians, Constantine was largely ignorant of the depth of the Judaic roots of Christianity. To use his own example of the date of Easter, the Jewish Gospel writers had clearly intended to emphasize the symbolism of Jesus' death, burial, and resurrection on Jewish festival days. They emphasized His death on Passover as the spotless "Lamb of God" whose blood would save sinners from spiritual death, just as the original Passover lamb had saved Jewish households in Egypt from the angel of death, His time in the grave during the Feast of Unleavened Bread when leaven (symbolizing the world's sin, which Jesus had taken upon Himself) was removed from the world, and His resurrection on the Feast of Firstfruits, symbolizing His status as the firstfruits of the Resurrection (1 Corinthians 15:23).

One consequence of the new anti-Semitism was the increased popularity of replacement theology, which contended that God had abandoned the Jews because of their rejection of Jesus and that all of the Bible's end-time prophecies concerning the now-defunct nation of Israel actually referred to the Christian Church. This nonsensical view—nonsensical because nearly all of the end-time prophecies were quite specific to the geography and statehood of Israel—was all the more remarkable given that replacement theology clearly contradicted the eleventh chapter of Paul's letter to the Romans. Paul began that chapter: "I say then, has God cast away His people? God forbid. For I also am an Israelite, of the seed of Abraham, of the tribe of Benjamin. God has not cast away His people whom He foreknew." Paul went on to declare that, though most of his fellow Jews were proceeding through a period of spiritual blindness, they would eventually see the light, recognize the true Messiah, and be regrafted into the tree of God. Although Paul was the self-styled "apostle of the Gentiles," he also warned them (Romans 11:20–21, 24–27):

> Do not be arrogant, but fear. For if God spared not the natural branches, take heed lest he not spare you. . . . If you were cut out of the olive tree, which is wild by nature, and were grafted, contrary to nature, into a good olive tree, how much more shall these, which be the natural branches, be grafted into their own olive tree? For I would not, brothers, that you

should be ignorant of this mystery, lest you should be wise in your own imagination; that blindness has come upon Israel, until the fullness of the Gentiles comes in. And so all Israel shall be saved; as it is written, "There shall come out of Zion the Deliverer, and shall turn away ungodliness from Jacob [Israel]. For this is my covenant unto them."

Here Paul clearly stated the early Church's conception of two chosen peoples bound by different covenants, though serving the same Lord and destined for the same glory by different paths. Paul wrote this even while suffering intense persecution at the hands of Jewish religious authorities nearly everywhere he preached. (It is important to note that in the twentieth and twenty-first centuries a series of popes have denounced anti-Semitism, that Pope John Paul II specifically repudiated replacement theology, and that for centuries a great many Protestants, beginning with Martin Luther, also exhibited a virulent anti-Semitism and embraced replacement theology, positions renounced by most Protestants only fairly recently.)

Though the replacement theology of the late empire was largely the product of a new anti-Semitism that accompanied the increasing Romanization of a once Judaic religion, it was also partly the result of the destruction of the nation of Israel and the dispersion of the Jews by Vespasian and Hadrian. Fourth- and fifth-century Christians could not imagine that Israel would ever be restored as a nation; therefore, they naturally inclined to the view that the Bible's end-time prophecies must refer to "spiritual Israel," the Christian Church, God's new (and exclusive) chosen people.

Since such an interpretation of Scripture was extraordinarily nonliteral, it also serves as an illustration of another development of the late empire—the increasing tendency to interpret Scripture allegorically. In the hands of theologians like Augustine, the Millennium of Christ's rule became a figurative reference to the Church Age, another interpretation that involved an extraordinary departure from the literal biblical text.

Church leaders like Jerome increasingly employed a harsh style of rhetoric based on pagan models. Steeped in classical literature, especially Roman comedy and satire and Cicero's invective-laden speeches, and a frequenter of Roman tribunals where insults flowed, Jerome treated his numerous perceived enemies—be they pagan, Jewish, heretic, or as orthodox as he—to a copious diet of rhetorical abuse: ridicule, sarcasm, invective, and even slanderous accusations of avarice, gluttony, lechery, and other faults commonly satirized in pagan harangues. No form of rhetoric could have been more inimical to the spirit of the New Testament, with its ubiquitous calls for humility, charity, harmony, and unity and its numerous admonitions against slander and even gossip. In some forms, such as Jerome's descriptions of the hypocritical behavior of some clergymen, his satirical writing served a moral purpose. It powerfully illustrated his thesis that the Church, whose task had been to purify the mass of society, had instead been corrupted by wealth and power until it was little better than its pagan counterparts. Jerome wrote regarding the Church, "After it passed under Christian emperors, it became greater indeed in power and riches, but weaker in virtues." But Jerome was also a retailer in unedifying, often hypocritical assaults on a large number of personal foes, whom he always conveniently categorized as enemies of God, thereby imbuing his own personal animus with a holy zeal. Thus did the harsher elements of pagan rhetoric combine with Christian self-righteousness to form a toxic brew. By the late imperial period, such rhetoric even led to violence on occasion, as competing factions, such as the Trinitarians and the Arians, not content with slandering one another in writing, began engaging in bloody feuds.

Just as medieval feudalism had its roots in the late Roman Empire, so did many of the doctrines and practices commonly associated with medieval Catholicism. Belief in the intercession of Mary and the saints, purgatory, and the efficacy of relics, as well as the practice of pilgrimages to holy sites, were all late Roman additions.

The veneration of Mary and the saints arose first among the newly converted, who missed certain aspects of paganism, such as the worship of goddesses and of specialized deities from whose ranks one could claim a personal patron by virtue of possessing a certain status or practicing a particular craft. Absent from first-century Christianity, the veneration of Mary was especially popular among newly converted pagans unaccustomed to the exclusive worship of a masculine God. Indeed, some statues of Isis and her baby Horus were simply renamed "Mary and Jesus."

Mary was now given characteristics that the New Testament had reserved for Jesus, such as an immaculate conception (a conception in which original sin was not transmitted), perpetual virginity, the power of intercession, and an ascension into heaven. The New Testament had made no mention of Mary's immaculate conception, her power of intercession, or her ascension into heaven, and had stated (Matthew 1:25) that Joseph "knew her not until she had brought forth her firstborn son," implying sexual relations between Joseph and Mary thereafter (a conclusion fortified by the numerous scriptural references to Jesus' "brothers"). Furthermore, when Jesus had been informed by someone in a crowd that His mother and brothers were waiting to speak to Him, rather than using the opportunity to exalt His mother and her powers of intercession, He had replied, "Who is my mother? Who are my brothers?" He had then pointed to His disciples and said, "Behold my mother and my brothers! For whoever shall do the will of my Father in heaven is my brother and sister and mother." Yet, by the seventh century, the veneration of Mary had been carried to such a height within the Church that the Qur'an

(Sura 5:73–75, 116) claimed that Christians worshipped three gods: the Father, the Mother (Mary), and the Son.

The veneration of the saints began with the veneration of martyrs, whose intercessory blessings from prison were believed to efface sin. The doctrine of their intercession, like the doctrine of Mary's intercession, contradicted 1 Timothy 2:5, in which Paul had stated, "For there is one God and one mediator between God and men, the man Christ Jesus." Paul taught that only Jesus was sinless and, thus, able to mediate between God and man as both the high priest and the sacrificial lamb. Yet Roman artists now depicted saints with haloes, a pagan symbol of divinity that would soon become one of the most characteristic elements of Christian art. Romans who had instructed their teenage boys to dedicate their first beard at a pagan temple now had them do so at martyrs' shrines.

Purgatory, which is nowhere found in the Bible, was the natural product of a new theology that taught salvation by a combination of faith and works, in contradiction to Paul's theology of salvation by faith alone. If salvation was earned at least partly by works, it remained a mystery how many good deeds were required, and thus it seemed only just that there should be a place besides hell for those well-meaning souls whose service was insufficient to redeem their sins. By contrast, in Paul's theology all sins were redeemed by the blood of Christ, making faith in Christ's atonement the only requirement of salvation. For this reason Paul had called salvation "a free gift." Finally, the veneration of relics, whose authenticity was often highly questionable, and pilgrimages to holy sites appealed to the deeply ingrained Roman tendency to invest material objects and places with magical powers.

The result of all of these innovations to first-century Christianity was a syncretism of biblical Christianity with Roman paganism. As Gibbon once put it: "The most respectable bishops had persuaded themselves that the ignorant rustics would more cheerfully renounce the superstitions of Paganism if they found some resemblance, some compensation, in the bosom of Christianity. The religion of Constantine achieved, in less than a century, the final conquest of the Roman empire; but the victors themselves were insensibly subdued by the arts of their vanquished rivals."

The three greatest of what are commonly called the "Early Church Fathers"—though they lived in the fourth and early fifth centuries after Christ—Jerome, Ambrose, and Augustine, were all Roman citizens who approved the introduction of these Roman elements into Christianity. Indeed, early medieval writers gave them the title "Early Church Fathers" in spite of their relatively late appearance precisely because they were the most influential writers of the century who first presented Christianity in what was to become the Roman Catholic form.

Yet if the Catholicism that emerged in the late imperial period constituted a merger of biblical Christianity and Roman paganism, it was one that still embodied the most crucial elements of the former. By the standards of Paul—"If you confess with your mouth that Jesus is Lord, and believe in your heart that God raised Him from the dead, you shall be saved" (Romans 10:9)—the Church was still recognizably Christian.

Indeed, by the standards of Paul, it was now more so in some respects. For instance, the increasing insistence on clerical celibacy comported with the assertions of Paul (1 Corinthians 7:1–2, 7–9, 38) that celibacy was a spiritually superior lifestyle, though he had considered marriage an acceptable, if inferior, alternative. Thus, as Gibbon famously quipped, while the Roman pagans had difficulty finding six women qualified to be Vestal Virgins, the Christians of the late empire had whole communities of celibates, including monasteries. Monasticism spread rapidly in the fourth century, in part as a protest against a perceived moral decline among the regular clergy.

THE SURVIVAL OF CHRISTIANITY: AUGUSTINE OF HIPPO (354–430)

The most important of the so-called Early Church Fathers was Augustine, who was born into a middle-class family in the town of Thagaste (Souk Ahras, Algeria). The son of a Christian mother and a pagan father, Augustine had become acquainted with Manichaeism while studying rhetoric at Carthage and had been a Manichaean for nine years before his conversion to orthodox Christianity in 387. Named after Mani, its third-century Mesopotamian founder, Manichaeism was a combination of Zoroastrianism and Gnostic Christianity that spread westward to the Roman Empire and eastward to the gates of China. It envisioned existence as a constant struggle between good and evil. God was a benevolent being whose limited power absolved him of any responsibility for evil in the world. Though human souls were the product of this good God, their bodies, which distracted them from the good, were the product of the evil Satan. This view differed from Christianity, a religion that considered the body a good creation of God that had been corrupted by the fall of Adam and that hardly placed Satan on the same level as God. Christians viewed God as creator of the whole universe, Satan as a mere fallen angel—a disgruntled employee.

Instrumental in Augustus' conversion to Christianity was another of the Church Fathers, Ambrose. A former governor of Liguria, Ambrose (334–397), the bishop of Milan, was a man of great conviction and courage who gave nearly all of his substantial wealth to the Church. In 390 Ambrose won the respect of both Christians and non-Christians by threatening the emperor Theodosius I with excommunication from his diocese after the emperor massacred thousands of Thessalonians in retribution for the murder of a Roman governor. Such was Ambrose's moral authority that the emperor was obliged to come to the bishop's basilica without his royal insignia and publicly express his sorrow and repentance. Ambrose also excited his congregation by chanting the psalms to the tune of new Eastern melodies. He urged discrimination between the worthy and the unworthy in the distribution of alms, since indiscriminate giving to liars and lazy people discouraged congregants from giving alms. He defended a widow whom an official was trying to marry against her will. He wrote concerning divorce, which left women financially destitute in his day: "How wicked it is if you abandon her in her old age whom you enjoyed in her youth! . . . You think you may divorce your wife because you are not forbidden by human law, but you are by the divine." He melted down his churches' gold and silver vessels to ransom captives of the Goths after Adrianople fell, saying, "The Church does not have gold to be stored up but to be laid out and spent for those in need." He prayed, "Grant first that I may know how to have heartfelt compassion for sinners . . . that I may not be proud in reproaching them, but that I may weep and grieve with them."

While bishop of Hippo Regius (Annaba, Algeria), Augustine wrote *Confessions* (397–401). Addressed to God in the style of the psalms, this deeply personal book began with an account of Augustine's past sinful life and conversion to Christianity at age thirty-two and ended with a series of passionate philosophical reflections. Augustine's somber self-criticism, enlivened by a tremendous eloquence and talent for metaphor, marked a radical break with the classical past and the inauguration of a new Christian literary tradition. In language remarkable for its combination of reason and passion he flouted the conventions of contemporary Christian literature by portraying conversion as merely the beginning of an arduous journey, not as a panacea for earthly troubles.

Augustine's stinging indictment of himself represented no less than an indictment of the classical world and of humankind in general. Augustine rebuked himself for a life spent pursuing all the fleeting and ultimately unsatisfying pleasures of the material world—sex, prestige, wealth, even smug intellectualism—rather than seeking the lasting and satisfying pleasures of the spirit. He had frequented the immoral Roman theater, had fathered an illegitimate child by a mistress ("a union of wanton love, in which a child is born but not wanted, though when born it compels one to love it"), had been swollen with ambition for wealth and fame as a teacher of rhetoric (a "vender of verbosity"), had heeded the ridiculous superstitions of the Manichaeans, had consulted astrologers (whose few accurate prophesies occurred by chance), and had wasted his talents pursuing the vain commendations of a self-deluded intellectual elite. Seeing his former vanity in the scientists of his day, Augustine wrote: "Through impious pride, falling away from and lacking in Thy great light, they foresee an eclipse of the sun, but they do not see their own eclipse in the present—for they do not search conscientiously for the source of the talent which they have, whereby they search out these things. . . . They say many true things about creation, yet they do not seek the Truth, the artificer of creation, with piety and therefore do not discover Him. Or, if they do make this discovery, in knowing God, they do not honor Him or give thanks to Him as God." It was better to be termed ignorant by the intellectual elite for possessing faith than to secure their praise by emulating their arrogance. Had not Paul written (1 Corinthians 3:19), "The wisdom of the world is foolishness to God"?

Augustine concluded that although earthly pleasures were both good and necessary (the taste of food was a necessary incentive to eating, just as sexual pleasure was a necessary incentive to procreation), their very goodness rendered them enormously susceptible to abuse. One must be on constant guard against them since they so quickly and easily became ends in themselves. Augustine himself had become so corrupted by lust that he had been reluctant to pray for chastity, lest his prayer be answered. After Augustine had attempted to achieve chastity on his own and failed, he finally heard "the voice of Chastity" whisper to his tortured soul concerning the chaste Christians he often saw: "Can you not live as these men and women do? In fact, do these men and women live by their own powers and not by the Lord their God? . . . Why do you stand upon yourself and so have naught to stand on?" Overwhelmed by the realization that his stubborn quest to become virtuous without divine assistance was, in fact, the greatest of his many sins of pride, Augustine's tears "burst forth in rivers," and he cried out to God, who healed Augustine through the Holy Spirit.

Augustine published his greatest theological work, *The City of God* (413–426), in response to the Visigoths' destruction of Rome in 410. Pagans cried that the destruction of the city represented the wrath of the Roman gods against Christians and others for abandoning that old-time religion, paganism. In *The City of God* Augustine ridiculed this theory, noting that other empires had arisen without the help of the Roman gods and that the earlier paganism had failed to prevent similar disasters, ranging from the fall of Troy to the Gauls' destruction of Rome (387 B.C.) and the bloody civil wars of the late republican period. In granting material goods, such as empires, to the wicked as well as the good, God acted mysteriously, but probably intended to show that temporal goods should not be valued too highly. Those who valued temporal, alienable goods like wealth and power over such eternal, unalienable goods as faith and love were condemned either to a perpetual desire for them or to a perpetual fear of their loss.

Augustine also criticized the Roman gods for denying their followers immortality and for failing to provide the Romans with moral instruction. Indeed, the Roman gods had personified vice itself, as even the Romans were forced to admit. After all, at the same time that the Romans had vividly recounted the immoral acts of the gods in their plays, they had made it a capital crime for a playwright to slander any citizen on the same stage by attributing the same actions to him.

Augustine pleaded with the Roman people to redirect their enormous energy and genius for territorial conquest toward the quest for the spiritual triumphs. Perhaps remembering Paul's statement (Romans 8:37), "In all these things we are more than conquerors through Him who loved us," as well as the Book of Revelation's numerous promises of glory for "him who conquers" sin, Augustine wrote: "This, rather, is the religion worthy of your desires, O admirable Romans. . . . Lay hold now on the celestial country, which is easily won, and in which you will reign truly and forever."

Augustine contended that there were two worlds, the Earthly City and the City of God. The dark Earthly City, animated by the love of self, had begun with the fall of Adam and Eve, a fall from truth and unity to falsehood and division. Just as the souls of Adam and Eve were divided by sin, their progeny were divided against one another by selfishness. As punishment for humans' stubborn pride in seeking to be their own satisfaction, God granted their wish, abandoning them to themselves. Thenceforth, humans were doomed to die in body as they had willingly died in spirit, condemned to death because they had forsaken eternal life. The punishment for humanity's rebellion against God was the rebellion of their own bodies against their souls, the transformation of human bodies from good and faithful servants into cruel and erratic masters. The tree from which Adam and Eve ate, in defiance of God's law, was called the Tree of Knowledge because by eating of it they learned, for the first time, the true value of the life they were now to lose.

Planned by God to repair the damage caused by Adam and Eve, the bright, celestial City of God, animated by love of God, had been constructed through the death and resurrection of Jesus. Citizens of both the Earthly City and the City of God occupied the same world. In their blindness the citizens of the Earthly City created strife by competing with one another for the finite material goods of the temporal world. By contrast, the wiser citizens of the City of God lived in harmony, sharing the limitless goods of the spirit. While the former were enslaved by their very lust for rule, the latter were truly free. While the former valued earthly things as ends in themselves, the latter merely accepted them as necessary to survival during their brief "sojourn on earth." The opposing values of the two cities divided them irreparably, often leading to the persecution of the righteous by the worldly. But while the worldly wallowed in the futility of their earthly existence until their day of destruction arrived, the righteous awaited positions in the true kingdom of love and justice.

Augustine referred to God's elect as "resident aliens" in the Earthly City, a status his readers understood well. The elect were uprooted and homesick during their period of exile from God's kingdom. Though they had to make peace with their temporary residence for practical reasons, it would never feel like home.

History was both an endless cycle of the rise and fall of futile civilizations and a divinely propelled progression toward an otherworldly utopia. Augustine assured his readers that the decline and fall of civilizations had been a natural occurrence in the Earthly City since Adam's fall, indicating no particular divine disfavor. Only the heavenly City of God was eternal. Introspective, intellectual, imaginative, and articulate, Augustine continues to delight readers of all faiths.

The immediate impact of Augustine's *City of God* was crucial to the survival of Christianity. At a time when Romans may well have been tempted to blame Christianity for the sack of Rome by the Visigoths, and for the general decline of Roman civilization, Augustine persuaded many Roman intellectuals that the unthinkable, the collapse of the Roman Empire, was, in fact, natural and inevitable. In place of loyalty to the worldly empire that so many people over so many centuries had mistakenly considered eternal, Augustine substituted fidelity to the spiritual Kingdom of God, which he presented as the only truly everlasting empire. The City of God, the New Jerusalem, displaced pagan Rome, the so-called Eternal City, as the ideal—even as Rome itself was becoming the seat of the Christian Church in the West.

Augustine's theology dominated the early medieval period. Jeffrey Burton Russell once aptly summarized Augustine's influence on medieval theology: "Philosophy and theology were for six hundred years after Augustine's death largely devoted to the elaboration of his thought." Not until the High Middle Ages, when the Scholasticism of Thomas Aquinas, a merger of Christianity with Aristotelian philosophy, gained prominence, was Augustine's theology displaced.

Augustine's influence on Martin Luther, John Calvin, and other Protestant reformers was equally great. Luther, who began his religious career as a Catholic monk of the Augustinian order, claimed that he had derived his doctrine of justification by faith alone from the psalms, from the apostle Paul, and from Augustine's *Confessions*. Luther was impressed by the fact that Augustine, like the psalmist and Paul, had found no hope in himself whatsoever, but had relied solely on God's promise of salvation.

Yet Catholics continued to cite Augustinian passages—especially those concerning the intercession of the saints and the existence of purgatory—that were more suitable to their own theology than to that of the Protestants. Augustine's writings were rich enough to provide some fodder for both sides during the Reformation.

THE PROTESTANT REFORMATION:
A REBELLION AGAINST ROMANIZATION

Nevertheless, despite the appreciation of Luther and Calvin for certain aspects of Augustinian theology, especially his emphasis on original sin and on the importance of faith, they were engaged in an effort to reverse the Romanization of Christianity that Augustine had helped promote in the fourth century. They wrote of the need to return to a religion more similar to first-century Christianity—a return to the original Hebrew and Greek scriptural texts (at least as the source material for new vernacular Bibles), to a stricter interpretation of Scripture that would discard many Catholic practices lacking biblical support, to a simpler liturgy conducted in the vernacular languages, to more spartan churches, and to a more democratic polity.

A nascent nationalism contributed to the success of the Reformation. Germans like Martin Luther, Frenchmen like John Calvin, and Swiss like Ulrich Zwingli resented Italian control of the papacy and the resultant redistribution of wealth from northern Europe to Italy. Like the Germanic tribes of the ancient world, they fought against the might of Rome. It is surely no accident that the reformers failed in those nations whose languages were most influenced by the Latin tongue (Italy, France, and Spain) and succeeded where that influence was less powerful (Britain and the Netherlands, which had been located at the far reaches of the Roman Empire, and much of Germany, which the Romans had never conquered).

CONCLUSION

Though Christianity began as a sect within Judaism, and was long regarded as such by Roman authorities, it was the peace, unity, and roads of the Roman Empire that allowed its rapid expansion among the Gentile population, and it was a trio of Roman citizens, Paul, Constantine, and Augustine who contributed most to the spreading and preservation of the religion. The fact that none of these three Roman citizens was ethnically Roman—Paul was a Jew,

Constantine a Serb, and Augustine a Berber—is a testament to the Romans' uncommon willingness to incorporate people of diverse cultures into their empire. Furthermore, Christianity became partly Romanized in the years after Constantine's conversion.

There is little doubt that the Roman Catholic Church, whose approximately one billion members constitute the largest Christian denomination in the world today, bears the indelible marks of its Roman ancestry. Because Protestantism was formed in rebellion against Roman Catholicism, it too was profoundly influenced by Rome. Like those atheists who are obsessed with rooting out and opposing every inkling of religion, thus leading them to develop a heightened sensitivity to every vestige of it, Protestants have been, from the very birth of their religious tradition, acutely sensitive to all forms of Roman influence. Thus, even the opponents of Rome cannot escape its influence.

Epilogue

$\mathcal{T}$hroughout this book I have noted the influence of various Romans on the United States in order to demonstrate that the profound impact of Rome has extended well beyond the borders of western Europe. But western Europe has a unique relationship with the Roman Empire. It has never quite gotten over the fall of the empire, the last time it was unified for a considerable length of time. In the eighth century Charlemagne, king of the Franks, attempted to re-create the Roman Empire. In 800 the pope crowned him "emperor of the Romans"; in fact, his empire subsequently became known as the "Holy Roman Empire." Charles V, the king of Spain and the Holy Roman Empire, attempted to reestablish the Roman Empire in the sixteenth century, Louis XIV of France in the seventeenth. Assuming the title of First Consul and surrounding himself with Roman symbols (the most massive being the Arc de Triomphe), Napoleon pursued the same goal in the nineteenth century. (Like Charlemagne, Napoleon had himself crowned in Rome, but, at the last second, snatched the crown from the pope's hands and placed it on his own head to demonstrate that his authority exceeded the pope's.) Even two nations never incorporated into the Roman Empire, Germany and Russia, named their respective kings "kaiser" and "czar" after "Caesar." In the twentieth century both Hitler and Mussolini tried to re-create the Roman Empire, Mussolini going so far as to name his political party after the fasces, the Roman symbol of executive authority. He also widened the avenue in front of the Colosseum and Forum as the favored site for his military parades, thus juxtaposing the ancient empire with his own modern version. All of these efforts at restoring by force the unity of Europe failed because they were blocked by those Europeans who did not care to live under the monarch or dictator in question.

Nevertheless, still aching for the unity that died with the Roman Empire—especially after two world wars that began in Europe made unity seem a matter of survival—western Europeans created the European Union (then called the European Economic Community) in 1957. The treaty establishing this alliance of western European nations was signed, quite purposely, on Capitoline Hill, in the very heart of the old Roman Empire. One of the signatories later stated that the men who signed the treaty felt great pride and joy that they were at last re-creating the Roman Empire. The union began as a common market but has since added a common currency and constitution. Moreover, its political elements—its Parliament and bureaucracy in Brussels, its common police force (Europol), its court system, and its foreign policy and military establishments—have all grown steadily in size and power. The hope is for European reunification by peaceful means—the Roman Empire but without the conquest and subjugation.

But, as the new millennium dawns, Christian millennialists have drawn upon the Book of Daniel, the Book of Revelation, and other apocalyptic texts to contend that the European Union is the revived Roman Empire that will provide the economic and military power base for the Antichrist, the world dictator who will demand that everyone worship him, will brand everyone with a mark on the head or right hand, without which a person will be unable to buy or sell, and will slaughter Christians and others who refuse to worship him and accept the mark. A quite different conception from that of the baffled bureaucrats in Brussels!

Regardless of whether biblical prophecy is fulfilled in the manner anticipated by the millennialists, it remains clear that the Roman legacy in western Europe is different than in the United States. While the United States, even as it has built a cultural, commercial, and military empire exceeding that of Rome, has mostly looked to early Rome's republican principles for inspiration, western Europe, first out of ambition and then from a survival instinct, has been in an epic quest for the stability and peace afforded by the Roman Empire. Ironically, since World War II, it has been the imperial power of the United States that has guaranteed an unprecedented period of stability and peace in western Europe, conditions that Europeans have sought to perpetuate through a closer union.

Suggestions for Further Reading

$\mathcal{T}$here are many well-written histories of, and historical commentaries on, ancient Rome that are geared to general readers. These include: R. H. Barrow, *The Romans* (Penguin, 1949); John Boardman et al., *The Oxford History of the Classical World* (Oxford, 1986); Mary T. Boatwright et al., *The Romans: From Village to Empire* (Oxford, 2004); Karl Christ, *The Romans: An Introduction to Their History and Civilization* (University of California, 1984); Michael Grant, *The Founders of the Western World: A History of Greece and Rome* (Scribner's, 1991); Antony Kamm, *The Romans: An Introduction* (Routledge, 2008); and Kevin M. McGeough, *The Romans: An Introduction* (Oxford, 2009). Excellent studies of specific periods of Roman history include: Averil Cameron, *The Later Roman Empire, A.D. 284–430* (Harvard, 1993); Tim Cornell, *The Beginnings of Rome: Italy from the Bronze Age to the Persian Wars* (Routledge, 1995); Arthur Eckstein, *Mediterranean Anarchy, Interstate War, and the Rise of Rome* (University of California, 2009); Tom B. Jones, *In the Twilight of Antiquity* (University of Minnesota, 1978); Christopher Kelly, *The End of Empire: Attila the Hun and the Fall of Rome* (Norton, 2009); R. M. Ogilvie, *Early Rome and the Etruscans* (Humanities Press, 1976); H. H. Scullard, *From the Gracchi to Nero: A History of Rome from 133 B.C. to A.D. 68* (5th ed., Routledge, 1982); and Colin M. Wells, *The Roman Empire* (Stanford, 1984).

Highly readable works on Roman law, politics, and administration include: John A. Crook, *The Law and Life of Rome* (Cornell, 1967); Anthony Everitt, *Cicero: The Life and Times of Rome's Greatest Politician* (Random House, 2003); Bruce W. Frier and Thomas A. J. McGinn, eds., *A Casebook on Roman and Family Law* (Oxford, 2004); J. M. Kelly, *Roman Litigation* (Clarendon, 1966); Wolfgang Kunkel, *An Introduction to Roman Legal and Constitutional History* (Clarendon, 1966); Paul Petit, *Pax Romana* (University of California, 1976); and Lily Taylor, *Roman Voting Assemblies* (University of Michigan, 1966).

Excellent works on Roman art, architecture, and engineering include: H. P. L'Orange, *Art Forms and Civic Life in the Late Roman Empire* (Princeton, 1965); William Lloyd MacDonald, *The Pantheon: Design, Meaning, and Progeny* (Harvard, 1976); Brunilde Sismondo Ridgway, *Roman Copies of Greek Sculpture: The Problem of the Originals* (University of Michigan, 1984); Lino Rossi, *Trajan's Column and the Dacian Wars* (Cornell, 1971); Frank Sear, *Roman Architecture* (Cornell, 1983); Nigel Sitwell, *Roman Roads of Europe* (St. Martin's, 1981); Peter Stewart, *Roman Art* (Oxford, 2004); Donald Emrys Strong, *Roman Art* (Penguin, 1976); and K. D. White, *Greek and Roman Technology* (Cornell, 1984).

Highly readable works on the various branches of Roman literature include: Susan H. Braund, *Roman Verse Satire* (Oxford, 1992); Michael Coffey, *Roman Satire* (Barnes and Noble, 1976); Shaye J. D. Cohen, *Josephus in Galilee and Rome* (Brill, 1979); Philip B. Corbett, *Petronius* (Twayne, 1970); John Francis D'Alton, *Horace and His Age: A Study in Historical Background* (Russell & Russell, 1962); Walter E. Forehand, *Terence* (Twayne, 1985); Hermann Ferdinand Frankel, *Ovid: A Poet between Two Worlds* (University of California, 1969); Karl Galinsky, *Ovid's Metamorphoses: An Introduction to the Basic Aspects* (University of California, 1975); Miriam T. Griffin, *Seneca: A Philosopher in Politics* (Clarendon, 1976); Elizabeth Hazelton Haight, *Apuleius and His Influence* (Cooper Square, 1963); Karl Pomeroy Harrington, *Catullus and His Influence* (Cooper Square, 1963); Christopher P. Jones, *Plutarch and Rome* (Clarendon, 1971); Ronald Mellor, *Tacitus* (Routledge, 1993); Clarence W. Mendell, *Tacitus: The Man and His Work* (Yale, 1957); Paul Nixon, *Martial and the Modern Epigram* (Cooper Square, 1963); John M. Rist, *Plotinus: The Road to Reality* (Cambridge, 1967); Henry Dwight Sedgwick, *Horace: A Biography* (Harvard, 1947); Charles Segal, *Lucretius on Death and Anxiety: Poetry and Philosophy in* De Rerum Natura (Princeton, 1990); Niall W. Slater, *Persius in Performance: The Theatre of the Mind* (Princeton, 1985); Sir Ronald Syme, *Sallust* (University of California, 1964); and P. G. Walsh, *Livy: His Historical Aims and Methods* (Cambridge, 1961).

Excellent works on Roman women's history include: Maureen B. Fant and Mary R. Lefkowitz, *Women's Life in Greece and Rome* (Johns Hopkins, 1982); Judith P. Hallett, *Fathers and Daughters in Roman Society: Women and the Elite Family* (Princeton, 1984); and Sarah B. Pomeroy, ed., *Women's History and Ancient History* (University of North Carolina, 1991).

Highly readable works on Roman science include: John M. Riddle, *Dioscorides on Pharmacy and Medicine* (University of Texas, 1985); George Sarton, *Galen of Pergamon* (University of Kansas, 1954); and William Stahl,

Roman Science: Origins, Development, and Influence to the Later Middle Ages (University of Wisconsin, 1962).

Other valuable works include: Michael Grant, *Gladiators* (Barnes and Noble, 1967); Elizabeth Rawson, *Intellectual Life in the Late Roman Republic* (Johns Hopkins, 1985); Brent D. Shaw, ed., *Spartacus and the Slave Wars* (St. Martin's, 2001); Peter Wells, *The Battle That Stopped Rome: The Emperor Augustus, Arminius, and the Slaughter of the Legions in the Teutoburg Forest* (Norton, 2003); and Thomas Wiedemann, *Greek and Roman Slavery* (Johns Hopkins, 1981).

Well-written works concerning early Christianity include: Stephen Benko, *Pagan Rome and the Early Christians* (Indiana University, 1984); Peter Brown, *Augustine of Hippo: A Biography* (University of California, 1967) and *The Rise of Western Christendom: Triumph and Diversity, A.D. 200–1000* (2d ed., Blackwell, 2003); Henry Chadwick, *The Early Church* (Penguin, 1969); E. R. Dodds, *Pagan and Christian in an Age of Anxiety* (Cambridge, 1968); Robin Lane Fox, *Pagans and Christians* (Knopf, 1987); Arnold H. M. Jones, *Constantine and the Conversion of Europe* (Collier, 1962); Angelo Paredi, *St. Ambrose: His Life and Times* (Notre Dame, 1964); and David S. Wiesen, *St. Jerome as a Satirist: A Study in Christian Latin Thought and Letters* (Cornell, 1964).

The past two and a half decades have witnessed the publication of a plethora of books concerning the Roman influence on Western civilization, especially on the United States. Such works include: E. Christian Kopff, *The Devil Knows Latin: Why America Needs the Classical Tradition* (ISI, 1999); Margaret Malamud, *Ancient Rome and Modern America* (Wiley-Blackwell, 2009); Paul A. Rahe, *Republics, Ancient and Modern: Classical Republicanism and the American Revolution* (University of North Carolina, 1992); Meyer Reinhold, *Classica Americana: The Greek and Roman Heritage in the United States* (Wayne State University, 1984); Carl J. Richard, *The Founders and the Classics: Greece, Rome, and the American Enlightenment* (Harvard, 1994), *Greeks and Romans Bearing Gifts: How the Ancients Inspired the Founding Fathers* (Rowman & Littlefield, 2008), and *The Golden Age of the Classics in America: Greece, Rome, and the Antebellum United States* (Harvard, 2009); M. N. S. Sellers, *American Republicanism: Roman Ideology in the United States Constitution* (New York University, 1994); Eran Shalev, *Rome Reborn on Western Shores: Historical Imagination and the Creation of the American Republic* (University of Virginia, 2009); Garry Wills, *Cincinnatus: George Washington and the Enlightenment* (Doubleday, 1984); Susan Ford Wiltshire, *Greece, Rome, and the Bill of Rights* (University of Oklahoma, 1992); and Caroline Winterer, *The Culture of Classicism: Ancient Greece and Rome in American Intellectual Life, 1780–1910* (Johns Hopkins, 2002) and *The Mirror of Antiquity: American Women and the Classical Tradition, 1750–1900* (Cornell, 2007).

Nearly all of the classics of Roman and early Christian literature can be found in good English translations in paperback editions published by Penguin. The Loeb Classics contain older translations that are less amenable to modern readers but also feature the original Latin on the opposite page from the translation. Other translations worthy of mention include: Lionel Casson, *Six Plays of Plautus* (Anchor, 1963); Robert Fitzgerald, *The Aeneid* (Random House, 1981); Horace Gregory, *The Poems of Catullus* (Covici-Friede, 1931); Moses Hadas, *The Stoic Philosophy of Seneca: Essays and Letters of Seneca* (P. Smith, 1966); W. S. Merwin, *Satires* (of Persius) (Indiana University, 1961); and Dorothea Wender, *Roman Poetry from the Republic to the Silver Age* (Southern Illinois University, 1980).

Index of Translations for Long Quotations

p. 131 Columella on the neglect of farms: Columella, *On Agriculture*, trans. by Harrison Boyd (Loeb Classical Library; Cambridge, Mass.: Harvard University Press, 1941), 1:13–15.

p. 146 Epicurus on virtue and pleasure: first two sentences, Diogenes Laertius, *Lives of the Eminent Philosophers*, trans. by Robert Drew Hicks (Loeb Classical Library; London: W. Heinemann, 1950), 2:657; last sentence, John Boardman et al., eds, *The Oxford History of the Classical World* (Oxford: Oxford University Press, 1986), p. 372.

p. 148 Lucretius on other worlds: R. E. Latham, trans., *On the Nature of the Universe*, revised by John Godwin (New York: Penguin, 1994), p. 64.

pp. 149–50 Lucretius in praise of Epicurus: Barrow, *Romans*, p. 148.

pp. 152 Cicero on natural law: Dagobert Runes, ed., *The Selected Writings of Benjamin Rush: Physician and Citizen, 1746–1813* (Philadelphia: University of Pennsylvania Press, 1934), pp. 181–182.

pp. 152–3 Cicero on nature: Maryanne Cline Horowitz, "The Stoic Synthesis of the Idea of Natural Law in Man: Four Themes," *Journal of the History of Ideas* 35 (January–March 1974):6, 9–10, 12–15.

p. 161 Marcus Aurelius on hardship and death: first six sentences, Marcus Aurelius, *The Meditations*, trans. by G. M. A. Grube (Indianapolis: Bobbs-Merrill, 1963), pp. 35–6, 53; last two sentences, F. W. Bussell, *Marcus Aurelius and the Later Stoics* (Edinburgh: T & T Clark, 1910), pp. 153, 189.

pp. 161–2 Marcus against vengeance: *Meditations*, pp. 49, 65, 71–72, 114, 117.

p. 163 Marcus Aurelius on fame: *Meditations*, pp. 22, 29, 81–2, 123.

pp. 181–2 Tacitus on Agricola: H. Mattingly, trans., *Tacitus: The Agricola and the Germania*, revised by S. A. Handford (New York: Penguin, 1970), pp. 98–99.

p. 215 Juvenal on the female gladiator: Michael Grant, *Gladiators* (New York: Barnes and Noble, 1967), p. 34.

p. 216 Martial on Maxine: Martial, *Selected Epigrams*, trans. by Rolfe Humphries (Bloomington: Indiana University Press, 1963), pp. 39–40.

p. 218 Martial to Ligurra: *Selected Epigrams*, p. 111.

p. 219 Martial on leaving Rome: *Selected Epigrams*, pp. 109–10.

p. 240 Epictetus on freedom: first two sentences, Boardman, *Oxford History of the Classical World*, p. 710; last seven sentences,

Bradley P. Nystrom and Stylianos Spyridakis, eds. and trans., *Ancient Greece: Documentary Perspectives* (Dubuque: Kendall-Hunt, 1985), pp. 111–3.

All translations from the Bible are taken from the New Revised Standard Version.

Index

About the Author

Carl J. Richard received his Ph.D. in history from Vanderbilt University in 1988. His books include *The Founders and the Classics: Greece, Rome, and the American Enlightenment* (Harvard University Press, 1994), *Twelve Greeks and Romans Who Changed the World* (Rowman & Littlefield, 2003), *The Battle for the American Mind: A Brief History of a Nation's Thought* (Rowman & Littlefield, 2004), *Greeks and Romans Bearing Gifts: How the Ancients Inspired the Founding Fathers* (Rowman & Littlefield, 2008), and *The Golden Age of the Classics in America: Greece, Rome, and the Antebellum United States* (Harvard University Press, 2009).